THE RIGHT TO MENTAL HEALTH: A HUMAN RIGHTS APPROACH

Human Rights Research Series, Volume 100.

The titles published in this series are listed at the end of this volume.

The Right to Mental Health:
A Human Rights Approach

Natalie ABROKWA

Cambridge – Antwerp – Chicago

Intersentia Ltd
8 Wellington Mews | Wellington Street
Cambridge | CB1 1HW | United Kingdom
Tel.: +44 1223 736 170
Email: mail@intersentia.co.uk
www.intersentia.com | www.intersentia.co.uk

Distribution for the UK and the rest of the world (incl. Eastern Europe):
NBN International
1 Deltic Avenue, Rooksley
Milton Keynes MK13 8LD
United Kingdom
Tel.: +44 1752 202 301 | Fax: +44 1752 202 331
Email: orders@nbninternational.com

Distribution for Europe:
Lefebvre Sarrut Belgium NV
Hoogstraat 139/6
1000 Brussels
Belgium
Tel.: +32 3 680 15 50 | Fax: +32 3 658 71 21
Email: mail@intersentia.be

Distribution for the USA and Canada:
Independent Publishers Group
Order Department
814 North Franklin Street
Chicago, IL 60610
USA
Tel.: +1 800 888 4741 (toll free) | Fax: +1312 337 5985
Email: orders@ipgbook.com

The Right to Mental Health: A Human Rights Approach
© Natalie Abrokwa 2023

The author has asserted the right under the Copyright, Designs and Patents Act 1988, to be identified as authors of this work.

No part of this book may be reproduced, stored in a retrieval system, or transmitted, in any form, or by any means, without prior written permission from Intersentia, or as expressly permitted by law or under the terms agreed with the appropriate reprographic rights organisation. Enquiries concerning reproduction which may not be covered by the above should be addressed to Intersentia at the address above.

Cover design by Danny Juchtmans / www.dsigngraphics.be
Artwork on cover © Rikke / Shutterstock

ISBN 978-1-83970-359-1 (paperback)
ISBN 978-1-83970-360-7 (PDF)
D/2023/7849/78

British Library Cataloguing in Publication Data. A catalogue record for this book is available from the British Library.

'not only is there no health without mental health, but there is no mental health without human rights'.[1]

---

[1] Audrey Chapman and others, 'Reimagining the Mental Health Paradigm for Our Collective Well-Being' (2020) 22(1) Health and Human Rights Journal 1, 1.

ACKNOWLEDGEMENTS

To Kofi

Writing a dissertation is like a wild rollercoaster ride: there are many ups and downs; it is very exciting but also a bit scary here and there. From the first step until the last keystroke, there were wonderful people to whom I am deeply grateful for – without their encouragement, trust, support, and love, I would have not mastered this ride.

A heartfelt thank you goes out to my two supervisors, Prof. Birgit Toebes and Prof. Aart Hendriks. I could have not asked for a better team. Brigit, you recognised the value of my research project when few others did. You supported me from day one and I am deeply grateful for your mentoring, your trust in me and the opportunities you gave me along the way. Aart, I would like to extend my sincere thanks for your academic encouragement, and your critical reflection on law and the bigger picture. Your critical questions have improved my work tremendously. You both offered me a mixture of freedom and guidance that helped me develop as a scholar. I would like to express my sincere gratitude for your time and ideas. I would also like to offer my special thanks to the members of my Assessment Committee, Prof. van der Wolf, Prof. Sinding Aasen, and Prof. Degener for their insightful comments and suggestions.

I would have never gotten on this wild ride if it was not for my dear friend Samory and my friend and former colleague Wendy. You both believed that I could master a PhD and it was through your support and friendship, that I dared to take on this next academic challenge. At this point, I also need to take the opportunity to thank all my colleagues in the wider mental health community in Ghana – some of whom became interviewees for my dissertation – it is through them that I found the motivation (and passion) to research on the right to mental health.

Despite having been an external PhD student and only occasionally visiting the University of Groningen, I would like to express my special thanks to my colleagues in the Transboundary Legal Department for their colleagiality and challenging debates. I remember many warm get-togethers in the office, over coffee or dinner – in addition to all the online meetings. Even from a distance, you made me feel part of our department. An experience I will always cherish.

Last but certainly not least, I wish to pay my deepest gratitude to my family. *Mama* and *Papa*, I am proud to share this moment with you. You have supported me through many wild rollercoaster rides in my life. Thank you for teaching me to dream big and giving me the freedom to discover unknown paths. To my big sister Evelyn, thank you

Acknowledgements

for showing me and encouraging me at crucial moments in my life that it is okay to take unknown paths. I would also like to thank my son Kuno, who joined our family during my PhD process, for giving me boundless happiness, and for making me stronger and better. Nobody has been more important to me in the pursuit of my PhD than my husband Kofi, whose love and encouragement are always with me. Kofi, where do I begin thanking you? Thank you for being there for me at every step of the way in my PhD process. Thank you for reading early drafts and providing feedback, for the thought-provoking discussions, for your late-night-proof readings, for supporting my international work-related travels – especially as a new mother, thank you for believing in me when I was struggling to believe in myself, and for helping me unwind during the difficult times of my PhD journey. I appreciate every step you take with me in this life. *Me do wo.*

LIST OF ABBREVIATIONS

AAAQ	Availability Accessibility Acceptability Quality
ACHR	American Convention on Human Rights
AfChHPR	African Charter on Human and Peoples' Rights
CAT	Convention against Torture and Other Cruel, Inhuman or Degrading Treatment or Punishment
CHPS	Community-based Health Planning and Services
CoE	Council of Europe
CPT	European Committee for the Prevention of Torture and Inhuman or Degrading Treatment or Punishment
CRC	Convention on the Rights of the Child
CRPD	Convention on the Rights of Persons with Disabilities
CteeCRC	Committee on the Rights of the Child
CteeESCR	Committee on Economic, Social and Cultural Rights
CteeRPD	Committee on the Rights of Persons with Disabilities
ECHR	European Convention on Human Rights
ECOSOC	United Nations Economic and Social Council
ECT	Electroconvulsive therapy
ECtHR	European Court of Human Rights
EU	European Union
EUCFR	Charter of Fundamental Rights of the European Union
FRA	European Union Agency for Fundamental Rights
HICs	High-income countries
HRCtee	Human Rights Committee
IACtHR	Inter-American Court of Human Rights
ICCPR	International Covenant on Civil and Political Rights
ICESCR	International Covenant on Economic, Social and Cultural Rights
LMIC	Low- and middle-income country
NCDs	Non-communicable diseases
NCPD	National Council of Persons with Disabilities
NGOs	Non-governmental Organisations
NHIS	National Health Insurance Scheme
OHCHR	Office of the High Commissioner for Human Rights
OPCAT	Optional Protocol of the Convention Against Torture
UDHR	Universal Declaration of Human Rights

List of Abbreviations

UN	United Nations
UNDP	United Nations Development Programme
UNGA	United Nations General Assembly
WGAD	Working Group on Arbitrary Detention
WHO	World Health Organization

CONTENTS

Acknowledgements vii
List of Abbreviations ix

PART 1.
CONCEPT AND PROBLEM 1

Chapter 1.
Introduction 3

1.1 Background and Problem 3
1.2 Research Questions and Structure 7
    1.2.1 Research Questions 7
    1.2.2 Research Structure 8
1.3 Methodology 9
1.4 Concluding Summary 12

Chapter 2.
Mental Health and Mental Healthcare: Background and Content 13

2.1 Introduction 13
2.2 The Meaning of Relevant Terms 13
    2.2.1 The Concept of 'Mental Health' 14
        2.2.1.1 The Definition of 'Mental Health' 14
    2.2.2 The Concept of 'Psychosocial Disability' 16
        2.2.2.1 The Debate on Terminology 17
        2.2.2.2 The Definition of 'Psychosocial Disability' 18
    2.2.3 The Concept of 'Mental Healthcare' 21
        2.2.3.1 The Definition of 'Mental Healthcare' 21
            2.2.3.1.1 Institutional Mental Health Services 22
            2.2.3.1.2 Integrated Mental Health Services 22
            2.2.3.1.3 Community-based Mental Health Services 23
2.3 The Influence of Culture on Accessing Mental Healthcare 24
    2.3.1 Health-seeking Behaviour and the Perception of Mental Health
        Conditions and Psychosocial Disabilities 25
    2.3.2 The Therapeutic Relationship 27
    2.3.3 Different Approaches to Mental Healthcare 28

		2.3.3.1	Conventional Mental Healthcare........................	28
		2.3.3.2	Traditional Mental Healthcare..........................	30
			2.3.3.2.1 The Concept of Traditional Healthcare	30
			2.3.3.2.2 The Governance of Traditional Healthcare.......	32
		2.3.3.3	Is There a Benefit of Combining Both Approaches?.........	32
2.4	Challenges Associated with the Mental Healthcare Context			33
	2.4.1	Barriers to Accessing Mental Healthcare Services		33
		2.4.1.1	Stigma and Discrimination.............................	33
		2.4.1.2	Different Perceptions of Psychosocial Disability...........	34
		2.4.1.3	Financial Barriers.....................................	34
		2.4.1.4	Availability of Services.................................	35
	2.4.2	Specific Human Rights Violations in Mental Healthcare Settings.....		36
		2.4.2.1	Denial of Free and Informed Consent...................	36
		2.4.2.2	Involuntary Treatment and Hospitalisation...............	37
2.5	Concluding Summary			38

PART 2.
THE RIGHT TO MENTAL HEALTH AND THE APPLICABLE HUMAN RIGHTS FRAMEWORK.. 39

Chapter 3.
Mental Health as a Human Right: The Evolving Framework 41

3.1	Introduction	41
3.2	Mental Health in International Human Rights Law......................	42
3.3	Mental Health in Regional Human Rights Law	46
3.4	Mental Health in Domestic Law	48
3.5	Taking a Broader View: Mental Health in International Soft Law Instruments	50
3.6	The Meaning of the Right to Mental Health	52
	3.6.1 Scholarly Debate over the Right to Health and Mental Health........	52
	3.6.2 Delineating a Human Rights Framework in the Mental Health Context...	54
3.7	Concluding Summary	57

Chapter 4.
The Right to Health Norm and Mental Health................................. 59

4.1	Introduction	59
4.2	Normative Content of the Right to the Highest Attainable Standard of Mental Health	60
	4.2.1 The Scope of the Right to Health and Mental Health...............	61
	4.2.1.1 Underlying Determinants of Mental Health	61
	4.2.1.2 Access to Mental Healthcare............................	62
	4.2.2 The Core Content of the Right to Health and Mental health..........	67

4.3	State's Obligations Arising from the Right to Health and Mental Health.		69
	4.3.1	Obligation to Respect the Right to Health regarding Mental Health.	70
	4.3.2	Obligation to Protect the Right to Health regarding Mental Health	70
	4.3.3	Obligation to Fulfil the Right to Health regarding Mental Health.	71
4.4	Mental Health as a Justiciable Element of the Right to Health		72
	4.4.1	Case Law at the UN Level	74
	4.4.2	Regional Case Law on the Right to Health and Mental Health.	74
		4.4.2.1 A Violation of the Right to Health Norm and Related Rights.	74
		4.4.2.2 A Violation of other Human Rights Explicitly Linked to the Right to Health.	76
		4.4.2.3 Opportunities and Challenges	78
4.5	Concluding Summary		79

Chapter 5.
A Human Rights Approach to Psychosocial Disability. ... 81

5.1	Introduction		81
5.2	Protection against Discrimination		87
	5.2.1	Non-discrimination and the Right to Health Norm.	88
	5.2.2	The Scope of Article 5 CRPD and Mental Healthcare	90
		5.2.2.1 The Legal Dimension of Equality.	91
		5.2.2.2 The Legal Dimension of Prohibiting Discrimination.	92
		5.2.2.3 The Duty to Ensure Reasonable Accommodation.	95
		5.2.2.4 Specific Measures as Legitimate Differential Treatment	97
	5.2.3	Obligations Derived from the Right to Equality and Non-discrimination in regard to Mental Healthcare.	98
	5.2.4	Synopsis	100
5.3	Legal Capacity and the Protection of Persons not Able to Give Consent		101
	5.3.1	Legal Capacity and the Right to Health Norm.	102
	5.3.2	The Scope of Article 12 CRPD and Mental Healthcare	104
		5.3.2.1 The Right to Legal Capacity and Mental Capacity to Consent.	104
		5.3.2.2 The Right to Supported Decision-making and Safeguards	108
	5.3.3	Obligations Derived from the Right to Legal Capacity in regard to Mental Healthcare	111
	5.3.4	Controversial Issue: Disadvantages Emerging from Universal Legal Capacity.	115
	5.3.5	Synopsis	118
5.4	Protection from Non-consensual Mental Health Treatment		119
	5.4.1	Non-consensual Treatment and the Right to Health Norm	122
	5.4.2	Involuntary Treatment and the Protection of Integrity (Article 17 CPRD).	123
		5.4.2.1 The Scope of the Right to Protect the Integrity of the Person	124

		5.4.2.2	Limitations on the Enjoyment of Personal Integrity	126
	5.4.3	Situations Amounting to Torture or Ill-treatment (Article 15 CRPD)		130
		5.4.3.1	The Scope of the Right to be Free from Torture or Ill-treatment	132
			5.4.3.1.1 The Definition of Torture and Ill-treatment in regard to Mental Healthcare	132
			5.4.3.1.2 Treatment without Consent	136
		5.4.3.2	Seclusion and Restraints	137
		5.4.3.3	Living Conditions in Mental Health Institutions	141
		5.4.3.4	Controversial Issue: Justifications for Restrictive Interventions	142
	5.4.4	A Broader Protection against Non-consensual Treatment: The Opportunities of Article 16		145
		5.4.4.1	The Scope of the Right to be Free from Exploitation, Violence and Abuse	146
		5.4.4.2	The Inherent Tension between Protection and Autonomy	151
	5.4.5	Obligations Derived from the Right to be Free from Non-consensual Treatment in Mental Healthcare		152
	5.4.6	Synopsis		156
5.5	Protection from Involuntary Placement in an Institution			158
	5.5.1	Involuntary Placement and the Right to Health Norm		160
	5.5.2	Freedom from Involuntary Hospitalisation (Article 14 CRPD)		161
		5.5.2.1	The Scope of the Right to Liberty and Security	163
			5.5.2.1.1 Deprivation of Liberty on the Basis of Psychosocial Disability	165
		5.5.2.2	Controversial issue: Suicide Prevention versus the Right to Liberty	172
		5.5.2.3	Involuntary Treatment as an Alternative to Involuntary Hospitalisation?	174
	5.5.3	Deinstitutionalisation and Independent Living Arrangements (Article 19 CRPD)		175
		5.5.3.1	The Scope of the Right to Live Independently and be Included in the Community	179
			5.5.3.1.1 The Right to Live Independently	179
			5.5.3.1.2 The Right to be Included in the Community	182
		5.5.3.2	Institutionalisation as a Threat to Life	184
	5.5.4	Obligations Derived from the Right to be Free from Involuntary Placement in a Mental Healthcare Institution		185
5.6	Concluding Summary			189

PART 3
COUNTRY STUDY ANALYSIS 193

Chapter 6.
Bridging Theory and Practice through Country Studies 195

6.1 Introduction 195
6.2 Design 196
    6.2.1 Research Approach 196
    6.2.2 Methodology 197
        6.2.2.1 Rationale for Country Selection 198
        6.2.2.2 Methods of Data Collection for the Case Study on Ghana .. 199
6.3 Country Study I: Ghana 201
    6.3.1 Background of Ghana 202
        6.3.1.1 Geographic, Demographic and Economic Characteristics .. 202
        6.3.1.2 Legal and Administrative Context 202
        6.3.1.3 Mental Health Service Provision 204
    6.3.2 Ghana's Mental Health Legislative Framework 209
        6.3.2.1 Relevant Legislation 209
        6.3.2.2 Relevant Policies, Guidelines and Programmes 213
    6.3.3 Persisting Key Challenge: Interventions Amounting to Ill-Treatment 216
        6.3.3.1 The Legal Framework regarding Voluntary and
                Involuntary Interventions 216
        6.3.3.2 The Legal Framework to Protect against Ill-treatment 220
        6.3.3.3 The Role of Traditional Healthcare: A Pathway or a
                Challenge? 226
    6.3.4 Concluding Summary 231
6.4 Country Study II: Germany 234
    6.4.1 Background of Germany 234
        6.4.1.1 Geographic, Demographic and Economic characteristics ... 234
        6.4.1.2 Legal and Administrative Context 235
        6.4.1.3 Mental Health Service Provision 236
    6.4.2 Germany's Mental Health Legislative Framework 240
        6.4.2.1 Relevant Legislation 241
            6.4.2.1.1 Involuntary Admission 242
            6.4.2.1.2 Involuntary Treatment 244
            6.4.2.1.3 Complaint Procedures 245
            6.4.2.1.4 Community-based Care 246
        6.4.2.2 Relevant Strategies, Plans and Programmes 247
    6.4.3 Persisting Key Challenge: Guardianship Regulation
        (Betreuungsrecht) 249
        6.4.3.1 The Legal Framework regarding the Question of
                Incompetence 249

		6.4.3.1.1	Restriction of the Capacity to Act 250
		6.4.3.1.2	Avoidance of Heteronomy in Situations of Impaired Decision-making Skills 251
	6.4.3.2	The Legal Framework regarding the System of Representation... 254
	6.4.3.3	Accessible Supportive Measures as Alternatives 260
6.4.4	Concluding Summary 261

PART 4.
ADVANCING THE RIGHT TO MENTAL HEALTH: CONCLUSIONS AND RECOMMENDATIONS 267

Chapter 7.
Conclusions and Recommendations 269

7.1 Introduction 269
7.2 Conclusions 270
7.3 Recommendations 276
    7.3.1 States (and State Actors)....................................... 276
    7.3.2 The Committee on the Rights of Persons with Disabilities (CteeRPD) 278
    7.3.3 Non-governmental Organisations (NGOs) 278
7.4 Final Remarks 278

List of Instruments 281
List of Cases.. 285
United Nations Documents.. 287
Documents of Other Bodies... 295
List of Tables 301
Samenvatting (Dutch Summary) 303
Selected Bibliography... 309
Curriculum Vitae 321

PART 1
CONCEPT AND PROBLEM

CHAPTER 1

INTRODUCTION

1.1 BACKGROUND AND PROBLEM

As expressed by the High Commissioner for Human Rights, Michelle Bachelet, 'through COVID-19, mental health has finally emerged as a global priority, as it should always have been'.[1] Before the COVID-19 pandemic, in 2019, one in every eight persons (970 million people) around the world was said to be living with a mental health disorder, with anxiety and depressive disorders being the most common (301 million and 280 million, respectively).[2] In 2020, this number rose significantly, due to the impact of, and measures against, the pandemic. The World Health Organization (WHO) estimates that, in just one year, cases of anxiety increased by 26 per cent, and cases of depressive disorders by 28 per cent.[3] For a long time these effects were underestimated. Due to the high stress levels experienced by people across the globe, particularly in the time of the pandemic, more attention must be given to mental health prevention. Health systems all around the world are significantly under-resourced, and have not yet adequately responded with interventions to prevent or reduce mental health disorders. There is a wide gap between the demand for treatment and the access to mental health support services that respond to the needs of affected individuals. This leaves approximately two-thirds of persons with mental health conditions without access to mental health services for treatment.[4] Another concern is that, even when they are able to access mental health support services, many individuals are caught in a vicious cycle of violence in interaction with these services.[5] Deputy Director General of the WHO, Zsuzsanna

---

[1] See Office of the High Commissioner for Human Rights (OHCHR) Consultation Mental Health and Human Rights, HRC RES 43/13, 15 November 2021, speech of Michelle Bachelet, <https://conf.unog.ch/digitalrecordings/index.html?embed=-h&mrid=DE3A94BD-A240–450A-91DD-FC6323A179F1> accessed 14 November 2022.

[2] World Health Organization (WHO), 'Mental disorders' (8 June 2022), <https://www.who.int/news-room/fact-sheets/detail/mental-disorders> accessed 14 November 2022.

[3] WHO, 'Mental Health and COVID-19: Early evidence of the pandemic's impact: Scientific brief, 2 March 2022', <https://www.who.int/publications/i/item/WHO-2019-nCoV-Sci_Brief-Mental_health-2022.1> accessed 14 November 2022.

[4] See WHO, 'Mental Health Atlas 2020' (WHO 2021), <https://www.who.int/publications/i/item/9789240036703> accessed 14 November 2022; Modhurima Moitra and others, 'The global gap in treatment coverage for major depressive disorder in 84 countries from 2000–2019: a systematic review and Bayesian meta-regression analysis' (2022) 19(2) PLoS Med.

[5] See OHCHR (n 1).

Jakab, articulates that 'the COVID-19 pandemic ... has ... served to highlight and compound the inadequate and outdated nature of mental health systems and services worldwide'.[6] While there has been an increase in demand due to the pandemic, mental health services have been disrupted, or even closed, in 93 per cent of countries around the globe.[7] People with mental health disorders living in mental health institutions have faced a worsening of their conditions, including higher risks of involuntary treatment and hospitalisation, over-medicalisation, isolation, or even death.[8] The pandemic has widened the gap that already existed in the provision of quality psychosocial support. Thus, the need is now higher than ever to adopt, implement, update, strengthen and monitor existing mental health laws, policies and practices, to adhere to human rights principles.

Although the last two decades have been marked by a growing awareness of the need to improve mental health services, has the response by governments around the world been sufficient? And do laws, policies and programmes align with international human rights? It is specifically through the work of former United Nations (UN) Special Rapporteur of the Right to Health (2014–2020), Dainius Pūras, that mental health has grown in prominence on the global stage. From the beginning of his mandate, he highlighted the need to advance the realisation of a right to mental health.[9] In 2015, the UN pledged to promote mental health and well-being in its Sustainable Development Goal 3, Target 3.4, which is to 'reduce by one-third pre-mature mortality from non-communicable diseases (NCDs) through prevention and treatment, and promote mental health and wellbeing'.[10] The right to mental health has also become a subject of ever-increasing importance at the UN Human Rights Council. In recent years, the Council has adopted several resolutions on mental health and human rights, recognising the need to fully integrate a human rights perspective into mental health,[11] and recognising the importance of providing effective mental health and other community-based services that protect, promote and respect the enjoyment of the rights to liberty and security of a person, as well as the right to live independently and be included in the

---

[6] See OHCHR Consultation Mental Health and Human Rights, HRC RES 43/13, 15 November 2021, speech of Zsuzsanna Jakab, <https://conf.unog.ch/digitalrecordings/index.html?embed=-h&mrid=DE3A94BD-A240-450A-91DD-FC6323A179F1> accessed 14 November 2022.

[7] WHO, 'World Mental Health Day on 10 October to highlight urgent need to increase investment in chronically underfunded sector' (5 October 2020), <https://www.who.int/news/item/05-10-2020-covid-19-disrupting-mental-health-services-in-most-countries-who-survey> accessed 5 July 2022.

[8] See OHCHR (n 1).

[9] United Nations General Assembly (UNGA), 'Report of the Special Rapporteur on the right of everyone to the enjoyment of the highest attainable standard of physical and mental health, Dainius Pūras' (28 March 2017) UN Doc A/HRC/35/21.

[10] See UNGA, 'Resolution adopted by the General Assembly on 25 September 2015, 70/1. Transforming our world: the 2030 Agenda for Sustainable Development' (21 October 2015) UN Doc A/RES/70/1, p 16.

[11] See UNGA, 'Resolution adopted by the Human Rights Council on 1 July 2016, 32/18. Mental health and human rights' (18 July 2016) UN Doc A/HRC/RES/32/18.

community, on an equal basis with others.[12] The most recent resolution, of July 2020 (resolution 43/13), voices concern that persons with mental health disorders, including mental health patients[13]:

> Continue to be subject to, inter alia, widespread, multiple, intersecting and aggravated discrimination, stigma, stereotypes, prejudice, violence, abuse, social exclusion and segregation, unlawful and arbitrary deprivation of liberty and institutionalization, overmedicalization and treatment practices that fail to respect their autonomy, will and preferences.[14]

It adds that such practices may constitute, or lead to, human rights violations, which could sometimes amount to torture or other cruel, inhuman or degrading treatment or punishment.[15] The resolution urges states to promote a paradigm shift in mental health, 'through the promotion of community-, evidence- and human rights-based and people-centred services and supports that protect, promote and respect the enjoyment of the rights'.[16] The WHO has also, increasingly, developed guidelines and programmes to address the needs of persons with mental health issues. Building upon its predecessor (the Mental Health Action Plan 2013–2020), the WHO Comprehensive Mental Health Action Plan 2013–2030 sets out actions for states to promote mental health and well-being, and to prevent mental health disorders.[17] More recently, the WHO provided, with its *Guidance on community mental health services: Promoting person-centred and rights-based approaches*, a set of publications with information and support to transform mental health systems and services to align with international human rights standards.[18] In his final report in 2020, Special Rapporteur Pūras clarified that, '[t]he

---

[12] See UNGA, 'Resolution adopted by the Human Rights Council on 28 September 2017, 36/13. Mental health and human rights' (9 October 2017) UN Doc A/HRC/RES/36/13.

[13] After careful consideration of the various terms and their implications, the author has chosen to use the term 'patient' generally in this book, rather than 'service user', 'client', 'survivor' or 'consumer'. The term 'patient' appropriately describes a temporary role in healthcare and implies that patients with mental disorders are valued in the same way as patients in physical healthcare. In this book, the term 'patient' is preferred when individuals are treated in the formal (and informal) healthcare setting. The term 'service user' was not chosen because it would imply that individuals were actively using the service or that the service was 'useful' to them. This term is particularly critical in the context of non-consensual mental health interventions. Depending on the context, e.g. when referring to other mental health (support) services, the term 'client' might be used in this book.

[14] UNGA, 'Resolution adopted by the Human Rights Council on 19 June 2020, 43/13. Mental health and human rights' (1 July 2020) UN Doc A/HRC/RES/43/13, p 2.

[15] Ibid.

[16] UNGA, 'Resolution adopted by the Human Rights Council on 19 June 2020, 43/13. Mental health and human rights' (n 14), para 7.

[17] See WHO, 'Comprehensive Mental Health Action Plan 2013–2030' (2021), <https://www.who.int/publications/i/item/9789240031029> accessed 14 November 2022.

[18] See WHO, 'Guidance on community mental health services: Promoting person-centred and rights-based approaches' (2021), <https://www.who.int/publications/i/item/9789240025707> accessed 14 November 2022.

global message is clear: there can be no good mental health without human rights'.[19] In May of the following year, at the World Health Assembly, various governments collectively and publicly recognised the importance of scaling up access to quality and human rights-based mental health services.[20]

This international recognition is to be welcomed. However, is it possible that more needs to be done at the global, regional and national levels regarding how mental health should be understood and addressed in light of a human rights approach? Despite promising trends, are human rights violations sufficiently addressed in mental healthcare systems worldwide? While many states have enacted legislation to promote and regulate mental health, the question remains whether these laws adequately protect the human rights of persons with mental health conditions. Obligations stemming from international human rights law should influence legislative, administrative, budgetary and other measures states have to take. But how does international human rights law precisely define the right to mental health?

The right to the highest attainable standard of health is well defined under international human rights law, and Article 12 of the International Covenant on Economic, Social and Cultural Rights (ICESCR) is recognised as a core norm for its protection. Although the provision does not prioritise physical health per se, academic debate has mostly scrutinised the right to health generally, or has focused primarily on physical health.[21] The limited existing legal scholarship covering mental health and human rights typically focuses on one component of the right to mental health, usually legal capacity or non-consensual treatment.[22] Against this background, this book aims to establish a comprehensive human rights framework, which takes into account specific legal challenges, in order to formulate a 'right to mental health'. It does so by amplifying the importance of mental health within the right to the highest attainable standard of health norm, and by emphasising the unique and interdependent relationship between mental health and the full enjoyment of other human rights. At the same time, the

---

[19]   UNGA, 'Report of the Special Rapporteur on the right of everyone to the enjoyment of the highest attainable standard of physical and mental health, Dainius Pūras' (15 April 2020) UN Doc A/HRC/44/48, para 2.

[20]   WHO, Seventy-fourth World Health Assembly, 'Resolution on strengthening WHO preparedness for and response to health emergencies' (31 May 2021), <https://apps.who.int/gb/ebwha/pdf_files/WHA74/A74_R7-en.pdf> accessed 14 November 2022.

[21]   See eg Brigit Toebes and others (eds), *The Right to Health: a Multi-Country Study of Law, Policy and Practice* (Springer 2014); John Tobin, *The Right to Health in International Law* (Oxford University Press 2012), Marie-Elske Gispen, *Human Rights and Drug Control: Access to Controlled Essential Medicines in Resource-constrained Countries* (Intersentia 2017); and Jamie Enoch and others, 'Human Rights in the Fourth Decade of the HIV/AIDS Response' 19(2) (2017) Health and Human Rights Journal 177.

[22]   Eilionóir Flynn and others (eds), *Global perspectives on legal capacity reform: our voices, our stories* (Routledge 2018); Anna Arstein-Kerslake, *Restoring voice to people with cognitive disabilities: realizing the right to equal recognition before the law* (Cambridge University Press 2017); Dinesh Bhugra and others (eds), 'The right to mental health and parity' 57(2) (2015) Indian Journal of Psychiatry 117; Peter Barlett and others, 'Urgently awaiting implementation: The right to be free from exploitation, violence and abuse in Article 16 of the Convention on the Rights of Persons with Disabilities (CRPD)' 53 (2017) The International Journal of Law and Psychiatry 2.

peculiarities of regional differences, and the influence of traditions at the domestic level, are considered. Analysis on the right to the highest attainable standard of health, and its shortcomings in the context of mental health, is scarce. This book illustrates why the right to the highest attainable standard of health norm might be insufficient to protect a comprehensive right to mental health, and examines what other human rights might be needed to mitigate the existing gaps. By considering human rights challenges in accessing mental health services, a range of mental health-related human rights are identified, to promote the right to mental health.[23] Offering the highest human rights standard for the protection of rights of persons with psychosocial disabilities, the Convention on the Rights of Persons with Disabilities (CRPD) will play a crucial role in this book. International human rights norms serve to ensure that regional and domestic law is adjusted accordingly: especially the latter, since treaty provisions are binding upon each state party. In many instances, regional human rights bodies have held states responsible for their failure to fulfil their legal obligations to protect the right to mental health.[24] By including Ghana and Germany as country studies, this research seeks to uncover to what extent international human rights on mental health are applicable and implemented in domestic settings. Taking this contextual approach may assist in revealing the complexities and shortcomings of international human rights law relating to mental health provision. If any complexities and shortcomings exist at all, it will further help to clarify the scope of the right to mental health.

With all the above in mind, the aim of this book is to utilise, and create an understanding of, the existing law, in order to guide law- and policy-making, and regulations for the thorough promotion of mental health at the international, regional and domestic level.

1.2 RESEARCH QUESTIONS AND STRUCTURE

1.2.1 RESEARCH QUESTIONS

The central research questions of this study are:

- Which rights and obligations exist for the protection of mental health under international human rights law?
- How should access to mental healthcare services be regulated from a human rights perspective?

---

[23] Henceforth in this paper, 'right to mental health' refers to the comprehensive right to mental health as being established in this book, not only to Article 12 of the International Covenant on Economic, Social and Cultural Rights.
[24] As examples, *Purohit and Moore v The Gambia*, Communication No. 241/2001, Sixteenth Activity report 2002–2003, Annex VII; *Varbanov v Bulgaria*, ECHR 2000-X 457; *Ximenes-Lopes v Brazil* (Merits, Reparations and Costs) IACtHR Series C No 149 (4 July 2006).

The central research questions encompass the following subquestions:

- What is meant, in this study, by 'mental health', 'psychosocial disability' and 'mental healthcare'?
- What are the human rights challenges that persons with mental disorders face in the mental healthcare context?
- What does the right to mental health entail?
- To what extent does the right to the highest attainable standard of physical and mental health, in particular Article 12 ICESCR, respect, protect and fulfil mental health as a stand-alone norm?
- Which additional human rights are relevant for guaranteeing access to mental healthcare, and what are the derived obligations?
- To what extent has mental health as a human right been given effect to in Ghana and Germany?
- How, if at all, can the chosen case studies serve as examples to advance the understanding of the right to mental health, and the right to accessing mental healthcare in particular?

The primary goal of this book is to examine whether international human rights law promotes and protects the right to mental health. In doing so, this book synthesises two different human rights treaties, the ICESCR and the CRPD,[25] and integrates them into an analytical framework for 'the right to mental health'. Through theoretical and partly empirical analysis (see section 1.3 on methodology) of the outlined subquestions, the research provides a better understanding of a human rights approach to accessing mental healthcare. This book is expected to establish a comprehensive right to mental health framework that can assist regional and domestic law- and policy-making, as well as for advancing rights-based and person-centred mental healthcare.

1.2.2 RESEARCH STRUCTURE

This book is divided into four parts: concept and problem (Chapters 1 and 2); normative analysis (Chapters 3, 4 and 5); country studies (Chapter 6); and conclusions and recommendations (Chapter 7).

Part 1 lays the foundation for the book. Chapter 1 introduces the research problem, the research design, and the methodology employed in this book. It briefly highlights the issues at hand. Chapter 2 discusses further context and explores the background and content of mental health and mental healthcare. It pays attention to the various mental health(care) terminologies, and explains the influence of culture on accessing mental healthcare, and why this matters. The chapter concludes with the identification of persisting human rights challenges associated with the mental healthcare context.

---

[25] The reason why this book focuses on these two treaties will be explained further in chapter 3.

The human rights challenges set the scene for the book and build the basis for the normative analysis.

Part 2 offers the normative analysis, and consists of Chapters 3, 4 and 5. Chapter 3 explores the evolving framework of the right to mental health, which gives rise to the question whether the right to the enjoyment of the highest attainable standard of physical and mental health protects and promotes mental health in the same fashion as physical health, and whether this is sufficient for the mental health context. Chapter 4 looks at the analysis of the normative content of the right to the highest attainable standard of health, and the derived state obligations. While the right to the highest attainable standard of health provides for the right of access to adequate mental health facilities, goods and services, there is growing consensus that a human rights approach to disability strengthens the right to mental healthcare. Hence, Chapter 5 scrutinises a set of human rights provisions to ensure humane and dignified mental healthcare. Besides exploring the scope and content of these provisions, as well as the derived state obligations, Chapter 5 also addresses various controversial issues and offers a way forward. In this way, the right to mental health framework is further strengthened.

Subsequently, in Part 3 and Chapter 6, the research moves to an appraisal of the domestic implementation of the right to mental health in Ghana, and in Germany. After a brief introduction to the case studies, and general country profiles, Chapter 6 maps out and analyses various legal and policy provisions regarding mental health(care) enacted by Ghana and Germany. The purpose of the country studies in Chapter 6 is twofold. First, they identify the gaps that exist between international human rights norms and domestic legislation. Second, they seek to explore how domestic norms and practices might offer possible (and practical) solutions to remaining challenges flowing from the rather black-and-white interpretation of international norms by the respective treaty bodies. By doing so, the understanding of the right to mental health framework can be advanced. Together with Part 2, the case studies in Chapter 6 build the core of the research.

Chapter 7 summarises the main findings of this research, and identifies several overall conclusions. Additionally, it offers a set of recommendations to international, regional and national actors to use as a basis for laws and policies to implement certain human rights standards under the right to mental health, to promote mental health, ensure access to humane and dignified mental healthcare, and protect the human rights of persons with mental health conditions and psychosocial disabilities.

1.3 METHODOLOGY

In this study, the author uses mixed methods to ensure that the research questions are fully addressed. The mixed methods approach provides a holistic understanding of how a human rights situation arose or developed, and how such a situation can be addressed. Ultimately, this leads to a deeper understanding of the subject area addressed by the central research questions.[26] As the title of the book indicates, the study follows a human rights-based approach, which can be defined as respecting human rights principles and ensuring the realisation of human rights. Furthermore, such an approach aims to strengthen the capacities of rights-holders, once they and their entitlements have been identified, as well as the corresponding human rights obligations of duty-bearers, once they and their duties have been identified.[27] Descriptive, normative and empirical research methods, as applied throughout the chapters, contribute to the understanding of what the respective human rights standards are, what they mean, and how their protection can be strengthened.[28] Based on Smith's explanation of a human rights-based approach,[29] the book also follows the 'human rights in context' approach, which contributes to properly understanding the actual human rights situation. The 'human rights in context' approach considers, among other matters, cultural, religious, and socio-economic factors that influence how the law is interpreted and applied. The advantage of such an approach is that understanding the law in context maximises the chance that human rights can be meaningfully realised on the national level.[30] The remainder of this section describes, in detail, which research methods are applied, in each of the chapters, to answer the individual subquestions and, thus, the central research questions, in the best possible way.

Chapter 2 adopts a descriptive research approach for the analysis of the content and background. Given that mental health, mental healthcare and human rights challenges are concepts recognised in different disciplines, secondary sources across the disciplines of public health, psychology, psychiatry, anthropology, law and human rights are analysed.

To delineate the normative content of the right to mental health in Part 2, the study carries out a normative analysis within the limits of a doctrinal analytical approach. The doctrinal research approach applied in this book is what Egan defines as 'reform-oriented doctrinal research': it not only describes what the law *is*, but also advocates for what the law *ought to be*.[31] In this additional dimension of doctrinal research, the author, as a researcher, not only establishes and discovers facts, but also makes normative decisions about the relevance of legal text.[32] In Chapters 3, 4 and 5, the author reviews relevant international, regional and domestic legal frameworks, including hard

---

[26] Rhona Smith, 'Human rights based approaches to research' in Lee McConnell and Rhona Smith (eds), *Research Methods in Human Rights* (Routledge 2018) 12.

[27] See United Nations Sustainable Development Group, 'The Human Rights Based Approach to Development Cooperation Towards a Common Understanding Among UN Agencies' (2003), <https://unsdg.un.org/resources/human-rights-based-approach-development-cooperation-towards-common-understanding-among-un> accessed 14 November 2022; Rhona Smith & Lee McConnell, 'Introduction to human rights research methods' in Lee McConnell and Rhona Smith (eds), *Research Methods in Human Rights* (Routledge 2018) 3.

[28] Rhona Smith (n 26) 9.

[29] Rhona Smith (n 26) 12.

[30] Rhona Smith & Lee McConnell, (n 27) p 3.

[31] Emphasis added.

[32] Suzanne Egan, 'The doctrinal approach in international human rights law scholarship' in Lee McConnell and Rhona Smith (eds), *Research Methods in Human Rights* (Routledge 2018) 28.

law, soft law and case law. Besides primary legal documents, the secondary data analysis includes reports, general comments and concluding observations by UN treaty bodies, reports by UN Special Rapporteurs, and academic publications. The normative analysis of Chapter 4 focuses on the key concepts and components derived from the right to the highest attainable standard of physical and mental health, Article 12 ICESCR, and its General Comment 14, as well as other related treaty interpretation. By applying the same research methods as in the two preceding chapters, the legal analysis in Chapter 5 defines the scope and remit of various additional human rights norms under the CRPD, which are considered under the right to mental health framework. Where appropriate and necessary, Chapter 5 presents opposing arguments and different opinions. The analysis aims to establish a valid and logical argumentation, while knowing well that the presented analysis cannot be considered as the only possibility. Throughout the book, but especially in Part 2, the interaction between human rights treaties – namely the ICESCR and CRPD – plays an integral role. Rather than focusing on the analysis of one treaty or regime, the author aims to demonstrate, with this study, that there is utility in analysing the interaction of different regimes in the form of 'regime complexes'. Regime complexes can be defined as 'an array of partially overlapping and nonhierarchical institutions governing a particular issue-area'.[33] As will be illustrated throughout the chapters of this book, the right to mental health is best conceptualised as a regime complex comprised of interconnected regimes.

For the country study analysis in Part 3,[34] the research takes descriptive, normative and empirical approaches. Taking a descriptive approach, the background information on Ghana and Germany is based on literature review across the disciplines of political science, public administration, public health and law. Regarding the domestic implementation of the right to mental health, the author conducts a normative analysis of existing domestic mental health laws and policies. The author obtained the legal documents that were selected for analysis, as well as the health-related and human rights-related documents, from official governmental websites, where available, or directly from governmental institutions or non-governmental organisations. In Ghana, these included the Ministry of Health, Mental Health Authority, the Traditional Medicine Practice Council and the Mental Health Society of Ghana. In Germany, these included the Federal Ministry of Health and the German Institute for Human Rights (which is the National CRPD Monitoring Body). When investigating the national laws and policies for the purpose of identifying the countries' practices, and to ensure the accuracy of the author's analysis, the author took a specific approach for each country study. This is further explained in the methodology section of the country studies (see subsection 6.2.2). While the study is legal at its core, a selection of qualitative empirical methods was used to gain local insights to produce an answer for the country study-related research questions.

---

[33] Kal Raustiala & David G Victor, 'The Regime Complex for Plant Genetic Resources' (2004) 58 (2) International Organization 277, 279.
[34] See subsection 6.2.2 for rationale for country selection.

1.4. CONCLUDING SUMMARY

This book seeks to contribute to the global discussion of mental health by examining a right to mental health approach. The academic relevance of the book is to better understand the human right to mental health and the implications of international human rights norms, particularly with respect to access to mental healthcare. By looking at the relationship between legal norms, regulations, traditions and culture, in relation to mental health, the book hopes to stimulate and inform policy debates on this issue. In addition to its academic relevance, the book hopes to contribute to a societal debate. It is the author's hope that implementing the recommendations offered in this book may help create better standards for persons with mental health conditions and psychosocial disabilities and enable them to access humane and dignified mental healthcare, which will have a positive impact not only on their lives, but also on society as a whole.

CHAPTER 2
MENTAL HEALTH AND MENTAL HEALTHCARE: BACKGROUND AND CONTENT

2.1 INTRODUCTION

This chapter lays the foundation for evaluating the normative framework of the right to mental health. Before proceeding with the normative analysis of the research, this chapter offers an introduction to the background and content. It establishes a basis upon which the book can be built. Throughout the sections, the concepts of mental health, psychosocial disability, mental healthcare and human rights challenges will be evaluated and defined from medical, philosophical, anthropological, socio-economical and legal perspectives, and their connection under the topic of the right to health will be illustrated.

The chapter is divided into further sections. Section 2.2 commences by defining relevant terms in the mental health context. Subsequently, the contextualisation of mental healthcare approaches is demonstrated (section 2.3) to address the different contexts in which the later-established right to mental health is supposed to apply. Then, section 2.4 elaborates on the prevalent human rights challenges in the mental healthcare context. This section highlights the vulnerability of persons with mental disorders when seeking mental healthcare.

2.2 THE MEANING OF RELEVANT TERMS

The terminologies associated with mental health and psychosocial disability differ among various schools of thought. The three definitions that are important for this book are 'mental health', 'psychosocial disability' and 'mental healthcare', which are all interconnected. According to the World Health Organization (WHO), mental health is a state of mental well-being, and is more than the absence of mental disorders.[1] Potentially, mental health conditions can lead to psychosocial disability,

---

[1] World Health Organization (WHO), 'Mental health: strengthening our response' (17 June 2022), <https://www.who.int/news-room/fact-sheets/detail/mental-health-strengthening-our-response> accessed 14 November 2022.

and psychosocial disability is a state that affects mental well-being. There are different kinds of psychosocial disabilities but, for all, healthcare and social services are key.[2] Therefore, after clarifying what mental health implies, and defining psychosocial disability, the author will explain what mental healthcare comprises: a service provision that is integral in the discussion about mental health, psychosocial disability and the human rights protection of persons with mental health conditions and psychosocial disabilities. Thus, the following sections will analyse essential terms and discuss: (i) which individuals belong to the vulnerable group addressed by the later-established right to mental health; and (ii) in which kind of mental healthcare contexts does the right to mental health need to be considered.

2.2.1 THE CONCEPT OF 'MENTAL HEALTH'

The origins of the concept of mental health can be traced back to developments in public health. According to literature dating back to the 1840s, the objectives of public health included the 'healthy mental and physical development of the citizen', and 'the concept of mental hygiene'.[3] Initially, the mental hygiene movement was primarily concerned with improving the care of persons with psychosocial disabilities: eradicating neglect, brutalities and abuses. With the foundation of the American National Committee for Mental Hygiene in 1909, the implications of environmental conditions were then also considered under the concept of mental hygiene. At this point, preventive activities, and not just the cure, also gained importance.[4] In 1948, the WHO was created within the United Nations (UN) system, to further international cooperation for identifying, addressing and improving public health issues; it was then that the terms 'mental hygiene' and 'mental health' were connected. As the WHO Expert Committee on Mental Health stated in 1951, 'mental hygiene consists of the activities and techniques which encourage and maintain mental health'.[5] In fact, with the entry into force of the WHO Constitution in 1948, a new definition of health was introduced, in which 'mental health' no longer referred to a specific discipline, but rather to a dimension of health.

2.2.1.1 *The Definition of 'Mental Health'*

The preamble to the 1946 WHO Constitution provides that, '[h]ealth is a state of complete physical, mental and social well-being and not merely the absence of

---

[2] WHO, Fact Sheet 'Mental disorders' (28 November 2019), <https://www.who.int/news-room/fact-sheets/detail/mental-disorders> accessed 14 November 2022.
[3] José Bertolote, 'The roots of the concept of mental health' (2008) 7(2) World Psychiatry 113, 113.
[4] José Bertolote (n 3) 113–114.
[5] WHO Expert Committee on Mental Health & WHO, 'Expert Committee on Mental Health: report on the second session, Geneva, 11–16 September 1950' (1951) <https://apps.who.int/iris/handle/10665/37982> accessed 14 November 2022, p 4.

disease or infirmity'.[6] This definition of 'health' is significant for various reasons. It is pragmatic, as it incorporates a social dimension into medicine. It is also holistic, and aims to overcome the dichotomy between body and mind. It further sets out to change the narrow biomedical definition, which classifies mental health as 'absence of mental disorder'. While the WHO definition of health received criticism for being too broad and lacking value for advancing the human right of health,[7] it is important to point out that in 1951 the WHO Expert Committee on Mental Health drafted a more detailed definition of 'mental health'. Then, mental health was understood as a condition subject to fluctuation, influenced by biological and social factors, which enabled individuals to achieve a balanced satisfaction of their own potentially conflicting, instinctive drives; to form and maintain harmonious relationships with others; and to participate constructively in their physical and social environment.[8] As the concept of positive mental health has changed over time, the WHO eventually revised its original definition of mental health to offer a more conclusive definition that understands mental health as 'a state of mental well-being that enables people to cope with the stresses of life, realize their abilities, learn well and work well, and contribute to their community.'[9]

In this definition, mental health is described as an integral component for well-being and the effective functioning of an individual. In other words, mental health is understood as being fundamental to the individual and collective ability of persons to think, interact with one another, emote, earn an income and enjoy life.[10] Scholars suggest that, specifically for children and adolescents, mental health implies that individuals are capable of achieving and maintaining optimal psychological functioning and well-being.[11] According to the former UN Special Rapporteur on the Right to Health, Dainius Pūras, the modern understanding of mental health further includes good emotional and social well-being, and healthy non-violent relations between individuals or groups, together with mutual trust of, tolerance of, and respect for the dignity of, every person.[12] In addition to the WHO definition, Pūras highlights the interaction between mental health and interpersonal relationships.

---

[6] Constitution of the World Health Organization (WHO Constitution) (adopted 22 July 1946, entered into force 7 April 1948) 14 UNTS 185, preamble.

[7] See eg Stephen Marks, 'The Emergence and Scope of the Human Right to Health' in José Zuniga, Stephen Marks and Lawrence Gostin (eds), *Advancing the Human Right to Health* (Oxford University Press 2013) 6–7; or Vahid Yazdi-Feyzabadi and others, 'The World Health Organization's Definition of Health: A Short Review of Critiques and Necessity of A Shifting Paradigm' (2018) 13(5) Iranian Journal of Epidemiology 155.

[8] WHO Expert Committee on Mental Health & WHO (n 5).

[9] WHO (n 1).

[10] Ibid.

[11] Melvyn WB Zhang & Roger CM Ho, 'Specific Mental Health Disorders: Child and Adolescent Mental Disorders' in Stella R Quah (ed), *International Encyclopedia of Public Health, second edition* (Elsevier 2017), 22–28.

[12] United Nations General Assembly (UNGA), 'Report of the Special Rapporteur on the right of everyone to the enjoyment of the highest attainable standard of physical and mental health, Dainius Pūras' (2 April 2015) UN Doc A/HRC/29/33, para 74–77.

In the 1960s, social scientist Bradburn asserted in his book, titled *The Structure of Psychological Well-Being*, that mental well-being is created by balancing two independent dimensions, which he considered positive and negative affect. In his view, a high level of mental well-being is characterised by 'positive affect'. If 'negative affect' dominates, individuals experience a low level of mental well-being. The ten-item scale Bradburn created to measure the positive and negative facets of psychological well-being[13] has been recognised as a parameter for measuring well-being, but has also been criticised for being too situation-specific.[14] Nowadays, it is acknowledged that mental health is 'a complex continuum, which is experienced differently from one person to the next, with varying degrees of difficulty and distress and potentially very different social and clinical outcomes.'[15] Mental health has a range of determinants, including social, economic, psychosocial, biological and environmental factors. Due to, inter alia, violence, persisting socio-economical pressure, specific personality factors or genetic factors, some individuals are more vulnerable to mental health conditions than others.[16] Mental health conditions, according to the WHO, 'include mental disorders and psychosocial disabilities as well as other mental states associated with significant distress, impairment in functioning, or risk of self-harm.'[17] It is therefore important to emphasise that psychosocial disability cannot simply be understood as the flip side of mental health.

2.2.2 THE CONCEPT OF 'PSYCHOSOCIAL DISABILITY'

Understanding the concept of 'psychosocial disability' is crucial for this book, as the right to mental health is specifically intended to protect people affected by psychosocial disabilities (as this vulnerable group is particularly susceptible to serious human rights infringements). After demonstrating the concept and definition of mental health, this section scrutinises the origins, terminology and definition of psychosocial disability.

Historically, psychosocial disabilities have been considered supernatural, psychological and biological, as the following will show. According to the supernatural belief, psychosocial disabilities are caused by agents outside the body and the environment that influence the person's behaviour and emotions. For instance, in the Persian Empire from 900 to 600 BC, psychosocial disabilities were regarded as the work

---

[13] The Bradburn Scale includes five positive affect questions and five negative affect questions that can be answered with yes or no. For every 'yes', the participant receives one point. In the end, the negative affect score is subtracted from the positive affect score to create the overall 'balance' score.
[14] Vivianne Kovess-Masfety and others, 'Evolution of Our Understanding of Positive Mental Health' in Helen Herrman, Shekhar Saxena & Rob Moodie (eds), *Promoting Mental Health: concepts, emerging evidence, practice* (World Health Organization 2005) 35.
[15] WHO (n 1).
[16] Ibid.
[17] Ibid.

of the devil.[18] A few centuries thereafter, the notion of psychological and biological causation of psychosocial disabilities was developed in ancient Greece. In the second half of the millennium BC, various philosophers distinguished between non-medical psychic disturbances and medical mental disorders. On the one hand, they believed in 'psychophysiological temperaments', influenced by cultural and social environments as well as early learning, as being 'diseases of the soul'.[19] This can be considered as an early stage of viewing mental ill health in terms of psychological phenomena. The 'diseases of the soul' were treatable with philosophical therapy, which aimed to gradually develop an individual's greater enlightenment and self-control.[20] This kind of therapy was introduced for persons troubled by dissatisfaction, fear and worries. On the other hand, ancient Greek philosophers believed that 'severe forms of mental disorders' were diseases of the head, heart or brain, and thus physical disorders that required medical treatment.[21] Thus, ancient philosophers understood mental disorders – at least in its severe forms – along the same lines as ancient medical doctors, namely as biological phenomena. Starting around 400 BC, Greek physician Hippocrates and Roman physician Gale both suggested, separately, that mental disorders, located in the brain, could be treated like any other disease. They associated mental disorders with an imbalance of four bodily fluids: an approach that is now widely recognised as 'chemical imbalance'.[22] While the physicians believed that mental disorders were caused by disease, head trauma or genetics, they also already recognised the interpersonal and psychological influence, such as the negative effects of stress.[23] Hippocrates' and Gale's findings paved the way for mental healthcare as it is widely implemented today. Although the supernatural, psychological and biological dimensions have their origins in ancient times, they have been developed over time, and continue to be considered today.

2.2.2.1   The Debate on Terminology

'Mental health condition', 'mental illness', 'mental ill health', 'mental disorders', 'psychosocial disorder', 'mental disability', 'psychosocial disability', 'intellectual disability' and various other terms can be used when discussing the topic of this book. Different scholars use different terms. Some of these terms have different connotations and shades of meaning; others reflect sensitive debates, such as the medical or social model of functioning.[24] For instance, 'mental illness' reinforces the medical model

---

[18]   David H Barlow & V Mark Durand, *Abnormal Psychology: An Integrative Approach*, eighth edition (Cengage Learning 2017), 9–10.
[19]   See eg Marke Ahonen, 'Ancient philosophers on mental illness' (2019) 30(1) History of Psychiatry 3, 3–5; or David H Barlow & V Mark Durand (n 18) 16.
[20]   Marke Ahonen (n 19) 3–5.
[21]   Marke Ahonen (n 19) 12–15.
[22]   David H Barlow & V Mark Durand (n 18) 13.
[23]   Ibid 9–10.
[24]   Paul Hunt & Judith Mesquita, 'Mental Disabilities and the Human Right to the Highest Attainable Standard of Health' (2006) 28(2) Human Rights Quarterly 332, 336.

of disability. Likewise, most international clinical documents use the term 'mental disorder'.[25] Adopting the language of health professionals, lawyers also commonly use 'mental disorders' in legal texts.[26] Moreover, the terminology has evolved over the years. For example, instead of 'mental disability', international human rights actors, the WHO and the disability community now commonly use the term 'psychosocial disability'.

In this book, the author chooses to use the term 'persons with mental health conditions and psychosocial disabilities'. 'Persons with mental health conditions' refers to people with a variety of experiences of mental distress, also including milder forms of mental health problems. 'Persons with psychosocial disabilities' refers to people with mental disorder which, in interaction with a social environment, presents barriers that hinder their full and effective participation in society on an equal basis with others. Psychosocial disability is not a synonym for mental disorder, but disability (or, in other words, impairment) can be an intrinsic sign or consequence of a mental disorder. For example, even persons who have recovered from their mental disorder may still face disabilities; the same is true for persons with an enhanced chance of suffering a new episode of their mental disorder.[27] Thus, psychosocial disability can be seen as a result of an underlying mental disorder. Bertolote and Sartorius find that psychosocial disability directly refers to the effects the underlying mental disorder has on the lives of affected individuals, and their needs or limitations.[28]

Using the term 'persons with mental health conditions and psychosocial disabilities' is useful for the positive protection of human rights. It includes all persons with mental health conditions, regardless of their severity, with particular attention to barriers that impede a person's participation in society due to their severe mental health problem.

2.2.2.2 The Definition of 'Psychosocial Disability'

When considering psychosocial disabilities as disabilities arising from mental disorders, it is helpful to examine the terms 'mental disorder' and 'disability' separately.

Firstly, mental disorders are a group of disorders that may share some similarities, ranging from mild to severe, and changing over time. There is no universal definition of mental disorder. In fact, regional courts and national mental health laws have defined mental disorders differently, depending on the international or national classification. The WHO defines 'mental disorder' as compromising a wide range of mental problems generally characterised as a combination of abnormal or disturbed

---

[25] Eg Classification of Mental and Behavioural Disorders: Clinical Descriptions and Diagnostic Guidelines (ICD-10); and Diagnostic and Statistical Resource Book on Mental Disorders (DSM-V).
[26] Which has the advantage that legal professionals can directly see whether a person is entitled to certain health benefits, support etc.
[27] José Bertolote & Norman Sartorius, 'WHO initiative of support to people disabled by mental illness: Some issues and concepts related to rehabilitation' (1996) 11(2) European Psychiatry 56.
[28] Ibid.

thoughts, emotions, behaviour and relationships with others, including anxiety disorders, depression, bipolar disorder or schizophrenia.[29] The most-recent edition of the American Diagnostic and Statistical Manual of Mental Disorders (DSM) defines mental disorder as:

> a syndrome characterized by clinically significant disturbance in an individual's cognition, emotion regulation, or behavior that reflects a dysfunction in the psychological, biological, or developmental processes underlying mental functioning. Mental disorders are usually associated with significant distress or disability in social, occupational, or other important activities.[30]

Secondly, the term 'disability' can be delineated by drawing inspiration from the most authoritative disability and human rights document, the Convention on the Rights of Persons with Disabilities (CRPD). The Preamble of this Convention indicates that no absolute definition of disability is possible, as 'disability is an evolving concept [that] results from the interaction between persons with impairments and attitudinal and environmental barriers that hinder their full and effective participation in society'.[31] By recognising disability as an evolving concept, the Convention endorses the understanding of disability as – at least in part – a social construct where attitudinal and environmental barriers create the condition 'disability'. Consequently, the notion of 'disability' is not rigid, and may be perceived differently depending on the societal context. This social concept contrasts with the medical concept that focuses only on a 'broken body'.[32] The CRPD does not see disability as resulting from a deficiency of the person, but rather, considers the interaction between the impairment and the surrounding environment.[33] Several scholars have interpreted the CRPD's definition of disability. Flynn, for instance, argues that the disability definition is based on the understanding 'that disability is not solely the result of a medical impairment, but also stems from societal barriers to participation',[34] including both the impairment and the barrier. Importantly, deriving from the use of the term 'interaction', the CRPD definition does not understand disability statically, as a result of barriers that exclude

---

[29] WHO, 'Mental Health Action Plan 2013–2020' (2013), <https://www.who.int/publications/i/item/9789241506021> accessed 14 November 2022, p 38.

[30] American Psychiatric Association (APA), Diagnostic and Statistical Manual of Mental Disorders, fifth edition (APA Washington 2013).

[31] UNGA, Convention on the Rights of Persons with Disabilities (CRPD) (adopted 13 December 2006, entered into force 3 May 2008) 2515 UNTS 3, preamble (e).

[32] A term commonly used in the explanation of the CRPD's disability concept, see eg Office of the United Nations High Commissioner for Human Rights (OHCHR), 'The Convention on the Rights of Persons with Disabilities, Training Guide, Professional Training Series No. 19' (2014), <https://www.ohchr.org/Documents/Publications/CRPD_TrainingGuide_PTS19_EN%20Accessible.pdf> accessed 14 November 2022.

[33] However, using the rather medical term 'impairment' could be interpreted as if the CRPD does not only embrace a social model; OHCHR (n 32) 24–28.

[34] Eilionóir Flynn, *From Rhetoric to Action: Implementing the UN Convention on the Rights of Persons with Disabilities* (CUP 2011) 18.

persons with impairments, but dynamically, considering the interactive process between individuals and their environments.[35] Similarly, the WHO also embraces disability as an umbrella term for impairments that limit a person's activity and restrict their participation.[36] Furthermore, Article 1 of the CRPD clarifies that 'persons with disabilities' refers to persons with long-term (psychosocial) impairments,[37] indicating a certain duration of the impairment. Therefore, it can be argued that persons with short-term mental health conditions are not included in the concept of psychosocial disabilities as used in the CRPD.

In conclusion, psychosocial disability exists when a mental disorder, regardless of self-identification ('perceived impairment') or diagnoses ('actual impairment'), becomes pervasive and interferes in a person's functioning. While mental disorders can be treated with, for example, drugs or therapy, it takes more to change the state of a psychosocial disability. In the words of the former UN High Commissioner for Human Rights, Seid al-Hussein, psychosocial disabilities restrict persons 'in the exercise of their rights and [pose] barriers to participation based on an actual or perceived impairment'.[38] The argumentation of the former UN High Commissioner al-Hussein can be seen as the cornerstone of this book, as the analysis aims to strengthen specifically the rights of persons with psychosocial disabilities and remove existing barriers.

Persons with mental health conditions and psychosocial disabilities encompass a variety of profoundly different conditions. In this book, the term refers to conditions such as anxiety, depression, bipolar disorders, schizophrenia and other psychoses – ranging from mild to severe forms, and it includes persons who identify themselves as having a mental health condition or psychosocial disability, as well as current or ex-users of mental health services.[39] The purpose for adopting this seemingly broad categorisation is in line with the very essence of this book: ensuring the promotion, protection and inclusion of all persons with mental health conditions, irrespective of their severity. Nevertheless, intellectual disabilities such as Down's syndrome or dementia are not covered as they are highly distinct in their causes and effects and cannot be equated with a mental disorder. Although these are typical conditions of disability covered by the CRPD, and although some of the sections analysed in this book could also be applicable to persons with intellectual disabilities (for instance the issue of over-medicalisation), these conditions require different approaches regarding

---

[35] Katerina Kazou, 'Analysing the Definition of Disability in the UN Convention on the Rights of Persons with Disabilities: is it really based on a 'Social Model' approach?' (2017) 23 International Journal of Mental Health and Capacity Law 25.
[36] WHO, 'International Classification of Functioning, Disability and Health (ICIDH-2)' (2001), <https://www.who.int/standards/classifications/international-classification-of-functioning-disability-and-health> accessed 14 November 2022.
[37] UNGA (n 31) art 1.
[38] UNGA, 'Report of the United Nations High Commissioner for Human Rights, Mental health and human rights' (31 January 2017) UN Doc A/HRC/34/32, para 5.
[39] Natalie Drew and others 'Human rights violations of people with mental and psychosocial disabilities: an unresolved global crisis' (2011) 378(9803) The Lancet 1664.

healthcare, so the right to mental health would need to be interpreted and implemented differently in these contexts.

2.2.3 THE CONCEPT OF 'MENTAL HEALTHCARE'

Access to mental healthcare offering treatment and support is key for persons with mental health conditions and psychosocial disabilities. In terms of the origins and developments of mental healthcare, institutions that care for persons with psychosocial disabilities have existed for many centuries, although the care provided has changed substantially over time. In the sixth century BC, the Greek Asclepiad temples accommodated persons with psychosocial disabilities, among others. Here, individuals were cared for and provided with music therapy and massages.[40] This practice was also found in Middle Eastern countries.[41] Nevertheless, the norm in many societies was to restrain persons with psychosocial disabilities, and to confine them at home.[42] The Middle Ages then marked the rise of actual mental asylums: institutions where people were taken because of their psychosocial disabilities.[43] Unlike the Greek or Middle Eastern temples, the conditions in mental asylums resembled prisons, as persons were often isolated in cells or chained up.[44] This slowly started to change in the late eighteenth century, when French psychiatrists instituted humane psychological interventions, and started removing chains in asylums. What can be viewed as the rise of therapeutic care and habitable institutions[45] gradually turned into the mental hygiene movement – a concept introduced in subsection 2.2.1 – leading to mental health services as we know them today.

2.2.3.1   *The Definition of 'Mental Healthcare'*

While 'healthcare' has previously been equated with medical care,[46] which is care provided by medical professionals, this book considers mental healthcare in line with the broader definition of healthcare of the WHO, which embraces 'a full range of services covering [mental] health promotion and protection, ... prevention, diagnosis, treatment, care and rehabilitation'.[47] This definition embraces the fact that, in mental healthcare, many more paramedical and non-medical care providers are involved, as

---

[40]   David H Barlow & V Mark Durand (n 18) 16.
[41]   Ibid.
[42]   Marke Ahonen (n 19) 5.
[43]   Edward Shorter, *A History of Psychiatry: From the Era of the Asylum to the Age of* Prozac (John Wiley & Sons, Inc. 1997).
[44]   David H Barlow & V Mark Durand (n 18) 17.
[45]   Ibid 16–17.
[46]   See eg UNGA, 'Report of the Special Rapporteur on the Right of Everyone to the Enjoyment of the Highest Attainable Standard of Physical and Mental Health, Paul Hunt' (31 January 2008) UN Doc A/HRC/7/11, para 45.
[47]   WHO, A Declaration of the Promotion of Patients' Rights in Europe (WHO 1994) 6.

compared to somatic healthcare. Zhang argues that the terms 'healthcare' and 'health services' need to be distinguished, because the latter may also include environmental services that have health benefits, such as sanitation or housing.[48] Yet, the WHO's definition of 'mental health services' encompasses all services that deliver effective interventions for mental health,[49] thus resembling its definition of healthcare. Hence, in this book, the terms 'mental healthcare' and 'mental health services' will be used interchangeably.

Existing mental healthcare from around the world can be mapped into three categories: institutional mental health services, integrated mental health services and community-based mental health services.[50] Where used, throughout this book, the terms 'mental healthcare' and 'mental health services' refer to either the mental health services as a whole, to a specific category of such services, or to a particular service within the defined range of such services.

2.2.3.1.1 Institutional Mental Health Services

Institutional mental health services are divided into two types: (i) specialist private or public hospital-based facilities offering inpatient wards or outpatient services; and (ii) dedicated mental hospitals that also offer long-stay care. In both types, specialist professionals provide mental healthcare.[51]

In many parts of the world, especially in low- and middle-income countries, mental hospitals are the most prevalent form of mental health services, and consume most of the countries' human and financial resources dedicated to mental healthcare. Despite their prevalence, mental hospitals often have poor outcomes, due to the nature of institutionalisation, lack of rehabilitation and poor clinical care; hence, the WHO classifies them as the least desirable type of mental health service.[52]

2.2.3.1.2 Integrated Mental Health Services

Integrated mental health services include treatment and promotional and preventive measures conducted in primary care clinics or by primary care workers, and mental health services in general secondary or tertiary hospitals. Such services include psychiatric wards, psychiatric beds in general wards, and outpatient clinics. Here, mainly primary healthcare professionals provide the services, including general practitioners or nurses trained in detecting and treating mental health conditions and psychosocial disabilities.[53]

---

[48] Yi Zhang, Advancing the Right to Health Care in China towards Accountability (Intersentia 2019) 26.
[49] WHO (n 29), p 39.
[50] WHO, Organization of services for mental health: WHO mental health policy and service guidance package (WHO 2003) 4–6.
[51] Ibid 4.
[52] Ibid.
[53] Ibid 2–3.

The benefits of integrated mental healthcare are that it is generally more accessible than specialist services, and usually more accepted by persons with mental health conditions and psychosocial disabilities, due to the reduced stigma associated when utilising such facilities. However, one of the disadvantages is that significant investment is needed to appropriately train general healthcare professionals.[54]

2.2.3.1.3 Community-based Mental Health Services

Community-based mental health services facilitate access to services, and provide an opportunity for persons with mental health conditions and psychosocial disabilities to continue to live in, and be included in, the community. They can be formal or informal. Formal services include 'community-based rehabilitation services, hospital diversion programmes, mobile crisis teams, therapeutic and residential supervised services, home help and support services'.[55] They are not based in hospital settings, but are usually linked to general or mental hospitals. However, guaranteeing good quality in formal community mental healthcare services is more costly, and places more demands on personnel, when compared with hospital-based services.[56]

Informal community mental health services are provided mostly by locals from the community who are not categorised as general health personnel or formally recognised professionals connected to mental healthcare delivery. Besides family members and local workers, traditional and faith-based healers classify as informal mental healthcare providers. In cases where no formal community mental health service is available, informal mental healthcare providers can often be found.[57] These informal services play an important role in mental healthcare delivery. There are fewer access barriers, and they are usually highly acceptable in local communities. Based on this, traditional and faith-based healers could potentially be considered a helpful complement to formal mental health services (as will be illustrated in section 6.2). Nonetheless, such service providers may charge high fees. Moreover, informal treatment methods have raised concerns about human rights violations,[58] as will be elaborated later.

Based on the above, it is the author's impression that, in certain situations (as will be explained in section 6.2), the best mental healthcare provision may be a combination of formal community mental health services, informal mental healthcare services, and primary healthcare services. This could enable accessible care – and, depending on the need, both inpatient and outpatient care – by, or at least with the involvement of, trained healthcare personnel, while being (culturally) acceptable. The influence that culture has on accessing mental healthcare should not be underestimated, as the next section will show.

---

[54] Ibid 11–14.
[55] Ibid 3.
[56] Ibid 15–16.
[57] Ibid 3.
[58] Ibid 17–18.

Table 2.1: Overview of the various terms and their definitions as adopted in this book

Term	Definition
Mental health	– A state of mental well-being that enables people to cope with the stresses of life, realize their abilities, learn well and work well, and contribute to their community (WHO); – Including good emotional and social well-being, together with mutual trust of, tolerance of and respect for the dignity of every person (Dainius Pūras); – A complex continuum, which is experienced differently from one person to the next, with varying degrees of difficulty and distress and potentially very different social and clinical outcomes (WHO)
Mental disorder	A wide range of mental problems generally characterized as a combination of abnormal or disturbed thoughts, emotions, behaviour, and relationships with others (WHO).
Psychosocial disability	– When a mental disorder, regardless of self-identification or diagnoses, becomes pervasive and interferes in a person's functioning. – Restriction in exercising rights and posing barriers to participation, based on an actual or perceived impairment.
Mental healthcare	A full range of services covering mental health promotion, protection, prevention, diagnosis, treatment, care and rehabilitation.
Institutional mental health services	– Specialist private or public hospital-based facilities/mental hospitals. – (Long-term) inpatient and outpatient care. – Specialist professionals provide care.
Integrated mental health services	– Primary care clinics or general secondary or tertiary hospitals. – Inpatient or outpatient care. – Mainly primary care workers (including physicians and/or psychiatrists) provide care.
Community-based mental health services	Formal community mental health services: – Rehabilitation services, hospital diversion programmes, mobile crisis teams, therapeutic and residential supervised services, home help and support services, etc.; – Usually linked to general/mental hospital; – Formally recognised professionals provide services. Informal community mental health services: – Informal care providers, such as family members, village workers, or traditional and faith-based healers.

2.3 THE INFLUENCE OF CULTURE ON ACCESSING MENTAL HEALTHCARE

Ideally, every individual living with mental health conditions and psychosocial disabilities would have access to appropriate mental healthcare. To achieve this, it is important to acknowledge the strong influence of culture. A basic understanding thereof is crucial for identifying a universally applicable right to mental health. The author is convinced that, by considering cultural values, international human rights norms are more likely to be domesticated and implemented, which would then be beneficial to the promotion and protection of mental health on the ground.

Mental health conditions and psychosocial disabilities are prevalent in all countries. However, cultural diversity across the world impacts significantly on many aspects of mental health.[59] These impacts affect a range of issues, from how mental health and psychosocial disability are perceived, to health-seeking behaviour and the attitudes of the patient and practitioner, and to the overall supply of mental healthcare services. Culture, according to Hernandez and others, 'influences what gets defined as a problem, how the problem is understood and which solutions to the problem are acceptable'.[60] For the purpose of this analysis, mental health conditions and psychosocial disability can be seen as 'the problem'.

The following subsections explore the various effects of culture on the perception of mental health conditions and psychosocial disabilities and health-seeking behaviour, as well as on the therapeutic relationship. This section will analyse how culture shapes different approaches to mental healthcare, and whether the goal of ensuring access to mental healthcare for all could benefit from incorporating different approaches. Insights from cross-cultural psychology, anthropology and public health will help to clarify this complex topic.

2.3.1 HEALTH-SEEKING BEHAVIOUR AND THE PERCEPTION OF MENTAL HEALTH CONDITIONS AND PSYCHOSOCIAL DISABILITIES

In many instances, affected individuals are unable to recognise symptoms of a mental health problem. They could suffer from long-lasting depressive episodes and want to hurt themselves, but might ascribe the onset of disease to a problem detached from their personal being, such as the possession of evil spirits.[61] Memon and others found that their interviewee from Africa had never heard of depression or mental health before.[62] Even if individuals recognise their symptoms as a mental health problem, they might be afraid to speak about it because of the fear of stigma and the concomitant rejection

---

[59] See eg Narayan Gopalkrishnan, 'Cultural Diversity and Mental Health: Considerations for Policy and Practice' (2018) 6(179) Frontiers in Public Health 179; Emil Kraepelin, 'Comparative psychiatry' (reprinted; originally published in 1904) in Roland Littlewood & Simon Dien (eds), *Cultural psychiatry and medical anthropology: In introduction and reader* (The Athlone Press 2000) 38–42; Anthony J Marsella & Ann Marie Yamada, 'Culture and mental health: An introduction and overview of foundations, concepts and issues' in Israel Cuéllar & Freddy Paniagua (eds), *Handbook of multicultural mental health* (Academic Press 2000) 3–24; and David L Sam & Virginia Moreira, 'Revisiting the Mutual Embeddedness of Culture and Mental Illness' (2012) 10(2) Online Readings in Psychology and Culture.
[60] Mario Hernandez and others, 'Cultural Competence: a literature review and conceptual model for mental health services' (2009) 60(8) Psychiatric Services 1046, 1047.
[61] Narayan Gopalkrishnan (n 59) 2.
[62] Anjum Memon and others, 'Perceived barriers to accessing mental health services among black and minority ethnic (BME) communities: a qualitative study in Southeast England' (2016) 6(11) BMJ Open, p 3.

and discrimination, or simply because mental health is not openly discussed in their culture.[63]

Diverse views in terms of etiology (the cause or causes of disease) impact on whether, and how, persons living with mental health conditions and psychosocial disabilities seek care and treatment. While some groups of people are less likely in general to seek mental health treatment, there are also differences in the types of treatment sought: some individuals rely on a mental health specialist, while others turn to primary care, traditional healers or family and friends.[64] As another interview by Memon and others shows, persons in West Indian communities mistrust psychiatrists, and turn only to family and friends when facing mental health problems.[65] Sam and Moreira demonstrate the effects of culture by drawing the following comparison:

A person who until recently has been well started to behave strangely. If the person lives in Western Europe, relatives might start to think the person is sick and seek help from a psychiatrist. Upon examination, including medical history, interviews and test results, the psychiatrist comes up with a diagnosis and outlines the methods of treatment, namely psychotherapy and medication. After careful administration over a few months, the person starts to get well again. If that person lives in Southeast Asia, relatives might start to think the person lost his spirits and seek help from a shaman. Upon examination, including a night ceremony with sacred chants calling upon deities to enter the shaman's body, offering of animal sacrifices to please the deities, and a spirit hooking ritual, the shaman tracks down the lost spirits, brings them back, deposits them in food which the affected person then must eat, and cleanses the person and his home of poisonous harms. After following the rituals and rites for a few months, the person starts to get well again. If that person lives in Africa, relatives might start to think evil spirits possess the person and seek help from a traditional herbalist. Upon examination including interviews with family members and friends, the evil spirit is identified, and rites and rituals are being carried out, such as drinking herbs from the forest, sacrificing animals, or making the person change daily routines. After the prescribed methods are carried out for a few months, the person starts to get well again. If that person lives in Northeastern Latin America, relatives might start to think the person is voodooed and seek help from the pai de santo. Upon examination including incorporation of various spirits, the pai de santo comes up with a diagnosis and outlines the form of treatment, including baths of herbs, lighting of candles and coming to the weekly sessions with the pai de santo. After carefully carrying out these methods for a few months, the person starts to get well again.[66]

Although there is truth in these examples, they can by no means be seen as universal practice in each of the cultural contexts. Nevertheless, they demonstrate the important

---

[63] US Department of Health and Human Services, *Mental Health: Culture, Race, and Ethnicity – A Supplement to Mental Health: A Report of the Surgeon General* (US Public Health Services 2001) 29–30.
[64] Ibid 28.
[65] Ibid.
[66] David L Sam & Virginia Moreira (n 59) 3–4.

role and influence of culture – and specifically religion and spirituality – on mental healthcare.

2.3.2 THE THERAPEUTIC RELATIONSHIP

Cultural impacts on the therapeutic relationship between the mental healthcare professional and the patient are also a significant factor in mental healthcare delivery. The cultural contexts of the practitioner and the patient are central to the therapeutic relationship.[67] The different cultural contexts that will be addressed in the following paragraph include educational, communicational and ethnic-related differences.

Ideally, practitioner and patient will be from the same culture, as a key problem in successfully reaching persons with mental health conditions and psychosocial disabilities lies in the gap between mental health professionals' understandings of mental health problems and how the patient or the community conceptualises psychological suffering.[68] In the therapeutic relationship, culture can unfold in two distinct ways. Firstly, the professionalism and education of the practitioner can create a cultural gap from the outset. This tension especially arises where a mental health specialist has undergone a training rooted in the biomedical model of disability, but is treating persons who believe in mental health conditions and psychosocial disabilities having deeper spiritual roots. A second, even more profound, problem arises if the mental health practitioner comes from a different culture altogether, or if their practice does not consider the cultural context at all. A worker in a mental hospital in Rwanda expressed the view that the foreigners who came after the genocide caused a lot of trouble because:

> they came … [and] did not identify the illness as an invasive external thing. They did not get the entire village to come together and acknowledge it together and all participate in trying to support the person who was getting treated. Treatment was not out in the bright sunshine where you feel happy. There was no music or drumming to get the heart running as the heart should run. Instead, they took people one at a time into sort of dingy little rooms for an hour at a time and asked them to talk about the bad things that had happened to them. Which, of course, just made them feel much worse, almost suicidal. [The local mental health workers] had to put a stop to it.[69]

Horstman argues that, for good public health outcomes, the social credibility of health interventions may be more valuable to the patient than the scientific credibility.[70] A

---

[67] Narayan Gopalkrishnan, '(n 59) 4.
[68] Vikram Patel, 'Rethinking mental health care. Bridging the credibility gap' (2014) 12 Intervention Journal 15.
[69] Andrew Solomon, 'Depression, Too, is a Thing with Feathers' (2008) 44(4) Contemporary Psychoanalysis 509, 522.
[70] Which is made up of same or similar values or norms.

clash between the social reality of the affected group and the mental health promotion and provision concept can threaten the credibility of mental health in the eyes of affected persons. Moreover, instead of seeking to develop programmes that are more effective, the focus should be on aiding people to make their own choices about how they want to be treated, and how they want to live, in light of the best understanding of the good life for themselves.[71] The latter can be interpreted as resembling the so-called 'health capability approach' identified by Sridhar Venkatapuram. With his conception of 'health justice', Venkatapuram proposes that individuals must have the ability to achieve the health goals they value, and act as agents of their own health.[72] Although the author's own conception of the right to mental health, which will be established later in this book, will incorporate Venkatapuram's health capability approach to some extent, analysing his 'health justice' concept in more depth lies beyond the scope of this book.

2.3.3 DIFFERENT APPROACHES TO MENTAL HEALTHCARE

Culture influences the perception of mental health conditions and psychosocial disabilities, the health-seeking behaviour, and the relationship between patient and practitioner. Because of cultural diversity, there are different approaches to mental healthcare. Conventional mental healthcare – that is, mental health services as they are widely implemented today – has emerged from a Western understanding of the human condition and mental health. While this understanding has, in many ways, provided strong frameworks to alleviate psychosocial disability, it has been – and still is – problematic when applied in a strict manner in non-Western cultures, without considering the cultural influence on the condition.[73] Thus, despite conventional mental healthcare offering new opportunities to work in a holistic way, it is also important to consider traditional approaches to mental healthcare. The following subsections illustrate the implications of each approach, and conclude with a description of the benefits of combining the two.

2.3.3.1 *Conventional Mental Healthcare*

The achievements of Western medicine have become the cornerstone of mental healthcare worldwide, and are thus often referred to as 'conventional mental healthcare'. Traditionally, the Western approach was based on the biomedical model, which

---

[71] Klasien Horstman, keynote speech at Aletta Jacobs School of Public Health Research Meet-up, 5 April 2019, Groningen, the Netherlands; see also Mare Knibbe and others 'Bianca in the neighborhood: moving beyond the 'reach paradigm' in public mental health' (2016) 26(4) Critical Public Health Journal 434.
[72] See eg Sridhar Venkatapuram, *Health Justice: An Argument from the Capabilities Approach* (Polity Press 2011).
[73] Narayan Gopalkrishnan (n 59) 1–2.

understood the origin of psychosocial disabilities to be fundamentally biological, caused mainly by neurological problems, substance misuse and genetics.[74] More recently, in the late twentieth century, the biopsychosocial model was proposed. This model acknowledges the role of biological, psychological and social factors in the causation of psychosocial disabilities and their treatment. This approach offers a more holistic approach to psychosocial disability and mental healthcare delivery. By reducing the separation between mind and body, which was prominent in the biomedical approach, mental health became more integrated in the primary healthcare sector, and a more client-centred and multidisciplinary approach was initiated.[75] Thereby, the needs and the social and environmental context of the individual were taken into consideration. This essentially led to a better quality of treatment and, therefore, improved the promotion and protection of the right to (mental) health.[76] The biopsychosocial model is endorsed by international organisations, and has been applied successfully to improve the situations of persons with psychosocial disabilities in various countries. It is considered to be the 'conceptual status quo'.[77]

Despite being perceived as the 'conceptual status quo', the biopsychosocial approach is often not realised in practice. Scholars argue that actual mental health service provision still shows a bias towards biomedical and not psychosocial disturbances. For instance, former Special Rapporteur Pūras stated that most mental healthcare funds in all countries around the world invest disproportionately in mental health services based on the biomedical model. And the first-line treatment of psychosocial disabilities tends to be with psychotropic medicines, which not uncommonly leads to over-medicalisation.[78] As Babalola and others point out, the application of the biopsychosocial approach is time- and cost-consuming, requiring human resources, training opportunities and financial resources. This poses a particular problem for low-

---

[74] See eg Jo Thakker & Tony Ward, 'Culture and classification: The cross-cultural application of the DSM-IV' (1998) 18(5) Clinical Psychology Review 501, 502; or UNGA, 'Report of the Special Rapporteur on the right of everyone to the enjoyment of the highest attainable standard of physical and mental health, Dainius Pūras' (28 March 2017) UN Doc A/HRC/35/21, para 18.

[75] When referring to the separation between mind and body in this sentence, the author wants to draw attention to the benefit the separation causes for the treatment of mental health issues, namely to not only 'fix the body'. However, the author does recognise that patients often face a combination of mental and somatic health issues (and thus, mind and body cannot strictly be separated). For the purpose of this section, however, this will not be addressed in more detail.

[76] Robert C Smith and others, 'An evidence-based Patient centered method makes the biopsychosocial model scientific' (2013) 91(3) Patient Education and Counseling 185; Ross White & Sashi P Sashidharan, 'Towards a more nuanced global mental health' (2014) 204(6) British Journal of Psychiatry 415; and Shane McInerney, 'Introducing the biopsychosocial model for good medicine and good doctors' (2002) 324(1533) BMJ.

[77] Basic Needs 'Better Mental Health, Better Lives' (nd), <https://basicneedsghana.org/> accessed 14 November 2022; and Graham Thornicroft and others, 'Capacity Building in Global Mental Health Research' (2012) 20(1) Harvard Review of Psychiatry 13.

[78] UNGA, 'Report of the Special Rapporteur on the Right of Everyone to the Enjoyment of the Highest Attainable Standard of Physical and Mental Health, Dainius Pūras' (n 74) para 19.

and middle-income countries.[79] While there are issues with the implementation of the biopsychosocial approach, the approach itself also receives criticism. Despite putting the individual in a social context, it is accused of disregarding the local context and traditions because it focuses on the individual in the centre of the analysis.[80] Babalola and others conclude that, for the biopsychosocial approach to be truly holistic, it cannot neglect the relational aspect of religion and spirituality. It must acknowledge the diversity of belief and practice regarding mental health conditions and psychosocial disabilities, and thus the approach of traditional healthcare, which is embraced by many societies.[81]

2.3.3.2 *Traditional Mental Healthcare*

In many regions of the world, and especially in low- and middle-income countries, large parts of society rely on traditional forms of healthcare. This has, firstly, to do with the perception of etiology of mental health conditions and psychosocial disabilities, as previously discussed. And, secondly, it might be the only available source of healthcare. In fact, traditional practitioners form a major part of the global mental health workforce. Therefore, the approach of traditional mental healthcare as a complement to the biopsychosocial approach will be outlined.

2.3.3.2.1 The Concept of Traditional Healthcare

Some forms of traditional healthcare are recognised throughout the world, such as traditional Chinese medicine or Ayurveda, while others are mostly practised in the region they originate from, such as traditional African medicine. Notwithstanding their diversity, all forms of traditional medicine can be defined as:

> the sum total of the knowledge, skill, and practices based on the theories, beliefs, and experiences indigenous to different cultures, whether explicable or not, used in the maintenance of health as well as in the prevention, diagnosis, improvement or treatment of physical and mental illness.[82]

In 2013, former WHO Director-General Chan stated that traditional medicine of proven quality, safety and efficacy can contribute to the goal of ensuring access to healthcare for all people around the world. Traditional healthcare is highly culturally

---

[79] Emmanuel Babalola and others, 'The biopsychosocial approach and global mental health: Synergies and opportunities' (2017) 33(29) Indian Journal of Social Psychiatry 291.
[80] Suman Fernando, *Mental health worldwide: Culture, globalization and development* (Palgrave Macmillan 2014).
[81] Emmanuel Babalola and others (n 79) 295.
[82] WHO, 'WHO traditional medicine strategy: 2014–2023' (2013), <https://www.who.int/medicines/publications/traditional/trm_strategy14_23/en/> accessed 14 November 2022, p 15.

acceptable care, and is accessible throughout communities. Chan, therefore, sees traditional medicine as specifically helpful in dealing with the rise of chronic non-communicable diseases under which psychosocial disabilities can be categorised.[83]

The safe use of quality products and practices is key to the efficiency of traditional medicine for mental health conditions and psychosocial disabilities. Traditional medicine products include herbs, parts of plants, minerals or even animal products. The practices involve medication therapy; procedure-based therapy; mental, spiritual and mind-based therapies; or a combination thereof.[84] Becoming an established practitioner depends highly on the region. While in Europe, North America or specific countries in Asia, practitioners must complete an official training programme or graduate from university, in many low- and middle-income countries the task of a traditional practitioner is carried on through generations, or taken up because of a special calling.[85]

Researchers have evaluated the actual effectiveness of traditional healers in treating mental health conditions and psychosocial disabilities.[86] Some conclude that, in particular, people with mild or moderate mental health conditions, and who have positive expectations of the procedure, benefit from the treatments of their chosen traditional or spiritual practitioner. On the other hand, their research was not able to prove the effectiveness of traditional healing on severe psychiatric disorders such as schizophrenia, especially with regards to its impact on the long-term progression of the disorder.[87] Despite its wide use, traditional medicine is exposed to strong criticism. Risks associated with traditional medicine include unqualified practitioners; the use of poor quality or adulterated products; danger of toxicity; delayed diagnoses or misdiagnoses; exposing patients to misleading or unreliable information; the failure to use effective conventional, evidence-based or humane treatment methods; and unwanted treatment interactions or adverse events.[88]

---

[83] Speech given by WHO Director-General, Dr Margaret Chan, at the International Conference on Traditional Medicine for South-East Asian Countries. New Delhi, India, 12–14 February 2013.
[84] WHO (n 82) 31.
[85] Tuviah Zabow, 'Traditional healers and mental health in South Africa' (2007) 4(4) International Psychiatry 81, 82.
[86] See eg Catherine Abbo, 'Profiles and outcome of traditional healing practices for severe mental illnesses in two districts of Eastern Uganda' (2011) 4 Global Health Action; Carolyn M Audet and others 'Mixed methods inquiry into traditional healers' treatment of mental, neurological and substance abuse disorders in rural South Africa' (2017) 12(12) PLoS ONE; Gareth Nortje and others 'Effectiveness of traditional healers in treating mental disorders: a systematic review' (2016) 3(2) Lancet Psychiatry 154, 167; Mario Incayawar, 'Efficacy of Quichua healers as psychiatric diagnosticians' (2008) 192(5) British Journal of Psychiatry 390; and Lily NA Kpobi and others, 'Traditional herbalists' methods of treating mental disorders in Ghana' (2019) 56(1) Transcultural Psychiatry 250.
[87] See Catherine Abbo (n 86); Carolyn M Audet (n 86); and Gareth Nortje (n 86) 167.
[88] See eg Lily NA Kpobi (n 86); and WHO (n 82).

2.3.3.2.2 The Governance of Traditional Healthcare

Regulating and managing traditional healthcare poses multiple difficulties. There are national, regional and global regulatory bodies for herbal medicine, for example the Global Regulatory Cooperation Network for Herbal Medicines. Notwithstanding this, it remains a challenge to guarantee the safety and high quality of the practice and products, especially when these are made by the practitioners themselves. Yet, it is the responsibility of states and their national healthcare stakeholders not only to coordinate traditional healthcare better, but also to ensure the protection of the patient's human rights. In recent years, many countries have developed strategies, policies and legislation to regulate traditional healthcare, and have integrated the practice into the primary healthcare system.

Ultimately, organised and well-trained traditional practitioners can potentially play an important role in quality mental health treatment, as collaboration partners to, and referral resources for, the formal mental healthcare system, especially in regions with scarcity of formal mental health services.[89]

2.3.3.3   Is There a Benefit of Combining Both Approaches?

A difference in culture has numerous implications for mental health practice, and may create challenges when accessing mental health services. According to Notje and others, if the cultural and spiritual beliefs of the patient are not in line with the conventional practitioner, a potentially more successful care would be provided through a mix of the biopsychosocial and traditional mental healthcare approaches.[90] Such a collaborative approach entails that mental health providers take the culture of communities into consideration when treating patients, or that mental health providers and traditional healers build on synergies between their approaches. In various countries, a collaborative approach has been practised with success.[91] Taking culture into account, as Gopalkrishnan finds, is an opportunity to develop holistic and integrated approaches for an effective mental healthcare provision.[92] While a combination of both approaches seems beneficial at first, the following questions remain: are there any potential challenges that arise with combining conventional mental healthcare (evidence-based healthcare) and traditional mental healthcare (often not evidence-based healthcare)? In what ways can both approaches, and even collaboration between their practitioners, be successfully enshrined in legislation and implemented in practice, to promote and protect mental health? The country study on Ghana in section 6.2 will explore this matter in more detail.

---

[89]   Karl Peltzer and others, 'HIV/AIDS/STI/TB knowledge, beliefs and practices of traditional healers in KwaZulu-Natal, South Africa' (2006) 18(6) AIDS Care 608.
[90]   Gareth Nortje (n 86) 167.
[91]   Oye Gureje and others, 'The role of global traditional and complementary systems of medicine in treating mental health problems' (2015) 2(2) Lancet Psychiatry 168, 176.
[92]   Narayan Gopalkrishnan (n 59) 6.

2.4 CHALLENGES ASSOCIATED WITH THE MENTAL HEALTHCARE CONTEXT

The goal of mental health services is, undoubtedly, to protect and promote mental well-being, and to address the needs of persons with mental health conditions and psychosocial disabilities.[93] For twenty-first century mental health services, recovery is a guiding principle of mental healthcare and treatment.[94] Recovery-oriented mental healthcare includes fostering relationships, promoting well-being, strengthening resilience, offering treatment, improving social inclusion, and supporting individuals to take responsibility for their own recovery by defining their goals and wishes.[95] Many people with (former) mental health conditions and psychosocial disabilities have identified the positive contribution that mental health services can make to their recovery, and thus their mental health.[96]

Nevertheless, worldwide, individuals with mental health conditions and psychosocial disabilities face particular challenges relating to mental health services. The first major concern is the initial barriers to accessing mental healthcare services, for people who want treatment. These barriers include stigma, people's different perceptions of their conditions, financial barriers, and availability of services. The second major concern is the specific human rights issues that arise when accessing mental health institutions, and thus in the mental healthcare setting. These include receiving treatment or being hospitalised against one's will. The danger of human rights violations holds particularly true when individuals are submitted to segregated services, such as mental hospitals or residential psychiatric institutions.

This section illustrates the main challenges associated with the mental healthcare context. It will set the scene for this book, and will be used as the basis for the subsequent normative analysis of the right to mental health.

2.4.1 BARRIERS TO ACCESSING MENTAL HEALTHCARE SERVICES

2.4.1.1 Stigma and Discrimination

Stereotyping, prejudice and stigmatisation associated with mental health conditions and psychosocial disabilities, which are present in every sphere of life, are major barriers for individuals seeking to access mental healthcare. Negative beliefs

---

[93] WHO (n 1).
[94] Mike Slide, 'The contribution of mental health services to recovery' (2009) 18(5) Journal of Mental Health 367.
[95] Ibid; and WHO (n 1).
[96] Mike Slide (n 94).

around mental health conditions include that they are signs of personal weakness or possession by evil spirits, or that persons with mental health conditions and psychosocial disabilities cannot contribute positively to the community.[97] In many societies, persons with mental health conditions and psychosocial disabilities are ostracised from their communities. However, social stigma reaches beyond even the individual, as a mental health diagnosis can stigmatise their whole family, resulting in loss of trust and respect from the broader community.[98] The fear of shame and stigma prevents persons with mental health problems and their families from seeking support, diagnoses or treatment.[99]

However, also when seeking to access mental healthcare services, persons with psychosocial disabilities are frequently denied treatment because of their condition. The root cause is often the assumption that they are deemed unworthy of treatment.[100]

2.4.1.2 Different Perceptions of Psychosocial Disability

As well as individuals who do not want to seek support due to the fear of stigma and discrimination, there is another group of individuals that chooses not to access care because they consider themselves not to be mentally ill, or not ill enough for treatment (as was addressed in subsection 2.3.1). In this sense, the perception of psychosocial disability can be seen as barrier to accessing mental healthcare services.

2.4.1.3 Financial Barriers

There are also financial barriers that prevent patients from accessing mental healthcare services. Medical insurance schemes might only partly cover the costs of mental healthcare services, or not cover them at all. Insurances also often incorporate terms that discriminate against persons mental health conditions and psychosocial disabilities. For instance, pre-existing mental health conditions may disqualify individuals from obtaining full health coverage.[101] Furthermore, statistics show that persons with psychosocial disabilities are less likely able to afford healthcare, including expensive psychotropic medicine.[102]

---

[97] UNGA, 'Report of the United Nations High Commissioner for Human Rights, Mental health and human rights' (n 38) para 15.
[98] Narayan Gopalkrishnan (n 59) 6.
[99] Paul Hunt & Judith Mesquita (n 24) 349.
[100] UNGA, 'Report of the Special Rapporteur on the rights of persons with disabilities, Catalina Devandas-Aguilar, Rights of persons with disabilities' (16 July 2018) UN Doc A/73/161, para 38.
[101] UNGA, 'Report of the United Nations High Commissioner for Human Rights, Mental health and human rights' (n 38) para 16.
[102] UNGA, 'Report of the Special Rapporteur on the rights of persons with disabilities, Catalina Devandas-Aguilar, Rights of persons with disabilities' (n 100) paras 35–36.

2.4.1.4 Availability of Services

In many countries, individuals cannot access mental healthcare due to a lack of available services.[103] At the heart of this issue are insufficient and poorly distributed resources, including mental healthcare facilities, goods, services and personnel. The main reasons for this shortage are inadequate funding, growing populations, and the growing need for mental healthcare.[104]

Insufficient resources affect the availability of mental health facilities and mental healthcare workers. If mental health staff are not available in adequate numbers, effective and qualitative mental health treatment might be at risk.[105] For instance, if a person successfully contacts a mental health facility, but the trained psychiatrist or psychologist must tend to numerous patients simultaneously, the diagnosis and treatment quality may be limited.

Closely connected to insufficient resources is the poor distribution of resources. Research shows that, especially in low- and middle-income countries – for instance in Nepal, Botswana or Costa Rica – modern mental health services are mostly located in the capital city, or in urban areas.[106] This can create a severe lack of available practising psychiatrists throughout the country, as can be seen, for instance, in South Africa or Tanzania; and also a lack of available psychotropic medication supply throughout the country, as has been seen in Ghana.[107] If mental health facilities, goods and services are disproportionately concentrated in urban areas and not sufficiently offered throughout the country, they remain inaccessible for many people.

The absence of community-based mental healthcare hinders persons from living and participating in the community, and ultimately creates a reliance on segregated psychiatric institutions as the main source of mental healthcare provision. Nowadays, psychiatric healthcare providers and institutions offer increasingly ambulant care, which can be classified as community-based mental healthcare. Nonetheless, many persons with psychosocial disabilities around the world remain in institutional settings, despite not needing long-term care, because of the unavailability of alternative mental health and social support systems.[108] According to Drew and others, these institutions are frequently associated with gross human rights violations.[109] Here, overcrowding,

---

[103] Many can also not access mental healthcare because of the need to have a reference by a medical specialist. However, this lays beyond the scope of this section.
[104] Natalie Drew and others (n 39).
[105] Megan Sambrook Smith and others, 'Barriers to accessing mental health services for women with perinatal mental illness: systematic review and meta-synthesis of qualitative studies in the UK' (2019) 9(1) BMJ Open.
[106] Martin Knapp and others, 'Economic barriers to better mental health practice and policy' (2006) 21(3) Health Policy and Planning 157, 161.
[107] Ibid.
[108] Lela Sulaberidze and others, 'Barriers to delivering mental health services in Georgia with an economic and financial focus: informing policy and acting on evidence' (2018) 18(1) BMC Health Services Research 108.
[109] Natalie Drew and others (n 39).

understaffing and inefficiency are sufficiently common that the WHO refers to such institutionalised settings as 'more penal than therapeutic'.[110] This brings the discussion to the next category of challenges: human rights violations specific to mental healthcare delivery.

2.4.2 SPECIFIC HUMAN RIGHTS VIOLATIONS IN MENTAL HEALTHCARE SETTINGS

2.4.2.1 Denial of Free and Informed Consent

The denial of free and informed consent, as a human rights problem, is omnipresent within mental health service delivery. Free and informed consent is denied frequently, and for various reasons, as described in more detail in Chapter 5. In such circumstances, the authority to make a decision in relation to a person's care is then given to a third person. Judges, representatives or guardians, as well as doctors or healthcare personnel, regularly make healthcare-related decisions on behalf of persons with psychosocial disabilities. Discriminatory labels such as 'unsoundness of the mind' are commonly used as a basis to deprive a person with psychosocial disabilities of their legal right to make a decision.

This can result in people being involuntarily admitted to mental health facilities, as well as being treated against their will. The European Union Agency for Fundamental Rights (FRA) found that persons with mental health conditions in Bulgaria and Latvia were not offered any choice when it comes to their admission to psychiatric institutions or treatments, after the imposition of guardianship. The FRA further found that, upon the recommendation of psychiatrists, parents initiated proceedings to revoke the rights of their children to make their own decisions, in order for them to be admitted and treated against their will. According to the FRA report, affected persons are also threatened with the need to take medicine in order not to become legally incapacitated (restricted from making their own decisions).[111] In addition to formal denials of people's rights to make their own decisions, and guardianship regimes, the FRA discovered that informal restrictions on decision-making also exist, with parents, community members or even mental health personnel curtailing the decision-making power of affected individuals. For instance, doctors discussed the treatment of these individuals only with family members, or institutional personnel told patients that, within the hospitals, they were not able to take their own decisions.[112]

---

[110] WHO, 'Mental Health: A Call for Action by World Health Ministers, Ministerial Round Tables 2001, 54th World Health Assembly' (2001), <https://www.who.int/mental_health/advocacy/en/Call_for_Action_MoH_Intro.pdf> accessed 14 November 2022, p 27.
[111] European Union Agency for Fundamental Rights (FRA), *Legal capacity of persons with intellectual disabilities and persons with mental health problems* (FRA 2013) 45.
[112] Ibid 49–50.

2.4.2.2 Involuntary Treatment and Hospitalisation

Former Special Rapporteur Pūras observes that power imbalances in mental healthcare delivery 'dominate the relationship between psychiatric professionals and users of mental health services, ... disempower users and undermine their right to make decisions about their health'.[113] Such power asymmetries regularly lead to problems of involuntary and coercive treatment and hospitalisation where this is not justified. Ideally, every person with mental health conditions and psychosocial disabilities should initially be assumed to have capacity, and to be able to accept or refuse voluntary treatment or admission. However, rates of involuntary treatment and hospitalisation of persons with mental health conditions and psychosocial disabilities continue to increase around the world, especially in high-income countries.[114] Unjustified solitary confinement, and the use of mechanical restraint mechanisms such as magnets, straps and chains, are frequent practices in many mental health settings all over the world, for example in the USA, in Scandinavian countries, the Czech Republic, Ghana and Kenya.[115] Often used to enforce compliance with medication and treatment, or as punishment, these practices have no therapeutic objective.[116] And it is especially the other harmful practices, such as over-medication or forced medication (chemical restraints), that are barely contested. Instead of improving the situation, coercion is, in fact, found to negatively affect the treatment outcomes of persons with mental health conditions and psychosocial disabilities.[117] Furthermore, it may discourage persons with mental health conditions from seeking support in the first place, which in turn becomes a barrier to accessing mental healthcare services.

---

[113] UNGA, 'Report of the Special Rapporteur on the Right of Everyone to the Enjoyment of the Highest Attainable Standard of Physical and Mental Health, Dainius Pūras' (n 74) para 22.

[114] See eg Mental Health Europe, 'Mapping and Understanding Exclusion: Institutional, coercive and community-based services and practices across Europe' (2017), <https://mhe-sme.org/wp-content/uploads/2018/01/Mapping-and-Understanding-Exclusion-in-Europe.pdf> accessed 14 November 2022.

[115] Andrew Molodynski and others, 'Coercion in mental healthcare: time for a change in direction' (2016) 13(1) BJPsych International 1; Human Rights Watch, 'Like a Death Sentence: Abuses Against Persons with Mental Disabilities in Ghana' (2012), <https://www.hrw.org/report/2012/10/02/death-sentence/abuses-against-persons-mental-disabilities-ghana> accessed 17 May 2021; Mental Disability Advocacy Center, 'The Right to Legal Capacity in Kenya' (2014), <http://sro.sussex.ac.uk/id/eprint/48143/1/mdac_kenya_legal_capacity_2apr2014_0.pdf> accessed 14 November 2022; and Mental Disability Advocacy Center, 'Cage Beds and Coercion in Czech Psychiatric Institutions' (2014), <www.mdac.info/sites/mdac.info/files/cagebed_web_en_20140624_0.pdf> accessed 14 November 2022.

[116] UNGA, 'Report of the Special Rapporteur on the rights of persons with disabilities, Catalina Devandas-Aguilar, Rights of persons with disabilities' (n 100) para 42.

[117] See eg Thomas Kallert and others, 'Coerced hospital admission and symptom change – a prospective observational multi-centre study' (2011) 6(11) PLOS One 1; or Tuula Wallsten and others, 'Short-term outcome of inpatient psychiatric care – impact of coercion and treatment characteristics' (2006) 41(12) Social Psychiatry and Psychiatric Epidemiology 975.

2.5 CONCLUDING SUMMARY

This chapter has provided an overview of the various concepts and definitions surrounding the topic of mental health and psychosocial disabilities, and has illustrated how culture impacts on access to mental healthcare. As a basis for the subsequent legal analysis, it has also addressed persisting challenges associated with mental healthcare delivery. Persons with mental health conditions and psychosocial disabilities experience inappropriate access to mental healthcare owing to various factors, such as the limited availability of mental health services, and serious human rights concerns in mental healthcare settings. Mainstreaming the needs and rights of persons with mental health conditions and psychosocial disabilities is crucial to ending the persisting inequality they experience in the mental healthcare system. Inclusive mental healthcare systems need to be implemented to ensure access to mental health services (as a solution to the barriers outlined in subsection 2.4.1). Moreover, mental healthcare services must include a human rights approach to disability (as a solution to the human rights violations as outlined in subsection 2.4.2), in order to guarantee that the services offered are non-discriminatory, and that they respect the requirement for informed consent prior to any medical measure, and are, as far as possible, free from involuntary treatment and hospitalisation.[118]

Mental health is not merely a medical or health concern; it is a matter of dignity and respect, as well as of equal opportunities and other human rights. The above analysis of the various challenges faced by persons with mental health conditions and psychosocial disabilities suggests there is a need to strengthen the protection of their rights. But how exactly does international human rights law provide adequate legal entitlements for affected persons, to promote and protect their mental health? The following chapters of this book focus on an analysis of relevant human rights norms to determine how to ensure the enjoyment of an adequate right to mental health that respects the autonomy, self-determination and human dignity of those affected, and ensures access to quality mental health services.

---

[118] As will be explored in depth in Chapter 5, there may be situations where treatment and hospitalisation against a person's will is needed to protect themselves and others.

PART 2
THE RIGHT TO MENTAL HEALTH AND THE APPLICABLE HUMAN RIGHTS FRAMEWORK

CHAPTER 3
MENTAL HEALTH AS A HUMAN RIGHT: THE EVOLVING FRAMEWORK

3.1 INTRODUCTION

Part 2 of this work identifies the global and regional human rights frameworks that are relevant for the protection and promotion of mental health around the globe. It analyses the legal recognition of the right to mental health by scrutinising key provisions, standards and developments under international human rights law, as well as relevant legislative and policy measures.

Chapter 3 does not aim to offer an exhaustive legal analysis of specific human rights that can be discussed in relation to mental health. Rather, this chapter sets the stage for the normative analysis that follows in the ensuing chapters. It does so by addressing the emergence of mental health as a human right, and by clarifying which legal provisions protect and promote mental health. The ultimate question that will be addressed is: what does the right to mental health entail?

To answer this question, it is necessary to start with the origins of the recognition of health – notably mental health – as a right. At the foundation of the mental health and human rights analysis lies the international human right to the enjoyment of the highest attainable standard of physical and mental health, as identified in the Constitution of the World Health Organization (WHO), and under international human rights law.

Given that the recognition of health as a right is a key element in the analysis set out in this book, this chapter firstly analyses its evolution, and discusses which international human rights instruments particularly address mental health as part of the right to health (section 3.2). To complement international human rights law, a brief overview of the regional human rights treaties is provided (section 3.3). Domestic legal systems offer the primary legal protection of human rights guaranteed under international and regional law. Thus, section 3.4 evaluates how mental health is protected and promoted in a range of domestic legal regimes. Although mental health does not go unmentioned in the international and regional treaties, it is domestic mental health law in particular that underlines the need for a more extended framework for mental health as a human right. The domestic mental health law illustrates that mental health cannot simply be promoted and protected without considering other human rights standards. This is further supported in the examination of non-binding instruments in section 3.5. Subsequently, section 3.6 identifies a normative framework for the protection and promotion of mental health as the fundament for this book. It clarifies that the term 'right to mental health' must be understood as embracing other important human rights related to mental health, not just the right to the highest attainable standard of health norm.

3.2 MENTAL HEALTH IN INTERNATIONAL HUMAN RIGHTS LAW

The normative concept of the right to mental health can be traced back to the Constitution of the WHO, which was adopted in 1946, and entered into force in 1948. As briefly stated above, the WHO Constitution defines health as 'a state of complete physical, mental and social well-being and not merely the absence of disease or infirmity'.[1] In addition, it refers to the enjoyment of health as 'one of the fundamental rights of every human being'.[2] Meier, who looked closely at the travaux préparatoires of the WHO Constitution, describes the comprehensive definition of health as a 'sweeping vision of "complete" health'.[3] This WHO definition explicitly includes mental well-being as an element of health, and defines health as being more than the absence of disease. These alone can be seen as breakthroughs. Additionally, the WHO Constitution also deemed health a fundamental right, which set in motion a shift from regarding health merely within the social justice framework to conceptualising 'complete health' as a human right.

Two years later, the United Nations (UN) formally recognised health as a human right in Article 25(1) of its 1948 Universal Declaration of Human Rights (UDHR), which stipulates that everyone has 'the right to a standard of living adequate for the health and well-being of himself … including … medical care and necessary social services, and the right to security in the event of … sickness and disability'.[4] Notably, the Article provides the right to health and well-being in circumstances such as sickness and disability,[5] which can be interpreted as including mental health conditions and

---

[1] Constitution of the World Health Organization (WHO Constitution) (adopted 22 July 1946, entered into force 7 April 1948) 14 UNTS 185, preamble.
[2] Ibid.
[3] Benjamin Meier, 'Making Health a Human Right: The World Health Organisation and the United Nations Programme on Human Rights and Scientific and Technological Developments' (2012) 13 Journal of the Historical Society 195, 201.
[4] United Nations General Assembly (UNGA), Universal Declaration of Human Rights (UDHR) (10 December 1948) UNGA RES 217A (III), art 25(1).
[5] The travaux préparatoires of the UDHR shows that before Article 25 was drafted as it is written in the final Declaration, various countries suggested to include specific provision for social security in the event of unemployment, sickness, disability, old age and the loss of livelihood in circumstances beyond his control (pp 139, 1002, 1612, 1622, 1825, 1854). A new Article was drafted, namely the right to social security, which entails 'the right to a standard of living and social services adequate for the health and wellbeing' (p 1866) and includes disability, among other events. It was then discussed whether sickness, disability or invalidity should be used as term (of which sickness and disability was chosen because the latter covers invalidity) and that the usage of 'social security' is unwise in that

psychosocial disabilities. Nevertheless, the Article has been criticised for lacking a definition of the term 'health', which could result in reducing the right to 'a right to medical care and to sickness benefits'.[6] Moreover, the Article does not explicitly refer to mental health.

Subsequently, in 1966, the right to the highest attainable standard of health was codified in the International Covenant on Economic, Social and Cultural Rights (ICESCR or Covenant). Article 12 ICESCR reflects the statement of Chisholm (the first Director-General of the WHO), that 'without mental health, there can be no true physical health'.[7] Article 12(1) of the ICESCR defines the right to health as 'the right of everyone to the enjoyment of the highest attainable standard of physical and mental health'. From examining the travaux préparatoires of the ICESCR, Saul and others found that the UN Commission on Human Rights was persuaded by the WHO's ambitious perspective of 'complete health' and, thus, integrated a more extensive definition of health in Article 12 than was envisaged by the UDHR.[8] In the Commission's original submission, health was referred to as 'a state of complete physical, mental and social well-being'.[9] In a discussion regarding the nature of the right, the Commission debated whether the 'highest attainable standard' should be confined to 'physical and mental health', or also encompass 'social well-being' or even 'moral well-being'. Although none of the additional states of well-being was endorsed, mental health was considered as a fundamental part of the right from the outset.[10] In addition to the definition of the right to health, Article 12 further stipulates, in a non-exhaustive list, actions states must take to achieve the full realisation of the right to health. In 2000, the Committee on Economic, Social and Cultural Rights (CteeESCR) adopted General Comment 14, to explain the implications of the right to the highest attainable standard of health, and thus offer more clarity. General Comment 14 is a non-binding yet authoritative statement. For instance, Article 12 must be understood as encompassing the right to healthy natural and workplace environments, which brings attention to the need to ensure an adequate supply of safe water, food, sanitation, housing and other social determinants of health, in light of promoting the right to the highest attainable standard of health.[11] States also have to recognise the right to

---

context in regard to how the International Labor Organization is already using it because it is broader than social insurance (pp 1867–1869, 1872, 2581). After new drafts, amendments and suggestions by different countries, Article 25 was then finalised to what it is now. See William Schabas, *The Universal Declaration of Human Rights: The Travaux Préparatoires* (Cambridge University Press 2013).

[6] Brigit Toebes, *The Right to Health as a Human Right in International Law* (Intersentia/Hart 1999) 40.

[7] Brock Chisholm, 'Outline for a study group on World Health and the survival of the human race: material drawn from articles and speeches' (1951), <https://apps.who.int/iris/handle/10665/330666> accessed 14 November 2022.

[8] Ben Saul and others, *The International Covenant on Economic, Social and Cultural Rights. Commentary, Cases, and Materials* (Oxford University Press 2014) 980.

[9] See UN General Assembly, Draft International Covenant on Human Rights: Report of the Third Committee (9 February 1957) UN Doc A/3525.

[10] Ben Saul and others (n 8).

[11] Committee on Economic, Social and Cultural Rights (CteeESCR), 'General Comment No. 14: The Right to the Highest Attainable Standard of Health (Art. 12)' (General Comment 14) (11 August 2000) UN Doc E/C.12/2000/4, para 15.

prevention as a component of the right to health, which embraces the establishment of prevention and educational programmes, and specifically the promotion of the social determinants of good health.[12] Moreover, under the ambit of the right to health facilities, goods and services, states have to take all necessary steps to create 'conditions which would assure to all medical service and medical attention in the event of sickness'.[13] The CteeESCR recognises two dimensions of the right to health: it covers the underlying determinants for health, including environmental health, and also embraces a right to access healthcare.[14] It further stipulates that health facilities, goods and services must be available, accessible, acceptable and of quality:[15] elements which will further be explored in subscesction 4.2.1.2 and in Chapter 6.

Besides being considered the fundamental instrument for the protection of the right to health, the ICESCR also provides the legal basis for mental health as a human right in international human rights law. The right to the highest attainable standard of health provision specifically refers to mental health, which means that mental health, just like physical health, is addressed as part of the right to health norm.[16] Therefore, the steps outlined in this provision, identifying the states' obligations, can be interpreted as also covering the mental health context, and – for persons with mental and physical health problems – the provision offers grounds for an interaction between mental and physical healthcare. Whether Article 12 ICESCR sufficiently covers the mental health context will be elucidated further in Chapter 4. For now, it is important just to establish that the ICESCR framework embraces mental health as a human right. In addition to the ICESCR, mental health is also embedded in other international human rights instruments, i.e. the 1989 Convention on the Rights of the Child (CRC), and the 2006 Convention on the Rights of Persons with Disabilities (CRPD); see also Table 3.1 below.

The CRC identifies a broad right to health of children, including access to healthcare and the underlying determinants of health, emphasising the right to the highest attainable standard of health of children with disabilities, in particular.[17] The CRC recognises that disability comprises both mental and physical disability.[18] Unlike the ICESCR, the CRC does not explicitly mention mental health in the right to health norm; yet it can be derived from the text of the CRC that the definition of health embraces

---

[12] Ibid para 16.
[13] UNGA, International Covenant on Economic, Social and Cultural Rights (ICESCR) (adopted 16 December 1966, entered into force 3 January 1976) 993 UNTS 3, art 12(2)(d).
[14] CteeESCR (n 11) para 11; see also Brigit Toebes, 'Introduction: Health and Human Rights in Europa' in Brigit Toebes, Mette Hartlev, Aart Hendriks & Janne Rothmar Herrmann (eds), *Health and Human Rights in Europe* (Intersentia 2012) 17.
[15] CteeESCR (n 11) para 12.
[16] It is important to emphasise that the author is referring here to 'mental health and not to 'the right to mental health'. While Article 12 ICESCR can also be considered as cornerstone of what the author refers to as 'the right to mental health', 'the right to mental health' as established in this book, goes beyond the right to the highest attainable standard of health norm and encompasses other human rights, see section 3.6.
[17] UNGA, Convention on the Rights of the Child (CRC) (adopted 20 November 1989, entered into force 2 September 1990) 1577 UNTS 3, arts 23–24.
[18] Ibid art 23(1).

both physical and mental health. For instance, Article 25 CRC clarifies what needs to be done if a child is placed away from home for the 'care, protection or treatment of his or her physical or mental health'.[19] The Convention further stipulates a right of access to adequate treatment and rehabilitation services for children and adolescents with mental ill health and psychosocial disorders.[20] According to the Committee on the Rights of the Child (CteeCRC), the human right to mental health includes healthcare services that are designed for the specific needs of children with mental disorders, as well as psychosocial support approaches that address mental health conditions without relying on institutionalisation or unnecessary medication. Furthermore, states are encouraged to scale up interventions to promote mental health, prevent mental disorders, and identify the earliest signs of mental ill health.[21] The conclusion is, therefore, that the CRC framework provides for a human right to mental health for children and adolescents with mental health conditions and psychosocial disabilities, which includes access to healthcare and rehabilitation services.

The third international human rights treaty encompassing mental health as a human right is the CRPD. It recognises the right to enjoy the highest attainable standard of health, and the right to health-related rehabilitation of persons with physical and psychosocial disabilities,[22] and adds that the right should be enjoyed 'without discrimination on the basis of disability'.[23] The Convention expressly provides for a right to the health services and rehabilitation that are needed because of the psychosocial disability. These services must entail early identification and appropriate intervention, to minimise or prevent further disability, and the services must be as close as possible to the community of the person, which can be read as favouring non-institutional settings.[24] Moreover, the CRPD highlights that health professionals have to offer care to persons with psychosocial disabilities on the basis of free and informed consent, protecting their autonomy and dignity.[25] In conclusion, similarly to the CRC, the CRPD framework not only recognises mental health as a human right, but also calls attention to other crucial human rights elements connected to mental health, such as non-discrimination and informed consent.

In conclusion, the right to the highest attainable standard of health norm, within international human rights law, may be seen as the fundament for mental health as a

---

[19] Ibid art 25.
[20] Ibid, arts 24(1), 23(3).
[21] See eg Committee on the Rights of the Child (CteeRC), 'General Comment No. 4 (2003): Adolescent Health and Development in the Context of the Convention on the Rights of the Child' (1 July 2003) CRC/GC/2003/4, para 25; CteeRC, 'General Comment No. 9 (2006): The rights of children with disabilities' (27 February 2007) CRC/C/GC/9, paras 51–52, 56–57; and CteeRC, 'General Comment No. 15 (2013) on the right of the child to the enjoyment of the highest attainable standard of health (art. 24)' (17 April 2013) CRC/C/GC/15, para 39.
[22] UNGA, Convention on the Rights of Persons with Disabilities (adopted 13 December 2006, entered into force 3 May 2008) 2515 UNTS 3, arts 25–26.
[23] Ibid art 25.
[24] Ibid art 25(b)(c).
[25] Ibid art 25(d).

human right. Yet, the following needs to be kept in mind: firstly, mental health is only one aspect of the broader right to the highest attainable standard of health; secondly, the content of the right to mental health is not fully reflected in the right to the highest attainable standard of health norm, as the previous paragraphs indicate. The right to mental health must also address issues such as consent or institutionalisation.

Table 3.1: Major international human rights treaties recognising mental health as human right

Treaty	Provision
1966 ICESCR	'[T]he right of everyone to the enjoyment of the highest attainable standard of physical and mental health', followed by 'steps to be taken by the States Parties to the present Covenant to achieve the full realization of this right' (Art. 12(1)(2)).
1989 CRC	'[A]ssistance … shall be designed to ensure that the disabled child has effective access to and receives … health care services [and] rehabilitation services' (Art. 23(3)).
	'[T]he right of the child to the enjoyment of the highest attainable standard of health and to facilities for the treatment of illness and rehabilitation of health. States Parties shall strive to ensure that no child is deprived of his or her right of access to such health care services', including measures to be taken to 'pursue full implementation of this right' (Art. 24(1)(2)).
2006 CRPD	'[T]he right to the enjoyment of the highest attainable standard of health without discrimination on the basis of disability', including measures to be taken 'to ensure access for persons with disabilities to health services that are gender-sensitive, including health-related rehabilitation' (Art. 25).
	'States Parties shall organize, strengthen and extend comprehensive habilitation and rehabilitation services and programmes, particularly in the areas of health' (Art. 26).

3.3 MENTAL HEALTH IN REGIONAL HUMAN RIGHTS LAW

Regional human rights instruments help to localise international human rights standards to apply to the particular human rights context of a region. They play an important role for the promotion and protection of human rights, and for the implementation of international human rights norms on the domestic level. Hence, in addition to the international human rights standards, it is worthwhile to examine these regional human rights provisions. The following overview analyses how the three main regional human rights systems recognise mental health as part of the right to the highest attainable standard of health norm. As this section is only meant to give a brief overview of the applicable regional human rights treaties to complement the discussion of international human rights law above, it will not offer an in-depth analysis of these regional treaties.

Article 16 of the 1981 African Charter on Human and Peoples' Rights (Banjul Charter or AfChHPR) recognises the 'right to enjoy the best attainable state of physical and mental health', which resembles the provision of the ICESCR discussed above, as well as setting out the measures that states need to take to 'protect the health of their people and to ensure that they receive medical attention when they are sick'.[26] As a supplement to the provisions of the Banjul Charter, the 2018 Protocol to the African Charter on Human and Peoples' Rights on the Rights of Persons with Disabilities in Africa defines a more detailed right to the highest attainable standard of health for persons with psychosocial disabilities. It declares, in Article 17(2), that access to health services involves, inter alia:

b) Providing ... health services designed to minimise or prevent further disability;
c) Prohibiting discrimination against persons with disabilities by providers of health services or providers of insurance;
d) Ensuring that all health services are provided on the basis of free, prior and informed consent;
e) Providing persons with disabilities with health-care in the community;
...
g) Ensuring that persons with disabilities are provided with support in making health decisions, when needed.

...

Ensuring that the training of health-care providers takes account of the disability specific needs and rights of persons with disabilities, and ensuring that the formal and informal health services do not violate the rights of persons with disabilities.[27]

Hence, the African human rights framework identifies precise regulations regarding the human right to mental health, setting an important example.

The equivalent provision within the Inter-American human rights system resembles the WHO Constitution's definition. The 1988 Additional Protocol of the American Convention on Human Rights in the Area of Economic, Social and Cultural Rights (Protocol of San Salvador) mandates that, '[e]veryone shall have the right to health, understood to mean the enjoyment of the highest level of physical, mental and social well-being'.[28] This provision continues by declaring health as a public good, and listing measures states have to take in order to ensure the right. Moreover, the 1999 Inter-American Convention on the Elimination of All Forms of Discrimination Against Persons with Disabilities (resolution AG/RES. 1608) stipulates the early detection, intervention, treatment and rehabilitation of persons with mental health conditions and

---

[26] Organization of African Unity, African Charter on Human and Peoples' Rights (Banjoul Charter) (adopted 27 June 1981, entered into force 21 October 1986) 1520 UNTS 271, art 16(1)(2).
[27] African Union, Protocol to the African Charter on Human and Peoples' Rights on the Rights of Persons with Disabilities in Africa (adopted 29 January 2018), art 17(2).
[28] Organization of American States, Additional Protocol of the American Convention on Human Rights in the Area of Economic, Social and Cultural Rights (Protocol of San Salvador) (adopted 17 November 1988, entered into force 21 October 1986) 1520 UNTS 271, art 10(1)(2).

psychosocial disabilites as priority areas for state parties, 'to ensure the optimal level of independence and quality of life'.[29]

Lastly, under the European human rights system, the 1996 European Social Charter (revised) stipulates that, '[e]veryone has the right to benefit from any measures enabling him to enjoy the highest possible standard of health attainable'.[30] For persons with psychosocial disabilities specifically, Article 15 of the Charter provides the right to rehabilitation and social resettlement. The 1997 Convention on Human Rights and Biomedicine holds that, when a person cannot give consent to interventions because of a mental health condition or psychosocial disability, the procedure can only be carried out if the person's representative authorises it. It further declares that, if there is serious risk to the health of persons living with mental health conditions or psychosocial disabilities, protective interventions can be carried out without the person's consent.[31] The matters of representation and interventions without consent will be elaborated further in Chapter 5.

3.4 MENTAL HEALTH IN DOMESTIC LAW

In addition to international and regional human rights law, many countries promote and protect mental health in their domestic legal systems, i.e. in constitutional provisions or domestic legislation. As Zhang elaborates, the figure given for the number of constitutions that provide a right to health norm varies in different publications, ranging from 56 to 135 countries.[32] The specific health rights protection also varies between countries, guaranteeing, for example, 'health care', 'health and medical care', 'public health', 'health security', 'health protection', 'overall health' or 'the highest attainable standard of physical and mental health'.[33] Heymann and others have established that only 12 national constitutions guarantee the right to health or medical care specifically for persons with disabilities.[34] However, not all of these constitutions refer explicitly to psychosocial disabilities, with only some constitutions containing a

---

[29] Organization of American States, Inter-American Convention on the Elimination of All Forms of Discrimination Against Persons with Disabilities (adopted 7 June 1999, entered into force 4 September 2001) AG/RES. 1608 (XXIX-O/99), art 3(2)(b).

[30] Council of Europe, European Social Charter (revised) (adopted 3 May 1996, entered into force 1 July 1999) ETS 163, art 11.

[31] Council of Europe, Convention for the Protection of Human Rights and Dignity of the Human Being with regard to the Application of Biology and Medicine: Convention on Human Rights and Biomedicine (Oviedo Convention) (adopted 4 April 1997, entered into force 1 December 1999) ETS 164, arts 6(3), 7.

[32] Yi Zhang, *Advancing the Right to Health Care in China towards Accountability* (Intersentia 2019) 32–35.

[33] See eg Lawrende Gostin, *Global Health Law* (Harvard University Press 2014), 263; and Jody Heymann and others, 'Constitutional rights to health, public health and medical care: the status of health protections in 191 countries' (2013) 8(6) Global Public Health 639.

[34] Jody Heymann and others (n 33) 651.

reference to mental health in particular.[35] For example, mirroring the right to health norm, the 1993 Constitution of the Republic of the Seychelles (amended) recognises 'the right of every citizen to protection of health and to the enjoyment of the highest attainable standard of physical and mental health'.[36] Likewise, the 2011 Constitution of the Republic of Hungary (amended) enshrines the right of everyone to 'physical and mental health', together with the state obligation to ensure access to the underlying determinants for health.[37] Some constitutions even predate the ICESCR, such as the 1972 Constitution of Panama (amended), which recognises that every individual 'is entitled to promotion, protection, conservation, recovery and rehabilitation of his/her health and the obligation to preserve it, health being understood to be complete physical, mental and social well-being',[38] adding an obligation (rather than a right) being placed on the individual. It further declares that the state shall particularly 'protect the physical, mental and moral health of minors and shall guarantee their rights to … health'.[39] The 1993 Constitution of Peru (amended) addresses mental health in a different way, by highlighting mental deficiency, stipulating that 'everyone has the right to protection of his health [and] anyone unable to take care of himself because of a physical or mental deficiency has the right to respect for his dignity and to a legal system of protection, care, rehabilitation, and security.'[40] Some constitutions indicate an entitlement to the right to mental health, such as the 2006 Constitution of the Republic of Serbia, which declares the right of everyone 'to protection of their mental and physical health'.[41] Others impose a duty on the government, such as the supply of free medicines to those who cannot afford them.[42]

Mental health may, further, be regulated in more detail in domestic legislation such as general health laws, disability-related legislation, capacity legislation, or criminal law, as well as in specific mental health legislation. As of 2020, 111 countries had stand-alone mental health laws, and 74 of those had developed or updated their laws in line with international and regional human rights standards.[43] Domestic mental health legislation typically focuses on issues regarding the civil and human rights protection of persons with mental health conditions and psychosocial disabilities; it regulates involuntary admission and treatment, as well as guardianship, professional training and the mental health service structure. The WHO further categorises the provisions of mental health laws into five types:

---

[35] Katrina Perehudoff, *Health, Essential Medicines, Human Rights & National Constitutions* (WHO 2008).
[36] The Constitution of the Republic of the Seychelles (adopted 1993, amended 2000), art 29.
[37] The Constitution of the Republic of Hungary (adopted 2011, amended 2013), art 20.
[38] The Constitution of the Republic of Panama (adopted 1972, amended 2004), art 109.
[39] Ibid 56.
[40] The Constitution of Peru (adopted 1993, amended 2009), art 7.
[41] The Constitution of the Republic of Serbia (adopted 2006), art 68.
[42] See eg The Constitution of the Republic of Panama (n 38) art 110(5); or The Constitution of the Republic of Ecuador (adopted 2008) art 47.
[43] WHO, 'Mental Health Atlas 2020' (2021), < https://www.who.int/publications/i/item/9789240036703> accessed 14 November 2022, pp 3, 21.

- the right of persons with mental health conditions and psychosocial disabilities to exercise their legal capacity;
- the transition towards community-based mental health services;
- the promotion of alternatives to coercive practices;
- procedures to ensure that the rights of persons with mental health conditions and psychosocial disabilities are protected, and to enable them to file complaints if rights are violated; and
- regular inspections of human rights conditions in mental health facilities by an independent body.[44]

Clearly, domestic mental health legislation not only reflects a 'right to the highest attainable standard of mental health', comprising the availability and enjoyment of social determinants of mental health and access to mental healthcare; it also reflects broader issues relating to the right to mental health, such as legal capacity or involuntary treatment and hospitalisation. While this may seem relatively groundbreaking for the protection of the rights of persons with mental health conditions and psychosocial disabilities, international norms and instruments already reflected these dimensions in the 1970s. This will be discussed in the following section.

3.5 TAKING A BROADER VIEW: MENTAL HEALTH IN INTERNATIONAL SOFT LAW INSTRUMENTS

The international, regional and domestic laws outlined above are all binding on state parties. In contrast, soft law instruments are not legally binding. Yet, they are not without legal significance. While binding treaties form the backbone of human rights law, soft law instruments contribute to the development of legal principles, offer authoritative treaty interpretations, and act as guides to treaty implementation – or can be seen as alternatives to treaty law – among other applications.[45] Hence, it is worth analysing applicable non-binding declarations and resolutions. Since 1975, the soft law instruments described below have guided states in identifying their obligations to protect the right to health of persons with mental health conditions and psychosocial disabilities.

The 1975 Declaration on the Rights of Disabled Persons recognises a right of persons with (psychosocial) disabilities to medical, psychological and functional treatment, and to medical and social rehabilitation in order to develop their capabilities and to empower their reintegration in society.[46] Although the Declaration reflects

---

[44] Ibid 37.
[45] See Marcel Brus, 'Soft Law in Public International Law: A Pragmatic or a Principled Choice? Comparing the Sustainable Development Goals and the Paris Agreement' in Pauline Westerman, Jaap Hage, Stephan Kirste & Anne Ruth Mackor (eds), *Legal Validity and Soft Law* (Springer 2018) 249; or Joost Pauwelyn and others, *Informal International Lawmaking* (Oxford University Press 2012).
[46] UNGA, 'Declaration on the Rights of Disabled Persons' (9 December 1975) UN Doc A/RES/30/3447, para 6.

Chapter 3. Mental Health as a Human Right: The Evolving Framework

the 'medical model' of disability, focusing on the medical problems of persons with psychosocial disabilities, its emphasis on healthcare as a right, and other important human rights principles, such as ensuring that persons with disabilities enjoy the same rights as persons without disabilities,[47] marks a shift from a 'caring approach' to a 'rights-based approach'.[48]

In 1991, the UN General Assembly adopted a second instrument aimed specifically at protecting and promoting the human rights of persons with mental health conditions and psychosocial disabilities: the 1991 Principles for the Protection of Persons with Mental Illness and the Improvement of Mental Healthcare (Resolution 46/119). These Principles, which are more elaborate than the above-mentioned Declaration, propose the right to the best available mental healthcare as a basic right, and identify a set of rules for personal representation in cases of lack of capacity. In order to protect affected persons, the Principles comprise a list of provisions aimed at improving the quality of mental healthcare. These include the right to live in the community (Principle 3), the right to treatment suitable to one's cultural background (Principle 7), the right to receive health and social care appropriate to one's mental health needs (Principle 8), and the right to be treated in the least restrictive manner (Principle 9). The most extensive Principle addresses and regulates consent to treatment (Principle 11). Moreover, the instrument stipulates rights and conditions in mental health facilities (Principle 13), and discusses involuntary admission (Principle 16) and access to information (Principle 19).[49] The Principles establish substantive human rights standards for persons with mental health conditions and psychosocial disabilities, and provide guidance for the implementation of state obligations regarding mental healthcare. The regulations within the Principles apply to all persons having a 'mental illness', established in accordance with 'internationally accepted medical standards'.[50] By stipulating procedural guarantees for involuntary admission or treatment in mental health institutions, and by providing protection against serious human rights abuses within the mental healthcare system, the Principles represented an important instrument to clarify human rights law in regard to the particularities of mental health conditions and psychosocial disabilities. They served as a model for the drafting of mental health legislation in various countries,[51] and were referred to by different human rights treaty bodies and human rights courts.[52] Nevertheless, the Principles can be criticised for lacking explicit regulations on guardianship arrangements, and organisations such as the World Network of Users and Survivors of Psychiatry have questioned the Principles' consistency with already-existing human rights standards regarding involuntary

---

[47] UNGA, 'Report of the Secretary-General, Progress of efforts to ensure the full recognition and enjoyment of the human rights of persons with disabilities' (24 July 2003) UN Doc A/58/181, para 11.
[48] Ibid.
[49] UNGA, 'The protection of persons with mental illness and the improvement of mental health care' (17 December 1991) UN Doc A/RES/46/119, annex.
[50] Ibid principle 4(1).
[51] UNGA, 'Report of the Secretary-General, Progress of efforts to ensure the full recognition and enjoyment of the human rights of persons with disabilities' (n 47) paras 12–13.
[52] See eg *Fernandes de Oliveira v Portugal*, App no 78103/14 (ECtHR, 31 January 2019) para 68.

treatment and admission.[53] Furthermore, and as already observed, given their non-binding nature, the Declaration and the Principles cannot impose binding legal obligations on states.

A third instrument adopted by the UN General Assembly Resolution 48/96 is the 1993 Standard Rules on the Equalization of Opportunities for Persons with Disabilities. Although, unlike the preceding document, the Standard Rules do not focus only on mental health conditions, they do also apply to 'people disabled by mental illness'.[54] The Standard Rules contain regulations on, inter alia: raising awareness in society about persons with disability, including their rights and needs (Rule 1); ensuring effective medical care, including adequate training of local community workers (Rule 2); the provision of rehabilitation services (Rule 3); and the development and supply of support services (Rule 4). They also define target areas for equal participation, such as accessibility, education, employment, family life and religion. Rather than addressing the specific human rights challenges of persons with mental health conditions and psychosocial disabilities (as the above-mentioned instruments do), this document identifies a broad range of rights that persons with disabilities should enjoy, also beyond the healthcare system.

Despite their differences, all three of these documents emphasise dignity and autonomy as fundamental principles. By placing mental health in a broader human rights context, they can be seen as important tools for the promotion and protection of human rights in mental health, although the established safeguards have often been rendered meaningless for mental health practice.[55] Nonetheless, these non-binding norms can now be found, in various forms, in the CRPD provisions. And, as will be illustrated next, the CRPD, which supersedes the previously developed soft law, plays a crucial role in how mental health can be framed as a human right today.

3.6 THE MEANING OF THE RIGHT TO MENTAL HEALTH

3.6.1 SCHOLARLY DEBATE OVER THE RIGHT TO HEALTH AND MENTAL HEALTH

It is widely recognised that mental health falls within the provision of the highest attainable standard of physical and mental health.[56] Yet, various scholars have

---

[53] World Network of Users and Survivors of Psychiatry, 'Position Paper on the Principles for the Protection of Persons with Mental Illness' (2001), <www.wnusp.net/index.php/position-paper-on-principles-for-the-protection-of-persons-with-mental-illness.html> accessed 14 November 2022.

[54] UNGA, 'Standard Rules on the Equalization of Opportunities for Persons with Disabilities' (20 December 1993) UN Doc A/RES/48/96, annex, para 17.

[55] UNGA, 'Report of the Special Rapporteur on the right of everyone to the enjoyment of the highest attainable standard of physical and mental health, Dainius Pūras' (28 March 2017) UN Doc A/HRC/35/21, para 32.

[56] See eg Paul Hunt & Judith Mesquita, 'Mental Disabilities and the Human Right to the Highest Attainable Standard of Health' (2006) 28(2) Human Rights Quarterly 332; or UNGA, 'Report of the

emphasised persisting challenges regarding the promotion and protection of *mental health* in particular.[57] Hunt and Mesquita, for instance, call mental health, 'among the most grossly neglected elements of the right to health'.[58] Additional tensions may arise, given that the specific context of mental health allows for restrictions on the enjoyment of the right to health. Previous Special Rapporteur on the Rights of Persons with Disabilities, Catalina Devandas-Aguilar, illustrates these tensions with two examples:[59] firstly, the 1991 Principles for the Protection of Persons with Mental Illness and the Improvement of Mental Health Care, which impose several restrictions to the right to free and informed consent; and, secondly, the 1997 Convention on Human Rights and Biomedicine of the Council of Europe, which allows for non-consensual interventions aimed at treating persons with mental health conditions and psychosocial disabilities.[60] As asserted by Devandas-Aguilar, these instruments, which are aimed at protecting the very right to health, establish a lower standard of protection in the mental healthcare setting than the (other) international and regional human rights treaties presented above. As will be elaborated later in this book, the notions of 'medical necessity' or 'dangerousness' are often used by UN treaty bodies, or in jurisprudence, to justify such restrictions.[61]

Despite acknowledging that persons with mental health conditions and psychosocial disabilities are protected by the general right to the highest attainable standard of health, Quinn and Degener argue that the international human rights norms providing for a right to health paid little attention to the specific (health) needs of persons with psychosocial disabilities until the CRPD was adopted.[62] Stavert and McGregor have asserted that, in order to realise the right to mental health, other enforceable, relevant human rights are required. Social, cultural, economic and political, as well as environmental, factors impact on mental health and its attainment, and must therefore be considered. Stavert and McGregor propose that human rights law must provide a framework to prevent the occurrence of mental health conditions and minimise the impact of mental health conditions on individuals, and that, additionally, such a framework must also offer adequate support and safeguards for persons with mental

---

Special Rapporteur on the rights of persons with disabilities, Catalina Devandas-Aguilar, Rights of persons with disabilities' (16 July 2018) UN Doc A/73/161, paras 9–20.

[57] Emphasis added.
[58] Paul Hunt & Judith Mesquita (n 56) p 333.
[59] UNGA, Report of the Special Rapporteur on the rights of persons with disabilities, Catalina Devandas-Aguilar' (n 56) para 11.
[60] Council of Europe, Oviedo Convention (n 31) arts 6, 7.
[61] See eg UNGA, 'Report of the Special Rapporteur on torture and other cruel, inhuman or degrading treatment or punishment, Juan E. Méndez' (1 February 2013) UN Doc A/HRC/22/53; or Human Rights Committee (HRCtee), 'General Comment No. 35 Article 9 (Liberty and security of person)' (16 December 2014) UN Doc CCPR/C/GC/35.
[62] Gerard Quinn & Theresia Degener, 'Human rights and disability: the current use and future potential of United Nations human rights instruments in the context of disability' (2002), <https://www.ohchr.org/Documents/Publications/HRDisabilityen.pdf> accessed 14 November 2022.

health conditions and psychosocial disabilities.[63] In the words of Bartlett, recognising that existing laws and human rights approaches were not working for persons with psychosocial disabilities was an impetus for the CRPD.[64]

The CRPD supersedes the above-mentioned standards.[65] It emphasises the need to remove all practices that limit the right of persons with psychosocial disabilities to enjoy the highest attainable standard of health, and provides sufficient safeguards to that end. Fundamentally, the CRPD framework offers a human rights approach to disability which, ultimately, advances the right to mental health, as will be outlined throughout this book. Consequently, the CRPD will be considered more thoroughly when delineating a human rights framework for the mental health context in the following subsection.

3.6.2 DELINEATING A HUMAN RIGHTS FRAMEWORK IN THE MENTAL HEALTH CONTEXT

In his final report, in 2020, former Special Rapporteur on the Right to Health, Dainius Pūras, states that human rights violations in the area of mental health must be addressed, and that the 'vicious cycle of discrimination, disempowerment, coercion, social exclusion and injustice' must be broken.[66] During his mandate, he indicated that the evolving human rights framework in mental health connects the right to the highest attainable standard of health, including the entitlement to social determinants, to 'the freedom to control one's own health and body'.[67] This freedom entails being free from discrimination, having legal capacity, and not being subject to non-consensual interferences, including violence and abuse. In addition to guaranteeing these freedoms, the entitlements to treatment and integration in the community must also be included. In fact, Pūras sees the failure to secure these entitlements as a primary driver for non-consensual interferences and violence in the mental health context.[68] Treatment for psychosocial disabilities is often provided far from home, in institutional settings.[69] Therefore, the human rights context around mental health must also link

---

[63] Jill Stavert & Rebecca McGregor, 'Domestic legislation and international human rights standards: the case of mental health and incapacity' (2018) 22(1) The International Journal of Human Rights 70, 71.

[64] Peter Bartlett, 'Implementing a Paradigm Shift: Implementing the Convention on the Rights of Persons with Disabilities in the Context of Mental Disability Law' in *Torture in Healthcare Settings: Reflections on the Special Rapporteur on Torture's 2013 Thematic Report* (Centre for Human Rights and Humanitarian Law, American University Washington College of Law 2014) 170.

[65] Including standards set by legally binding and non-binding human rights instruments, UN treaty bodies and jurisprudence.

[66] UNGA, 'Report of the Special Rapporteur on the right of everyone to the enjoyment of the highest attainable standard of physical and mental health, Dainius Pūras' (15 April 2020) UN Doc A/HRC/44/48, summary.

[67] Ibid para 31.

[68] Ibid para 32.

[69] See eg UNGA, 'Report of the United Nations High Commissioner for Human Rights, Mental health and human rights' (31 January 2017) UN Doc A/HRC/34/32, para 30; or United Nations Economic

Chapter 3. Mental Health as a Human Right: The Evolving Framework

the right to health to the 'integration and treatment in the community with appropriate support'.[70] This implies that persons must not be subjected to institutionalisation. These four components: being free from discrimination; legal capacity; and not being subject to either non-consensual interferences or institutionalisation, are protected by seven key human rights that can be found in the CRPD. Together with the right to the highest attainable standard of health, these additional human rights are delineated under a normative framework for mental health in Table 3.2 below. Article 12 ICESCR is acknowledged as the most authoritative right to the highest attainable standard of health norm. The CRPD, however, details essential building blocks for ensuring respect, promotion, protection and fulfilment of the right to mental health. Therefore, the additional human rights for the protection of persons with mental health conditions and psychosocial disabilities are drawn from the CRPD.

Table 3.2: Human rights to ensure the protection and promotion of mental health

Mental health	The right to the enjoyment of the highest attainable standard of health (Art. 12 ICESCR, Art. 25 CRPD).
Freedom from discrimination	The right to be free from discrimination (Art. 5 CRPD).
Legal capacity	The right to equal recognition before the law (Art. 12 CRPD).
Freedom from non-consensual interferences	The right to respect for his or her physical and mental integrity (Art. 17 CRPD).
	The right to be free from torture or cruel, inhuman or degrading treatment or punishment (Art. 15 CRPD).
	The right to be free from exploitation, violence and abuse (Art. 16 CRPD).
	The right to liberty and security of the person (Art. 14 CRPD).
Not being subjected to institutionalisation	The right to live independently and be included in the community (Art. 19 CRPD).

While the right to the enjoyment of the highest attainable standard of health is a key right in the debate about mental health and human rights, it cannot, in the author's view, be seen as an umbrella right that covers the normative framework. The other established human rights play a central role in the promotion and protection of mental health.

Table 3.2 connects each component (on the left-hand side) to only the most relevant applicable human rights (on the right-hand side), to avoid repetition. However, it must be pointed out that some of the listed human rights apply to more than one component.

---

and Social Council, 'Report of the Special Rapporteur on the right of everyone to the enjoyment of the highest attainable standard of physical and mental health, Paul Hunt' (11 February 2005) UN Doc E/CN.4/2005/51, para 14.

[70] UNGA, 'Report of the Special Rapporteur on the right of everyone to the enjoyment of the highest attainable standard of physical and mental health, Dainius Pūras' (n 66) para 31.

Intersentia

For instance, the right to equal recognition before the law, the right to liberty and security of the person, and the right to respect for his or her physical and mental integrity can all also be linked to not being subjected to institutionalisation. Ultimately, all of the outlined human rights are indivisible, interdependent and interrelated,[71] as the following examples show. To receive treatment (right to health), informed consent (the right to equal recognition before the law) is needed. The deprivation of liberty (the right to liberty and security of the person), in terms of non-consensual interferences such as involuntary admission, is often the result of denying persons with mental health conditions and psychosocial disabilities legal capacity (the right to equal recognition before the law). Involuntary treatment (the right to respect for his or her physical and mental integrity) can include seclusion or constraint mechanisms, which might amount to ill-treatment (the right to be free from exploitation, violence and abuse; or the right to be free from torture or cruel, inhumane or degrading treatment or punishment).

Despite their interconnection, it is worth noting that there are also potential conflicts between the rights identified above. For example, under the right to equal recognition before the law, a person can either give or withhold consent to treatment; in other words, a person has the right not to be treated.[72] Nevertheless, there is a duty to protect persons. The European Convention on Human Rights and Biomedicine, for instance, proclaims that persons with mental health conditions and psychosocial disabilities can be subjected to treatment against their will if, without treatment, serious harm is likely to result to their health.[73] Such conflicts will be examined further in the normative analysis in Chapter 5.

When reviewing the language employed in international, regional and domestic human rights treaties, the right to the enjoyment of the highest attainable standard of health embraces the right to mental health. However, in consideration of the preceding argumentation, the author would like to propose that the term 'right to mental health' extends beyond the right to health norm. Instead, the right to mental health, as evaluated in this book, must be understood as the sum of all human rights relevant under the normative framework for the promotion and protection of mental health. This view is supported by others, who also argue that the right to mental health is more than just the widely recognised right to the highest attainable standard of health. Within the UN system alone, former UN High Commissioner for Human Rights, Seid al-Hussein, discussed the right to legal capacity, free and informed consent, being free from ill-treatment and torture, as well as not being deprived of one's liberty, as important elements under the human rights-based approach to disability in the context of mental health.[74] Additionally, former Special Rapporteur Pūras claimed that the

---

[71] See UNGA, Vienna Declaration and Programme of Action (12 July 1993) UN Doc A/CONF.157/23, para 5.
[72] See eg World Medical Association, Declaration of Lisbon on the Rights of the Patient (revised) (October 2005) 2.
[73] Council of Europe (n 31) art 7.
[74] UNGA, 'Report of the United Nations High Commissioner for Human Rights, Mental health and human rights' (n 69) paras 22–33.

right to provide consent to treatment and hospitalisation is a core element under what he calls the right to mental health framework.[75]

3.7 CONCLUDING SUMMARY

The ICESCR offers a legally binding framework for the right to the enjoyment of the highest attainable standard of health. The Covenant explicitly states that health includes mental health. This legal norm is complemented by legal standards formed within the CRC and the CRPD, sometimes referring to health, and sometimes explicitly or exclusively referring to mental health. From these treaty provisions emerges the obligation of all state parties to respect, protect and fulfil mental health as a human right. However, as was discussed in this chapter, human rights with respect to mental health go beyond the right to health norm. Thus, the right to mental health is broader than the right to the highest attainable standard of health. The human rights framework in relation to mental health comprises a range of rights, including the right to health; but also the right to be free from discrimination; the right to equal recognition before the law; the right to respect for one's physical and mental integrity; the right to be free from torture or cruel, inhuman or degrading treatment or punishment; the right to be free from exploitation, violence and abuse; the right to liberty and security of the person; and the right to live independently and be included in the community.

The following chapters will analyse how the right to the highest attainable standard of health, as a standard under international human rights law, protects mental health, and how the other human rights under the established normative framework contribute to promoting and protecting what can be labelled 'the right to mental health'.

---

[75] UNGA, 'Report of the Special Rapporteur on the right of everyone to the enjoyment of the highest attainable standard of physical and mental health, Dainius Pūras' (n 55) para 63.

CHAPTER 4
THE RIGHT TO HEALTH NORM AND MENTAL HEALTH

4.1 INTRODUCTION

After the previous chapters suggested a human rights framework with respect to mental health and illustrated how it evolved, this chapter conducts a legal analysis of one of its key norms, namely the right to the highest attainable standard of physical and mental health. As explained in Chapter 3, 'the right to mental health' is considered broader than the right to the highest attainable standard of health norm (herein also referred to as the right to health[1]), as 'the right to mental health' entails other human rights as well. Nevertheless, this chapter aims to analyse relevant components of the right to the highest attainable standard of health to create conceptual clarity regarding the mental health dimension of the right. Ultimately, the findings of this chapter will form part of the broader right to mental health framework. The question that will be answered in this chapter is: to what extent does the right to the highest attainable standard of physical and mental health, in particular Article 12 of the International Covenant on Economic, Social and Cultural Rights (ICESCR), respect, protect and fulfil mental health as a stand-alone norm?

To answer this question, it is necessary to have a clear picture of the components of the right to the highest attainable standard of health. To identify the mental health elements within this right, this chapter commences by evaluating the normative content of the right to health (section 4.2), before sharpening the legal analysis by outlining state obligations arising from the right to the highest attainable standard of health with regard to mental health (section 4.3). To complement the analysis of the right to health in line with Article 12 ICESCR, section 4.4 sheds light on whether and how mental health has been interpreted as a justiciable element of the right to health. Here, case law from the international and regional human rights bodies in which mental health is recognised as an element of the right to health will be discussed.

---

[1] To avoid confusion, it is important to distinguish between 'the right to health' and 'the right to mental health', as they are considered as two different (but interconnected) concepts in this book.

4.2 NORMATIVE CONTENT OF THE RIGHT TO THE HIGHEST ATTAINABLE STANDARD OF MENTAL HEALTH

The right to health, as provided in Article 12 ICESCR, contains various obligations on states which correspond with freedoms and entitlements for individuals and, sometimes, groups and populations. According to the Committee on Economic, Social and Cultural Rights (CteeESCR), the freedoms can be broken down into different components: the right to make decisions affecting one's health and bodily integrity, including the right to free and informed consent; and the right to be free from interferences,[2] such as inhuman or degrading treatment or punishment, non-consensual medical treatments or being hospitalised involuntarily.[3] The freedom component, which once more underlines the interrelation of the right to health with other human rights, is particularly relevant to the experience of individuals with mental health conditions and psychosocial disabilities and is thus fundamental in the discussion about the right to mental health, as was already established in section 3.6. The entitlements consist of various elements for health prevention and protection. Several scholars, among them Zhang and San Giorgi, distinguish between entitlements under underlying determinants of health, and entitlements under the right to access healthcare, under which mental healthcare is just one of the entitlements, next to primary healthcare, preventive healthcare, child healthcare, rehabilitative healthcare, the provision of essential drugs and more.[4] Listing mental healthcare as an isolated entitlement under the right to access healthcare, next to many other forms of healthcare, fails to address the comprehensive approach of mental healthcare, which also includes the prevention of mental ill health, the provision of essential psychotropic medicine, and psychiatric rehabilitation.

Taking a different approach, and not considering mental healthcare solely as one of the entitlements under the right to access healthcare, the following subsections delineate the full normative content of the right to health in Article 12 ICESCR with regard to mental health. Various scholars have examined the right to health in line with the classification introduced by Toebes, who established three different elements of the right to health, namely scope, core content and overlapping elements.[5] To provide an illustrative overview of the scope and core content of the right to health in the particular context of mental health, this section is based on that classification.

---

[2] As will be elaborated in more detail in Chapter 5, non-consensual interferences are not absolute rights and might be subject to limitations.
[3] Committee on Economic, Social and Cultural Rights (CteeESCR), 'General Comment No. 14: The Right to the Highest Attainable Standard of Health (Art. 12)' (General Comment 14) (11 August 2000) UN Doc E/C.12/2000/4, para 8.
[4] See Yi Zhang, *Advancing the Right to Health Care in China towards Accountability* (Intersentia 2019) 40; and Maite San Giorgi, *The Human Right to Equal Access to Health Care* (Intersentia 2012) 15–16.
[5] Brigit Toebes, *The Right to Health as a Human Right in International Law* (Intersentia/Hart 1999) 243.

4.2.1 THE SCOPE OF THE RIGHT TO HEALTH AND MENTAL HEALTH

The scope of the right to the highest attainable standard of health can be understood as the general content of the right. This subsection identifies all of the elements embedded in the right to health provision (Article 12 ICESCR) that affirm mental health. As a point of departure, these elements are divided into underlying determinants of mental health, on the one hand, and access to mental healthcare, on the other.

4.2.1.1 Underlying Determinants of Mental Health

The right to underlying determinants of health is a precondition for securing the right to the highest attainable standard of mental health. Ensuring underlying determinants promotes mental health, and can, in one way or another, also be seen as preventing certain forms of psychosocial disabilities. The CteeESCR declares, in a non-exhaustive list, the following underlying determinants of health: access to safe and potable water; adequate sanitation facilities; adequate supply of safe food, nutrition and housing; healthy occupational and environmental conditions; and access to health-related education and information.[6] These determinants refer to the physical environment, and are widely recognised as affecting health outcomes and the enjoyment of the right to health. Yet, while people who face poverty and economic inequalities suffer disproportionately from poor mental health, people are also prone to mental health problems irrespective of whether material preconditions are met.[7]

Thus, a rights-based approach to the promotion of mental health further requires that specific conditions are created and sustained. In 2017, the then UN High Commissioner for Human Rights, Zeid al-Hussein, proposed particularly that, for mental health, the underlying determinants include 'low socioeconomic status, violence and abuse, adverse childhood experiences, early childhood development and whether there are supportive and tolerant relationships in the family, the workplace and other settings'.[8] Hence, conceptualising the determinants of mental health also requires a focus on people's emotional and psychosocial environments, including relationships, social connections and community identity between individuals. Furthermore, former Special Rapporteur on the Right to Health, Dainius Pūras, defines structural conditions as root causes for mental health conditions. He widens the conception of determinants, and claims that inequitable laws and structures of power and governance, and policies that stratify society, profoundly affect how people act and the relationships they have.[9]

---

[6] CteeESCR, General Comment 14 (n 3) para 11.
[7] Jessica Allen and others, 'Social determinants of mental health' (2014) 26(4) International Review of Psychiatry 392, 393.
[8] United Nations General Assembly (UNGA), 'Report of the United Nations High Commissioner for Human Rights, Mental health and human rights' (31 January 2017) UN Doc A/HRC/34/32, para 6.
[9] UNGA, 'Report of the Special Rapporteur on the right of everyone to the enjoyment of the highest attainable standard of physical and mental health, Dainius Pūras' (12 April 2019) UN Doc A/HRC/41/34, paras 4–5.

In his view, the focus of research and action on psychosocial, structural and political determinants is vital for the mental health determinants to be centred on human rights.[10]

Several treaty bodies, including the CteeESCR, have progressively adopted interpretations that include psychosocial and structural determinants to promote mental health and well-being. These determinants include, for example, participation in cultural life,[11] a non-violent environment for children,[12] ending violence against women,[13] and community inclusion.[14] In fact, Pūras proclaims that, '[g]iving effect to the full range of human rights is a core determinant of mental health' in and of itself.[15]

4.2.1.2 Access to Mental Healthcare

Article 12(2) ICESCR identifies a non-exhaustive set of state obligations.[16] In conjunction with the progressive realisation clause (Article 2(1) ICESCR),[17] it is not possible to determine in detail the kind of mental healthcare individuals must have access to, and to what extent. Notwithstanding this, a range of explanatory documents from the CteeESCR and beyond help concretise the mental health elements covered by the right to the highest attainable standard of health.

As elucidated in Chapter 3, Article 12(2)(d) ICESCR obliges states to create conditions that 'assure to all medical service and medical attention in the event of sickness … both physical and mental'.[18] Paragraph 12(2)(d) CteeESCR General Comment 14 sets out the right to health facilities, goods and services, including the provision of, and timely access to, 'appropriate mental health treatment and care'.[19] Along similar lines, the Committee of the Convention on the Rights of the Child

---

[10] UNGA, 'Report of the Special Rapporteur on the right of everyone to the enjoyment of the highest attainable standard of physical and mental health, Dainius Pūras' (15 April 2020) UN Doc A/HRC/44/48, paras 23, 26; see also WHO and Commission on Social Determinants of Health, 'Closing the gap in a generation: Health equity through action on the social determinants of health' (2008), <https://www.who.int/social_determinants/final_report/csdh_finalreport_2008.pdf> accessed 14 November 2022.

[11] CteeESCR, 'General comment No. 21: The right of everyone to take part in cultural life (Art. 15, para 1(a))' (21 December 2009) Un Doc E/C.12/GC/21, para 16.

[12] Committee on the Rights of the Child (CteeRC), 'General comment No. 13: The right of the child to freedom from all forms of violence' (18 April 2011) UN Doc CRC/C/GC/13, para 14.

[13] CteeESCR, 'General comment No. 22 on the right to sexual and reproductive health (Art. 12)' (2 May 2016) UN Doc E/C.12/GC/22, paras 7–8.

[14] Committee on the Rights of Persons with Disabilities (CteeRPD), 'General comment No. 5 (2017) on living independently and being included in the community' (27 October 2017) UN Doc CRPD/C/GC/5.

[15] UNGA, 'Report of the Special Rapporteur on the right of everyone to the enjoyment of the highest attainable standard of physical and mental health, Dainius Pūras' (n 9) para 13.

[16] See CteeESCR, General Comment 14 (n 3) para 7.

[17] See eg UNGA, International Covenant on Economic, Social and Cultural Rights (ICESCR) (adopted 16 December 1966, entered into force 3 January 1976) 993 UNTS 3, art 2; or CteeESCR, 'General Comment No. 3: The Nature of States Parties' Obligations' (General Comment 3) (14 December 1990) UN Doc E/1991/23.

[18] CteeESCR, General Comment 14 (n 3) para 17.

[19] Ibid.

(CteeRC) interprets the right to health to include the right to be treated and cared for as children and adolescents with mental disorders.[20] Similarly, the African Commission on Human and Peoples' Rights (African Commission) interprets the right to health as including access to humane and dignified care for persons with psychosocial disabilities.[21] Given their importance, Table 4.1 offers an overview of the three identified definitions of access to mental healthcare within the right to the highest attainable standard of health:

Table 4.1: The right to the highest attainable standard of health interpreted as including...

CteeESCR General Comment 14	Access to appropriate mental health treatment and care.
CteeCRC General Comment 4	The right to be treated and cared for as children and adolescents with mental disorders.
African Commission Pretoria Declaration	Access to humane and dignified care for persons with psychosocial disabilities.

Recalling the provisions of one of the CteeESCR's earlier general comments regarding persons with disabilities (General Comment 5) may help to clarify what is required with regard to mental health. Therein, the right to physical and mental health implies:

> the right to have access to, and to benefit from, those medical and social services ... which enable persons with disabilities to become independent, [and which] prevent further disabilities and support their social integration.[22]

The same paragraph also states that rehabilitation services must be offered. Moreover, General Comment 5 states that mental healthcare has to be with the same level of medical care as provided to other members of society, and must be provided in such a way that patients are able to maintain full respect for their rights and dignity.[23] Besides curative and rehabilitative services, the CteeESCR recognises the importance of preventive health services and education as well,[24] the latter including access to information about preventive and health-promoting behaviour.[25] Furthermore, the CteeESCR emphasises the need for the public health sector, as well as private mental health providers and facilities, to comply with the non-discrimination principle, and interprets the ICESCR as proscribing any discrimination in access to healthcare

---

[20] CteeRC, 'General Comment No. 4: Adolescent Health and Development in the Context of the Convention on the Rights of the Child' (General Comment 4) (1 July 2003) UN Doc CRC/GC/2003/4, para 25.
[21] African Commission, 'Pretoria Declaration on Economic, Social and Cultural Rights in Africa' (2004).
[22] CteeESCR, 'General Comment No. 5: Persons with Disabilities' (General Comment 5) (9 December 1994) UN Doc E/1995/22, para 34.
[23] Ibid para 34.
[24] CteeESCR, General Comment 14 (n 3) paras 17, 25, 44(d).
[25] Ibid para 22.

and underlying determinants of health on, inter alia, the ground of psychosocial disability.[26]

In addition to the right to health facilities, goods and services, the CteeESCR has also interpreted Article 12 ICESCR as containing a set of interrelated and essential elements of the right to (mental) healthcare, namely that (mental) healthcare facilities, goods and services should be available, accessible, acceptable and of good quality (referred to as AAAQ).[27] The meaning and implications of the AAAQ will be illustrated briefly, and in general, here. These principles will then be discussed in the context of each of the two countries analysed in Chapter 6, to set the stage for the discussion of the domestic implementation of the right to mental health(care).

The first element of the AAAQ – availability – requires a sufficient quantity of facilities, goods, services and programmes, such as hospitals and clinics, trained professional personnel and essential drugs.[28] Further indicators to evaluate availability include the number of healthcare providers per citizen, the number of hospital beds, and the waiting time for being admitted to a healthcare service.[29]

The second element of the AAAQ – accessibility – has four overlapping dimensions. Firstly, facilities, goods and services must be accessible to everyone, in particular to the most vulnerable and marginalised, without discrimination by law, before the law, or in fact.[30] Vulnerable and marginalised groups, such as persons with mental health conditions and psychosocial disabilities, should not be treated less favourably than others (non-discrimination). Secondly, facilities, goods and services must be within safe physical reach for everyone, including persons with psychosocial disabilities, even in remote areas (physical accessibility).[31] Thirdly, facilities, goods and services, whether public or private, must be affordable to everyone (economic accessibility). Socially and economically disadvantaged groups, to which persons with psychosocial disabilities often belong, should not be disproportionately burdened with health expenses.[32] In fact, it is especially mental healthcare, including costly medication, that is not always covered by national health insurance schemes (as discussed in subsection 2.4.1.3). The fourth and final dimension of accessibility is that information should be accessible so as to seek, receive and impart information and ideas in relation to mental health issues (information accessibility).[33]

The third element of the AAAQ – acceptability – provides that all facilities, goods and services must be respectful to medical ethics[34] and culturally appropriate.[35] The

---

[26] Ibid para 26.
[27] Ibid para 12.
[28] Ibid para 12(a).
[29] Maite San Giorgi (n 4) 52–53.
[30] CteeESCR, General Comment 14 (n 3) para 12(b); Maite San Giorgi (n 4) 65.
[31] CteeESCR, General Comment 14 (n 3) para 12(b).
[32] Ibid.
[33] Ibid.
[34] Commonly referred to as a set of moral principles, values and beliefs that guide practitioners when making medical choices.
[35] CteeESCR, General Comment 14 (n 3) para 12(c).

latter dimension implies that local cultural conceptions of mental health and ill health should be taken into consideration in service provision.[36]

The last of the four elements of the AAAQ is quality. Mental health facilities, goods and services must be scientifically and medically appropriate, and of good quality. This requires scientifically approved drugs and hospital equipment, as well as healthcare personnel adequately trained on (mental) health and human rights.[37] While the CteeESCR does not present a concrete interpretation of the term quality, the World Health Organization (WHO) stipulates that high quality mental health services 'require the use of evidence based practices and must incorporate human rights principles, respect autonomy and protect people's inherent dignity'.[38] When evaluating the AAAQ, resource scarcity needs to be taken into consideration. Zhang highlights that, in the process of allocating resources to fully ensure health facilities, goods and services with sufficient availability, accessibility, acceptability and quality, trade-offs may exist between the different elements. For instance, while a state may build up available services throughout the country, including in remote areas, the quality of these facilities might be poor.[39] Ultimately, the AAAQ principles can be seen as a yardstick to measure a country's compliance with the right to mental health.

Along with general comments, concluding observations may clarify how the CteeESCR defines requirements for states with respect to mental healthcare and treatment. The following non-exhaustive overview lists such further elements, deduced from concluding observations published between 2014 and 2019. Accordingly, mental health services include:

– activities to raise awareness of mental health issues and disorders, and activities to reduce the stigma of these[40]
– mental health services in general hospitals[41]
– a widely available and accessible comprehensive, integrated, and interdisciplinary system of community-based services, including peer support[42]

---

[36] Yi Zhang (n 4) 62.
[37] CteeESCR, General Comment 14 (n 3) 12(d); Maite San Giorgi (n 4) 60.
[38] WHO, 'WHO QualityRights: Service standards and quality in mental health care' (nd), <https://www.who.int/mental_health/policy/quality_rights/infosheet_hrs_day.pdf> accessed 14 November 2022.
[39] Yi Zhang (n 4) 62.
[40] See eg UN Economic and Social Council (ECOSOC), 'Committee on Economic, Social and Cultural Rights Concluding observations on the initial report of Cabo Verde' (27 November 2018) UN Doc E/C.12/CPV/CO/1, para 61.
[41] See eg ECOSOC, 'Committee on Economic, Social and Cultural Rights Concluding observations on the fourth periodic report of Argentina' (1 November 2018) UN Doc E/C.12/ARG/CO/4, para 54(g).
[42] See eg ECOSOC, 'Committee on Economic, Social and Cultural Rights Concluding observations on the fourth periodic report of Cameroon' (25 March 2019) UN Doc E/C.12/CMR/CO/4, para 56(c); ECOSOC (n 41) para 54(e); 'Committee on Economic, Social and Cultural Rights Concluding observations on the fourth periodic report of the Republic of Korea' (19 October 2017) UN Doc E/C.12/KOR/CO/4, para 58; and 'Committee on Economic, Social and Cultural Rights Concluding observations on the second periodic report of Lithuania' (24 June 2014) UN Doc E/C.12/LTU/CO/2, para 20.

- a sufficient amount of skilled personnel[43]
- health professionals trained on early diagnosis and care[44]
- mental healthcare in detention;[45]

and, specifically regarding the quality element of mental health treatment and care, concluding observations state that:

- treatment should be on the basis of free and informed consent, unless exceptional circumstances require otherwise.[46]
- coercive measures in mental health institutions should be reduced, including among children.[47]
- involuntary institutionalisation should be restricted, especially when treating children and adolescents.[48]

Nevertheless, the CteeESCR fails to clarify the meaning or details of these enumerated elements.

In conclusion, the right to the highest attainable standard of health covers access to mental healthcare and treatment, including preventive, medical, social and rehabilitative services. Any claim to access mental health services, therefore, falls within the scope of Article 12(2)(d) ICESCR. CteeESCR General Comment 14 and the CteeESCR's concluding observations further suggest that mental health facilities, goods

---

[43] See eg ECOSOC, 'Committee on Economic, Social and Cultural Rights Concluding observations on the fifth periodic report of Mauritius' (5 April 2019) UN Doc E/C.12/MUS/CO/5, paras 55–56; 'Committee on Economic, Social and Cultural Rights Concluding observations on the second periodic report of Greece' (27 October 2015) UN Doc E/C.12/GRC/CO/2, para 36(b); and 'Committee on Economic, Social and Cultural Rights Concluding observations on the initial report of Uganda' (8 July 2015) UN Doc E/C.12/UGA/CO/1, para 34.

[44] See eg ECOSOC, 'Committee on Economic, Social and Cultural Rights Concluding observations on the sixth periodic report of Bulgaria' (29 March 2019) UN Doc E/C.12/BGR/CO/6, para 43; and 'Committee on Economic, Social and Cultural Rights Concluding observations on the initial report of Indonesia' (19 June 2014) UN Doc E/C.12/IDN/CO/1, para 34.

[45] See eg ECOSOC, 'Committee on Economic, Social and Cultural Rights Concluding observations on the sixth periodic report of the United Kingdom of Great Britain and Northern Ireland' (14 July 2016) UN Doc E/C.12/GBR/CO/6, para 58.

[46] See eg ECOSOC, 'Committee on Economic, Social and Cultural Rights Concluding observations on the second periodic report of Kazakhstan' (29 March 2019) UN Doc E/C.12/KAZ/CO/2, para 45(a); ECOSOC (n 41) para 54(c); 'Committee on Economic, Social and Cultural Rights Concluding observations on the fifth periodic report of Australia' (11 July 2017) UN Doc E/C.12/AUS/CO/5, para 46(d); 'Committee on Economic, Social and Cultural Rights Concluding observations on the sixth periodic report of Poland' (26 October 2016) UN Doc E/C.12/POL/CO/6, para 52(c); and 'Committee on Economic, Social and Cultural Rights Concluding observations on the sixth periodic report of Sweden' (14 July 2016) UN Doc E/C.12/SWE/CO/6, para 44(c).

[47] See eg ECOSOC, 'Committee on Economic, Social and Cultural Rights Concluding observations on sixth periodic report of Denmark' (12 November 2019) UN Doc E/C.12/DNK/CO/6, para 57; and 'Committee on Economic, Social and Cultural Rights Concluding observations on the third periodic report of Slovakia' (14 November 2019) UN Doc E/C.12/SVK/CO/3, para 40.

[48] See eg ECOSOC, 'Committee on Economic, Social and Cultural Rights Concluding observations on the fourth periodic report of Argentina' (n 41) para 54(d)(f).

and services should be available, accessible, acceptable and of good quality, including treatment on the basis of free and informed consent (with exceptions), reduction of coercive measures and restriction of involuntary institutionalisation. In light of resource scarcity, however, a state may argue that it is unable to guarantee access to mental healthcare and treatment in line with the regulations as stated above.

4.2.2 THE CORE CONTENT OF THE RIGHT TO HEALTH AND MENTAL HEALTH

As briefly mentioned above, the right to the highest attainable standard of health is subject to progressive realisation, meaning that states are obliged to progressively work towards its realisation. While a state must take 'deliberate, concrete and targeted' steps 'to the maximum of its available resources',[49] the CteeESCR reaffirms, in its General Comment 14, that states have a core obligation to fulfil a minimum essential level of service provision, irrespective of resource availability.[50] In resource-poor settings, mental health is often considered an unaffordable luxury.[51] Compelling states to offer essential mental health services would send a strong signal. But do mental health services fall within the scope of the core obligation?

The Committee suggests that states have a core obligation to ensure 'essential primary healthcare'. It indicates that 'compelling guidance' should be drawn from contemporary instruments.[52] The 1978 Alma-Ata Declaration and 1994 Programme of Action of the International Conference on Population and Development contain no references to mental health. However, more recent documents embrace mental healthcare as part of their primary healthcare components, such as the WHO document titled *A vision for primary health care in the 21st century*,[53] or the UN Declaration on Universal Health Coverage, which refers to primary healthcare as 'first contact with the health system ... to enhance people's physical and mental health'.[54] Irrespective of mental health being part of primary healthcare, the CteeESCR has not provided definitional clarity as to exactly what constitutes *essential* primary

---

[49] CteeESCR, General Comment 14 (n 3) para 30; UNGA, ICESCR (n 17), art 2(1).
[50] CteeESCR, General Comment 14 (n 3) para 43.
[51] See eg Vikram Patel & Martin Prince, 'Global Mental Health' (2010) 303(19) The Journal of the American Medical Association 1976; or Office of the United Nations High Commissioner for Human Rights (OHCHR), 'Consultation on Human Rights and mental health: "Identifying strategies to promote human rights in mental health". Statement by UN High Commissioner of the United Nations for Human Rights Zeid Ra'ad Al Hussein' (14 May 2018), <https://www.ohchr.org/EN/NewsEvents/Pages/DisplayNews.aspx?NewsID=23080&LangID=E> accessed 14 November 2022.
[52] CteeESCR, General Comment 14 (n 3) para 43.
[53] World Health Organization and the United Nations Children's Fund, 'A vision for primary health care in the 21st century' (2018), <https://www.who.int/docs/default-source/primary-health/vision.pdf> accessed 14 November 2022.
[54] UN Member States, 'Political Declaration of the High-level Meeting on Universal Health Coverage "Universal health coverage: moving together to build a healthier world"' (23 September 2019), para 13.

healthcare.[55] Consequently, it remains unclear whether states have a core obligation to provide an essential level of mental healthcare, as part of primary healthcare.

In paragraph 43 of General Comment 14, the CteeESCR outlines six core obligations applicable to the right to the highest attainable standard of health, and holds that a state can, under no circumstances, justify its non-compliance with these core obligations.[56] According to the former UN High Commissioner for Human Rights, these core obligations apply as much to mental health as to physical health.[57] States are, without exception, obliged to carry out the actions listed in Table 4.2 below:

Table 4.2: Core obligations under the right to health

Healthcare	(i)	Ensure the right of access to health facilities, goods and services on a non-discriminatory basis, especially for vulnerable or marginalized groups.
	(ii)	Provide essential drugs, as from time to time defined under the WHO Action Programme on Essential Drugs.
	(iii)	Ensure equitable distribution of all health facilities, goods and services.
	(iv)	Adopt and implement a national public health strategy and plan of action, giving particular attention to all vulnerable or marginalised groups.
Underlying determinants	(v)	Ensure access to the minimum essential food which is nutritionally adequate and safe, to ensure freedom from hunger to everyone.
	(vi)	Ensure access to basic shelter, housing and sanitation, and an adequate supply of safe and potable water.

Some scholars argue that it remains unspecified which types of health facilities, goods and services (i/ii/iii) fall within the scope of the core content.[58] However, according to former Special Rapporteur on the Rights of Persons with Disabilities, Catalina Devandas-Aguilar, access to essential health services needed by persons with psychosocial disabilities owing to their impairment, including essential habilitation and rehabilitation, should be considered as core obligations.[59] Similarly, former Special Rapporteur Pūras proposed that, for individuals in the most marginalised situations, it is a core obligation not just to provide equitable access to mental health interventions, but also equitable access to the core determinants (v/vi). Regarding the national mental health strategies (iv), he clarified that these must be formulated and implemented across public policy sectors, and not just within the healthcare framework.[60] Moreover, national mental health strategies must constitute a road map that leads from coercive

---

[55] Emphasis added; Lisa Forman and others, 'What could a strengthened right to health bring to the post-2015 health development agenda?: interrogating the role of the minimum core concept in advancing essential global health needs' (2016) 13 BMC International Health and Human Rights 1, 6.
[56] CteeESCR, General Comment 14 (n 3) paras 43, 47.
[57] UNGA, 'Report of the United Nations High Commissioner for Human Rights, Mental health and human rights' (n 8) para 8.
[58] Lisa Forman and others (n 55) 6; and Yi Zhang (n 4) 51.
[59] UNGA, 'Report of the Special Rapporteur on the rights of persons with disabilities, Catalina Devandas-Aguilar, Rights of persons with disabilities' (16 July 2018) UN Doc A/73/161, para 18.
[60] UNGA, 'Report of the Special Rapporteur on the right of everyone to the enjoyment of the highest attainable standard of physical and mental health, Dainius Pūras' (n 10) para 22.

mental health treatment towards appropriate and acceptable rights-based mental health services and rights-based support, including access to services within the community, and the immediate upscaling of rights-based and non-coercive treatment alternatives (i/iii).[61]

Beyond the core obligations as enumerated by the CteeESCR (see Table 4.2 above), more mental health elements have been classified as core obligations that states must fulfil. These include providing services to promote mental health;[62] ensuring freedom from non-consensual medical treatment and experimentation (with possible exceptions, as will be discussed in Chapter 5);[63] promoting campaigns against stigmatisation of, and discrimination towards, persons with mental disorders; and including the recognition, care and treatment of mental health conditions in the training curricula of all health practitioners.[64]

Although various human rights scholars hold the CteeESCR's interpretation of the core content to be deficient in general,[65] the preceding analysis suggests that some mental health components can certainly be recognised within the scope of the core content of the right to health (Article 12 ICESCR). After all, the core obligations of the right to the highest attainable standard of health are just a starting point. With due consideration of progressive realisation, there are a set of duties that states have to fulfil to ensure the enjoyment of the right to the highest attainable standard of mental health. The following section clarifies these duties.

4.3 STATE'S OBLIGATIONS ARISING FROM THE RIGHT TO HEALTH AND MENTAL HEALTH

The identification of state obligations may guide decision-makers in formulating and implementing equitable mental health laws and policies which empower individuals to claim their rights to mental health before the national courts. Below, the meanings and implications of the obligations to respect, protect and fulfil the right to the highest attainable standard of health will be discussed, with an emphasis on mental health. Some examples of (potential) violations of these obligations will also be identified.

---

[61] UNGA, 'Report of the Special Rapporteur on the right of everyone to the enjoyment of the highest attainable standard of physical and mental health, Dainius Pūras' (28 March 2017) UN Doc A/HRC/35/21, para 37; and UNGA, 'Report of the Special Rapporteur on the right of everyone to the enjoyment of the highest attainable standard of physical and mental health, Dainius Pūras' (n 10) para 52.

[62] UNGA, 'Report of the Special Rapporteur on the right of everyone to the enjoyment of the highest attainable standard of physical and mental health, Dainius Pūras' (n 10) para 22.

[63] UNGA, 'Report of the Special Rapporteur on the rights of persons with disabilities, Catalina Devandas-Aguilar' (n 59).

[64] UNGA, 'Report of the Special Rapporteur on the right of everyone to the enjoyment of the highest attainable standard of physical and mental health, Paul Hunt' (11 February 2005) UN Doc E/CN.4/2005/51, para 35.

[65] John Tobin, *The right to health in international law* (Oxford University Press 2012) 239–253; Lisa Forman and others (n 55) 1–11; and Yi Zhang (n 4) 41–56.

As Chapman advocates, listing violations of the right to health can lead to a better understanding of the state's obligations to implement the right.[66] The findings of this section serve as starting point to detect the various obligations that states must comply with in order to protect and promote the right to mental health comprehensively, and will be expanded in Chapter 5.

4.3.1 OBLIGATION TO RESPECT THE RIGHT TO HEALTH REGARDING MENTAL HEALTH

The obligation to respect the right to the highest attainable standard of health is a negative obligation that requires states to refrain from interfering directly or indirectly with the enjoyment of this right.[67] States must refrain from denying or limiting equal access to mental health facilities, goods and services, as well as to the underlying determinants of mental health.[68] While states are generally required to refrain from prohibiting traditional health practices and medicine, and from applying coercive medical treatments, General Comment 14 identifies an exception with specific regard to mental health. It states that, when it comes to the treatment of mental health conditions, traditional healthcare can be prohibited, and coercive measures can be applied.[69] Both of these exceptions and their validity will be critically examined at later points throughout this book.

Violations of the obligation to respect the right to health would occur if a state were to deny or limit access to mental healthcare and related support services to individuals as a result of de facto or de jure discrimination. This occurs when public healthcare providers deny or limit access to healthcare to individuals because of their mental health conditions. Other examples of violations would be the failure to enforce relevant mental health laws and policies; or the adoption of laws and policies that interfere with the enjoyment of any component of the right to the highest attainable standard of mental health.[70]

4.3.2 OBLIGATION TO PROTECT THE RIGHT TO HEALTH REGARDING MENTAL HEALTH

The second obligation – the obligation to protect the right to health – implies that states must take measures to prevent third parties from violating the right to the highest attainable standard of mental health of an individual. This includes that states have the duty to adopt legislation or other necessary measures to ensure that individuals

---

[66] Audrey Chapman, 'Conceptualizing the Right to Health: A Violations Approach' (1998) 65 Tennessee Law Review 389, 395.
[67] CteeESCR, General Comment 14 (n 3) para 33.
[68] Ibid para 34.
[69] Ibid para 34.
[70] Ibid para 50.

have equal access to mental health facilities, goods and services.[71] States are further required to ensure that third parties do not limit individuals' access to mental health-related information and services, and that medical personnel and health professionals have the appropriate skills and education on health and human rights.[72]

The obligation to protect the right to the highest attainable standard of health would be violated if a state failed to take all necessary measures to prevent third parties from interfering with the guarantees provided by Article 12 ICESCR.[73] When it comes to mental health, third parties not only include private mental hospitals or health centres, but also independent mental health practitioners, the pharmaceutical industry, and even relatives of the affected individual. States need to regulate the activities of third parties to protect individuals from infringements of their right to mental health. For instance, when relatives do not give permission for their family members with psychosocial disabilities to receive treatment,[74] when pharmaceutical companies disseminate biased information about mental health issues,[75] or when private practitioners use religious rituals instead of science to treat mental health conditions (especially those rituals that are questionable from a human rights perspective),[76] positive and proactive action is required from the state.[77] In particular, religious rituals instead of science to treat mental health conditions are common in many countries around the world, as will be illustrated in the ensuing chapters. According to former Special Rapporteur Pūras, these practices result from insufficient investment in rights-based mental health policies and services, as well as from over-reliance on coercive practices and over-medicalised measures. He suggests that the practices even reflect a failure of the obligation to fulfil the right to health, as they demonstrate a lack of political will.[78]

4.3.3 OBLIGATION TO FULFIL THE RIGHT TO HEALTH REGARDING MENTAL HEALTH

The obligation to fulfil the right to the highest attainable standard of health implies that states are required to facilitate, provide and promote conditions in which mental

---

[71] Ibid para 35.
[72] Ibid paras 35, 44(e).
[73] Ibid para 33.
[74] The role and rights of relatives or others regarding the mental health situation of an individual will be addressed in different sections of this book, for instance with regards to guardianship regulations in section 6.3 or the protection of others from persons with mental health conditions and psychosocial disabilities, which will be discussed under non-consensual mental health treatment in section 5.4.
[75] However, in the European Union and many other countries, the information pharmaceutical companies disseminate are assessed before a pharmaceutical drug is given access to the market; UNGA, 'Report of the Special Rapporteur on the right of everyone to the enjoyment of the highest attainable standard of physical and mental health, Dainius Pūras' (14 July 2017) UN Doc A/72/137.
[76] This will be discussed in more detail in section 6.2.
[77] UNGA, 'Report of the Special Rapporteur on the right of everyone to the enjoyment of the highest attainable standard of physical and mental health, Dainius Pūras' (n 10) para 19.
[78] Ibid.

health can be realised. States have a positive duty to make accessible mental health-related services which enable and assist individuals to enjoy their right to the highest attainable standard of mental health. States should adopt appropriate legislative, administrative, budgetary, judicial, promotional and other measures to ensure access to quality mental health services, and the provision of public mental health interventions that protect individuals from risk factors for poor mental health.[79] Consequently, the right to the highest attainable standard of mental health must be reflected adequately in national legislation, policies and programmes, and in the domestic budget.[80] In line with social and psychosocial determinants of mental health, states are required to provide interventions that protect members of society from key risk factors for poor mental health, including actions beyond the healthcare sector, namely in homes, schools, workplaces and the wider community. Instead of focusing on the individual, therapeutic efforts must include promotion of a healthy society. Ensuring the coverage of immediate social, psychosocial, and material needs is central for promoting mental health, and recovery from poor mental health.[81]

Violations of the obligation to fulfil the right to health include: (i) failure to recognise or implement the right to the highest attainable standard of mental health in the national legal system; (ii) failure to adopt national public mental health strategies or programmes across sectors to realise the right to mental health; (iii) failure to allocate sufficient resources, including budget and workforce, resulting in the non-enjoyment of the right to the highest attainable standard of mental health; (iv) failure to equitably distribute mental health facilities, goods and services; (v) failure to provide access to information about human rights to individuals with mental health conditions who may be institutionalised; and (vi) failure to monitor progress, including in regard to reducing medical coercion.[82]

4.4 MENTAL HEALTH AS A JUSTICIABLE ELEMENT OF THE RIGHT TO HEALTH

The previous sections of this chapter identified how Article 12 ICESCR, as the most authoritative right to the highest attainable standard of health norm, promotes and protects mental health. A subsequent question is whether there is case law that reflects

---

[79] Ibid para 20.
[80] UNGA, 'Report of the Special Rapporteur on the right of everyone to the enjoyment of the highest attainable standard of physical and mental health, Paul Hunt' (n 64) para 50.
[81] UNGA, 'Report of the Special Rapporteur on the right of everyone to the enjoyment of the highest attainable standard of physical and mental health, Dainius Pūras' (n 10) para 67.
[82] CteeESCR, General Comment 14 (n 3) para 52; Yi Zhang (n 4) 71; UNGA, 'Report of the Special Rapporteur on the right of everyone to the enjoyment of the highest attainable standard of physical and mental health, Dainius Pūras' (n 10) para 20; UNGA, 'Report of the Special Rapporteur on the right of everyone to the enjoyment of the highest attainable standard of physical and mental health, Paul Hunt' (n 64) para 50; UNGA, 'Report of the Special Rapporteur on the right of everyone to the enjoyment of the highest attainable standard of physical and mental health, Dainius Pūras' (n 61) para 36.

Chapter 4. The Right to Health Norm and Mental Health

the protection of mental health under the right to the highest attainable standard of health. This section aims to give an impression of how judicial and quasi-judicial bodies have interpreted mental health under the right to health. For that purpose, this section will discuss a range of decisions from international and regional judicial and quasi-judicial bodies. As it is impossible to be comprehensive, and to identify all relevant cases from around the world, a selection has been made which is by no means meant to be exhaustive. As such, the aim of this section is to shed light on the justiciability of mental health as a right.

In the 1990s, there was much debate about the justiciability of economic, social and cultural rights.[83] Currently, however, in human rights doctrine, the focus is more on the wider concept of 'accountability', which not only embraces legal accountability, but also the possibility of using administrative, political and other mechanisms to seek accountability for human rights violations.[84] Nevertheless, this section does not intend to analyse the legal enforceability of mental health but, rather, examines to what extent judicial and quasi-judicial bodies have dealt with the right to the highest attainable standard of health when adjudicating on complaints with regard to mental health. While enforceability is sometimes employed as a synonym for justiciability, the two concepts can be distinguished. Justiciability, as defined by the International Commission of Jurists, 'refers to the ability to claim a remedy before an independent and impartial body when a violation of a right has occurred or is likely to occur'. Enforceability additionally implies the question of whether the decision by the judicial or quasi-judicial body can be executed or put into effect.[85] Supplementarily, Toebes has pointed out that justiciability does not necessarily refer, for example, to the right to the highest attainable standard of health as such, but rather to elements of the right.[86] Thus, mental health could be regarded as a justiciable element of the right to health.[87]

---

[83] See eg Fons Coomans & Fried van Hoof (eds), *The right to complain about economic, social and cultural rights: proceedings of the expert meeting on the adoption of an optional protocol to the International covenant on economic, social and cultural rights held from 25–28 January 1995 in Utrecht* (SIM 1995); Matthew CR Craven, *The International Covenant on Economic, Social and Cultural Rights: A Perspective on its Development* (Clarendon Press 1998); or Virginia A Leary, 'Justiciability and Beyond: Complaint Procedures and the Right to Health' (1995) 55 International Commission of Jurists Review.

[84] See eg Alicia Yamin, 'Beyond Compassion: The Central Role of Accountability in Applying a Human Rights Framework to Health' (2008) 10(2) Health and Human Rights 1,1; Helen Potts, 'Accountability and the Right to the Highest Attainable Standard of Health' (2008), <http://repository.essex.ac.uk/9717/1/accountability-right-highest-attainable-standard-health.pdf> accessed 14 November 2022; Marlies Hesselman and others (eds), *Socio-Economic Human Rights for Essential Public Services Provision* (Routledge 2017); Paul Hunt and others, 'Implementation of Economic, Social and Cultural Rights' in Schott Sheeran and Nigel Rodley (eds), *Routledge Handbook of International Human Rights Law* (Routledge 2013) 550–554; or Yi Zhang (n 4) 208–214.

[85] Kitty Arambulo, Strengthening the Supervision of the International Covenant on Economic, Social and Cultural Rights. Theoretical and Procedural Aspects (Intersentia 1999) 55, 57.

[86] Brigit Toebes (n 5) 168.

[87] Given the complexity of the debate around justiciability, which is not discussed in more detail as it is not the focus of this book, it needs to be kept in mind that justiciability also highly depends on place and context. One (quasi-)judicial body may decide that mental health is a justiciable element of the

Part 2. The Right to Mental Health and the Applicable Human Rights Framework

Exploring whether and how a complaint concerning mental health is addressed under the right to the highest attainable standard of health, by judicial and quasi-judicial human rights bodies, can contribute to further recognition of mental health as part of the right to health norm within the human rights jurisprudence.

4.4.1 CASE LAW AT THE UN LEVEL

At the international level, since the first Optional Protocol to the ICESCR entered into force in 2013, the CteeESCR has been authorised to receive individual complaints. At the time of writing, no case has been submitted which addresses mental health.[88] Just like the CteeESCR, the CteeRC and the Committee on the Rights of Persons with Disabilities (CteeRPD) can both receive individual communications, relating to violations of the CRC and CRPD, respectively. As previously discussed, both Conventions provide for a right to the highest attainable standard of mental health. Therefore, their interpretation could strengthen the conceptual clarity of the right to health relating to mental health. Although the complaints received by these committees have included some involving the right to health, none of these have required the inherent element of mental health to be interpreted further.[89] In *Noble v Australia*, the CteeRPD adopted views regarding the exercise of legal capacity, and the deprivation of liberty, of persons with mental and intellectual disabilities.[90] However, since the case does not discuss the rights to legal capacity and liberty in relation to the right to health, or in the healthcare context, it will not be examined in this section. As this short overview shows, the outcome at the UN level is extremely limited.

4.4.2 REGIONAL CASE LAW ON THE RIGHT TO HEALTH AND MENTAL HEALTH

4.4.2.1 A Violation of the Right to Health Norm and Related Rights

A landmark case for the African region, but also for the world in general, is *Purohit and Moore v The Gambia*, in which mental health advocates represented mental health patients detained in the psychiatric unit of a hospital. The applicants alleged that the mental health legislation of the Gambia, the Lunatics Detention Act, as well as the

---

right to health in relation to one case, but in a different setting (different case or different court) the outcome might be different.

[88] For an overview of individual complaints before any UN treaty body see OHCHR, 'Jurisprudence' (nd), <https://juris.ohchr.org/en/search/results?Bodies=9&sortOrder=Date> accessed 14 November 2022.

[89] Ibid.

[90] CteeRPD, Noble v Australia, Communication No 7/2012 (10 October 2016) UN Doc CRPD/C/16/D/7/2012.

way mental health patients were being treated at the psychiatric unit, amounted to a violation of various rights protected by the African Charter on Human and People's Rights (AfChHPR), including the right to health. The African Commission on Human and People's Rights (African Commission) held that the Gambia had fallen short of satisfying the requirements of Article 16, the right to the highest attainable state of physical and mental health, and Article 18(4), the right of the disabled to special measures of protection in keeping with their physical and moral needs, of the African Charter.[91] The African Commission pointed out that the enjoyment of the right to health 'is crucial to the realisation of all the other fundamental human rights and freedoms',[92] and that this right includes the right to access mental health facilities, mental health goods and mental health services guaranteed to everyone without discrimination of any kind.[93] Furthermore, by virtue of their disabilities, and due to their health conditions, persons with psychosocial disabilities should be 'accorded special treatment which would enable them not only attain but also sustain their optimum level of independence and performance'.[94] This includes the highest attainable standard of mental healthcare in the: (i) analysis and diagnosis of the mental health condition; (ii) treatment of the mental health condition; and (iii) rehabilitation.[95] The Commission assessed the legislative regime of the Gambia for persons with mental health conditions and psychosocial disabilities, the Lunatic Detention Act, and found that it lacked a standard of treatment, and did not provide resources and programmes of treatment to persons with mental health conditions and psychosocial disabilities to match their needs.[96] Importantly, being aware that millions of Africans cannot enjoy the right to health maximally because of the prevailing poverty that renders African countries incapable of providing the necessary resources, infrastructure and amenities to facilitate the full enjoyment of the right to health, the African Commission stated that state parties have an obligation to 'take concrete and targeted steps, while taking full advantage of … available resources, to ensure that the right to health is fully realised in all its aspects without discrimination of any kind'.[97]

In this way, the Commission implicitly considered the concept of 'progressive realisation', as identified under Article 2(1) ICESCR (see subsection 4.2.2.) However, the Commission did not specify details of possible constraints due to the limits of available resources, as elaborated on in CteeESCR General Comment 3. Despite commending the steps already taken by the Gambia, the African Commission found that the measures were insufficient in light of the progressive realisation obligation. It concluded that the 'right to proper health care, which is crucial for [the] survival [of

---

[91] *Purohit and Moore v The Gambia*, Communication No. 241/2001, Sixteenth Activity report 2002–2003, Annex VII, paras 77–85.
[92] Ibid para 80.
[93] Ibid.
[94] Ibid para 81.
[95] Ibid para 82.
[96] Ibid para 83.
[97] Ibid para 84.

persons with psychosocial disabilities] and their assimilation into and acceptance by the wider society',[98] should never be denied. In the context of mental healthcare, the African Commission further found that persons with psychosocial disabilities 'have a right to enjoy a decent life, as normal and full as possible, a right which lies at the heart of the right to human dignity'.[99] By accepting that the conditions in the psychiatric unit amounted to inhumane and degrading treatment, the African Commission ruled that the provisions of the domestic mental health law also amounted to a violation of Article 5 AfChHPR, the right to be free from inhumane and degrading treatment.[100]

4.4.2.2 A Violation of other Human Rights Explicitly Linked to the Right to Health

In due consideration of the fact that the right to the highest attainable standard of health is not directly enforceable before the European or Inter-American Courts of Human Rights, there is a line of jurisprudence in which these courts have protected some elements of mental health by specifically linking the right to health with other human rights, such as the right to life and personal integrity, or the right to humane treatment. Given their relevance for the promotion and protection of mental health, and without being exhaustive, some of these cases will be discussed here.

The Inter-American Court of Human Rights (IACtHR) emphasised in *Ximenes-Lopes v Brazil* that, in line with 'the right to effective healthcare', the state has a duty to guarantee the provision of effective mental healthcare services.[101] This duty entails the obligation to ensure the promotion of mental health, the prevention of mental health conditions, and the provision of mental health services in the least restrictive ways.[102] In that respect, the Court determined whether the medical care provided 'ha[d] been in keeping with the minimum requirements to preserve the patient's dignity'.[103] The IACtHR found that the general conditions of the mental health facility, and the medical treatment provided there, had been precarious, and therefore that they did not appropriately respect and protect the right to personal integrity and the right to life of people with mental health conditions and psychosocial disabilities contained in Articles 5(1) and 4(1) of the American Convention on Human Rights (ACHR), respectively.[104]

In *Luis Eduardo Guachalá Chimbó v Ecuador*, the Inter-American Commission of Human Rights (IACHR) considered 'the right to health' as constituting one of the economic and social provisions mentioned in Article 26 ACHR,[105] and thus that it was

---

[98] Ibid para 85.
[99] Ibid para 61.
[100] Ibid paras 56–61.
[101] *Ximenes-Lopes v Brazil* (Merits, Reparations, and Costs) IACtHR Series C no 149 (4 July 2006), para 128.
[102] Ibid.
[103] Ibid para 131.
[104] Ibid para 132.
[105] Article 26 ACHR obliges states to undertake measures to achieve 'progressively [...] the full realization of the rights implicit in the economic, social, educational, scientific, and cultural standards set forth

protected under this Article. According to the Commission, states are, accordingly, obliged 'to seek to achieve [the right to health's] progressive development as well as to respect, ensure, and adopt the measures necessary for upholding that right'.[106] Regarding the content of the right to health, the IACHR then indicated that states should ensure that 'adequate mental health establishments and services' are available, and that these are 'integrated to the general social services, limiting the approach of segregated, centralized, and long-term psychiatric care'.[107] In that regard, states should provide health systems that:

> empower the persons with particular mental health needs, prioritizing the defense of their own interests, seeking greater control and independence over their health, promoting their inclusion in the community, and offering treatments based on their rights and psychosocial support that protect them from harmful medical practices that contribute to their exclusion or mistreatment.[108]

In the context of institutionalising people in mental health facilities, the IACHR adopts the view that the state is the entity responsible for ensuring the integrity and health of such people.[109] This is because it is necessary to guarantee the right to health, and to ensure that the free and informed consent of persons is respected, according to the IACHR.[110] Consequently, confinement or treatment in mental health institutions without informed consent violates the right to health and, thus, constitutes a violation of Article 26 ACHR.

Despite generating extensive case law regarding mental health, the European Court of Human Rights (ECtHR) has not yet addressed alleged violations in mental healthcare practice under the right to health, as has been done by the Inter-American Court and Commission. This is because the right to health is not covered by the European Convention on Human Rights (ECHR), as demonstrated in section 3.3. Nevertheless, there is case law regarding the provision of medical services to persons with psycyhosocial disabilities in prisons, which would, presumably, also apply to persons detained in psychiatric institutions.[111] The ECtHR has held, in several cases, that a lack of access to appropriate mental healthcare in custody is capable of engaging state responsibility under Article 3 ECHR, which prohibits inhuman and degrading treatment. In *Venken and Others v Belgium*, for instance, the ECtHR found that compulsory confinement of people with mental health conditions and psychosocial disabilities for a significant amount of time in the psychiatric wing of a prison, without

---

in the Charter of the Organization of American States as amended by the Protocol of Buenos Aires.'
[106] *Luis Eduardo Guachalá Chimbó v Ecuador* (Merits) IACHR Report No 111/18 (5 October 2018), para 155.
[107] Ibid para 156.
[108] Ibid para 157.
[109] Ibid para 168.
[110] Ibid para 159.
[111] See eg Peter Bartlett and others, *Mental Disability and the European Convention on Human Rights* (International Studies in Human Rights Volume 90) (Martinus Nijhoff Publishers 2007) 113–114.

appropriate medical support and with no prospects of change, amounted to degrading treatment, and thus constituted a violation of Article 3 ECHR.[112] Furthermore, in *Murray v The Netherlands*, the ECtHR reiterated that states are under an obligation to provide detainees suffering from mental health problems with appropriate medical care, which includes examination, diagnoses, proper treatment for the mental health condition, and suitable medical supervision.[113]

4.4.2.3 Opportunities and Challenges

Determining that persons with mental health conditions and psychosocial disabilities should have access to appropriate mental healthcare services under the right to health is an important breakthrough in the human rights jurisprudence. It makes visible the vulnerable situation of a highly marginalised group, and demonstrates that the right to the highest attainable standard of mental health can be protected. Some scholars, including Guarnizo-Peralta, claim, however, that the interpretations of the courts often remain limited when it comes to developing disability rights further, as their judgments often lack detail on the identification of state duties to provide healthcare services required by persons with psychosocial disabilities because of their impairments.[114] The above-mentioned case of *Luis Eduardo Guachalá Chimbó v Ecuador* nonetheless reflects a move towards encompassing a disability rights approach to improving mental healthcare. In the Merits section of the judgment, the Inter-American Commission recognised the CRPD as important, and called it a 'specific instrument that contributes to adequate and broader interpretation of the American Convention' in cases of persons with psychosocial disability, to 'clarif[y] the state's obligations to respect and ensure enjoyment of their rights by persons with disabilities'.[115] Specifically, the IACHR established that free and informed consent is a fundamental element for guaranteeing the right to health in the area of mental health, where coercive measures perpetuate the power imbalance between practitioners and patients.[116] In particular, it stated that it is the duty of the state to train medical and health personnel working with persons with mental health conditions and psychosocial disabilities on inclusive care.[117] Mental health staff must ensure that: '(i) accurate and accessible information is provided on the options of available services; (ii) non-medical alternatives are offered; and (iii) access is provided to independent support'.[118] Ultimately, the IACHR found a violation of the right to legal capacity under the right to the recognition of juridical personality (Article 3 ACHR),[119] and a violation of the right to access to information

---

[112] *Venken and Others v Belgium*, App no 46130/14 (ECtHR, 6 April 2021).
[113] *Murray v The Netherlands*, App no 10511/10 (ECtHR, 26 April 2016), paras 106, 117.
[114] Diana Guarnizo-Peralta, 'Disability rights in the Inter-American System of Human Rights: An expansive and evolving protection' (2018) 36(1) Netherlands Quarterly of Human Rights, pp 55–56.
[115] *Luis Eduardo Guachalá Chimbó v Ecuador* (n 106) para 121.
[116] Ibid. para 169.
[117] Ibid para 170.
[118] Ibid para 171.
[119] Ibid. para 179.

for giving consent in relation to health matters under the right to freedom or thought of expression (Article 13(1) ACHR).[120] For both findings, the IACHR drew inspiration from Article 12 CRPD, and CteeRPD General Comment 1, regarding the right to equal recognition before the law.[121] Throughout the report, the Inter-American Commission leaned mostly on the CRPD when interpreting the different elements of the case. As a recent case, it demonstrates the increasing tendency by human rights treaty bodies to rely on disability norms, and to outline state duties to improve (access to) mental healthcare. The ECtHR rarely uses the CRPD to advance an ECHR point. Nevertheless, it has cited the CRPD as 'relevant international law' in judgments relating to mental health,[122] and scholars such as Lewis claim that the ECtHR also uses CRPD stock phrases, such as 'special care', in its judgments.[123] The following chapter will illustrate how, in addition to the right to the highest attainable standard of health as analysed in the present chapter, a human rights approach to accessing mental healthcare will, ultimately, benefit from a stronger disability rights approach.

4.5 CONCLUDING SUMMARY

Including the right to the highest attainable standard of health norm as a key element of the right to mental health framework implicitly ensures that unique elements of the right to health norm (Article 12 ICESCR) are included in this framework. Firstly, states have the duty to promote underlying determinants of mental health. Secondly, states must provide mental health facilities, goods and services, including preventive, medical, social and rehabilitation services, that are available, accessible, acceptable and of good quality, according to the maximum available resources. Lastly, there is the state duty to progressively realise conditions that promote and protect mental health in line with the outlined obligations to respect, protect and fulfil the right to health, with due consideration of the core content of this right and, thus, core obligations of immediate effect.[124]

Undoubtedly, Article 12 ICESCR contributes important components to the broader right to mental health. To answer the question from the beginning of this chapter,[125] the legal analysis stipulates that the right to the highest attainable standard of health

---

[120] Ibid. para 183.
[121] Ibid. paras 123–130, 169–170.
[122] See eg *Glor v Switzerland*, App no 13444/04 (ECtHR, 30 April 2009), para 53; *Stanev v Bulgaria*, App no 36760/06 (ECtHR, 17 January 2012), para 245; or *Guberina v Croatia*, App no 23682/13 (ECtHR, 22 March 2016), para 6.
[123] See eg, Oliver Lewis, 'Stanev v. Bulgaria: On the Pathway to Freedom' (2012) 19(2) Human Rights Brief, 2–7.
[124] UNGA, 'Report of the Special Rapporteur on the right of everyone to the enjoyment of the highest attainable standard of physical and mental health, Dainius Pūras' (n 10) para 8.
[125] Namely: To what extent does the right to the highest attainable standard of physical and mental health, in particular Article 12 of the International Covenant on Economic, Social and Cultural Rights (ICESCR)?

norm, in fact, provides the right to underlying determinants of mental health, and the right to access mental health facilities, goods and services. As evidenced in this chapter, especially the right to access mental health facilities, goods and services is also supported by the interpretations of the CteeRC and the African Commission. However, the previous chapters of this book elucidated that simply providing access to mental health facilities, goods and services is not enough. While the aim of mental health services is to contribute positively to the health and well-being of persons with mental health conditions and psychosocial disabilities, there are instances where their rights and autonomy are being violated. Indeed, the selected case law discussed above shows that mental health may be interpreted as a justiciable element of the right to health. Nevertheless, the cases presented also indicate that human right concerns in the mental healthcare context go beyond the right to health norm, notably touching upon related rights. In all cases, the judicial or quasi-judicial bodies interpreted a violation as falling – solely or additionally – under other human rights, such as the right to life, to integrity, or to be free from inhuman or degrading treatment.

Altogether, the preceding normative analysis of Article 12 ICESCR and the case law supports the proposition that, in the context of mental health, attention has to be given to elements that undoubtedly have impacts on the provision of mental healthcare, such as informed consent.[126] Toebes refers to such elements as overlapping elements, suggesting that they do not fall within the scope of the right to the highest attainable standard of health because: (i) they are not contained in the text of Article 12 ICESCR; and (ii) they are already protected by other human rights.[127] Regarding the impact of these other elements/rights on people's mental health, and keeping in mind the human rights violations occurring in mental healthcare practice, however, it is submitted that, without considering these other elements/rights more elaborately under the right to mental health framework, mental health cannot comprehensively be promoted and protected. Therefore, in addition to the right to the highest attainable standard of (mental) health, as examined and established in this chapter, the ensuing chapter will analyse other rights complementing 'the right to mental health'. These additional elements/rights focus particularly on human rights-based access to mental healthcare, to address the persisting human rights challenges in mental health services comprehensively. The following analysis will also include controversial debates, such as whether persons with mental health conditions and psychosocial disabilities have the right to refuse treatment, even if this leads to unrestorable health damage or death.

---

[126] See eg CteeESCR concluding observations in subsection 4.2.1 or the case of *Ximenes-Lopes v Brazil* in subsection 4.4.2.2.
[127] Brigit Toebes (n 5) 259.

CHAPTER 5
A HUMAN RIGHTS APPROACH TO PSYCHOSOCIAL DISABILITY

5.1 INTRODUCTION

People with mental health conditions and psychosocial disabilities are protected by the right to the highest attainable standard of health, like everybody else. While access to adequate mental health facilities, goods and services is provided under the (general) right to health, as described in the previous chapter, the question is whether the mere right to access mental healthcare is sufficient to ensure adequate mental health treatment. It will be argued in this chapter that it is not: states can fulfil their obligations to provide sufficient care but still violate human rights in the delivery of mental healthcare.[1]

As noted in section 2.4, mental healthcare generally contributes positively to the recovery of persons with mental health conditions and psychosocial disabilities. Often, mental health services are indispensable to guaranteeing affected individuals a humane and dignified life. A lack of mental health services or poor-quality services can have a negative impact on mental health treatment and, in many cases, hinder recovery.[2] Evidence reveals disturbing trends in violence, institutionalisation, and the overuse of non-consensual interferences.[3] As Mental Health Europe states:

> 'Violence in psychiatry is ubiquitous. They hold us with mental belts to reality. They talk about us without us. They do everything so we cannot integrate back into society, depriving us of personality and individuality. They often take away our dignity by forcing us to take

---

[1] The author acknowledges that not everybody with persons with mental health conditions and psychosocial disabilities may need mental healthcare, and that human rights violations also affect individuals who do not belong to the specific group with healthcare needs. However, as this chapter focuses specifically on (access to) mental healthcare, human rights violations in the wider mental health context will not be analysed in depth.

[2] Shekhar Saxena & Fahmy Hanna, 'Dignity- a fundamental principle of mental health care' (2015) 142(4) Indian Journal of Medical Research 355.

[3] Mental Health Europe & Tizard Centre at the University of Kent, 'Mapping and Understanding Exclusion: Institutional, coercive and community-based services and practices across Europe' (Mental Health Europe 2018), <https://mhe-sme.org/wp-content/uploads/2018/01/Mapping-and-Understanding-Exclusion-in-Europe.pdf> accessed 14 November 2022.

medication. They do it with stubbornness and without thinking about the violence that comes within.' – user of psychiatric services from Poland.[4]

The prevailing human rights infringements against persons with mental health conditions and psychosocial disabilities (as also outlined in section 2.4) and the existing case law (some of it mentioned in section 4.4) suggest that the care provided by mental health services can inhibit the enjoyment of the right to mental health. There is a shared agreement about the unacceptability of frequent human rights violations in mental health settings,[5] and former Special Rapporteur on the Right to Health, Dainius Pūras, has declared that change is needed.[6] With a human rights approach to disability, this chapter sets out to strengthen the right to access mental healthcare.

Rather than justifying the status quo with legal arguments, the framework of the Convention on the Rights of Persons with Disabilities (CRPD) offers a pathway to eliminate prevalent human rights infringements. Thus, this chapter scrutinises which mental health-related human rights need to be protected to provide adequate mental healthcare, in order to guarantee the right to mental health (including underlaying determinants) comprehensively. As a point of departure, each section in this chapter will firstly delineate to what extent the right to health norm grants protection against the respective human rights restrictions. However, the international human rights system paid little attention to the specific health needs of persons with psychosocial disabilities up until the adoption of the CRPD. Hence, the analysis of CRPD provisions will form the main part of the normative analysis of mental health-related human rights as key elements of the right to mental health framework. The difference this makes for the promotion and protection of mental health will be illustrated throughout this chapter.

What is the role or position of the CRPD with respect to the promotion of the right to mental health and the protection of persons with mental health conditions and psychosocial disabilities? As briefly indicated in Chapter 2, the CRPD moves away from a medical approach to disability, to a human rights approach to disability, and thus lays a foundation for a paradigm shift in the promotion of mental health.[7] According to the medical approach, persons with psychosocial disabilities are considered to be persons that need to be cured, treated or protected, even from themselves. Special laws

---

[4] Mental Health Europe, 'What we really need is support, not coercion' (10 December 2019), <https://www.mhe-sme.org/hrd19/> accessed 14 November 2022.

[5] See eg Oddný Mjöll Arnardóttir, 'The rights of persons with disabilities in the context of healthcare' in Brigit Toebes, Mette Hartlev, Aart Hendriks & Janne Rothmar Herrmann (eds), *Health and Human Rights in Europe* (Intersentia 2012) 249–271.

[6] United Nations General Assembly (UNGA), 'Report of the Special Rapporteur on the right of everyone to the enjoyment of the highest attainable standard of physical and mental health, Dainius Pūras' (28 March 2017) UN Doc A/HRC/35/21, para 66.

[7] UNGA, 'Report of the Special Rapporteur on the rights of persons with disabilities, Catalina Devandas-Aguilar, Rights of persons with disabilities' (16 July 2018) UN Doc A/73/161, paras 11–12.

were established to govern practices relating to mental health, for instance regarding guardianship, institutionalisation or residential care. These laws and programmes have often resulted in isolation, social exclusion and social disadvantages.[8] The question that was predominantly asked and clarified through such laws was: when, how and to what extent can the rights of persons with psychosocial disabilities be restricted?[9] The CRPD adopted a human rights approach to disability, where persons with psychosocial disabilities are considered to be rights-holders, rather than just recipients of treatment, protection and welfare.[10] While the Convention does not provide for new human rights, it tailors and applies existing regulations to the specific human rights challenges of persons with psychosocial disabilities. The treaty has been received as 'a long-overdue articulation of the rights of people with disabilities'.[11] It highlights not merely the legal, but also the moral, obligation to remove barriers that persons with psychosocial disabilities experience, and to remove structures and practices that limit their full enjoyment of their human rights. The question that the CRPD seeks to answer is: what is needed to ensure that persons with psychosocial disabilities can fully enjoy and exercise all human rights, and how can they be supported?[12]

At this point, however, it is important to voice criticism toward the absolutist position of the CRPD, and especially the Committee of the CRPD (CteeRPD) and its interpretations of the Convention's provisions. An international group of clinicians has complained that members of the medical profession were not involved in the negotiation of the draft treaty. This omission of clinical voices has also become apparent at the later stage of actually interpreting the Convention, since members of the Committee with a clinical or related background are limited.[13] From a legal perspective, scholars such as Dawson have observed that the Committee's interpretations fail 'to offer adequate guidance on how, when situations arise where rights articulated in the CRPD are in conflict, this can be resolved'.[14] The text of the CRPD itself is ambiguous. Szmukler notes that '[t]his points to whether – in a particular instance – autonomy, on the one hand, or protection of the interests of a vulnerable person, on the other, should

---

[8] Lecture of Rosemary Kayess on 'Introduction to the UN Convention on the Rights of Persons with Disabilities' at the 9th International Disability Law Summer School of the Centre for Disability Law & Policy National University of Ireland (Galway) on 19 June 2017.
[9] Keynote address of Catalina Devandas Aguilar at the 9th International Disability Law Summer School of the Centre for Disability Law & Policy National University of Ireland (Galway) on 23 June 2017.
[10] UNGA, 'Report of the Special Rapporteur on the right of everyone to the enjoyment of the highest attainable standard of physical and mental health, Dainius Pūras' (n 7) para 12.
[11] Brendan Kelly, *Dignity, Mental Health and Human Rights* (Ashgate 2015) 93.
[12] Keynote address of Catalina Devandas Aguilar (n 9).
[13] See eg Melvyn Freeman and others, 'Reversing hard won victories in the name of human rights: a critique of the General Comment on Article 12 of the UN Convention on the Rights of Persons with Disabilities' (2015) 2(9) The Lancet Psychiatry 844.
[14] John Dawson, 'A realistic approach to assessing mental health laws' compliance with the UN-CRPD' (2015) 40 International Journal of Law and Psychiatry 70; and George Szmukler, '"Capacity", "best interests", "will and preferences" and the UN Convention on the Rights of Persons with Disabilities' (2019) 18(1) World Psychiatry 34, 36.

prevail'.[15] Accepting the standpoint of the Committee, Scholten and Gather argue, could even lead to serious adverse consequences for persons with mental health conditions and psychosocial disabilities.[16] As other scholars claim, the Committee's interpretation of the CRPD norms 'threatens to undermine hard-won, critical rights of people with mental health disabilities',[17] including the right to the highest attainable standard of health. The author therefore aims not only to outline the advantages of establishing a right to mental health framework with CRPD norms, but also (especially under the 'Controversial Issue' sections of this chapter) to uncover gaps in the CRPD framework that need to be addressed to ensure that the implementation of the CRPD generates laws and practices that safeguard the right to mental health.

The roots of a human rights approach to disability, which is the main theme of this chapter, can be traced back to what is called the social model of disability.[18] The central idea of the social model is that disabilities result from persons with impairments attempting to interact with a barrier-filled environment. The focus of the social model is on dismantling barriers, created by the physical environment or society, that limit persons with disabilities from fully participating in society and enjoying their human rights. By doing so, the social model also enhances the participation in society of persons with psychosocial disabilities. The social model of disability underpins the human rights model of disability. The difference between the social and human rights models is that the latter goes further, by considering persons with psychosocial disabilities to be entitled to the same rights as all other people. Barriers to enjoying these rights are seen as discriminatory. The human rights model recognises that persons with psychosocial disabilities have the right to have these barriers removed, as well as a right to claim their rights.[19] Discrimination in healthcare provision damages health, and experiencing discrimination is itself harmful to one's health and mental well-being. Health disadvantages associated with psycyhosocial disability are often overlooked, leading to an inappropriate allocation of mental health resources.[20] By applying the human rights model of disability, the CPRD forges new ground. It embraces the belief that the lives of persons with

---

[15] George Szmukler (n 14) 36.
[16] See Matthé Scholten & Jakov Gather, 'Adverse consequences of article 12 of the UN Convention on the Rights of Persons with Disabilities for persons with mental disabilities and an alternative way forward' (2017) 4 Journal of Medical Ethics, 226–33.
[17] George Szmukler (n 14) 36.
[18] Sheila Wildeman, 'Protecting Rights and Building Capacities: Challenges to Global Mental Health Policy in Light of the Convention on the Rights of Persons with Disabilities' (2013) 41(1) Journal of Law, Medicine & Ethics, 52.
[19] See eg Marno Retief & Rantoa Letšosa, 'Models of disability: A brief overview' (2018) 74(1) HTS Teologiese Studies/ Theological Studies; and World Health Organization (WHO), 'Mental health, disability and human rights: WHO QualityRights core training – for all services and all people: course guide' (2019), < https://apps.who.int/iris/handle/10665/329546> accessed 14 November 2022.
[20] Penelope Weller, 'Article 25: Health' in Ilias Bantekas, Michael Ashley Stein & Dimitris Anastasiou (eds), *The UN Convention on the Rights of Persons with Disabilities: A Commentary* (Oxford University Press 2018) 708.

(psychosocial) disabilities have the same value and dignity as the lives of able-bodied persons. To ensure that persons with (psychosocial) disabilities receive the care they need, health resources must be allocated appropriately, and healthcare services must be made accessible. With the introduction of the human rights model, the CRPD departs – at least in theory – from the charity model of disability, which perceives persons with psychosocial disabilities as helpless and passive recipients of welfare, as well as the medical model of disability, which considers affected persons as sick, incapable, dependent, and as to be fixed and healed through medical intervention.[21] These old models legitimise differential or discriminatory treatment against, or the isolation of, persons with psychosocial disabilities, through a medically driven incapacity approach.[22]

Consequently, the CRPD highlights the need to remove all barriers that limit the full and equal enjoyment of the right to health for persons with mental health conditions and psychosocial disabilities. In fact, the CRPD obliges states to take measures to modify or abolish existing laws, regulations, customs or practices that constitute discrimination against persons with mental health conditions and psychosocial disabilities.[23] While acknowledging that the underlying determinants of mental health are decisive factors for, and an important component of, the right to mental health, and without wishing to medicalise the right to mental health, this chapter focuses on ensuring access to humane and dignified mental healthcare. Therefore, the following sections are confined to an analysis of provisions that complement the right to health norm, and they seek to answer the following questions: which additional human rights are relevant for guaranteeing humane and dignified mental healthcare? And what are the obligations deriving therefrom? In addition to identifying a human rights approach to accessing mental healthcare, the findings from this chapter will essentially complement the normative framework of the right to mental health as a whole.

Arguably, the CRPD comprises various rights which are all essential. Considering these rights offers a new impetus for promoting the understanding and implementation of the right to mental health. The right to the highest attainable standard of health norm is, therefore, complemented by the following interconnected CRPD Articles, listed in the order in which they will be analysed:

---

[21] See eg Marno Retief & Rantoa Letšosa, 'Models of disability: A brief overview' (2018) 74(1) HTS Teologiese Studies/ Theological Studies; and WHO, 'Mental health, disability and human rights: WHO QualityRights core training – for all services and all people: course guide' (2019), < https://apps.who.int/iris/handle/10665/329546> accessed 14 November 2022.

[22] Committee on the Rights of Persons with Disabilities (CteeRPD), 'General Comment No. 6 (2018) on equality and non-discrimination' (General Comment 6) (26 April 2018) UN Doc CRPD/C/GC/6, para 8.

[23] UNGA, Convention on the Rights of Persons with Disabilities (CRPD) (adopted 13 December 2006, entered into force 3 May 2008) 2515 UNTS 3, art 4(1)(b).

Part 2. The Right to Mental Health and the Applicable Human Rights Framework

Table 5.1: Overview of sections and respective CRPD Articles[24]

Section	Article(s)	Type of article(s)
Section 5.2: Protection against discrimination	– Article 5: Equality and non-discrimination	– General obligation/principle, core value, taken into account in the interpretation and implementation of each specific obligation.
Section 5.3: Legal capacity and the protection of persons not able to give consent	– Article 12: Equal recognition before the law	– Specific obligations, specific human rights and fundamental freedoms.
Section 5.4: Protection from non-consensual mental health treatment	– Article 17: Protecting the integrity of the person – Article 15: Freedom from torture or cruel, inhuman or degrading treatment or punishment – Article 16: Freedom from exploitation, violence and abuse	
Section 5.5: Protection from involuntary placement in an institution	– Article 14: Liberty and security of person – Article 19: Living independently and being included in the community	

Various authors have demonstrated that the right to the highest attainable standard of health relates to additional human rights. In that respect, the right to health norm, as codified by Article 12 International Covenant on Economic, Social and Cultural Rights (ICESCR), has been connected to a set of health-related rights enshrined in the ICESCR.[25] Article 25 of the CRPD reaffirms the right to enjoy the highest attainable standard of health, in the context of (psychosocial) disability, including all elements of the right to health, such as the freedoms or entitlements.[26] This book is novel in the way it considers human rights that are particularly integral to the promotion of the right to access mental healthcare. The following analysis of CRPD norms will demonstrate the

---

[24] At this point, the author wants to note that the division within this table intentionally differs slightly from the division in table 3.2 'Human rights to ensure the protection and promotion of mental health' in Chapter 3, particularly regarding Article 14 CRPD. While table 3.2 pooled the respective CRPD norms with regards to common human rights violations, arranging the sections in Chapter 5 differently depicts the needed protection in a more informed manner, which ultimately will lead to a better protection against the common human rights infringements. The significance of this altered division will be illustrated throughout this chapter. In the end, both divisions aim at the same outcome: Promoting and protecting the right to (access) mental health comprehensively.

[25] See eg Brigit Toebes, 'The right to health and other health-related rights' in Brigit Toebes, Mette Hartlev, Aart Hendriks & Janne Rothmar Herrmann (eds), *Health and Human Rights in Europe* (Intersentia 2012) 83–110; or Maite San Giorgi, *The Human Right to Equal Access to Health Care* (Intersentia 2012) 18–19.

[26] UNGA, 'Report of the Special Rapporteur on the right of everyone to the enjoyment of the highest attainable standard of physical and mental health, Dainius Pūras' (n 7) para 13.

extent to which they offer stronger protection than the right to the highest attainable standard of health norm alone. This chapter encompasses rights that support and safeguard persons with mental health conditions and psychosocial disabilities. After all, under the 'right to mental health' framework, all of the Articles enumerated above must be considered in combination with the right to the highest attainable standard of health norm.

Each section in this chapter addresses one or more human rights relevant to its respective subject matter. All sections are structured similarly. First, each section illustrates how the right to the highest attainable standard of health norms of Article 12 ICESCR and Article 25 CRPD already grant (or do not grant) protection in relation to the topic under discussion. Subsequently, an analysis of the scope of the chosen CRPD norm(s) is made. And, lastly, the obligations deriving there from are examined. Where applicable, controversial issues will be used to enhance the discussion.

5.2 PROTECTION AGAINST DISCRIMINATION

> Due to prevalent stigma and inadequate support services, including mental health care, more than 57,000 Indonesians with psychosocial disabilities (mental health conditions) have been chained or locked in a confined space at least once in their lives.[27]

Discrimination and the associated marginalisation and exclusion have been described as the most common human rights violations against persons with mental health conditions and psychosocial disabilities.[28] Although freedom from discrimination is not a healthcare-specific concept, states do have an obligation to provide mental healthcare without discrimination. Every human rights treaty codifies the principle of equality and non-discrimination in one way or another. Yet, international human rights law does not have one uniform definition of 'equality and non-discrimination'.[29] Within the framework of the CPRD, disability-based discrimination is defined (in Article 2 CRPD) as:

> any distinction, exclusion or restriction on the basis of [mental] disability which has the purpose or effect of impairing or nullifying the recognition, enjoyment or exercise, on an equal basis with others, of all human rights and fundamental freedoms in the political,

---

[27] Human Rights Watch, 'World Report 2020, Events of 2019' (2020), <https://www.hrw.org/sites/default/files/world_report_download/hrw_world_report_2020_0.pdf> accessed 14 November 2022, p 278.

[28] Natalie Drew and others, 'Human rights violations of people with mental and psychosocial disabilities: an unresolved global crisis' (2011) 378(9803) The Lancet 1664, 1670.

[29] Jessica Lynn Corsi, 'Article 5: Equality and Non-Discrimination' in Ilias Bantekas, Michael Ashley Stein & Dimitris Anastasiou (eds), *The UN Convention on the Rights of Persons with Disabilities: A Commentary* (Oxford University Press 2018) 142.

economic, social, cultural, civil or any other field. It includes all forms of discrimination, including denial of reasonable accommodation.[30]

Article 3 CRPD establishes equality and non-discrimination as general principles, Article 4 refers to them as general obligations, and Article 5 enshrines equality and non-discrimination as a substantive right.[31] Because of their interconnection with human dignity, equality and non-discrimination are the cornerstones of the protection guaranteed by the CRPD, and they are invoked consistently throughout the substantive Articles of the Convention. A human rights approach to disability requires that equality and non-discrimination are unconditionally applied with regard to persons with psychosocial disabilities. This entails that no additional qualifier associated with the impairment can be used to justify the restriction of any human right.[32]

The benefits of the non-discrimination norm, as embodied in Article 5 CRPD, for the promotion and protection of mental health is that it directly applies to persons with psychosocial disabilities and the situations they find themselves in, one of these being the mental healthcare context. The questions that will be addressed here are: what are the implications of equality and non-discrimination? And what measures do states have to take to protect against or eliminate discrimination in the mental healthcare context? The aim of this section is to elaborate the role of the right to equality and non-discrimination for the realisation of the right to mental health.

This section first analyses the interface between non-discrimination and the right to health norm. Subsequently, the scope of the right to equality and non-discrimination, as enshrined in Article 5 CRPD, will be analysed. And, lastly, the obligations deriving from these rights will be illustrated. While most parts of this section will examine Article 5 generally, links to the mental healthcare context will be provided wherever possible. Despite it being a general provision, the author chose to include Article 5 CRPD in the delineated right to mental health framework, as it truly builds the foundation of the framework on which the discussion can be built. It is submitted that understanding the right to equality and non-discrimination of persons with psychosocial disabilities is a prerequisite for promoting the right to mental health.

5.2.1 NON-DISCRIMINATION AND THE RIGHT TO HEALTH NORM

Non-discrimination, as an element of the right to the highest attainable standard of health, is recognised in various international and regional human rights treaties.

---

[30] UNGA, CRPD (n 23) art 2.
[31] To describe the implications of the three different approaches: principles provide guidelines but are non-justiciable; obligations are legally binding duties of states; and rights must be understood as entitlements to do or have something, which can be claimed before a court.
[32] UNGA, 'Mental health and human rights, Report of the United Nations High Commissioner for Human Rights' (31 January 2017) UN Doc A/HRC/34/32, para 23.

For instance, within the framework of the most authoritative international right to health norm, Article 12 ICESCR, the CteeESCR proscribes any discrimination in accessing health facilities, goods and services on the ground of psychosocial disability, which applies to the public health sector, as well as to private health providers. Non-discrimination includes the notion that persons with psychosocial disabilities can access (mental) health facilities, goods and services that meet their needs according to law, and in fact.[33] In relation to (psychosocial) disability, the Committee specifically highlights that distinction, exclusion, limitation, or denial of reasonable accommodation based on disability has the effect of nullifying or impairing the recognition, enjoyment or exercise of economic, social or cultural rights, such as those under Article 12 ICESCR.[34] However, the CteeESCR has not clarified the implications of this non-discrimination principle in detail.

Within the CRPD framework, which is the basis of this chapter, Article 25 reaffirms the right of all persons with psychosocial disabilities to enjoy the highest attainable standard of health without discrimination on the basis of disability. The text of the Article explicitly defines non-discrimination as: (i) persons with psychosocial disabilities being provided 'with the same range, quality and standard' of healthcare as provided to other persons; (ii) health insurances not being discriminatory against persons with psychosocial disabilities; and (iii) not denying healthcare or health services or food and fluids on the basis of disability.[35] Under Article 25 CRPD, the principle of non-discrimination affirms that access to healthcare must be equitable, implying that a satisfactory degree of care can be obtained effectively.[36]

While this obligation exists on paper, many violations of this standard occur in practice. Former UN High Commissioner for Human Rights, Zeid al-Hussein, reported that, in public and private mental healthcare settings, practices commonly circumvent the equality approach, including through failure to provide reasonable accommodation for persons with psychosocial disabilities.[37] Consequently, there is a need to strengthen the enjoyment of the right to equality and non-discrimination in mental healthcare. For this purpose, it seems useful to connect the right to health norm to the right to equality and non-discrimination as enshrined in Article 5 CRPD. The latter elucidates in detail what non-discrimination means, and which derived state obligations need to be fulfilled. The following subsections address these topics.

---

[33] Committee on Economic, Social and Cultural Rights (CteeESCR), 'General Comment No. 14: The Right to the Highest Attainable Standard of Health (Art. 12)' (General Comment 14) (11 August 2000) UN Doc E/C.12/2000/4, paras 12(b), 18, 26.

[34] CteeESCR, 'General Comment No 5: Persons with Disabilities' (General Comment 5) (9 December 1994) UN Doc E/1995/22, para 16.

[35] UNGA, CRPD (n 23) art 25.

[36] Ilja Richard Pavone, 'Article 25 [Health]' in Valentina Della Fina, Rachele Cera & Giuseppe Palmisano (eds), *The United Nations Convention on the Rights of Persons with Disabilities* (Springer International Publishing 2017) 474.

[37] UNGA, 'Mental health and human rights, Report of the United Nations High Commissioner for Human Rights' (n 32) para 24.

5.2.2 THE SCOPE OF ARTICLE 5 CRPD AND MENTAL HEALTHCARE

Conceptually, equality and non-discrimination reflect the same idea. The ban on discrimination is intended to secure equality. The Explanatory Report to Protocol No. 12 of the European Convention on Human Rights explains that 'the principle of equality requires that equal situations are treated equally and unequal situations differently. Failure to do so will amount to discrimination unless an objective and reasonable justification exists.'[38] Article 5 CRPD, the right to equality and non-discrimination, provides a broad mandate to achieve equality, and to eradicate all forms of discrimination on the basis of psychosocial disability. It prohibits de jure and de facto discrimination in mental health services regulated by public authority. Read together with Article 4(1)(e), it becomes evident that it also extents to the private sector, including any person, practitioner or private institution.[39]

The normative content of the Article can be broken into four parts, each dealing with a different aspect of equality and non-discrimination. After requiring states to recognise: (i) that all persons are equal before and under the law, and thus entitled to the equal protection and equal benefit of the law, Article 5 calls on states to promote; (ii) the prohibition of discrimination and equal and effective legal protection. In addition, it urges states to ensure: (iii) reasonable accommodation; and (iv) to establish specific measures. Some scholars observe that, whereas the first three parts appear to be autonomous norms because they guarantee equality and non-discrimination in general, the last part could be interpreted as a subordinate norm, because it aims to prohibit discrimination only in the enjoyment of certain rights.[40]

On the whole, Article 5 demonstrates that equality for persons with psychosocial disabilities requires more than prohibiting discrimination. Prior to the drafting of General Comment No. 6 on equality and non-discrimination (General Comment 6), the CRPD was widely criticised for not defining the concept of 'discrimination on the basis of disability' or the meaning of treating persons with disability 'on an equal basis'.[41] However, the Committee on the Rights of Persons with Disabilities (CteeRPD) resolved such conceptual criticism through the interpretation of Article 5 CRPD in its General Comment 6.

---

[38] Council of Europe, 'Explanatory Report to the Protocol No. 12 to the Convention for the Protection of Human Rights and Fundamental Freedoms (ETS No 177)' (4 November 2000).
[39] CteeRPD, General Comment 6 (n 22) para 13.
[40] See Daniel Moeckli, 'Equality and Non-Discrimination' in Daniel Moeckli, Sangeeta Shah, and Sandesh Sivakumaran (eds), *International Human Rights Law, second edition* (Oxford University Press 2013) 161–162; or Jessica Lynn Corsi (n 29) 157.
[41] See eg John Dawson (n 14) 70–79; or Sergio Ramos Pozón, 'The convention on the rights of persons with disabilities and mental health law: A critical review' (2016) 10 ALTER, European Journal of Disability Research 301, 304.

5.2.2.1 The Legal Dimension of Equality

Article 5 CRPD embraces formal equality, referring to respect for non-discrimination, as well as substantial equality, which is achieved through equal opportunities.[42] Paragraph 1 provides that 'all persons are equal before and under the law and are entitled without any discrimination to the equal protection and equal benefit of the law'.[43] The central role of equality essentially gives effect to all Articles of the Convention.

Formal equality reflects the basic idea of treating individuals in similar situations alike.[44] 'Equality before the law', a term used in several international human rights treaties, is literal in meaning. It refers to the prohibition of discrimination in the administration of justice, or, in other words, equal treatment by law enforcement officers or the judiciary. This is, for example, violated when persons with psychosocial disabilities are perceived as less credible when filing complaints. 'Equality under the law', a term unique to the CRPD, stipulates that persons with psychosocial disabilities have a right to be protected effectively, meaning that the law itself should grant substantive equality. It refers to the content of the law rather than the practices of law enforcement officers. Violations of the right to equality under the law appear in the form of laws or policies that allow for treating persons with psychosocial disabilities differently than other individuals in similar situations, by allowing for specific restrictions or limitations,[45] a matter that will be addressed throughout this book. When interpreted broadly, 'equality under the law' could also be understood as 'affected by the law', which includes direct discrimination and indirect discrimination alike.[46] Ultimately, it is often negative stereotypes and prejudice that inhibit formal equality.

Substantive equality upholds the principle that individuals in different situations should be treated differently. The concept sets out to address disadvantages experienced by persons with psychosocial disabilities, and to correct the cycle of disadvantages.[47] Substantive equality comprises equality of opportunity and equality of result.[48] 'Equality of opportunity' is ensured through the 'equal protection of the law' component, which obliges states to refrain from maintaining or establishing discrimination, and to take positive actions to overcome barriers that prevent persons with psychosocial disabilities from enjoying rights equally to others. This includes the provision of reasonable accommodation or individual support (see subsection

---

[42] Rachele Cera, 'Article 5 [Equality and Non-Discrimination]' in Della Fina, Rachele Cera & Giuseppe Palmisano (eds), *The United Nations Convention on the Rights of Persons with Disabilities* (Springer International Publishing 2017) 161.
[43] UNGA, CRPD (n 23) art 5(1).
[44] Rachele Cera (n 42) 161.
[45] CteeRPD, General Comment 6 (n 22) para 14.
[46] See Daniel Moeckli (n 40) 164–165; or Jessica Lynn Corsi (n 29) 160.
[47] Rachele Cera (n 42) 161.
[48] See Sandra Fredman, *Discrimination Law*, second edition (Oxford University Press 2011).

5.2.2.3).[49] When properly implemented, the equality of opportunity approach ensures that (most) persons with psychosocial disabilities are generally able to enjoy their rights.[50] Yet, the CRPD stipulates an additional commitment to assist achieving de facto equality: it embraces a substantive equality concept that further entails the 'equality of result' approach. 'Equality of result' is ensured through the 'equal benefit of the law' component, which obliges states 'to promote, guarantee, and secure equality by taking proactive steps to eliminate structural patterns of disadvantage'.[51] Instead of focusing on the need for accommodation and modifications on a case-by-case basis, as in the equality of opportunity model, the equality of result approach aims to remove and eliminate the barriers that create such inequalities. To achieve equal results, the underlying causes of differential treatment need to be addressed, and societal change is required.[52] This is where the adoption of specific measures comes into play (see subsection 5.2.2.4). In general, substantive equality can be understood as the concept of transformative equality – redressing systemic discrimination by targeting structural inequalities – which permeates the entire CRPD. As Cera expresses, substantive equality 'acknowledges that positive action for change is necessary in order to overcome discrimination that is deeply interwoven in legal, political, economic, and cultural structures of society.'[53]

5.2.2.2   The Legal Dimension of Prohibiting Discrimination

Based on Article 5(2) CRPD, disability is a prohibited ground for discrimination. This paragraph of the Article basically contains the legal requirements for achieving equality. It states that all discrimination on the basis of disability must be prohibited, including the four main forms of discrimination: direct discrimination, indirect discrimination, the denial of reasonable accommodation (which will be explained below), and harassment.[54] Disability-based discrimination, grounded in Article 5 CRPD, has also been recognised as a human rights infringement by regional human rights courts. In 2009, *Glor v Switzerland* was the first case before the European Court of Human Rights (ECtHR) where a violation of disability-based discrimination (Article 14 European Convention on Human Rights (ECHR])) was found in conjunction with another right.[55] Here, the ECtHR argued that 'there is a European and worldwide consensus on the need to protect people with disabilities from discriminatory treatment [and] towards full social inclusion of people with disabilities, [as] adopted by the [CRPD]'.[56]

---

[49] CteeRPD, General Comment 6 (n 22) para 16.
[50] Rachele Cera (n 42) 162.
[51] Jessica Lynn Corsi (n 29) 160.
[52] Rachele Cera (n 42) 162.
[53] Ibid.
[54] CteeRPD, General Comment 6 (n 22) para 18.
[55] *Glor v Switzerland,* Aoo no 13444/04 (ECtHR, 30 April 2009) para 98.
[56] Ibid para 53.

The CRPD definition of disability-based discrimination, as referenced above, does not confine itself to a particular addressee. Rather, it applies to states and a broad range of state agents alike, including public mental health facilities, private persons, and institutions such as private mental healthcare providers.[57] Thus, it also imposes a duty on states to avert discrimination by non-state actors.

'All discrimination', under Article 5, comprises discrimination against persons with past, present or presumed psychosocial disabilities, and against persons with dispositions to psychosocial disabilities, as well as their associates, such as family members.[58] In *Guberina v Croatia*, the first case in ECtHR jurisprudence to provide protection from disability-based discrimination by association (under Article 14 ECHR),[59] the applicant could claim victim status based on the severe physical and psychosocial disability of his son, 'with whom he has close personal links and for whom he provides care'.[60] In this case, the Court insisted that states must take into account the obligations stemming from the CRPD when interpreting generally applicable legislation in a disability-sensitive manner.[61]

Additionally, Article 5(2) CRPD stipulates that equal and effective legal protection against discrimination on all grounds must be guaranteed, which is far-reaching and imposes, on states, positive duties to offer protection to rights-holders.[62] The ECtHR even decided that, vis-à-vis persons with psychosocial disabilities, a state's margin of appreciation – that is, the space for manoeuvre granted to states in fulfilling their obligations under the ECHR –[63] is narrow. The Court found in *Kiss v Hungary* that:

> if a restriction on fundamental rights applies to a particularly vulnerable group in society, who have suffered considerable discrimination in the past, such as the mentally disabled, then the State's margin of appreciation is substantially narrower and it must have very weighty reasons for the restrictions in question.[64]

The Court claimed that such an approach was necessary regarding groups that were historically subject to prejudice with lasting consequences, leading to their social exclusion.[65] In cases where persons with psychosocial disabilities have been discriminated against in practice, or by law, legal remedies and measures of redress must be available. In fact, within the CRPD framework, the CteeRPD has previously criticised the absence of information on legal remedies and the lack of accessible

---

[57] Rachele Cera (n 42) 164.
[58] CteeRPD, General Comment 6 (n 22) paras 17, 20.
[59] *Guberina v Croatia*, App no 23682/13 (ECtHR, 22 March 2016).
[60] Ibid para 79.
[61] Ibid para 92.
[62] CteeRPD, General Comment 6 (n 22) para 17.
[63] Steven Greer, The Margin of Appreciation: Interpretation and Discretion under the European Convention on Human Rights (Council of Europe 2000) 5.
[64] *Kiss v Hungary*, App no 38832/06 (ECtHR, 20 May 2010) para 42.
[65] Ibid.

complaint mechanisms, and has urged states to establish effective mechanisms whereby victims can obtain redress, including compensation, rehabilitation and non-repetition, and whereby perpetrators within public and private institutions can be identified and punished.[66]

Lastly, the CRPD definition goes beyond the definitions of discrimination contained in other international human rights treaties, by embedding a deeper understanding of equality. It includes the 'denial of reasonable accommodation' as a form of discrimination, and adds the term 'on an equal basis with others'. The latter is important for securing substantive and transformative equality, and must be understood in two ways. First, it implies that persons with psychosocial disabilities do not have more or fewer rights or benefits than the general population. Second, it requires states to take specific measures to achieve de facto equality for persons with psychosocial disabilities.[67] Hence, the right to non-discrimination can be violated if states fail to treat persons with disabilities differently due to their significantly different situations.[68] Cera suggests that:

> if people are not starting from the same position due to past systemic discrimination, treating them alike will not redress disadvantage, but it may actually create or perpetuate existing discrimination and social hierarchies.[69]

Therefore, the principle of equality, under Article 5 CRPD, requires the adaptation of universal rights to the unique situations of persons with psychosocial disabilities, through the provision of reasonable accommodations and the adoption of specific measures.[70] Both of these are key elements prescribed by Article 5 CRPD, and can be seen as vital measures for enabling persons with psychosocial disabilities to access mental health services, and to enjoy their rights to mental health. The concepts, and their implications in the mental health context, will be delineated next.

---

[66] See eg CteeRPD, 'Concluding Observations on the initial Report of South Africa' (23 October 2018) UN Doc CRPD/C/ZAF/CO/1, paras 8–9; 'Concluding Observations on the initial Report of the former Yugoslav Republic of Macedonia' (29 October 2018) UN Doc CRPD/C/MKD/CO/1, para 7; 'Concluding Observations on the initial Report of Rwanda' (3 May 2019) UN Doc CRPD/C/RWA/CO/1, para 9; 'Concluding Observations on the initial Report of Senegal' (13 May 2019) UN Doc CRPD/C/SEN/CO/1, para 7; 'Concluding Observations on the combined second and third periodic reports of Ecuador' (21 October 2019) UN Doc CRPD/C/ECU/CO/2-3, para 13; 'Concluding Observations on the initial Report of the Philippines' (16 October 2018) UN Doc CRPD/C/PHL/CO/1, para 10; 'Concluding Observations on the initial Report of Seychelles' (16 April 2018) UN Doc CRPD/C/SYC/CO/1, para 12; 'Concluding Observations on the initial Report of Haiti' (13 April 2018) UN Doc CRPD/C/HTI/CO/1, para 8; or 'Concluding Observations on the initial Report of Myanmar' (22 October 2019) UN Doc CRPD/C/MMR/CO/1, para 11.
[67] CteeRPD, General Comment 6 (n 22) para 17.
[68] CteeRPD, *HM v Sweden*, Communication No 3/2011 (21 May 2012) UN Doc CRPD/C/7/D/3/2011, para 8.3.
[69] Rachele Cera (n 42) 159.
[70] Ibid.

Chapter 5. A Human Rights Approach to Psychosocial Disability

5.2.2.3   The Duty to Ensure Reasonable Accommodation

In the context of disability, reasonable accommodation has been found to be an intrinsic part of the immediately applicable duty of non-discrimination.[71] The refusal to provide reasonable accommodation is recognised as a ground for discrimination in Article 2 CRPD. The Convention also provides, for the first time under human rights law, the free-standing and enforceable right to reasonable accommodation, which is contained in Article 5. The CRPD defines 'reasonable accommodation' in Article 2 as:

> necessary and appropriate modification and adjustments not imposing a disproportionate or undue burden, where needed in a particular case, to ensure to persons with disabilities the enjoyment or exercise on an equal basis with others of all human rights and fundamental freedoms.[72]

According to Article 5(3) CPRD, states have the positive obligation to take 'all appropriate steps to ensure that reasonable accommodation is provided'.[73] States taking necessary steps to ensure that the right to reasonable accommodation is fulfilled, instead of people having to rely on individual litigation, is a reflection of the social model of disability, which sees disability as result of societal barriers.[74] In *Luis Eduardo Guachalá Chimbó v Ecuador*, a case concerning the institutionalisation of a person with psychosocial disabilities, the Inter-American Commission on Human Rights (IACHR) emphasised the 'need for differential treatment' when, due to the specific circumstances that affect disadvantaged persons, 'equal treatment would entail suspending or limiting access to a service or good, or the exercise of a right'.[75] While it is the role of states to ensure that reasonable accommodation is provided, both public and private entities have a positive legal obligation to provide reasonable accommodation.[76]

While the concept of reasonable accommodation might be seen as functionally equivalent to prohibiting indirect discrimination, it is important to at least mention the differences here. The concept of indirect discrimination requires a group disadvantage, is usually more wide-ranging, and implies a much higher duty. The concept of reasonable accommodation aims for tailored measures that meet an individual's needs and situation. Like the duty to prohibit indirect discrimination, the duty to reasonably accommodate persons with psychosocial disabilities is not absolute. The duty to provide reasonable accommodation is limited by what is called 'disproportionate or undue burden' and, thus, requires a balancing of interests. A request for reasonable accommodation is bound by a possible unjustified burden on the accommodating party,

---

[71]   CteeRPD, General Comment 6 (n 22) para 23.
[72]   UNGA, CRPD (n 23) art 2.
[73]   Ibid art 5(3).
[74]   Rachele Cera (n 42) 168.
[75]   *Luis Eduardo Guachalá Chimbó v Ecuador* (Merits) IACHR Report No 111/18 (5 October 2018), para 119.
[76]   See CteeRPD, General Comment 6 (n 22) paras 13, 26(e) and 73(h); and Rachele Cera (n 42) 170.

such as high financial costs of accommodation, unavailability of resources, or negative impacts on other persons, to name a few.[77] In the context of indirect discrimination, the challenged measure must be objectively justified.[78]

The CteeRPD interprets 'reasonable accommodation' as an accommodation that is relevant, appropriate and effective for the individual with psychosocial disabilities. The accommodation must achieve the purpose for which it is being made, and has to be tailored to meet the requirements of the person with psychosocial disabilities.[79] Reasonable accommodation duties, although closely linked to accessibility, are different from accessibility duties (which arise under Article 9 CRPD). The duty to provide reasonable accommodation is tailored to individual needs in specific contexts, and is an ex nunc duty, meaning that it is valid for the future and not the past. Hence, states have to provide reasonable accommodation from the moment persons with psychosocial disabilities require access to non-accessible situations, or want to exercise their right to reasonable accommodation.[80] Accessibility duties instead refer to groups, and must be provided before the persons concerned seek redress.[81] In the mental healthcare context, reasonable accommodation includes making mental health facilities, services and information accessible to affected individuals, adjusting medical procedures, implementing advanced planning, and enabling access to support when needed.[82] However, it should not be confused with providing support, for instance support in decision-making (as will be elaborated in subsection 5.3.2.2), or support to be able to live independently and included in the community (as will be elaborated in subsection 5.5.3).[83]

In a range of Concluding Observations, the CteeRPD has emphasised that, in particular, persons with psychosocial disabilities are not being adequately provided with reasonable accommodation. To ensure the application of the concept of reasonable accommodation, the Committee has recommended that states take concrete measures to raise awareness about the concept in the private sector, and among the general public.[84] In recent years, refusal and failure to ensure reasonable accommodation has been recognised as disability-based discrimination several times in the jurisprudence. For example, in *Çam v Turkey*, before the ECtHR,[85] the Court found a violation because Turkey had not provided necessary and appropriate modifications and adjustments, which persons with disabilities are entitled to expect in order to enjoy

---

[77] CteeRPD, General Comment 6 (n 22) paras 25(b), 26(e).
[78] See Erica Howard, 'Indirect Discrimination, Reasonable Accommodation and Religion' in Daniël Cuypers & Jogchum Vrielink (eds), *Equal is not Enough* (Cambridge University Press 2018) 73–92.
[79] CteeRPD, General Comment 6 (n 22) para 25(b).
[80] Ibid para 24.
[81] Jessica Lynn Corsi (n 29) 164.
[82] UNGA, 'Report of the Special Rapporteur on the right of everyone to the enjoyment of the highest attainable standard of physical and mental health, Dainius Pūras' (n 6) para 50.
[83] CteeRPD, General Comment 6 (n 22) para 25(c).
[84] See eg CteeRPD, 'Concluding Observations on the initial Report of Senegal' (n 66) paras 7–8; or 'Concluding Observations on the initial Report of South Africa' (n 66) paras 8–9.
[85] *Çam v Turkey*, App no 51500/08 (ECtHR, 23 February 2016) para 67.

the exercise of their right on an equal basis with others. The applicant was denied the enjoyment of the right without any objective or reasonable justification.[86] Although the case concerned the right to education, and is, therefore, not directly relevant to the present study, it confirmed the importance of including reasonable accommodation in light of the right to non-discrimination in the context of disability. In fact, the CteeRPD had already paved the way for recognition of the denial of reasonable accommodation as a form of discrimination amounting to a violation of the right to health, in the case of *HM v Sweden*. Here, the CteeRPD held that the provision of the requested reasonable accommodation constituted the only effective means to protect the right to health of the applicant, who suffered from a chronic disease.[87] As these two cases show, the right to be provided with reasonable accommodation functions as a gateway to the exercise of all other rights.[88]

5.2.2.4 Specific Measures as Legitimate Differential Treatment

Former Special Rapporteur of the Sub-Commission on Prevention of Discrimination and Protection of Minorities, Marc Bossuyt, argues that:

> a persistent policy in the past of systematic discrimination of certain groups of the population may justify – and in some cases may even require – special measures intended to overcome the sequels of a condition of inferiority.[89]

Specific measures, as provided in Article 5(4) CRPD, are positive or affirmative actions, and are another concept seeking to achieve de facto equality. While reasonable accommodation implies that states must take action to ensure equal treatment, specific measures involve preferential treatment of persons with psychosocial disabilities over others, to address the systemic exclusion of the former group from enjoying their right to health.[90] Usually temporary in nature, specific measures entail adopting or maintaining certain advantages in favour of the marginalised group. In the mental health context, these include, for instance, mental health outreach programmes, peer support programmes, allocation of resources to the mental health sector, or the reallocation of resources to strengthen community-based mental healthcare. Consistently with the CRPD principles and regulations, specific measures adopted under Article 5(4) CRPD must not result in the perpetuation of stigmatisation, discrimination, segregation or isolation of persons with psychosocial disabilities.[91]

---

86   Ibid paras 65, 69.
87   CteeRPD, *HM v Sweden* (n 68).
88   Delia Ferri, 'Reasonable accommodation as a gateway to the equal enjoyment of human rights: from New York to Strasbourg' (2018) 6(1) Social Inclusion, 42.
89   United Nations Economic and Social Council, 'The Concept and Practice of Affirmative Action, Final report submitted by Mr. Marc Bossuyt, Special Rapporteur, in accordance with Sub-Commission resolution 1998/5' (17 June 2002) UN Doc E/CN.4/Sub.2/2002/21, para 101.
90   CteeRPD, General Comment 6 (n 22) para 28.
91   Ibid paras 28, 29.

Although specific measures are generally not mandatory, particular situations may require the enactment of specific measures. Therefore, depending on the context, a failure to adopt such measures could then amount to discrimination under Article 5.[92]

5.2.3 OBLIGATIONS DERIVED FROM THE RIGHT TO EQUALITY AND NON-DISCRIMINATION IN REGARD TO MENTAL HEALTHCARE

States must take measures to protect against, and eliminate, discrimination, which include the duties to ensure reasonable accommodation, and to adopt specific measures as justified differential treatment.[93] Based on the CteeRPD's General Comment 6, the right to equality and non-discrimination consists of three distinct duties of respecting, protecting and fulfilling the right.[94]

Firstly, based on the obligation to respect the right to equality and non-discrimination, states are obliged to refrain from any discriminatory action against persons with psychosocial disabilities, such as denying access to mental healthcare services. Furthermore, states must address all forms of discrimination that make facilities or information inaccessible, or that impede the right to health through violations of the right to receive mental healthcare on the basis of free and informed consent.[95]

The obligation to protect the right requires states to take actions to avoid discrimination by third parties. It concerns the responsibility to take appropriate measures to prevent private actors from discriminating against persons with psychosocial disabilities.[96] This is particularly important in the mental healthcare context, where discrimination by private entities, who often operate behind closed doors, may go unnoticed. In that regard, states are obliged to adopt various enforcement measures. According to the CteeRPD, these include: (i) measures to raise the awareness of all people (including mental health personnel) about the rights of persons with psychosocial disabilities, and specifically what their right to health entails and the meaning of discrimination; (ii) measures that ensure the provision of access to justice; and (iii) measures to provide sufficient and accessible legal aid.[97] Further, states must take all appropriate steps to ensure that non-state actors provide

---

[92] Jessica Lynn Corsi (n 29) 169.
[93] Rachele Cera (n 42) 164–173.
[94] The 'respect, protect, fulfil' framework was formally adopted in international law in the late 1990s and the first UN document to include this tripartite division of state obligations was the UN Committee on Economic, Social and Cultural Rights General Comment 12 on the right to food in 1999; CteeRPD, General Comment 6 (n 22) para 30.
[95] CteeRPD, General Comment 6 (n 22) para 25.
[96] United Nations Human Rights Committee (HRCtee), 'General Comment No. 31, The nature of the general legal obligation imposed on States Parties to the Covenant' (26 May 2004) UN Doc CCPR/C/21/Rev.1/Add.13, para 8.
[97] CteeRPD, General Comment 6 (n 22) para 31.

reasonable accommodation.[98] Thus, states have to impose reasonable accommodation obligations on private mental health facilities and providers, and have to take steps to raise awareness of the duty to accommodate, and of the measures that should be taken.[99]

To fulfil the non-discrimination obligation, states are obliged to modify or abolish existing laws, regulations, practices or customs that constitute (disability-specific) discrimination, such as discriminatory mental health laws that legitimise inappropriate non-consensual institutionalisation and treatment, or guardianship laws that deny or restrict legal capacity.[100] The reason for this is that limiting the enjoyment or exercise of certain human rights, based on psychosocial disability, is discriminatory. Moreover, states should ensure that domestic legislation incorporates disability as a prohibited ground of discrimination. Additionally, reasonable accommodation provisions, with an explicit definition in line with the CRPD, must be enshrined as an immediately enforceable right in all areas of law and policy, and the denial of reasonable accommodation must be recognised and punishable as a form of discrimination.[101] For example, Norway's Anti-Discrimination and Accessibility Act (No. 42 of 2008) contains the obligation to reasonably accommodate persons with psychosocial disabilities, regarding their access and enjoyment of social and healthcare services. A breach of this obligation is regarded as discrimination.[102] Besides enshrining a reasonable accommodation provision in law, the CteeRPD requires states to undertake systematic training on that matter at all levels, and across sectors, including private providers.[103] Unlike reasonable accommodations, specific measures are generally not obligatory unless they are deemed necessary to accelerate or achieve de facto equality.[104]

Promoting equality and tackling discrimination are cross-cutting obligations with immediate effect. As such, they are not subject to progressive realisation.[105] While accessibility (Article 9 CRPD) is subject to progressive realisation, states have the immediate obligation to provide reasonable accommodation to ensure that persons with psychosocial disabilities can access mental healthcare or support services when the need arises.[106]

---

[98] See Rachele Cera (n 42) 168; and UNGA, CRPD (n 23) art 5(3).
[99] Rachele Cera (n 42) 168.
[100] CteeRPD, General Comment 6 (n 22) para 30.
[101] See eg CteeRPD, 'Concluding observations on the initial report of Germany' (13 May 2015) UN Doc CRPD/C/DEU/CO/1, para 14(b).
[102] Norway, Anti-Discrimination and Accessibility Act (No 42 of 2008), sec 12.
[103] CteeRPD, General Comment 6 (n 22) para 55.
[104] CteeRPD, 'General Comment on Equality and Non- discrimination (Article 5): First draft as at 31 August 2017' (31 August 2017), <www.ohchr.org/Documents/HRBodies/CRPD/GCArt5.docx> accessed 14 November 2022, paras 30, 37.
[105] Ibid paras 30, 37.
[106] UNGA, 'Report of the Special Rapporteur on the right of everyone to the enjoyment of the highest attainable standard of physical and mental health, Dainius Pūras' (n 7) para 58.

5.2.4 SYNOPSIS

The CRPD codifies and promotes transformative equality. It seeks to advance the equality of persons with psychosocial disabilities by obliging states to make individually tailored and structural adjustments to tackle the specific situations of persons with psychosocial disabilities. It explicitly addresses transformative dimensions, such as reasonable accommodation to promote equality, or specific measures to redress disadvantages.[107] As Arnardóttir posits: 'Only by way of such accommodation can non-discrimination truly prevail.'[108]

The right to equal recognition and non-discrimination, as enshrined in Article 5 CRPD, prescribes the duty to promote equality, prohibit disability-specific discrimination and provide reasonable accommodation, spanning all human rights within the CRPD.[109] In the following analysis of mental health-related human rights, the phrase 'on an equal basis with others' will be recurrent, which underscores the importance of equality and non-discrimination. And while reasonable accommodation is often referred to in employment or education settings, many of the mental healthcare-related rights also require reasonable accommodations to achieve full implementation, as will be illustrated.

To conclude the subsection on protection against discrimination, the following table provides an overview of its scope and associated obligations, as analysed above:

Table 5.2: Summary of the scope of, and obligations arising from, Article 5 CRPD

Scope	– Acceptance of formal equality (respect for non-discrimination) and substantial equality (achieved through equal opportunities). – Prohibition of discrimination, including direct and indirect disability-based discrimination, the denial of reasonable accommodation, and harassment; and legal protection against the various forms of discrimination. – The duty to take all appropriate steps to ensure reasonable accommodation (tailored measures to meet an individual's needs and situation), not imposing a disproportionate or undue burden on the party making the accommodations. – Specific measures as legitimate preferential treatment to address systematic exclusion.
Obligations	– Providing reasonable accommodation (when required) and specific measures. – Taking measures to raise awareness about the rights of persons with psychosocial disabilities.

---

[107] Jessica Lynn Corsi (n 29) 141.
[108] Oddný Mjöll Arnardóttir (n 5) 255.
[109] Lisa Waddington & Andrea Broderick, *Promoting equality and non-discrimination for persons with disability, Contribution to the Council of Europe Strategy on the Rights of Persons with Disabilities* (Council of Europe 2017) 7.

5.3 LEGAL CAPACITY AND THE PROTECTION OF PERSONS NOT ABLE TO GIVE CONSENT

> 'Nothing could prepare me for the experience of being taken against my will – not by the police or even an ambulance, but by an older sister who felt she knew best. What followed was the most violent of admissions. Totally traumatized and in shock, the sheer panic of dealing with my new reality never went away. I was manhandled, forcibly injected and held against my will for more than a month' – survivor of the mental health system, Australia.[110]

Historically, persons with mental health conditions and psychosocial disabilities have been deprived of their right to legal capacity in many areas of life under guardianship laws or mental health laws. This has often been based on the Principles for the Protection of Persons with Mental Illness and the Improvement of Mental Health Care.[111] Such substituted decision-making regimes, regularly justified to mitigate the risk of self-harm or harming others, have proven to be paternalistic in their approach to providing mental health treatment and care.[112] Consequently, the legal capacity of persons with mental health conditions and psychosocial disabilities is often restricted, either formally, through a declaration of incapacity, or informally, through permitting acts that violate the bodily integrity of a person.[113] The denial of legal capacity occurs in various settings, among them inpatient and outpatient mental health services. It becomes apparent in different ways. Involuntary admission to, and treatment in, facilities denies the patient the right to exercise informed consent to mental healthcare. Even if they are not admitted involuntarily, legal capacity may be denied when a person is being treated, because mental health personnel assume that the person cannot make their own decisions. Additionally, threatening someone with involuntary admission and treatment in order for the person to accept unwanted practices is also an infringement of the right to legal capacity.[114] Article 12 CRPD, which contains the right to equal recognition before the law, addresses the issue of legal capacity. Although the right to legal capacity is not absolute (as will be discussed below), it offers protection against many of the interferences outlined above, and emphasises the social involvement of persons with mental health conditions and psychosocial disabilities.

---

[110] WHO, 'Legal capacity and the right to decide: WHO QualityRights core training: mental health and social services: course guide' (2019), < https://apps.who.int/iris/handle/10665/329539> accessed 14 November 2022.

[111] UNGA, 'The protection of persons with mental illness and the improvement of mental health care' (17 December 1991) UN Doc A/RES/46/119, annex.

[112] Marion Byrne and others, 'A new tool to assess compliance of mental health laws with the convention on the rights of persons with disabilities' (2018) 58 International Journal of Law and Psychiatry 122, 129.

[113] Lucy Series & Anna Nilsson, 'Article 12 CRPD: Equal Recognition before the Law' in Ilias Bantekas, Michael Ashley Stein & Dimitris Anastasiou (eds), *The UN Convention on the Rights of Persons with Disabilities: A Commentary* (Oxford University Press 2018) 350.

[114] WHO (n 110).

Depriving persons with mental health conditions and psychosocial disabilities of their right to legal capacity is a limitation on the exercise of any other human right. Thus, Article 12 CRPD is an essential building block to securing the enjoyment of all other human rights within and beyond the CRPD framework. While the right to legal capacity is a more general concept applied in the context of disability, for instance regarding marriage or owning property, there are two elements that are particularly important for the promotion and protection of mental health: mental capacity to consent and supported decision-making. As this section focuses specifically on decision-making within the context of mental health treatment and care, these two elements will be analysed in more detail. The questions that will be answered are: what does the right to legal capacity imply for the mental healthcare context? And what measures do states have to take? The aim of this section is to evaluate the role that the right to equal recognition before the law plays in the realisation of the right to mental health.

Examining Article 12 CRPD offers key advantages for the promotion and protection of mental health, as compared to the right to the highest attainable standard of health norm. A human rights approach to disability addresses structural inequalities, and implies the promotion of a mental healthcare continuum based on informed consent, as well as a paradigm change from substituted decision-making to supported decision-making.

This section of Chapter 5 commences by illustrating the intersection between legal capacity and the right to the highest attainable standard of health norm. It continues by analysing the scope of the right to equal recognition before the law, as enshrined in Article 12 CRPD, focusing on legal capacity and mental capacity to consent, as well as supported decision-making. Subsequently, this section will explore the obligations states have to fulfil with regard to mental healthcare, deriving from the various components of Article 12. The section concludes with a discussion on controversial issues under Article 12 CRPD.

5.3.1 LEGAL CAPACITY AND THE RIGHT TO HEALTH NORM

The recognition of legal capacity is indivisibly linked to the enjoyment of the right to the highest attainable standard of health. Article 12 ICESCR, the most authoritative right to health norm, does not, however, explicitly refer to legal capacity or the capacity to consent to, or refuse, a mental health intervention.[115] The CteeESCR's interpretation of Article 12 ICESCR provides that the right to health includes 'the right to control

---

[115] CteeESCR, General Comment 14 (n 33) para 34; see Yana Litins'ka, *Assessing capacity to decide on medical treatment: On human rights and the use of medical knowledge in the laws of England, Russia and Sweden* (Uppsala University 2018) 112. Note that ever since the CRPD has come into force, the CteeESCR has raised concerns about legally incapacitating persons with mental health conditions and psychosocial disabilities and coercive treatment in mental health facilities, see eg CteeESCR, 'Concluding observations on the second periodic report of Kazakhstan' (29 March 2019) UN Doc

one's health and body'.[116] However, the CteeESCR does not define its meaning in depth. The CteeESCR further interprets the right to health as containing the right to seek, receive and communicate information and ideas concerning one's health status.[117] While this cannot be understood as the right to legal capacity per se, it resembles the integral informed consent component thereof. But what about situations in which the mental capacity to seek, receive or communicate information is impaired? Under Article 12 ICESCR, states are obliged to take positive measures to enable or assist individuals to enjoy their right to health; supporting them in making informed choices about their health is one of these measures.[118] Nevertheless, the CteeESCR fails to clarify any details on support measures. And, fundamentally, this right to health norm and its interpretation by the Committee does not address the matter of substitution, i.e. substituted decision-making by a representative. This concept is very common in mental healthcare, and requires further examination.

Article 25 CRPD, the right to the highest attainable standard of health provision within the CRPD framework, provides standards and obligations that states have to guarantee when implementing the right to health. It explicitly requires health professionals to provide healthcare on the basis of free and informed consent, adding that public and private healthcare providers need to be trained on human rights, dignity and autonomy.[119] Valid consent has two separate characteristics, in the text of the CRPD: it should be free and informed. Important in this subsection of the book is, specifically, the concept of informed consent, which means to respect and protect the autonomous and self-determining choice of the person concerned to access and control the healthcare provision[120] (the concept of free consent will be elaborated in subsection 5.4.1). Under the duty to guarantee the right to health, states are obliged to involve persons with psychosocial disabilities in all decisions concerning their mental health therapy.[121] Indirectly, this regulation suppresses substitution. Still, situations in which persons with psychosocial disabilities might not be able to express free and informed consent remain obscure under Article 25 CPRD. For instance, what about situations of severe psychotic illnesses, which by definition impair decision-making skills?[122] Consequently, this right to health norm also leaves a gap that needs to be filled.

Without setting out additional rights, Article 12 CRPD provides specific measures and safeguards for persons with psychosocial disabilities to exercise their right to legal capacity. It describes precise obligations states must fulfil to protect affected individuals

---

E/C.12/KAZ/CO/2, para 45(a); and 'Concluding observations on sixth periodic report of Denmark' (12 November 2019) UN Doc E/C.12/DNK/CO/6, para 57.
[116] CteeESCR, General Comment 14 (n 33) para 8.
[117] Ibid para 12(b).
[118] Ibid para 37.
[119] UNGA, CRPD (n 23) art 25(d).
[120] Penelope Weller (n 20) 724–725.
[121] Ilja Richard Pavone (n 36) 478.
[122] See WHO, International Statistical Classification of Diseases and Related Health Problems, 10th Revision (ICD-10)-2015-WHO (World Health Organization 2015).

in areas in which they have traditionally been denied this right, as will be illustrated in the following subsection.

5.3.2 THE SCOPE OF ARTICLE 12 CRPD AND MENTAL HEALTHCARE

The right to legal capacity is guaranteed under Article 12 CRPD. Paragraph 1 reaffirms that persons with psychosocial disabilities are recognised before the law, with rights and responsibilities like anyone else. However, Article 12 also acknowledges that this recognition is not limited to the person's status, but also extends to performing actions, such as making decisions. Hence, Paragraph 2 stipulates that persons with psychosocial disabilities have the same right as everybody else to act under the law, meaning that they can create, modify or end legal relationships. This right to legal capacity includes that they can make their own decisions, and that others must respect these decisions. When it is difficult to make decisions on their own, persons with psychosocial disabilities have the right to receive support to make decisions, under Paragraph 3. If persons receive support to make decisions, Paragraph 4 grants protection against possible abuse.[123] The following normative analysis addresses each component in detail.

5.3.2.1 The Right to Legal Capacity and Mental Capacity to Consent

Legal capacity, as provided in Article 12(2) CRPD, is an inherent and inalienable right of all people. Throughout this section, two ways to ensure that persons with psychosocial disabilities can exercise their right to legal capacity, namely through informed consent, and through supported decision-making, will be highlighted.

There is no internationally agreed definition of the term 'legal capacity'.[124] Yet, when analysing the concept of legal capacity, two integral components have been defined: the capacity to hold rights and duties (also referred to as legal standing), and the capacity to exercise and act upon these rights and duties (also referred to as legal agency), which includes the capacity to sue.[125] Legal standing to hold rights is described in terms of being recognised as a legal person before the law. In simplified terms, legal capacity to hold rights exists for all human beings; it is a static status that does not change over time.[126] In the context of mental healthcare, legal standing, for example, entails that all persons have the right to seek medical assistance. Legal agency implies that one can

---

[123] UNGA, CRPD (n 23) art 12.
[124] European Union Agency for Fundamental Rights (FRA), *Legal capacity of persons with intellectual disabilities and persons with mental health problems* (FRA 2013) 9.
[125] Sarah Lees & Matthias Leicht-Miranda, 'Legal Opinion on Article 12 of the CRPD' (2008), <https://disability-studies.leeds.ac.uk/library/author/legalopiniononarticleofthecrpd/> accessed 14 November 2022; and CteeRPD, 'General Comment No. 1 (2014) Article 12: Equal recognition before the law' (General Comment 1) (19 May 2014) UN Doc CRPD/C/GC/1, paras 12–14.
[126] Yana Litins'ka (n 115) 33.

act on these rights and have these actions recognised. It can be described as creating, maintaining and extinguishing legal relations, and enforcing rights before the relevant authority.[127] In the context of mental healthcare, legal agency, for example, entails that persons have the right to make decisions regarding medical assistance. Legal scholarship commonly draws a distinction between the capacity to hold rights and duties and the capacity to exercise them.[128] Nevertheless, Dhanda argues in favour of abandoning this distinction, and instead sees capacity as a universal legal attribute. In her opinion, one must either recognise universal legal capacity or object to perceiving legal capacity as a universal human attribute.[129] The CteeRPD affirms this concept, declaring that both components – legal standing and legal agency – must be recognised, for the right to legal capacity to be fulfilled. However, the second component is frequently denied to persons with psychosocial disabilities.[130]

Legal capacity is distinct from the concept of mental capacity. Legal capacity can be described as 'the right to make a decision'. It relates to whether an individual's act or decision is legally recognised as valid and binding. Mental capacity, on the other hand, concerns a person's putative psychological 'ability to make a decision' which ought to be recognised as valid and binding – also referred to as their decision-making skills – which may vary from person to person, depending on numerous factors. In line with Article 12 CPRD, the right to legal capacity can never be denied to a person. Everyone must be able to enjoy and exercise their right to legal capacity irrespective of their decision-making skills. Hence, a psychosocial disability cannot justify the denial of legal capacity.[131]

As a general rule, obtaining informed consent to admission or treatment is essential for respecting the right to legal capacity.[132] Informed consent is a fundamental element of the right to mental health, as it serves to promote a person's autonomy, bodily integrity and self-determination.[133] Informed consent implies that a person using mental healthcare services has received, understood and made a decision based on all available information concerning their mental health treatment. The information needs to be provided in such a way as it can be understood by the person, and it should include information on the benefits and risks of the treatment, and alternatives to the treatment, as well as the benefits and risks of not undergoing this or other treatment.

---

[127] Ibid.
[128] See eg Nicholas Caivano, 'Conceptualizing Capacity: Interpreting Canada's Qualified Ratification of Article 12 of the UN Disability Rights Convention' (2014) 4(1) Western Journal of Legal Studies; or Lucy Series & Anna Nilsson (n 113).
[129] Amita Dhanda, 'Legal Capacity in the Disability Rights Convention: Stranglehold of the Past or Lodestar for the Future' (2007) 34(2) Syracuse Journal of International Law & Commerce, 457–458.
[130] CteeRPD, General Comment 1 (n 125) paras 12–14.
[131] Ibid para 13.
[132] While the right to legal capacity is closely linked to informed consent, the latter is a core element of Article 17 CRPD (protecting the integrity of the person) and thus, will also be analysed in more detail in subsection 5.4.2.
[133] UNGA, 'Report of the Special Rapporteur on the right of everyone to the enjoyment of the highest attainable standard of physical and mental health, Dainius Pūras' (10 April 2018) UN Doc A/HRC/38/36, para 25.

Informed consent requires that the person concerned has the right to refuse the treatment altogether.[134] Essentially, consent must be given voluntarily, meaning without threat, coercion, manipulation or undue influence.[135] Furthermore, informed consent assigns associated duties and obligations to mental healthcare providers.[136] These providers must provide information, and be cognisant of, and minimise threats to, voluntary decision-making. Despite being a core principle in healthcare provision, persons are often denied the exercise of informed consent in the context of mental health because they are found to lack the mental capacity to consent. In fact, UN treaty bodies and special procedures, as well as regional human rights conventions, allow exceptions to the requirement of informed consent on the basis of 'medical necessity' or 'dangerousness', as will be elaborated in section 5.4.[137] The CteeRPD has declared that, even in crisis situations, a person's autonomy and legal capacity to make a decision must be respected.[138] Does the Committee then propose not to interfere, for example, with a person experiencing a psychosis who tries to jump off a bridge? In that regard, the 1997 Convention on Human Rights and Biomedicine of the Council of Europe allows persons with serious mental health conditions and psychosocial disabilities to receive mental health treatment without their consent, if it is found that, without such treatment, the person's health would be seriously damaged. In situations where the law has declared persons with mental health conditions and psychosocial disabilities to lack the capacity to consent, a representative makes the decisions on behalf of the affected individual.[139] This is not uncommon in practice. When persons are considered to have impaired decision-making skills because of a mental health condition or psychosocial disability, their legal capacity to make a decision is often removed. The CteeRPD summarises three common approaches. Firstly, legal capacity may be removed because of a 'status', meaning simply on the basis of the diagnosis of a mental health condition. Here, mental capacity is perceived to be a permanent status; or it is removed because of being a hospitalised patient. Secondly, it may be removed because the affected person's decision is deemed unreasonable or has negative consequences. This is called the 'outcome approach'. And, thirdly, legal capacity may be removed on the basis of the 'functional approach': instead of being based on the outcome, the restriction of legal

---

[134] See Henriette Sinding Aasen and Mette Hartlev, 'Human Rights Principles and Patient Rights' in Brigit Toebes, Mette Hartlev, Aart Hendriks, Katharina O Cathaoir, Janne Rothmar Herrmann & Henriette Sinding Aasen (eds), *Health and Human Rights. Global and European Perspectives*, second edition (Intersentia 2022) 70ff.

[135] UNGA, 'Report of the Special Rapporteur on the right of everyone to the enjoyment of the highest attainable standard of physical and mental health, Anand Grover' (10 August 2009) UN Doc A/64/272, paras 9, 14, 15.

[136] Ibid paras 9, 25.

[137] UNGA, 'Report of the Special Rapporteur on the right of everyone to the enjoyment of the highest attainable standard of physical and mental health, Dainius Pūras' (n 7) para 14.

[138] CteeRPD, General Comment 1 (n 125) para 18.

[139] Council of Europe, Convention for the Protection of Human Rights and Dignity of the Human Being with regard to the Application of Biology and Medicine: Convention on Human Rights and Biomedicine (Oviedo Convention) (adopted 4 April 1997, entered into force 1 December 1999) ETS 164, arts 6, 7.

capacity is based on the process by which an individual makes a decision. According to this approach, a person's decision-making skill is considered deficient.[140] At the heart of the functional approach are functional or cognitive tests in the clinical assessment of competence. Cognitive tests, increasingly popular,[141] are especially criticised by the CteeRPD. On the one hand, they are discriminatorily applied to people with psychosocial disabilities and, on the other hand, they presume to accurately assess the human mind.[142] The Committee clarifies that none of the three approaches may serve as a legitimate ground to justify the denial of legal capacity of a person with perceived or actual deficits in their mental capacity to consent.[143] Jurisprudence of regional human rights courts affirms this reasoning to some extent, especially regarding the first enumerated approach, the 'status approach'. In *AN v Lithuania*, the ECtHR explicitly held that 'the existence of a mental disorder, even a serious one, cannot be the sole reason to justify full incapacitation'.[144] *Shtukaturov v Russia* (2008), the first legal capacity case before the ECtHR, is another example. Because of his mental disorder, the applicant in this case was declared fully incapacitated for an indefinite period, and deprived of his legal capacity without his knowledge, having been forcibly admitted to a psychiatric hospital, where he received medical treatment against his will, and was not allowed to obtain a review of his status. The full deprivation of legal capacity was found to constitute a 'very serious interference' in the applicant's private life, and to be disproportionate to the legitimate aim pursued, and thus a violation of the right to respect private life (Article 8 ECHR).[145] Besides laying the foundation to determine incapacity under Article 8, it is important to note that the Court also introduced possible limitations on the right to legal capacity. It declared that measures of interference have to be proportionate, and must be fair, to ensure due respect of the interests safeguarded by Article 8.[146] According to the ECtHR, a person's interests under Article 8 must be safeguarded to the extent that a guardian must be appointed if a person is unable to look after their own interests. In the case of *B v Romania*, the Court established that there had been a procedural violation of Article 8 because the authorities had failed to appoint a legal representative at the time of the applicant's hospitalisation.[147] Such judgments run counter to the approach adopted by the CRPD. Generally, the ECtHR is hesitant to declare restrictions on the right to legal capacity to be violations of Article 8 ECHR.

Article 12 CPRD states that, if a person is considered to have impaired decision-making skills because of a psychosocial disability, then instead of denying legal capacity

---

[140] CteeRPD, General Comment 1 (n 125) para 15.
[141] As they appear increasingly in legislation around the world, see Lucy Series & Anna Nilsson (n 113) 352.
[142] CteeRPD, General Comment 1 (n 125) para 15.
[143] Ibid, para 13.
[144] *AN v Lithuania*, App no 17280/08 (ECtHR, 31 May 2016) para 123.
[145] *Shtukaturov v Russia*, App no 44009/05 (ECtHR, 27 March 2008) paras 86, 88, 90, 96.
[146] Ibid para 89.
[147] *B v Romania*, App no 1285/03 (ECtHR, 19 February 2013) paras 93–101.

to the individual and appointing a legal guardian, the person is entitled to access the support they may want or require, to be able to exercise their right to legal capacity. This groundbreaking distinction will guide the discussion below in relation to the so-called right to supported decision-making.

5.3.2.2 The Right to Supported Decision-making and Safeguards

Supported decision-making is key to ensuring that persons with psychosocial disabilities are not, under any circumstances, formally deprived of their right to legal capacity. Under Article 12(3) CRPD, states are obliged to provide access to the support necessary to enable persons with psychosocial disabilities to make their own decisions. Under the system of supported decision-making, an individual can choose and control who supports them, and to what extent they are being supported. Specifically, the supported individuals themselves make the final decision.[148]

Series and Nilsson argue that 'support for the exercise of legal capacity' encompasses a range of support and adaptions, and that, therefore, it needs to be distinguished from 'supported decision-making', which is only one type of support in the exercise of legal capacity. They claim that the support paradigm is far broader than assisting individuals to make decisions for themselves.[149] This study, which relies on the interpretation of the CteeRPD, is particularly interested in forms of support for decision-making, including the development and recognition of advance planning instruments and alternative methods of communication. Hence, this book mainly discusses supported decision-making whenever speaking about support in exercising legal capacity.

When supporting someone to exercise and enjoy their right to legal capacity, all forms of support have to be based on the rights, will and preferences of the person concerned, and must never amount to substituted decision-making.[150] By way of contrast, in substituted decision-making, decisions are made on behalf of persons by third parties, such as family, practitioners or guardians, based on what they perceive as being in the person's best interest (also called 'the best interest principle'). Although the text of Article 12 CRPD remains silent on whether it permits or prohibits substituted decision-making, the CteeRPD's interpretation of the Article brings clarity. At this point, it needs to be highlighted that the CteeRPD acknowledges that there are circumstances in which the will and preferences of a person cannot be determined, despite efforts to do so, such as where that person has limited communication skills or is in coma. In situations where a person is unable to communicate their will and preferences, decisions must be based on the best interpretation of the person's will and preferences, and not in the person's best interest.[151] Although the notion of the best interest varies, it often relies on the external evaluation of what is considered 'good for them', which may be in

---

[148] Lucy Series & Anna Nilsson (n 113) 366.
[149] Ibid 364.
[150] CteeRPD, General Comment 1 (n 125) paras 16–17.
[151] Ibid para 21.

conflict to what the persons themselves want. The best interpretation of a person's will and preferences involves considering their past and present wishes, attitudes, values, and (non-verbal) everyday actions and feelings, a complex process that can be time- and resource-consuming. Such interpretative approaches to will and preferences have come to be known as facilitated decisions.[152] While some scholars argue that facilitated decisions are substituted decisions, especially where complete support is needed, they do not fall under the technical definition of substituted decisions, because the support, however intensive it may be, is still directed to the realisation of the will and preferences of the person concerned.[153] However, at this point the Committee's incomplete interpretation of 'respect for will and preferences' must be criticised. Szmukler highlights that there are specific situations (and these are not uncommon) where the 'will' and 'preferences' of a person diverge, or are even contradictory, with regard to a treatment decision. As an example, a person with unquestioned decision-making ability may express his or her 'will' in an advance directive with regard to a future episode in which he or she has impaired decision-making capacities. If, in that future episode, the person expresses a different or contradictory treatment 'preference', which of the two – 'will' or currently expressed 'preferences' – should be respected?[154] The CteeRPD is silent on this matter. Could it be that 'the best interest principle' should be applied in such situations after all?

Despite constituting a violation under Article 12 CPRD, numerous domestic laws still authorise substituted decision-making. Recently, case law of regional human rights bodies has addressed and criticised substitution. Ecuador, for instance, is a country that maintains a model of substituted decision-making despite ratifying the CRPD.[155] And the case of *Luis Eduardo Guachalá Chimbó v Ecuador* dealt with this issue. Here, the Inter-American Commission found that the applicant had been hospitalised and treated without his informed consent, and without giving him support to enable him to make his own decision. The Commission considered that the applicant had been denied the right to exercise legal capacity because the state had not provided the support needed to guarantee the right, such that the applicant would have been able to give his informed consent. On the contrary, the state had restricted his right to decide, based solely on his psychosocial disability.[156] Accordingly, the IACHR considered that there had been a violation of the right to legal capacity as a component of the right to the recognition of juridical personality (Article 3 of the American Convention on Human Rights).[157]

---

[152] Lucy Series & Anna Nilsson (n 113) 365.
[153] See eg Wayne Martin and others, 'The Essex Autonomy Project Three Jurisdictions Report: Towards Compliance with CRPD Art. 12 in Capacity/Incapacity Legislation across the UK' (2016), <https://autonomy.essex.ac.uk/resources/eap-three-jurisdictions-report/> accessed 14 November 2022, p 58.
[154] George Szmukler (n 14) 37.
[155] See CteeRPD, 'Concluding observations of the Committee on the Rights of Persons with Disabilities, Ecuador' (n 66) para 25.
[156] *Luis Eduardo Guachalá Chimbó v Ecuador* (n 75) paras 178–179.
[157] Article 3 IACHR stands for the right to recognition as a person before the law, which resembles Article 12 CRPD.

There are different formal and informal measures for supported decision-making. For instance, affected individuals can choose a person they trust to assist them when exercising their right to legal capacity, or they can call on peer, advocate or lawyer support. Support must be tailored to the individual ('issue-specific'), and can vary throughout their life ('time-specific').[158] Some people require support only for complex decisions, while others also require it for simple ones. Support can also constitute advance planning or advance directives, which give people the ability to plan in advance what will and preferences need to be followed in the event that they become unable to communicate a decision at a later date.[159] After all, supported decision-making is voluntary: a person can always choose not to have support.[160] According to Byrne and others, recognising support for the exercise of legal capacity comes with benefits: it can enhance the ability to access mental health services and treatment voluntarily, and early access to support might even prevent (coercive) emergency interventions.[161]

In a system of support, safeguards must be present to ensure that support is carried out rightfully. States have the obligation under Article 12(4) CRPD to create effective and appropriate safeguards for all measures that relate to the exercise of legal capacity. As their primary purpose, these safeguards must ensure that the rights, will and preferences of the person are respected, and they must provide protection against conflicts of interest, undue influence, exploitation and abuse.[162] The CteeRPD indicates that persons who rely on the support of others are at particular risk of being subject to conflicts of interest or undue influence. In this regard, the CteeRPD explicitly states that 'the best interest principle' can never be seen as a safeguard under Article 12, in relation to adults.[163] While safeguards must protect against undue influence, the Committee recognises that the protection must respect the rights, will and preferences of individuals, which also includes the right to take risks and make mistakes.[164]

Furthermore, the CteeRPD declares that safeguards must ensure that the support for decision-making is proportional and tailored to the individual, as well as that there is a complaint and redress mechanism in place.[165] In that regard, the Yokohama Declaration proposes that an individual who requires support should, further, be entitled to have a legal representative who, inter alia, protects the person from any form of ill-treatment, respects the person's civil and human rights, and takes action on their behalf if these rights are threatened.[166] However, it is questionable whether such a form of legal representation would not, in and of itself, be incompatible with the supported decision-making regime as envisioned by the CRPD, since legal representation,

---

[158] The World Congresses on Adult Guardianship Law 2010 and 2016, Yokohama Declaration (revised and amended) (16 September 2016), sec 3(3).
[159] CteeRPD, General Comment 1 (n 125) para 17.
[160] Ibid para 19.
[161] Marion Byrne and others (n 112) 134.
[162] CteeRPD, General Comment 1 (n 125) para 20.
[163] Ibid para 21.
[164] Ibid para 22.
[165] UNGA, CRPD (n 23) art 12(4).
[166] The World Congresses on Adult Guardianship Law 2010 and 2016 (n 159).

especially 'on behalf of a person', might ultimately include an element of substitution. This topic will be addressed in more detail in the case study about Germany conducted in section 6.4.

5.3.3 OBLIGATIONS DERIVED FROM THE RIGHT TO LEGAL CAPACITY IN REGARD TO MENTAL HEALTHCARE

States have an obligation to respect, protect and fulfil the right of all persons with mental health conditions and psychosocial disabilities to legal capacity. Universal legal capacity, the CteeRPD upholds, can only be fully recognised if states eradicate all denials of legal capacity that are discriminatory on the basis of a mental health condition.[167] This includes deprivation of formal decision-making, usually taken over by court-appointed guardians, health practitioners or families, as well as informal decision-making by others, particularly family, friends or the community. Relying on the proposal of three core obligations under Article 12 CRPD by Arstein-Kerslake and Flynn, this subsection distinguishes between three obligations: (i) abolishing regimes of substituted decision-making; (ii) making available support mechanisms to enable persons with psychosocial disabilities to exercise their legal capacity; and (iii) creating safeguards for support mechanisms.[168]

To abolish substituted decision-making regimes, states are obliged to refrain from any actions that deprive persons with mental health conditions and psychosocial disabilities of their right to legal capacity. States have the obligation to refrain from enacting new laws that permit substitution, and to remove substituted decision-making laws and develop alternatives of supported decision-making.[169] Ideally, legislation should provide for the right to make decisions freely, and to self-rule, think, decide and act independently without interference, on an equal basis with other members of society; and if support is required to enhance a person's autonomy and ability to think about, reflect on and express decisions regarding their mental health treatment and care, support based on the subjective will of the person concerned should be available.[170] Thus, legislation should provide an entitlement to support. Byrne and others propose that optimal mental health law should, further, give guidance on how a person's autonomy can be recognised, especially where will and preferences conflict, or where the person's mental health condition or psychosocial disability affects their will and

---

[167] CteeRPD, General Comment 1 (n 125) para 25.
[168] Anna Arstein-Kerslake & Eilionoir Flynn, 'The General Comment on Article 12 of the Convention on the Rights of Persons with Disabilities: A Roadmap for Equality Before the Law' (2016) 20(4) The International Journal of Human Rights 471, 478.
[169] See various Concluding observations of the Committee on the Rights of Persons with Disabilities, eg 'Concluding observations of the Committee on the Rights of Persons with Disabilities, Tunisia' (13 May 2011) UN Doc CRPD/C/TUN/CO/1, paras 22–23; or 'Concluding observations of the Committee on the Rights of Persons with Disabilities, Greece' (29 October 2019) UN Doc CRPD/C/GRC/CO/1, paras 17–18.
[170] Marion Byrne and others (n 112) 130.

choices.[171] Substituted decision-making regimes have three common characteristics: removing legal capacity (even if only partially); having substituted decision-makers appointed by a third person (even if this is against the will of the person concerned); and having decisions of substituted decision-makers being based on 'the best interest principle'.[172] Consequently, legislation that permits or enforces these matters is considered a violation of Article 12 CRPD, and must be abolished. The Irish Assisted Decision-Making (Capacity) Act 2015 has been acknowledged as a good example of how to avoid a violation of Article 12 CRPD.[173] By placing the will and preferences of persons with impaired mental capacity at the heart of decision-making, the Act outlines three stages of decision-making assistance: (i) decision-making assistance; (ii) co-decision-making; and (iii) decision-making representative as last resort. The decision-making assistant, appointed by the affected individual, assists and advises the affected individual to make and express a relevant decision. The co-decision-making involves joint decision-making by the affected individual and a relative or friend who has a relationship of trust with the affected individual, and who was appointed by the affected person. Only if there is no suitable co-decision-maker will the court appoint a decision-making representative, i.e. a substituted decision-maker. Despite making decisions on behalf of the affected individual, a decision-making representative must ascertain the will and preferences of the affected individual insofar as possible, and act accordingly.[174] Series and Nilsson point out, however, that even in countries where the law does not restrict the legal capacity of persons with mental health conditions and psychosocial disabilities, de facto substitution may remain because the customary practices of some societies systematically deny legal capacity.[175] Therefore, states are also obliged to take action, in the form of training or educational programmes, to prevent non-state actors, such as practitioners, legal service providers or family members, from interfering with the ability of persons with mental health conditions and psychosocial disabilities to realise their rights to legal capacity. Within the mental healthcare context, states are obliged to require all mental health personnel to obtain the free and informed consent of persons with mental health conditions and psychosocial disabilities prior to any mental health treatment. Under the state's obligation not to permit substituted decision-making, mental health staff must directly engage persons with mental health conditions and psychosocial disabilities in appropriate consultations.[176] Mental health staff can implement supported decision-making by trying to best understand, and act according to, the person's will and preferences. They could refer to what is known

---

[171] Ibid.
[172] CteeRPD, General Comment 1 (n 125) para 27.
[173] Brendan D Kelly, 'The Assisted Decision-Making (Capacity) Act 2015: what it is and why it matters' (2017) 186(2) Irish Journal of Medical Science 351–356.
[174] See The Republic of Ireland, Assisted Decision-Making (Capacity) Act 2015 (No 64 of 2015).
[175] Lucy Series & Anna Nilsson (n 113) 351; see also Lecture of Michael Njenga on 'The link between legal capacity and peer support for persons with psychosocial disabilities in Kenya' at the 9th International Disability Law Summer School of the Centre for Disability Law & Policy National University of Ireland (Galway) on 20 June 2017.
[176] CteeRPD, General Comment 1 (n 126) para 41.

about the person, or even to advance planning documents stating the person's will and preferences.[177] Importantly, however, according to the CteeRPD, developing supported decision-making systems in parallel with maintaining substituted decision-making regimes cannot be seen as being in accordance with Article 12.[178]

Key to establishing supported decision-making regimes is the recognition of the right to access and use support in decision-making. According to Byrne and others, with the right to access decision-making support comes the corresponding state obligation to provide access to such support mechanisms. First and foremost, legislation should provide a clear definition of will and preferences, the ways in which they can be expressed or determined, and guidance on how supporters can best interpret a person's will and preferences in circumstances where ongoing intensive support is required. Furthermore, legislation must clearly outline the duties, obligations and limitations of the supporter.[179] To comply with the obligation to develop and recognise support mechanisms for the exercise of legal capacity, states have to ensure that the established supported decision-making regimes incorporate certain dimensions. Based on CteeRPD General Comment 1, support for decision-making must be available to all persons, including to persons with severe psychosocial disabilities, and should be accessible at any time. Support should be contextual, and proportional to the decision-making ability of the person concerned. If affected persons are isolated and cannot rely on support in the community, for instance because of inpatient mental healthcare, states must facilitate the creation of support. Furthermore, states must ensure that financial resources are not a barrier to accessing support for exercising legal capacity. Thus, support must be available for free, or at minimal cost.[180] There are various examples of community-based supported decision-making models which have proven to be successful, such as the Personal Ombudsman in Sweden, the Open Dialogue in Finland, or the Circle of Support in Australia or the United Kingdom. The Personal Ombudsman model is a long-term engagement offered by several NGOs. The Personal Ombudsman is a skilled person who, for instance, helps clients with access to services, but only to the extent that the clients want help. The Open Dialogue approach aims to support the individual's network of friends and family in line with respecting the individual's decision-making. The Open Dialogue team seeks to engage social networks and rebuild relationships by inviting participants to voice and reflect on thoughts and feelings in non-hierarchical daily meetings. The Circle of Support is a group of persons who meet regularly to provide the affected person with support. The affected person decides, on their own, who to invite, and what to discuss in these meetings.[181] States are obliged to provide training to persons who require support on how to decide which kind of support is necessary, and for how long.[182] In mental health facilities, and in

---

[177] WHO (n 111).
[178] CteeRPD, General Comment 1 (n 125) paras 25, 26, 28.
[179] Marion Byrne and others (n 112) 135.
[180] CteeRPD, General Comment 1 (n 125) para 29.
[181] WHO (n 111) 13–14.
[182] CteeRPD, General Comment 1 (n 125) para 24.

circumstances where support persons are available, mental health personnel should ensure that these persons do not have undue influence or substitute the decisions of the affected persons.[183] This brings the discussion to the last of the three core obligations, namely to provide safeguards for support mechanisms.

In order to guarantee support that is free from abuse, misuse or unlawful interferences, states have the responsibility to set up safeguards in all processes relating to support in exercising legal capacity.[184] Such safeguards for support may consist of ensuring respect for will and preferences; acting according to the best interpretation of the will and preferences; prohibiting consent on behalf of an individual; setting up monitoring systems to ensure that the rights, will and preferences are respected at all times; ensuring assessment of support needs or time limits for support measures and judicial review; and setting up complaint mechanisms to seek damages from the supporter in the event that they act improperly.[185] While practitioners must ensure that persons with impaired decision-making can access the support they need, they should not be formal supporters themselves, because of conflict of interest and the concomitant risk of undue influence. Instead, independent support from advocates, peer supporters or others should be offered.[186]

According to Dhanda, legal obstruction is a major obstacle that undermines legal capacity, and thus its removal is essential to bring change. She argues that not only guardianship regimes should be abolished, but also laws that allow for the use of force. She further points out that, in addition to the removal of barriers, Article 12 CRPD urges states to enable participation. While this includes creating a range of support measures for decision-making and enacting them through law, enabling participation goes beyond legislation. Activities such as awareness-raising are required, and non-state actors, including community members, private mental health practitioners and judges need to be educated and trained on Article 12.[187] As a matter of fact, the CteeRPD also recommends raising awareness in society about the right to equal recognition before the law, and about how to realise the right to legal capacity, as can be derived from its Concluding Observations.[188]

The right to equality before the law, as provided in Article 12 CRPD, is recognised as a civil and political right. Civil and political rights apply from the moment of their ratification onwards, and require states to take steps to immediately realise them.[189]

---

[183] Ibid para 41.
[184] Ibid para 29.
[185] Lecture of Alberto Vásquez on 'Recognising Legal Capacity Law Reform Trends: Costa Rica, Peru and Colombia' at the 9th International Disability Law Summer School of the Centre for Disability Law & Policy National University of Ireland (Galway) on 20 June 2017.
[186] WHO (n 111).
[187] Lecture of Amita Dhanda on 'Article 12 CRPD – Understanding legal capacity' at the 9th International Disability Law Summer School of the Centre for Disability Law & Policy National University of Ireland (Galway) on 20 June 2017.
[188] See eg CteeRPD, 'Concluding observations of the Committee on the Rights of Persons with Disabilities, India' (29 October 2019) UN Doc CRPD/C/IND/CO/1, para 27(c).
[189] CteeRPD, General Comment 1 (n 125) para 30.

The CteeRPD has declared that, upon ratification of the CRPD, states must immediately begin to take deliberate and well-planned steps to realise the rights provided under Article 12, and that the provisions of Article 12 are not subject to progressive realisation.[190] Furthermore, unlike reasonable accommodation, the right to supported decision-making cannot be limited by the claim of a disproportionate or undue burden. The obligation to provide access to support in the exercise of legal capacity is absolute.[191] A common concern is the cost of establishing support structures. Yet, it needs to be acknowledged that systems of substituted decision-making also require financial resources. Furthermore, supported decision-making schemes, such as the Personal Ombudsman, have proven to reduce costs to the overall system, for example through reducing the need for healthcare services.[192] Other schemes simply formalise existing support networks, such as peer support groups.

The Committee states that there are 'no permissible circumstances ... in which a person may be deprived of the right to recognition as a person before the law, or in which this right may be limited'.[193] While some commentators propose that Article 12 should be interpreted as a non-derogable right, it is important to note that the CRPD does not include a prohibition on derogation of Article 12. Considering international law (specifically Article 16 International Covenant on Civil and Political Rights (ICCPR), the right to recognition everywhere as a person before the law), other commentators suggest that the non-derogability applies to Article 12(1) CRPD only – the recognition as a person before the law – but not to the exercise of legal capacity as contained in Article 12(2), meaning that the capacity to act can be limited.[194]

5.3.4 CONTROVERSIAL ISSUE: DISADVANTAGES EMERGING FROM UNIVERSAL LEGAL CAPACITY

The CteeRPD's objective to eliminate substituted decision-making is to be highly commended. Yet, Article 12 CRPD and the (lack of) interpretation by the CteeRPD may pose a challenge for the balance between the personal dignity and autonomy of the affected individuals (as embedded in the right to legal capacity), and the protection of their rights to health and against involuntary treatment, and even their right to life. As Szmukler questions:

---

[190] Ibid.
[191] Ibid para 34.
[192] Tommy Engman and others, 'A New Profession is Born – Personligt ombud, PO' (2008), <https://www.personligtombud.se/publikationer/pdf/A%20New%20Proffession%20is%20Born.pdf> accessed 14 November 2022, p 24.
[193] CteeRPD, General Comment 1 (n 125) para 5.
[194] Australian Human Rights Commission, 'Submission to the United Nations Committee on the Rights of Persons with Disabilities, Draft General Comment on Article 12 of the CRPD Committee' (28 February 2014), <https://humanrights.gov.au/our-work/legal/submissions-united-nations> accessed 14 November 2022, paras 15–27.

if all efforts at support have failed, or if the person refuses support, but there is still an inability to understand the facts pertinent to the decision in question, or to appreciate their relevance, or to use, weigh, or reason with that information in terms of what is important to that person, to his or her beliefs and values, to his or her personal life goals or personal conception of the good, is his or her choice to be nevertheless accepted?[195]

The text of Article 12, but also its related General Comment, leave open questions for the practical implementation of the Article. Central to arguments for the universal legal capacity regime are the concepts of equality and non-discrimination.[196] Yet, determining whether there has been discrimination depends on whether there is agreement on what constitutes disadvantages, which is the origin of debates concerning Article 12.

One argument is based on whether a specific legal capacity regime discriminates against persons with psychosocial disabilities in a disadvantageous manner. The supposition of the universal legal capacity proponents is that depriving legal capacity is in itself disadvantageous, and commonly results in more disadvantages, namely the appointment of substituted decision-makers, institutionalisation and forced treatment. These views, although advanced by many scholars, are not universally held.[197] Some scholars, such as Freeman and others or Dawson, claim that substituted regimes are a critical means of actually protecting and upholding the rights of persons with psychosocial disabilities.[198] Herring proposes that 'the best interest principle' is a way to safeguard interventions,[199] especially for persons with psychosocial disabilities who might fail to determine the best therapeutic.[200] Even the ECtHR jurisprudence frames life-saving medical treatments against the will of individuals whose mental capacity is impaired as a positive obligation under human rights law.[201] To protect someone's health, substituted decision-making on behalf of a person with serious psychosocial disability is also recommended under the Council of Europe's Recommendation No R (99) 4.[202] On the other hand, Serie and Nilsson have highlighted extensive literature showing the risks of limiting an individual's self-determination and self-expression, as well as the harm of guardianship, institutionalisation and forced treatment.[203]

The second argument in the universal legal capacity debate focuses on the harm that can arise if the universal legal capacity paradigm prohibits all forms of non-consensual interventions. Could securing another right within the CRPD be a legitimate aim for

---

[195] George Szmukler (n 14) 36.
[196] Namely that it applies to persons with mental health conditions and psychosocial disabilities on an equal basis with others.
[197] Lucy Series & Anna Nilsson (n 113) 362.
[198] See Melvyn Freeman and others (n 13); and John Dawson (n 14) 70–79.
[199] Jonathan Herring, *Vulnerable Adults and the Law* (Oxford University Press 2016) 63.
[200] Sergio Ramos Pozón, 'The convention on the rights of persons with disabilities and mental health law: A critical review' (2016) 10(4) European Journal of Disability Research 301, 306.
[201] See *Arskaya v Ukraine,* App no 45076/05 (ECtHR, 5 December 2013).
[202] See Council of Europe, Committee of Ministers, 'Recommendation No R (99) 4 on principles concerning the legal protection of incapable adults' (23 February 1999), principle 25.
[203] Lucy Series & Anna Nilsson (n 114) 362–363.

an intervention? It is often emphasised that securing the right to life (Article 10) or the right to health (Article 25), in relation to self-harm practices – meaning choices that are likely to bring death or a long-term deterioration of health – should allow for depriving a person of their right to legal capacity in order to actually 'save' or 'help' the person or the people surrounding the individual. As Litins'ka proposes, some self-harm practices have to be regarded as cries for help, and not as a wish or preference to die.[204] Under the ICCPR framework 'not every differentiation of treatment will constitute discrimination, if the criteria for such differentiation are reasonable and objective and if the aim is to achieve a purpose which is legitimate under the Covenant.'[205] Freeman and his colleagues raise a compelling argument by asking 'if a person having a severe exacerbation of affective or psychotic illness is not provided proven, effective treatment, can he or she be said to be receiving the highest attainable standard of health?'[206]

Would it undermine the right to mental health to allow a person to stay in a psychotic state instead of giving involuntary treatment, at least to the point of sufficient recovery to accept or refuse treatment in an informed manner?[207] The CRPD framework does not provide an answer to how potentially conflicting rights should be balanced. Especially in emergency situations, the interpretation of a person's will and preferences, which requires consideration of past information and engagement with families and friends, arguably poses a challenge.[208] The opinions of human rights scholars on this matter vary widely. Hendriks suggests that protecting the dignity of persons who are (temporarily) unable to make informed decisions requires and justifies, 'paradoxically as this may sound, in certain, carefully examined and exceptional circumstances', involuntary institutionalisation and forced treatment.[209] Arstein-Kerslake and Flynn emphasise that respecting a person's will and preferences should never amount to an abandonment of the person concerned. While Article 12 calls for respect for the will and preferences, that does not mean that state interventions are impermissible, especially if a person's will and preferences would result in serious harm to themselves or to others. Rather, according to Arstein-Kerslake and Flynn, Article 12 suggests that these interventions must be imposed on an equal basis on persons with or without psychosocial disabilities. Moreover, such interventions should not amount to substituted decision-making.[210] Possibly, this is how Article 12 CRPD should be understood, to ensure that it can be applied to *all* real-life situations,[211] especially emergency situations. In contrast to this viewpoint, Series and Nilsson submit that 'individual autonomy including the freedom to make one's own choices,

---

[204] Yana Litins'ka (n 115) 127.
[205] HRCtee, 'CCPR General Comment No. 18: Non-discrimination' (10 November 1989), para 13.
[206] Melvyn Freeman and others (n 13) 846.
[207] Ibid.
[208] Marion Byrne and others (n 112) 139.
[209] Aart Hendriks, 'UN Convention on the Rights of Persons with Disabilities' (2007) 14(3) European Journal of Health Law 273, 279.
[210] Anna Arstein-Kerslake & Eilionoir Flynn (n 169) 484–486.
[211] Emphasis added.

and independence of persons'[212] is within the first general principle of the Convention, whereas 'protection' does not appear amongst the CRPD principles (Article 3 CPRD). When taking General Comment 1 and responses to complaints before the CteeRPD into account, they discuss that the text of the CRPD can 'unlikely [be interpreted] to find measures such as forced treatment or institutionalisation as proportionate to serving any legitimate aims within the CRPD'.[213] But could interference with the autonomy of persons with mental health conditions and psychosocial disabilities be justified if it results in more autonomy and self-determined actions in the long run? In this book's sections on non-consensual treatment (section 5.4) and institutionalisation (section 5.5), this discussion of the balancing of conflicting rights (the right to health versus the right to be free from torture and ill-treatment, and the right to life versus the right to liberty, respectively) will be continued, including the balancing of interests between individuals with mental health conditions and psychosocial disabilities and society in general.

5.3.5 SYNOPSIS

The existing jurisprudence of regional human rights courts shows that the partial and, in exceptional cases, full, deprivation of legal capacity can be permitted, provided that procedural safeguards and proportionality requirements are met, and upon the condition that objective medical evidence shows that the degree of psychosocial disability warrants the deprivation of capacity.[214] This is in contrast to the new paradigm approach of Article 12 CRPD, under which an impairment, even a severe psychosocial disability, cannot be grounds for denying legal capacity. The right to legal capacity, as enshrined in Article 12, marks a shift from substitution to an era without paternalistic guardianship regimes: an era where persons with psychosocial disabilities receive help through supporters – if possible from the community. In summary, the right to mental health, coupled with the principle of support for legal capacity in Article 12, creates a new approach to decision-making in the context of mental health.

Despite ongoing controversies, Article 12 CRPD has influenced domestic, regional and international law-making bodies. It has been considered in domestic and regional jurisprudence,[215] national legal capacity legislation reforms,[216] and reports and

---

[212] UNGA, CRPD (n 23) art 3(a).
[213] Lucy Series & Anna Nilsson (n 113) 365.
[214] Phil Fennell, 'Article 15: Protection against Torture and Cruel or Inhuman or Degrading Treatment or Punishment' in Ilias Bantekas, Michael Ashley Stein & Dimitris Anastasiou (eds), *The UN Convention on the Rights of Persons with Disabilities: A Commentary* (Oxford University Press 2018) 439–440.
[215] Anna Lawson and Lisa Waddington (eds), *Domestic Interpretation of the UN Convention on the Rights of Persons with Disabilities: A Comparative Analysis* (Oxford University Press 2017).
[216] See eg Robert Dinerstein, 'Emerging international trends for practices in guardianship laws for people with disabilities' (2016) 22 ILSA Journal of International and Comparative Law 435–460.

procedures within the UN and WHO systems.[217] And while the interpretation of Article 12 is contested, the goal of ending substituted decision-making is considered central to lowering the risk of a wider range of human rights infringements, such as forced treatment and institutionalisation,[218] which will be addressed in the following sections 5.4 and 5.5.

To conclude the subsection on legal capacity and the protection of persons not able to give consent, the following table provides an overview of the scope of, and obligations arising from, Article 12, as analysed above:

Table 5.3: Summary of the scope of, and obligations arising from, Article 12 CRPD

Scope	– The right to legal capacity, meaning the capacity to hold rights and duties, and to exercise and act upon these rights and duties; or, in other words, the right to make a decision. • Recognition that legal capacity and mental capacity are distinct concepts, the latter being a person's putative psychological ability to make a decision (in other words, a person's decision-making skills). – The right to access supported decision-making in the event of impaired decision-making skills. • Support based on (the best interpretation of) the will and preferences of the person concerned. • Effective and appropriate safeguards to ensure that support is rightfully carried out.
Obligations	– Abolishing regimes of substituted decision-making. – Providing access to supported decision-making. – Creating safeguards for support.

5.4 PROTECTION FROM NON-CONSENSUAL MENTAL HEALTH TREATMENT

The key purposes of mental health services are to promote and protect the mental health and well-being of individuals. Any treatment of persons with mental health conditions and psychosocial disabilities should aim to preserve their dignity and autonomy, reduce the impact of their illnesses, and improve their quality of life.[219] Yet, in service provision around the world, people with mental health conditions and psychosocial disabilities are particularly vulnerable to coercion. Principally, coercion can be understood as any action which is inconsistent with the wishes of the affected individual, and which is undertaken without informed consent, to make the individual

---

[217] See eg UNGA, 'Report of the Special Rapporteur on torture and other cruel, inhuman or degrading treatment or punishment, Juan E. Méndez' (n 61); or WHO, Office of the High Commissioner for Human Rights and other UN Agencies, *Eliminating forced, coercive and otherwise involuntary sterilization: An interagency statement* (WHO 2014).
[218] Lucy Series & Anna Nilsson (n 113) 341.
[219] See WHO, 'Mental health care law: Ten basic principles' (1996), <https://www.who.int/gender-equity-rights/knowledge/mental-health-care-law/en/> accessed 14 November 2022.

behave or stop behaving in a specific way.[220] In the mental health context, coercion refers to non-consensual admission and non-consensual treatment. Non-consensual treatment, which is the focus of this section, includes various forms of forced treatment (such as forced medication); seclusion, such as isolating someone; and restraints, including physical restraint (holding someone down), mechanical restraint (using ropes or chains to tie someone down) or chemical restraint (using medication to control the behaviour of the individual).[221] Coercion against persons with mental health conditions and psychosocial disabilities can also be more subtle. For instance, individuals can be made to believe that negative actions will be taken against them, or that certain things will be refused to them, if they do not comply with a treatment; or individuals might be given medication without their knowledge (for example, hidden in food).[222] Non-consensual admission and the concomitant institutionalisation will be elucidated separately in section 5.5. Coercion is not exclusive to private or public psychiatric facilities, but can also occur in the community, at home, or in the provision of social services.

Former Special Rapporteur on the Rights of Persons with Disabilities, Catalina Devandas-Aguilar, considered the main problem of coercion in the context of mental health: that it is widely accepted, and that legal exceptions normalise coercion in mental health practice, which opens the door for human rights violations to occur.[223] The basis for coercive practices, says Devandas-Aguilar, is the existing power asymmetry. In some cases, coercion is authorised by national legislation, and exceptions under human rights rhetoric further legitimise coercion as a last resort, or for security reasons, to protect the person concerned or others. Irrespective of this, she argues that 'coercion is in no way protection', and that violating human rights cannot be used to protect other human rights.[224]

Non-consensual treatment by psychiatric personnel, other health or medical professionals and caregivers falls under the scope of the right to personal integrity (Article 17 CRPD); freedom from torture or cruel, inhuman or degrading treatment or punishment (Article 15 CRPD); and freedom from exploitation, violence and abuse (Article 16 CRPD). To address and stop coercive practices in mental health service provision, more respect must be given to these particular CRPD norms. Therefore, this section examines each of these provisions with respect to their roles in promoting and protecting the right to mental health.

---

[220] WHO, 'Freedom from coercion, violence and abuse: WHO QualityRights core training: mental health and social services: course guide' (2019), <https://apps.who.int/iris/handle/10665/329582> accessed 14 November 2022, p 4.
[221] Ibid p 5.
[222] Ibid.
[223] Keynote address of Catalina Devandas-Aguilar at the 9th International Disability Law Summer School of the Centre for Disability Law & Policy National University of Ireland (Galway) on 23 June 2017.
[224] Ibid.

Chapter 5. A Human Rights Approach to Psychosocial Disability

While all Articles of the CRPD are interrelated and relevant to this topic, the other most directly relevant Articles are Articles 12 and 14 CRPD. Article 12 CRPD, as already explained in more depth in section 5.3, requires states to ensure that service providers and others respect an individual's choices, and do not carry out any interventions against the individual's will and preferences. Article 14 CRPD, the right to liberty and security, is important, as detention in mental health services is often a setting for, and accompanied by, coercion. As mentioned above, involuntary admission and institutionalisation will be analysed in more detail in section 5.5. Acts of non-consensual treatment, and especially ill-treatment or torture, can also be the cause of mental health conditions and psychosocial disabilities. This aspect, however, goes beyond the scope of this section. The questions that will be addressed throughout this section are: what does the right to be free from non-consensual treatment imply in the mental healthcare context? And what measures do states have to take? The aim of this section is to evaluate the implications of the rights to respect for one's physical and mental integrity; to be free from torture or cruel, inhuman or degrading treatment or punishment; and to be free from exploitation, violence and abuse, for the realisation of the right to mental health.

A human rights approach to disability, in the context of consensual treatment, implies that mental healthcare counselling and treatment should be on a voluntary basis.[225] The CRPD always prioritises the importance of the autonomy and dignity of persons with psychosocial disabilities, including when undergoing mental healthcare treatment. Each of the norms analysed in this section are reminders that persons with mental health conditions and psychosocial disabilities are rights-holders when undergoing mental health treatment or using mental health services. In consideration of their vulnerability, the CRPD offers guidance on how to prevent coercion, and how best to safeguard the right to mental health when treating individuals.

This section is divided into five subsections. First, the interconnection of non-consensual treatment and the right to the highest attainable standard of health norm will be illustrated (subsection 5.4.1). Article 17 CRPD, as a general principle of non-consensual treatment and protection against forced treatment, will then be discussed (subsection 5.4.2). Following this is an examination of Article 15 CRPD and treatment amounting to torture and ill-treatment (subsection 5.4.3). The next subsection will examine the opportunities for Article 16 CRPD to provide broader protection against non-consensual treatment (subsection 5.4.4). Before drawing some conclusions, the state obligations with regard to mental healthcare, derived from the various components of Articles 15, 16 and 17 CRPD, will be outlined (subsection 5.4.5). Throughout the section, controversial issues will be raised and discussed.

---

[225] UNGA, 'Report of the Special Rapporteur on the right of everyone to the enjoyment of the highest attainable standard of physical and mental health, Anand Grover' (n 136) para 24.

5.4.1 NON-CONSENSUAL TREATMENT AND THE RIGHT TO HEALTH NORM

Some scholars classify forced psychiatric interventions as outright breaches of the right to the highest attainable standard of health.[226] But to what extent does the right to health norm, specifically as found in Article 12 ICESCR and Article 25 CRPD, implicate freedom from non-consensual treatment?

Indisputably, the CteeESCR has interpreted Article 12 ICESCR, in its General Comment 14, as including the right to be free from interferences, such as torture, non-consensual medical treatment and experimentation.[227] At the same time, however, the Committee specifically allows for applying coercive medical measures for the treatment of mental health conditions, without further elaborating to what extent, or under which circumstances.[228] It can be argued that this provision, found in General Comment 14, is outdated, and has been superseded by the standards set forth in the CRPD. Nevertheless, even since the CRPD came into force, the CteeESCR merely asks states to reduce the recourse to coercive treatment in the mental health context, and it still allows for treatment without informed consent when 'exceptional circumstances require otherwise'.[229] Once more, it is observed that the CteeESCR is reluctant to offer more clarification.

The travaux préparatoires reflecting the drafting process of Article 25 CRPD included a debate about involuntary psychiatric admission and treatment, which led to the adoption of a separate provision (now Article 17): the right to respect for one's physical and mental integrity.[230] Nevertheless, Article 25(d) CRPD can be seen as being of particular relevance to the right to be free from non-consensual treatment, as it enshrines that healthcare services should be provided to persons with psychosocial disabilities on the basis of valid consent, which (in practice) means free and informed consent. While informed consent has already been elaborated on in section 5.3, the characteristics of free consent, delineated from the CRPD's preparatory works, emphasise non-coercion.[231] If medical or therapeutic procedures are administered without free consent, they constitute involuntary treatment.[232] While the right to

---

[226] See eg We Shall Overcome, 'Forced psychiatric interventions as disability-based discrimination. Parallel Report to the 5th Periodic Report of Norway to the UN Committee on Economic, Social and Cultural Rights for the 51 session (4 – 29 November 2013)' (September 2013), p 4; or Tina Minkovitz, 'Prohibition of Compulsory Mental Health Treatment and Detention Under the CRPD' (2011) SSRN Electronic Journal.

[227] CteeESCR, General Comment 14 (n 33) para 8.

[228] Ibid para 34.

[229] See eg CteeESCR, 'Concluding observations on sixth periodic report of Denmark' (n 116) paras 56–57; or 'Concluding observations on the second periodic report of Kazakhstan' (n 116) para 45(a).

[230] Penelope Weller (n 20) 713. See definition of free consent also eg UN Human Rights Office of the High Commissioner, 'Free, Prior and Informed Consent of Indigenous Peoples' (September 2013), <https://ohchr.org/Documents/Issues/ipeoples/freepriorandinformedconsent.pdf> accessed 14 November 2022.

[231] Yana Litins'ka (n 115) 125.

[232] UNGA, 'Report of the Special Rapporteur on the right of everyone to the enjoyment of the highest attainable standard of physical and mental health, Dainius Pūras' (n 6) para 17.

health norm under the CRPD clearly implies that mental healthcare must be free of coercion, it does not indicate whether this regulation is absolute, irrespective of the circumstances.

By way of an additional remark, neither the CteeESCR nor the CteeRPD have made any statements on the possible need for compulsory treatment specifically in emergency situations. The state obligations deriving from the right to the highest attainable standard of health norms are to provide proper mental healthcare. The treaty bodies do not impose any obligation of forced treatment, for instance to prevent the deterioration of health. In that regard, the CteeESCR has explicitly stated that the right to health does not mean the right to be healthy.[233] Yet, mental healthcare is often accompanied with coercive practices based on 'the best interest principle', 'necessity' or 'dangerousness'. To ensure that the right to mental health framework protects persons with mental health conditions and psychosocial disabilities better against non-consensual treatment while accessing mental health services, the author will connect the right to the highest attainable standard of health norm, in turn, to Articles 17, 15 and 16 CRPD. The following analysis of the additional Articles will also help in finding a way forward with regard to exceptional circumstances.

5.4.2 INVOLUNTARY TREATMENT AND THE PROTECTION OF INTEGRITY (ARTICLE 17 CPRD)

> 'The nurses would make us have the medications in front of them. If I complained that there were too many tablets, the nurse would sometimes forcefully put the pills in my mouth and stroke my throat to send them down, the way I feed my dogs ... I woke up one night and I couldn't move; my body was in intense physical pain. A nurse came and jabbed an injection into my body, without even taking off my clothes. You are treated worse than animals; it's an alternate reality.' – 46-year-old woman with a perceived psychosocial disability, Delhi.[234]

According to the travaux préparatoires of the CRPD, the drafters initially discussed whether forced medical treatment is tantamount to torture, and should therefore be considered under the Article dealing with torture or cruel, inhuman or degrading treatment or punishment. Without considering forced medical treatment separately, however, members of the Ad Hoc Committee argued that abuses which did not amount to torture or cruel, inhuman or degrading treatment would then be left unregulated. Consequently, agreement was reached that involuntary interventions were connected more to personal integrity and, thus, should be considered under a separate Article.[235] Article 17 CRPD (then draft Article 12) was originally entitled 'Freedom from Violence

---

[233] CteeESCR, General Comment 14 (n 33) para 8.
[234] WHO (n 220) 13.
[235] See United Nations, Ad Hoc Committee, Daily summary of discussion at the fifth session, Vol 6, No 5, the positions of Costa Rica, Trinidad and Tobago, the EU, Liechtenstein, and New Zealand (28 January 2005), <www.un.org/esa/socdev/enable/rights/ahc5sum31jan.htm> accessed 14 November 2022.

and Abuse', but was later split into 'the protection of personal integrity' (now Article 17) and 'freedom from exploitation, violence, and abuse' (now Article 16). The reason for this split was that the Articles deal with related, but different, issues.[236]

Before the entry into force of the CRPD, no UN human rights treaty included the right to personal integrity. Nonetheless, the right to privacy, and the right to be free from torture or cruel, inhuman or degrading treatment or punishment, could be seen as its precursors. For example, the aim of the latter has previously been defined as 'protect[ing] both the dignity and the physical and mental integrity of the individual'.[237] Similarly to Article 17 CRPD, the Charter of Fundamental Rights of the European Union (EUCFR) provides, in Article 3, a stand-alone norm on the right to the integrity of the person. In relation to the specific field of medicine, the Article expounds respect for 'the free and informed consent of the person concerned, according to the procedures laid down by law'.[238] In the American Convention on Human Rights (ACHR), the right to have one's physical, mental and moral integrity respected is linked with the right to humane treatment,[239] whereas the African Charter for Human and People's Rights (AfChHPR) calls for the protection of integrity under its right to life norm.[240] Physical and mental integrity are, further, at the core of Article 8 ECHR, the right to respect for private life.[241] What differentiates Article 17 CRPD most from these regional human rights norms is the requirement of reasonable accommodation for enabling access to support when exercising the right to protection the integrity of the person, which is likely the most fundamental element of the CRPD.

5.4.2.1 The Scope of the Right to Protect the Integrity of the Person

Article 17 CRPD provides for 'the right to respect for his or her physical and mental integrity on an equal basis with others', and can be understood as a general principle regarding treatment in mental health institutions.[242] Instead of losing personal integrity due to disability, Article 17 reaffirms that persons with disabilities possess their own personal integrity, which has to be respected on an equal footing with that

---

[236] Francesco Seatzu, 'Article 17: Protecting the Integrity of the Person' in Ilias Bantekas, Michael Ashley Stein & Dimitris Anastasiou (eds), *The UN Convention on the Rights of Persons with Disabilities: A Commentary* (Oxford University Press 2018) 495.

[237] United Nations International Human Rights Instruments, 'Compilations of general comments and general recommendations adopted by Human Rights Treaty Bodies' (29 July 1994) UN Doc HRI/GEN/1/Rev.1, referring to General Comment 20, para 2.

[238] European Union, Charter of Fundamental Rights of the European Union (EUCFR), art 3(2)(a).

[239] Organization of American States, American Convention on Human Rights (adopted 22 November 1969, entered into force 18 July 1978) OAS Treaty Series No 36, 1144 UNTS 123, art 5(1).

[240] Organization of African Unity, African Charter on Human and Peoples' Rights (Banjoul Charter) (adopted 27 June 1981, entered into force 21 October 1986) 1520 UNTS 271, art 4.

[241] See eg *Storck v Germany*, App no 61603/00 (ECtHR, 16 June 2005) paras 103, 143, or *Glass v the United Kingdom*, App no 61827/00 (ECtHR, 9 March 2004) para 70.

[242] UNGA, CRPD (n 23) art 17.

of others.243 On the one hand, if a society as a whole accepts certain limitations on one's personal integrity, persons with (psychosocial) disabilities have no greater rights than others. On the other hand, and by virtue of Article 17, limitations singling out persons with (psychosocial) disabilities are prohibited.244 The text of Article 17 consists of a single sentence focusing on the issue of non-discrimination, using 'right to personal integrity' terminology and offering no further elaboration. At the time of this study, the CteeRPD had not (yet) released a General Comment on Article 17. To determine the scope of the Article, Concluding Observations issued by the Committee can be analysed. Recommendations drawn from the CteeRPD's reporting procedure reveal that informed consent is a key element of Article 17. In the Concluding Observations on Cyprus and Bosnia-Herzegovina, for instance, the CteeRPD has expressed its concern regarding medical treatments without the individual, prior, free and informed consent of the persons concerned, and the lack of support mechanisms for decision-making.245 This points to the inextricable link between Article 17 and Article 12 CRPD, considering that Article 12 is crucial in the event that the need for support to exercise free and informed consent arises. Keys suggests that addressing the issue of free and informed consent to (mental health) interventions can be understood as the main goal of Article 17, as the concept of free and informed consent is the gatekeeper to personal integrity.246 Mental health treatment that is based on valid consent would not, therefore, raise any issues under Article 17 CRPD. Treatment based on misinterpretation, or treatment given without full information, or under threat, would, however, constitute involuntary treatment, and thus, raise concerns under Article 17.247

In a general healthcare context, it has been proposed that, for simple medical procedures, implied consent from a patient is sufficient, whereas express consent is required for complex or invasive treatments.248 Arnardóttir argues that, given the extraordinary character of psychiatric treatment, mental health interventions should, as a rule, be regarded as invasive treatments and, thus, require express consent.249 This assertion is also supported by jurisprudence. In *Luis Eduardo Guachalá Chimbó*

---

243 Tina Minkowitz, 'The United Nations Convention on the Rights of Persons with Disabilities and the Right to Be Free from Nonconsensual Psychiatric Interventions' (2007) 34(2) Syracuse Journal of International Law and Commerce, 412.
244 Tina Minkovitz (n 226).
245 CteeRPD, 'Concluding Observations on the initial Report of Cyprus' (8 May 2017) UN Doc CRPD/C/CYP/CO/1, paras 41–42; and 'Concluding Observations on the initial Report of Bosnia and Herzegovina' (2 May 2017) UN Doc CRPD/C/BIH/CO/1, para 33.
246 May Keys, 'Article 17 [Protecting the Integrity of the Person]' in Valentina Della Fina, Rachele Cera & Giuseppe Palmisano (eds), *The United Nations Convention on the Rights of Persons with Disabilities* (Springer International Publishing 2017) 329.
247 UNGA, 'Report of the Special Rapporteur on the right of everyone to the enjoyment of the highest attainable standard of physical and mental health, Dainius Pūras' (n 6) para 17.
248 In this context, 'invasive treatment' means treatment that interferes with a person's physical integrity. Nevertheless, the author acknowledges that 'simple medical procedures' can also (indirectly) have profound health or other effects; UNGA, 'Report of the Special Rapporteur on the right of everyone to the enjoyment of the highest attainable standard of physical and mental health, Anand Grover' (n 136) para 13.
249 Oddný Mjöll Arnardóttir (n 5) 264.

v Ecuador, the IACHR found that the medical treatment performed had restricted the applicant's autonomy, integrity and health because his prior, full and informed consent had not been sought. The Inter-American Commission concluded that the treatment was, therefore, an unjustified paternalistic intervention amounting to a violation of, inter alia, the right to have his physical, mental and moral integrity respected under Article 5(1) of the American Convention.[250] Moreover, the ECtHR has clarified, in several instances, that even minor interferences with the personal integrity of a person with mental health condition and psychosocial disability are unlawful if they are carried out against the individual's will.[251] In *Storck v Germany*, the applicant resisted medical treatment, and had to be administered medication by force on several occasions while being involuntarily placed in a locked ward at a psychiatric institution. This treatment against her will was found to constitute an interference with her right to respect for private life.[252] Also, in *Glass v the United Kingdom*, the ECtHR held that the administration of forced medication in a mental health context amounts to a violation of the individual's personal integrity. This case concerned a child with mental and physical disabilities who was subject to medical treatment, notwithstanding the continuous objection to the proposed treatment by his mother, who acted as his legal proxy. Being unable to challenge his status, and the conclusion that a fair balance had not been struck between the child's health needs and his right of dignity, the ECtHR considered that the treatment, against the will of the mother, breached the applicant's right to respect for private life, and in particular his right to personal integrity.[253]

5.4.2.2 Limitations on the Enjoyment of Personal Integrity

Despite consensus on the need to respect the personal integrity of persons with mental health conditions and psychosocial disabilities, coercive mental health treatment and other restrictive practices have been legitimised to some extent. Under the ECHR framework, limitations to personal integrity are allowed if they are in accordance with the law and proportionate to the legitimacy of the aim pursued, for instance to protect the person concerned or others.[254] For example, in *Grare v France* (1992), the applicant was forcibly given psychiatric medication, which had distressing side effects. He claimed that this constituted inhuman and degrading treatment, and a breach of respect for his private life. Whether the medical treatment was administered with or without the applicant's consent remained unclear. The former European Commission of Human Rights rejected the application, arguing that, even though the treatment had unpleasant side effects, it did not reach the minimum level of severity necessary to engage Article 3, the prohibition of torture or cruel, inhuman or degrading treatment. According to the

---

[250] *Luis Eduardo Guachalá Chimbó v Ecuador* (n 75) paras 182–183.
[251] *Storck v Germany* (n 241) para 143.
[252] Ibid paras 142–153.
[253] *Glass v the United Kingdom* (n 241) paras 70–72.
[254] Council of Europe, European Convention for the Protection of Human Rights and Fundamental Freedoms, as amended by Protocols Nos 11 and 14, 4 November 1950, ETS 5, art 8(2).

Commission, if the treatment in question had been an invasion of his right to private life under Article 8(1) ECHR, it could have been justified under Article 8(2) ECHR because of the need to preserve public order, and to protect the applicant's health.[255] Along similar lines, The IACHR has recognised that, in emergency situations where medical treatment must be given in order to preserve the individual's life or health, and where the individual cannot give consent, the informed consent requirement (including the right to refuse treatment) does not apply. Importantly, the exception to obtaining informed consent must be based on a specific emergency situation, and not merely the fact of the individual having a mental health conditions and psychosocial disabilities.[256] The IACHR reasoned that it is the state that bears the responsibility for ensuring the integrity and health of persons institutionalised in mental health centres.[257] With regard to these justifications, it is worthwhile looking into the negotiations relating to Article 17 CRPD. One of the members of the Ad Hoc Committee stated that:

> [t]he problem is that disability is often wrongly characterised as a medical emergency. An episode of madness or psychosis is not a medical emergency, it is a disability that requires a solution arrived at in consultation with the person. In addition, social prejudice often leads to the incorrect characterisation of disability as a threat to public health.[258]

The text of Article 17 and the CteeRPD interpretations so far do not reveal whether the right to personal integrity can be limited in exceptional situations under the Convention. On previous occasions, the CteeRPD has merely recommended ensuring that decisions relating to a person's physical or mental integrity require the free and informed consent of the person concerned; and that access to independent support must be provided, if needed.[259] Emerging from the CteeRPD's case law is the Committee's approach towards the issue that any mental health treatment should be rejected without the consent of the person involved.[260] In searching for possible limitations on Article 17, it may be helpful to look into the drafting history and related negotiations and discussions about the topic at stake. According to the Vienna Convention on the Law of Treaties, the drafting history of a treaty can be used to supplement the interpretation of an Article if its meaning is ambiguous or obscure.[261] It emerges from the travaux of Article 17 that involuntary treatment, in line with specific safeguards, might be authorised in the contexts of medical emergencies or risk to public health. The Ad Hoc Committee on a Comprehensive and Integral International Convention on

---

[255] See *Grare v France*, App no 18835/91 (ECtHR, 2 December 1992) (Admissibility Decision).
[256] *Luis Eduardo Guachalá Chimbó v Ecuador* (n 75) paras 138, 167.
[257] Ibid para 168.
[258] Ad Hoc Committee, 7th Session, 'Draft Art 17 – Protecting the integrity of the person, International Disability Caucus' (19 January 2006), <www.un.org/esa/socdev/enable/rights/ahc7docs/ahc7idcchairamend1.doc> accessed 14 November 2022.
[259] CteeRPD, General Comment 1 (n 125) para 42.
[260] Francesco Seatzu (n 236) 504.
[261] United Nations, Vienna Convention on the Law of Treaties (adopted 23 May 1969, entered into force 27 January 1980), 1155 UNTS 331, art 32.

the Protection and Promotion of the Rights and Dignity of Persons with Disabilities published the working text of Article 17 as follows:

1. States Parties shall protect the integrity of the person or persons with disabilities on an equal basis with others.
2. States Parties shall protect persons with disabilities from forced interventions or forced institutionalization aimed at correcting, improving or alleviating any actual or perceived impairment.
3. In cases of medical emergency or issues of risk to public health involving involuntary interventions, persons with disabilities shall be treated on an equal basis with others.
4. [States Parties shall ensure that involuntary treatment of persons with disabilities is:
   a. Minimized through the active promotion of alternatives;
   b. Undertaken only in exceptional circumstances, in accordance with procedures established by law and with the application of appropriate legal safeguards;
   c. Undertaken in the least restrictive setting possible, and that the best interests of the person concerned are fully taken into account;
      a. Appropriate for the person and provided without financial cost to the individual receiving the treatment or to his or her family.][262]

Other Articles within the Convention are designed to apply to persons who are able to give consent, for instance Article 15(1) ('no one shall be subjected without his or her free consent') or Article 25(d) ('on the basis of free and informed consent'). Therefore, Paragraph 4 was meant for the protection of persons who are unable to consent to treatment.[263] However, Paragraph 4 was placed in brackets from the outset because of strong disagreement. It was argued that this paragraph would set a lower standard for persons with disabilities regarding informed consent. Additionally, Paragraph 3 was disputed by opponents who claimed that including regulatory safeguards provided legitimacy for non-consensual interventions.[264] As a consequence, the controversial paragraphs were rejected, any references to non-consensual interventions or institutionalisation were omitted, and Article 17 was reduced to how it currently stands. In its current form, the single sentence of Article 17 is silent on whether involuntary interventions are permitted, or whether the enjoyment of the right to personal integrity is subject to limitations. Kayess and French critically argue that, in order to avoid conflict during the negotiations, the Ad Hoc Committee adopted an Article that – without providing any specific regulations – fails to fulfil the very essence of its

---

[262] UNGA, 'Report of the Ad Hoc Committee on a Comprehensive and Integral International Convention on the Protection and Promotion of the Rights and Dignity of Persons with Disabilities on its seventh session' (13 February 2006) UN Doc A/AC265/2006/2.
[263] Bernadette McSherry, 'Protecting the Integrity of the Person: Developing Limitations on Involuntary Treatment' (2008) 26(2) Law in Context: Socio-Legal Journal 111, 114.
[264] Francesco Seatzu (n 236) 497.

existence, namely to regulate the use of coercion for the purpose of treatment.[265] So how can Article 17 be interpreted regarding (exceptional) non-consensual treatment? In spite of interpretations issued by the CteeRPD, Szmukler and others argue that, '[i]t seems unlikely that an intention behind the CRPD was to exclude the possibility of all forms of non-consensual treatment in all cases'.[266] If a person with no mental health conditions and psychosocial disabilities is treated, in an emergency situation, without his or her consent, due to a coma or semicoma, then it should also be permissible to treat persons with mental health conditions and psychosocial disabilities in emergency situations without their consent, if their decision-making skills are (temporarily) impaired. At least this is what the term 'on an equal basis with others', enshrined in Article 17, connotes. Drawing from regional interpretations, McSherry suggests that the right to personal integrity can best be understood as limiting some, but not all, non-consensual mental health interventions.[267] She proposes that the right protects 'the competent patient from unwanted treatment and the incompetent patient from unbeneficial treatment', and that it has to be understood as limiting 'overly intrusive treatment'.[268] For instance, she has referred to the European Committee for the Prevention of Torture and Inhuman or Degrading Treatment or Punishment (CPT)'s institutional standards, which recognise that the use of restraints can rarely be justified and should be limited, and that the use of electroconvulsive therapy can no longer be accepted in mental health treatment.[269] Keys reasons that Article 17 presents a broad right intended to protect personal integrity against various abuses of formal or informal power, with a scope that is theoretically limitless.[270] While many actions can potentially impact on physical or mental integrity, she suggests that the principles of self-determination, personal autonomy and inherent dignity, which can be seen as the ethical and legal normative justifications for informed consent,[271] can offer guidance when it comes to the application of Article 17.[272]

The emphasis of the final text of Article 17 is on guaranteeing informed consent.[273] This once again underlines the human rights approach of the CRPD, as discussed in the introduction of this chapter: instead of clarifying to what extent persons with disabilities can be deprived of their rights, the Convention aims at the full enjoyment of the rights; in this case, informed consent to treatment and, if needed, with support.

---

[265] Rosemary Kayess & Phillip French, 'Out of darkness into light? Introducing the Convention on the rights of persons with disabilities' (2008) 8(1) Human Rights Law Review 1, 30.
[266] George Szmukler and others. 'Mental health law and the UN Convention on the rights of persons with disabilities' (2014) 37(3) International Journal of Law and Psychiatry 245, 250.
[267] Bernadette McSherry (n 263) 114.
[268] Ibid pp 119, 121.
[269] See Council of Europe: European Committee for the Prevention of Torture and Inhuman or Degrading Treatment or Punishment (CPT), 'The CPT standards' (8 March 2011) CPT/Inf/E (2002) 1 – Revised 2010, paras 39, 47, 48.
[270] May Keys (n 246) 329.
[271] UNGA, 'Report of the Special Rapporteur on the right of everyone to the enjoyment of the highest attainable standard of physical and mental health, Anand Grover' (n 136) para 9.
[272] May Keys (n 246) 329.
[273] Ibid p 328.

Does the scope of this new right under international human rights law go beyond the substance of existing norms? Even before the enforcement of the CRPD, human rights courts had found violations of the right to personal integrity under other rights, such as the right to privacy, as discussed above (see subsection 5.4.2.1). Yet, the importance of Article 17 CRPD cannot be underestimated. For the first time, the right to respect for physical and mental integrity is set out at an international level instead of purely at the regional level. It is also important to understand the interpretation and application of the right to personal integrity, based on its interrelationship with Article 12 CRPD and the derived obligations to provide access to support.

As the CteeRPD Concluding Observations show, non-consensual interferences in mental healthcare not only raise concerns under Article 17; the Committee has also issued specific recommendations with respect to Article 15 CRPD, which contains the right to be free from torture or cruel, inhuman or degrading treatment or punishment. The protective scope of Article 17 does not have a minimum threshold of severity and thus, also encompasses minor non-consensual interventions. Yet, it is acknowledged that forced medical treatment can, in fact, also amount to torture or ill-treatment under Article 15 if a certain minimum level of severity is attained.[274]

5.4.3 SITUATIONS AMOUNTING TO TORTURE OR ILL-TREATMENT (ARTICLE 15 CRPD)

> Despite a 1977 government ban on the practice, people with psychosocial disabilities continue to be shackled by family members, traditional healers, and staff in state institutions, in some cases for years.[275]

In general, mental healthcare providers try to help people with mental health conditions and psychosocial disabilities understand and recover from their conditions. Recovery (which is more than treatment) can be supported but not imposed.[276] It is also not the norm for providers to intentionally mistreat and punish patients. Yet, people with mental health conditions and psychosocial disabilities continue to be subject to severe abuses in and outside of mental healthcare institutions around the world.[277] In this regard, non-consensual treatment and other harmful practices not only violate the right to informed consent as part of the right to personal integrity, but may also constitute cruel, inhuman or degrading treatment or punishment (ill-treatment), and may even amount to torture.

Article 15 CRPD prohibits ill-treatment and torture, acts that have been regulated extensively in international law since before the adoption of the CRPD. It is a recognised

---

[274] See eg Oddný Mjöll Arnardóttir (n 5) 265; or Francesco Seatzu (n 236) 504.
[275] Human Rights Watch (n 27) 278.
[276] Mike Slide, 'The contribution of mental health services to recovery' (2009) 18(5) Journal of Mental Health 367.
[277] UNGA, 'Report of the Special Rapporteur on torture and other cruel, inhuman or degrading treatment or punishment, Juan E. Méndez' (n 61) para 59.

prohibition in universal and regional human rights treaties, such as in Article 7 ICCPR, Article 5 ACHR, Article 5 AfChHPR and Article 3 ECHR, which are all provisions that allow no derogation from the right to be free from ill-treatment or torture, even in times of public emergency. Although persons with disabilities are a protected group under these provisions, there is an added value to such provisions in the context of the CRPD, for persons with psychosocial disabilities in general, and for persons with psychosocial disabilities living in institutions in particular. Firstly, when considering the degree of suffering and whether this reaches the threshold of ill-treatment or torture, the very circumstances of the person with psychosocial disabilities need to be considered. Secondly, there is ample evidence that persons with psychosocial disabilities who live in institutions are particularly vulnerable to ill-treatment, ranging from unspeakable indignities to neglect or severe forms of seclusion and restraint.[278] Of course, such ill-treatment can also take place outside of the institutional setting, at home. Violence and abuse also extend to treatment in the private sphere, and inside the home, at the hands of family members, community members, health professionals or other caregivers.[279] When such practices are perpetrated against persons with psychosocial disabilities, they often remain unseen, or it is claimed that they are justified. Therefore, it is valuable to incorporate Article 15 CRPD into the discussion, in order to delineate particularities for the mental healthcare context.

In the drafting process for Article 15 CRPD, a key issue for debate was whether to bring non-consensual treatment within the absolute prohibition in the anti-torture provision, as already mentioned above.[280] After several working group discussions, a prior, and still controversial, draft Article 15 (then Article 11) stated that:

1. States Parties shall take all effective legislative, administrative, judicial, educational or other measures to prevent persons with disabilities from being subjected to torture or cruel, inhuman or degrading treatment or punishment.
2. In particular, States Parties shall prohibit, and protect persons with disabilities from, medical or scientific experimentation without the free and informed consent of the person concerned, and shall protect persons with disabilities from forced interventions or forced institutionalization aimed at correcting, improving or alleviating any actual or perceived impairment.[281]

---

[278] See Antonio Marchesi, 'Article 15 [Freedom from Torture or Cruel, Inhuman or Degrading Treatment or Punishment]' in Valentina Della Fina, Rachele Cera & Giuseppe Palmisano (eds), *The United Nations Convention on the Rights of Persons with Disabilities* (Springer International Publishing 2017) 309–310; and UNGA, 'Interim report of the Special Rapporteur on torture and other cruel, inhuman or degrading treatment or punishment, Manfred Nowak' (28 July 2008) UN Doc A/63/175, para 38.

[279] UNGA, 'Interim report of the Special Rapporteur on torture and other cruel, inhuman or degrading treatment or punishment, Manfred Nowak' (n 278) para 39.

[280] Phil Fennell (n 214) 430–432.

[281] UNGA, 'Report of the Working Group to the Ad Hoc Committee on a Comprehensive and Integral International Convention on the Protection and Promotion of the Rights and Dignity of Persons with Disabilities' (27 January 2004) UN Doc A/AC265/2004/WG/1 Annex 1, 16–17.

The second part of Paragraph 2, regarding non-consensual interventions (both treatment and admission), was subject to vigorous debate throughout the drafting process, and did not find its way into Article 15 of the Convention. In the final version, the drafters adopted the verbatim text of Article 7 ICCPR, and Article 15(2), dealing with preventive measures, mirrored Article 2 of the UN Convention against Torture and Other Cruel, Inhuman or Degrading Treatment or Punishment (CAT). Article 15 CRPD reads as follows:

1. No one shall be subjected to torture or to cruel, inhuman or degrading treatment or punishment. In particular, no one shall be subjected without his or her free consent to medical or scientific experimentation.
2. States Parties shall take all effective legislative, administrative, judicial or other measures to prevent persons with disabilities, on an equal basis with others, from being subjected to torture or cruel, inhuman or degrading treatment or punishment.[282]

The text that emerged from the drafting process has been described as 'a relatively sparse provision', but if it is read together with other CRPD norms, this would 'most certainly expand its meaning and intended application'.[283] In the following subsections, the scope of Article 15 and its meaning within the disability context, and particularly mental health treatment, will be clarified.

5.4.3.1   The Scope of the Right to be Free from Torture or Ill-treatment

For non-consensual mental health treatment to be considered through the lens of ill-treatment and torture, it must be clarified whether, and under what circumstances, such treatment engages Article 15 CPRD.[284] Naturally, the voluntary use of certain substances or procedures in the course of mental health treatment must be distinguished from non-consensual interventions, and cannot be considered torture or ill-treatment.[285]

5.4.3.1.1   The Definition of Torture and Ill-treatment in regard to Mental Healthcare

Ill-treatment and torture, as included in Article 15(1) CRPD, have previously been defined in international law, and through the practices of international bodies such

---

[282]   UNGA, CRPD (n 23) art 15.
[283]   Janet E Lord, 'Shared Understanding or Consensus – Masked Disagreement? The Anti-Torture Framework in the Convention on the Rights of Persons with Disabilities' (2010) 33 Loyala of Los Angeles International and Comparative Law Review, p 27.
[284]   The author acknowledges that the denial of treatment or postponing necessary treatment also raises concerns under Article 15 CRPD, as will be briefly mentioned below. However, addressing these issues in more detail is beyond the scope of this chapter, which addresses human rights concerns that arise once persons are already part of the mental healthcare system.
[285]   Tina Minkowitz (n 243) 418.

Chapter 5. A Human Rights Approach to Psychosocial Disability

as treaty bodies and regional courts. The Inter-American Convention to Prevent and Punish Torture is a human rights instrument that directly prohibits 'the use of methods upon a person intended to obliterate the personality of the victim or to diminish his physical or mental capacities, even if they do not cause physical pain or mental anguish.'[286] The Inter-American Convention defines methods such as psychotropic drugs and psychosurgery as torture under this norm, irrespective of whether they cause severe pain or suffering.[287] The most widely endorsed definition of the crime of torture can be found in the CAT, although its relationship to non-consensual treatment is not as apparent as that in the Inter-American Convention. The CAT definition specifies that an act has to fulfil four elements, namely: (i) severe physical or mental pain or suffering; (ii) an element of intent; (iii) a specific purpose; and (iv) state involvement or the acquiescence of a public official.[288]

For the first element, Arnardóttir argues that whether the degree of pain and suffering reaches the threshold of torture depends on the nature and context of the treatment, the manner in which it is carried out, its duration, the physical and mental effects of the treatment, and the condition of the person concerned, among other factors.[289] Marchesi observes that the subjective nature of pain and suffering could lead to the conclusion that a treatment which is generally lawful could amount to torture, on account of the higher degree of pain and suffering in which it results for persons with psychosocial disabilities.[290] As Minkowitz explains, most persons are subject to non-consensual interventions 'in the midst of intense psychological experiences, so that the suffering caused by additional trauma can be unbearable'.[291] Moreover, pain and suffering should not only be understood as the conscious experience of the person concerned, but must also include the subsequent physical and psychological effects of the methods that were applied.[292]

Regarding the second element, the requirement of intent, it has been found that, in healthcare settings, this element is not only fulfilled through a state's action or inaction with the purpose of degrading, humiliating or punishing, but also where such action or inaction nevertheless leads to such a result.[293] Former Special Rapporteur on Torture, Manfred Nowak, considers that the requirement of intent 'can be effectively implied where a person has been discriminated against on the

---

[286] Organization of American States, Inter-American Convention to Prevent and Punish Torture (9 December 1985) OAS Treaty Series, No 67, art 2.
[287] Tina Minkowitz (n 243) 417.
[288] See UNGA, Convention Against Torture and Other Cruel, Inhuman or Degrading Treatment or Punishment (CAT) (adopted 10 December 1984, entered into force 26 June 1987) 1465 UNTS 85, art 1(1); and UNGA, 'Report of the Special Rapporteur on torture and other cruel, inhuman or degrading treatment or punishment, Manfred Nowak' (5 February 2010) UN Doc A/HRC/13/39/Add.5, para 30.
[289] Oddný Mjöll Arnardóttir (n 5) 265.
[290] Antonio Marchesi (n 278) 311.
[291] Tina Minkowitz (n 243) 420.
[292] Ibid p 419.
[293] UNGA, 'Report of the Special Rapporteur on torture and other cruel, inhuman or degrading treatment or punishment, Juan E. Méndez' (n 61) para 18.

basis of disability'.[294] In mental healthcare, this is particularly relevant because discriminatory practices are often masked as good intentions. This will not be prejudged here, as the good intention justification will be discussed shortly.

The third element of the CAT definition, the purpose requirement, includes as a purpose punishment, intimidation, coercion or discrimination of any kind, among others.[295] Punishment, according to Minkowitz, is often implicit in non-consensual treatment. She explains that it is not only punishment for specific acts, 'but for having caused concern, annoyance, or anger in others'.[296] This third requirement implies that, provided that the other three elements of the definition are present, mental health treatment aimed at discriminating against the person concerned would amount to torture. Marchesi reasons that medical treatment of persons with psychosocial disabilities which inflicts severe pain and suffering 'will amount to torture or to other prohibited ill-treatment whenever it is not justified by a therapeutic purpose as, in such an event, it would be likely to have [a] discriminatory nature'[297] and, possibly, one or more other purposes, such as intimidation or coercion. Furthermore, former Special Rapporteur on Torture, Juan Méndez, observes that, alongside supposedly therapeutic aims, the explicit or implicit aim of inflicting punishment or intimidation often exists.[298]

The fourth element, the requirement for the involvement of the state, has been defined as relating to public officials, whether acting in their official or private capacities, and also as applying to doctors or other healthcare and social workers, including those who work in private hospitals and institutions, as well as other private parties.[299] Thus, the fourth element is satisfied when personnel are involved that have control over, or responsibility for, the treatment and care of persons with psychosocial disabilities, especially but not exclusively in institutions. Special Rapporteur on Torture, Nils Melzer, refers to this constitutive element as 'powerlessness', which arises when individuals are deprived of their liberty, for instance through hospitalisation or institutionalisation, or even through the deprivation of legal capacity.[300]

Treatment that falls short of one or more elements of the torture definition may still amount to inhuman or degrading treatment. For example, Nowak considers that negligent conduct which lacks the intent criteria can still amount to ill-treatment if it

---

[294] UNGA, 'Interim report of the Special Rapporteur on torture and other cruel, inhuman or degrading treatment or punishment, Manfred Nowak' (n 278) para 49.
[295] UNGA, CAT (n 289) art 1(1).
[296] Tina Minkowitz (n 243) 422.
[297] Antonio Marchesi (n 278) 312.
[298] UNGA, 'Report of the Special Rapporteur on torture and other cruel, inhuman or degrading treatment or punishment, Juan E. Méndez' (n 61) para 22.
[299] See HRCtee, 'General comment No 20: Article 7 ((Prohibition of torture, or other cruel, inhuman or degrading treatment or punishment)' (27 May 2008), UN Doc HRI/GEN/1/Rev.9 (Vol. I) para 2; Phil Fennell (n 214) 447; and UNGA, 'Interim report of the Special Rapporteur on torture and other cruel, inhuman or degrading treatment or punishment, Manfred Nowak' (n 278) para 51.
[300] UNGA, 'Report of the Special Rapporteur on torture and other cruel, inhuman or degrading treatment or punishment, Nils Melzer' (20 March 2020) UN Doc A/HRC/43/49, para 40.

leads to severe pain or suffering.[301] The jurisprudence of the ECtHR has established that a mental health treatment is deemed to be 'inhuman' when 'it was premeditated, was applied for hours at a stretch and caused either actual bodily injury or intense physical or mental suffering'.[302] It is considered 'degrading' when 'it was such as to arouse in the victims feelings of fear, anguish and inferiority capable of humiliating and debasing them'.[303] Certainly, mental health treatment (or its consequences) must attain a minimum level of severity for it to fall under the scope of torture or ill-treatment.[304] For that reason, Article 15 CRPD is implicated in more serious cases that involve neglect, the use of force, or mental and physical abuse. Yet, the assessment of a minimum level of severity is relative. As explained above, in each case the methods used, duration, context and effects of the treatment must be considered. Despite deviating opinions regarding what kind of mental health treatment constitutes ill-treatment or torture, there seems to be general agreement regarding the administration of unmodified electroconvulsive therapy (ECT), meaning without anaesthetic and muscle relaxants. According to the Council of Europe's CPT Standards, the WHO, and Nowak, unmodified ECT qualifies as ill-treatment or torture.[305]

The ECtHR distinguishes between inhuman or degrading treatment and torture in such a way that a *deliberate* inhuman treatment that causes very serious or cruel suffering is usually classified as torture.[306] Thus, treatment with the sole purpose of disciplining persons with psychosocial disabilities would possibly be considered as torture under the ECtHR. The CteeRPD, on the other hand, characterises all sorts of ill-treatment as breaches of Article 15 CRPD, without differentiating between torture and cruel, inhuman or degrading treatment or punishment. In its Concluding Observations on Chile, for instance, the Committee expressed its deep concerns:

> about evidence that practices such as psychosurgery, electroconvulsive therapy, extended isolation in cells without heating or basic services, physical restraints and other types of treatment deemed to be cruel, inhuman or degrading are employed in the State party with the sole purpose of 'disciplining' or 'correcting deviant behaviour' in persons with psychosocial disabilities.[307]

---

[301] UNGA, 'Interim report of the Special Rapporteur on torture and other cruel, inhuman or degrading treatment or punishment, Manfred Nowak' (n 278) para 49.

[302] *Kudla v Poland*, App no 30210/96 (ECtHR, 26 October 2000) para 92.

[303] Ibid.

[304] This is based on the opinion of the European Commission of Human Rights that ill-treatment must attain a minimum level of severity to fall within the scope of the prohibition of torture; see *Ireland v United Kingdom*, App no 5310/71 (ECtHR, 18 January 1978) para 162.

[305] See Council of Europe, European Committee for the Prevention of Torture and Inhuman or Degrading Treatment or Punishment, 'Involuntary placement in psychiatric establishments' (31 August 1998), <https://www.coe.int/en/web/cpt/psychiatry> accessed 14 November 2022, para 39; UNGA, 'Interim report of the Special Rapporteur on torture and other cruel, inhuman or degrading treatment or punishment, Manfred Nowak' (n 278), para 61; and WHO, 'WHO QualityRights Tool Kit'(2012), <https://www.who.int/mental_health/publications/QualityRights_toolkit/en/> accessed 14 November 2022, p 83.

[306] Emphasis added; Phil Fennell (n 214) 443.

[307] CteeRPD, 'Concluding Observations on the initial Report of Chile' (13 April 2016) UN Doc CRPD/C/CHL/CO/1, para 33.

In its Concluding Observations on India, the Committee also described subjecting persons with psychosocial disabilities to physical and chemical restraints, forced medication, coercion, physical abuse, humiliation, electroconvulsive therapy and shackling as forms of violence and ill-treatment.[308]

5.4.3.1.2 Treatment without Consent

Medical *experimentation* (which is not the same as medical treatment) without one's free consent is explicitly prohibited in the second sentence of Article 15(1) CRPD.[309] Irrespective of efforts during the drafting process, this prohibition does not extend to non-consensual *treatment*.[310] Nevertheless, the right to be free from torture and ill-treatment has also been applied to the broader context of medical interventions. Shortly after the coming into force of the CRPD, where notably the second paragraph of Article 15 had been shortened regarding non-consensual treatment, Nowak offered significant support for the new CRPD paradigm. In his report he stated that 'medical treatments of an intrusive and irreversible nature, when they lack a therapeutic purpose, *or aim at correcting or alleviating a disability*, may constitute torture and ill-treatment if enforced or administered without the free and informed consent of the person concerned.'[311] Hence, non-consensual treatment that is intended to correct or alleviate psychosocial disability could constitute ill-treatment or torture. Administering lobotomy, psychosurgery and electroconvulsive therapy without the consent of the person concerned would, in Nowak's view, amount to a violation of Article 15.[312] In its Concluding Observation on Norway, the CteeRPD also expressed concerns, under Article 15, over the use of non-consensual electroconvulsive treatment in its modified form, and recommended that such practices should be abolished completely.[313] The same will likely be true for mind-altering drugs, such as neuroleptics, that cause trembling, shivering or contractions, or which make the individual apathetic; these are commonly used to manage psychosis, but are also used as a form of punishment. Neuroleptics have highly sedative effects and, thus, have been used as emergency sedation or rapid tranquilisation, despite their adverse side effects, ranging from Parkinsonian symptoms to type 2 diabetes.[314] In *Viana Acosta v Uruguay*, the Human Rights Committee (HRCtee) concluded that the mental health treatment of the complainant, which included injecting tranquilisers against his will, constituted inhuman treatment.[315] The CteeRPD refers to emergency sedation or rapid

---

[308] CteeRPD, 'Concluding Observations on the initial Report of the Republic of India' (n 188) para 32(c).
[309] Emphasis added; UNGA, CRPD (n 23) art 15(1).
[310] Emphasis added.
[311] Emphasis added; UNGA, 'Interim report of the Special Rapporteur on torture and other cruel, inhuman or degrading treatment or punishment, Manfred Nowak' (n 278) para 47.
[312] Ibid paras 40, 59.
[313] CteeRPD, 'Concluding Observations on the initial Report of Norway (7 May 2019) UN Doc CRPD/C/NOR/CO/1, paras 25–26.
[314] Phil Fennell (n 214) 451.
[315] *Antonio Viana Acosta v Uruguay*, Communication No 110/1981 (HRCtee, 29 March 1984), paras 2.7, 10, 14 and 15.

tranquilisation as 'chemical restraint', and condemns it as ill-treatment in its reports.[316] In the Committee's Concluding Observation on Germany, chemical restraints are even recognised as acts of torture.[317]

Despite obliging states to prevent persons with psychosocial disabilities from being subject to torture or ill-treatment in Article 15(2), matters that fall within the 'more serious harm' category of Article 15 CRPD are not precisely defined. Derived from jurisprudence, the matters of: (i) seclusion and restraints; and (ii) living conditions in institutions will be analysed in more detail below. Interestingly, human rights courts have also interpreted that the right to be free from torture and ill-treatment may be breached by a failure to provide adequate mental health treatment.[318] This is especially relevant for persons with a high risk of self-harm, or who are known to be suicidal. However, the issue of suicide, in connection with the right to life, will be analysed in more depth under the right to liberty, in section 5.5.

5.4.3.2 Seclusion and Restraints

Seclusion, also referred to as solitary confinement, is the involuntary confinement of a person alone in a room from which leaving is physically prevented.[319] The term 'restraint' can be defined as any method or equipment that cannot be removed, and that restricts an individual's freedom of movement.[320] In mental health services, seclusion and restraint are commonly used during severe distress or emotional crises, but also as a form of punishment.[321] Persons may be placed in solitary confinement, tied to beds for prolonged periods – including with chains and handcuffs – or be locked in caged beds, or over-medicated as a form of chemical restraint.[322]

In academic literature, seclusion and restraints are often discussed under Article 17 CRPD rather than under Article 15 CRPD.[323] However, given that solitary confinement and prolonged restraint in mental healthcare institutions have been declared as having no therapeutic justification, both measures – for even a short period of time – may constitute ill-treatment or torture.[324] Seclusion and physical, mechanical or chemical restraints are identified as violations of Article 15 in various Concluding Observations

---

[316] See eg CteeRPD, 'Concluding Observations on the initial Report of Serbia' (23 May 2016) UN Doc CRPD/C/SRB/CO/1, para 27–28; CteeRPD, 'Concluding Observations on the initial Report of Slovakia' (17 May 2016) UN Doc CRPD/C/SVK/CO/1, para 45.

[317] CteeRPD, 'Concluding Observations on the initial Report of the Republic of Germany' (n 101) para 33.

[318] See eg *Keenan v United Kingdom*, App no 27229/95 (ECtHR, 3 April 2001) paras 115–116; or *Luis Eduardo Guachalá Chimbó v Ecuador* (n 75) para 143.

[319] The author acknowledges that there are patients who choose for confinement or isolation. In this book, however, the term 'seclusion' includes a non-consensual component.

[320] Francesco Seatzu (n 236) 504.

[321] WHO (n 220) p xii.

[322] UNGA, 'Interim report of the Special Rapporteur on torture and other cruel, inhuman or degrading treatment or punishment, Manfred Nowak' (n 278) para 55.

[323] See eg May Keys (n 246); Bernadette McSherry (n 263); or Francesco Seatzu (n 236).

[324] UNGA, 'Report of the Special Rapporteur on torture and other cruel, inhuman or degrading treatment or punishment, Juan E. Méndez' (n 61) para 63.

of the CteeRPD.[325] The jurisprudence of regional human rights bodies affirms this characterisation. In the case of *Ximenes-Lopes v Brazil*, the victim was detained in a private psychiatric hospital. After refusing to come out of the bathroom during an aggressive episode, he was overpowered by a nurse and two other patients, during which he suffered severe injuries. He was then placed under physical restraint and medicated without consent. After becoming aggressive again later that day, he was once again physically restrained with his hands tied behind his back until the following day when his mother visited. Seeing her son's pain, she asked for medical assistance, which was not carried out properly. On the same day, Ximenes-Lopes died of injuries that were established to have been caused by a 'blunt instrument'.[326] Concerning practices at the institution, the Inter-American Court of Human Rights (IACtHR) found that patients were under the constant threat of physical attack by staff who were untrained to work with persons with psychosocial disabilities. It also recognised that patients were subject to violence while suffering from critical health conditions, as physical restraint and control techniques were frequently imposed during crisis situations.[327] The Court further considered that the type of physical restraint to which Ximenes-Lopes was exposed was inconsistent with the need to provide decent mental health treatment, and did not protect personal integrity. To be in accordance with Article 5 of the American Convention, the right to humane treatment, the Court declared that:

> [Restraint] should be used as a last resort and with the only purpose of protecting the patient, or else the medical staff or third persons, when the behavior of the patient involved is such as to pose a threat to their safety. Restraint can have no purpose other than the foregoing, and should be implemented only by qualified staff rather than by patients.[328]

An accompanying expert report by Eric Rosenthal stated that the excessive use of physical strength, the beating and the restraint constituted degrading treatment, especially because there was no evidence that indicated imminent danger for Ximenes-Lopes or others, and neither was there proven to have been any attempt to use less aggressive control methods.[329] Regarding the cruel, inhuman and degrading treatment suffered by Ximenes-Lopes, the Court found a violation of the right to humane treatment as established in Articles 5(1) and 5(2) of the Convention.[330] In Judge Sergio Garcia-Ramirez's reasoned opinion in the judgment, he pointed out that measures taken

---

[325] See eg CteeRPD, 'Concluding Observations on the initial Report of Slovakia' (n 316) paras 43–44; or CteeRPD, 'Concluding Observations on the initial Report of Germany' (n 101) para 35.
[326] *Ximenes-Lopes v Brazil* (Merits, Reparations, and Costs) IACtHR Series C no 149 (4 July 2006), para 112(1)-(15).
[327] Ibid para 120.
[328] Ibid para 134.
[329] Ibid p 13.
[330] Article 5(1) states: 'Every person has the right to have his physical, mental, and moral integrity respected.'; Article 5(2) states: 'No one shall be subjected to torture or to cruel, inhuman, or degrading punishment or treatment. All persons deprived of their liberty shall be treated with respect for the inherent dignity of the human person.'; *Ximenes-Lopes v Brazil* (n 326) para 150.

regarding persons with mental health conditions and psychosocial disabilities should be 'consistent with the characteristics of the suffering and the need for treatment, ... [as] reasonable and moderate as practicable and aim at relieving pain and foster[ing] well-being'.[331]

In *Rosario Congo v Ecuador*, the Inter-American Commission found that subjecting persons with mental health condition and psychosocial disabilities to solitary confinement (seclusion) can involve an even more serious violation than that of the right to have one's physical, mental and moral integrity respected. It established that solitary confinement constitutes inhuman and degrading treatment, and therefore a violation of Article 5(2) of the American Convention, which reads as follows:

> No one shall be subjected to torture or to cruel, inhuman, or degrading punishment or treatment. All persons deprived of their liberty shall be treated with respect for the inherent dignity of the human person.[332]

Congo, who suffered from a mental disorder, was detained at a social rehabilitation centre. Owing to his mental state, he was moved to an isolation cell where he remained for approximately 40 days until he died.[333] The Commission considered the violation of Article 5(2) to have been aggravated because Congo had been left in isolation, unable to satisfy his basic needs. In that regard, it concluded that Ecuador had violated his right to 'be treated with respect for the inherent dignity of the human person'.[334]

The ECtHR has also found violations of the right to be free from inhuman and degrading treatment (Article 3 ECHR) regarding the use of restraints in more recent cases. In *Bures v Czech Republic*, the applicant had been brought to a sobering-up centre after taking an overdose of medicine that was part of his mental health treatment. There, he was immediately put in a multiple-point restraint belt, and was subsequently placed in this belt for up to two hours at a time, on three occasions during one night. The belt caused severe bilateral paresis of the elbow nerves. In line with the medical necessity doctrine, the government tried to justify the treatment based on the restlessness of the applicant. The Court, however, observed that the strapping was applied as a matter of routine, and no alternative methods had been tried to calm the applicant. It concluded that, despite the government's attempted justification, it had failed to show that the application of restraint measures was necessary and proportionate in the circumstances.[335] In *MS v Croatia (No. 2)*, the applicant had been tied to a bed in a psychiatric hospital for 15 hours despite her diagnosed back pain problems, causing great distress and physical pain. The ECtHR found no evidence of her having been aggressive or posing immediate or imminent harm to herself or others. Therefore, the

---

[331] *Ximenes-Lopes v Brazil* (Merits, Reparations, and Costs) IACtHR Series C no 149 (4 July 2006), Reasoned Opinion of Judge Sergio Garcia-Ramirez, para 25.
[332] Organization of American States, American Convention on Human Rights (n 239) art 5(2).
[333] *Rosario Congo v Ecuador*, IACHR Report No 63/99 (13 April 1999), paras 55–59.
[334] Ibid para 59.
[335] *Bures v The Czech Republic*, App no 37679/08 (ECtHR, 18 January 2013) paras 83–100.

Court was not satisfied that the use of restraint had been necessary and proportionate in the circumstances, and thus found that there had been inhuman and degrading treatment, in violation of Article 3 ECHR.[336] In contrast to Bures and MS, in the case of *Aggerholm v Denmark* the ECtHR found that there had been sufficient grounds to strap the applicant to a restraint bed.[337] Aggerholm had originally been confined to a psychiatric hospital because of a criminal conviction involving violence, and at the time of his restraint, he allegedly posed an imminent danger to himself or others, and alternatives to the restraint measures were not available. The Court found, however, that the authorities had failed to prove that restraining the applicant for 23 hours had been 'strictly necessary', that it had respected the applicant's human dignity, and that it had not exposed him to pain and suffering. The Court, therefore, concluded that, with regard to the continuation and duration of the measure, there had been a violation of Article 3 ECHR.[338]

Caged beds, whether metal or netted, have been found to constitute ill-treatment, and various human rights bodies, including the European Committee for the Prevention of Torture, the UN Committee against Torture, and the UN Human Rights Committee, have called for them to be banned.[339] Instead of abolishing restraint measures, many countries resorted to alternative forms of restraint once the use of caged beds was officially banned. In the example of the Czech Republic, Fennell observed that, in recent years, psychiatric hospitals had initially changed from metal to netted caged beds, but due to the prohibition of these by law, institutions had then started to remove caged beds and make use of 'degrading alternatives'.[340] In its Concluding Observations on the Czech Republic, the CteeRPD clearly condemned these alternatives, and urged the state to 'immediately prohibit the use of mechanical and chemical restraints in psychiatric institutions on persons with psychosocial disabilities'.[341]

In various other Concluding Observations, the CteeRPD has expressed its concerns regarding seclusion and restraints, in particular the use of straps or belts for more than 48 hours, and the use of net beds, physical restraints, or, as elaborated above, chemical restraints.[342] The Committee has referred to these non-consensual practices in mental health institutions as amounting to ill-treatment and torture, and has thus urged states to eliminate the use of solitary confinement and restraints.[343] Former Special Rapporteur Méndez supports the views of the CteeRPD, and calls for an 'absolute

---

[336] *MS v Croatia (No 2)*, App no 75450/12 (ECtHR, 19 February 2015) paras 99–112.
[337] *Aggerholm v Denmark*, App no 45439/18 (ECtHR, 15 September 2020) paras 89–98.
[338] Ibid paras 102–114.
[339] Phil Fennell (n 214) 461.
[340] Ibid.
[341] CteeRPD, 'Concluding Observations on the initial Report of the Czech Republic' (15 May 2015) UN Doc CRPD/C/CZE/CO/1, para 32.
[342] See eg CteeRPD, 'Concluding Observations on the initial Report of Austria' (30 September 2013) UN Doc CRPD/C/AUT/CO/1, paras 32–33; or CteeRPD, 'Concluding Observations on the initial Report of Denmark' (30 October 2014) UN Doc CRPD/C/DNK/CO/1, paras 38–39.
[343] See eg May Keys (n 246) 333; or UNGA, 'Mental health and human rights, Report of the United Nations High Commissioner for Human Rights' (n 32) para 33.

ban' on such non-consensual measures, especially in all places where individuals are deprived of their liberty, including psychiatric and social care institutions. In his opinion, environments that allow for using seclusion and restraint also foster other non-consensual interventions, such as forced medication or ECT.[344] Moreover, in extreme cases, persons with mental health condition and psychosocial disabilities have also died from being secluded and restrained, including deaths resulting from asphyxia or cardiac arrest during the use of bodily force, or from overdoses in situations of chemical restraints to control their behaviour.[345]

5.4.3.3 Living Conditions in Mental Health Institutions

In several cases, persons with alleged psychosocial disabilities have been found to have been treated in a way that was inhuman or degrading because of having been admitted to a mental health facility with conditions that were incompatible with the respect for their dignity.[346] This infringement of the right to be free from torture and ill-treatment is closely linked to institutionalisation, which will be discussed in section 5.5. In the interests of coherence, however, the matter of living conditions will be analysed under this section relating to situations amounting to ill-treatment and torture.

As early as 1980, the European Commission held that keeping a person in isolation in a psychiatric hospital under inhuman conditions, namely without clothing, toilet facilities, furniture or ventilation, was a violation of Article 3 ECHR: the right to be free from torture or inhuman or degrading treatment.[347] Later jurisprudence shows that the general living conditions in mental health institutions can also amount to cruel, inhuman and degrading treatment. One of these cases is *Purohit and Moore v The Gambia*, which was heard before the African Commission. Drawing from previous case law, the African Commission found that cruel, inhuman or degrading treatment must be interpreted so as to extend the widest possible protection against physical or mental abuses, and that exposing persons with mental health conditions and psychosocial disabilities to personal suffering and indignity violates their right to human dignity. The Commission argued that persons with mental health conditions and psychosocial disabilities have the right to enjoy a decent life, as normal and full as possible: a right that should be guarded and forcefully protected. Consequently, the Commission found that the living conditions, among other things, at the mental health institution

---

[344] UNGA, 'Report of the Special Rapporteur on torture and other cruel, inhuman or degrading treatment or punishment, Juan E. Méndez' (n 61) para 63.
[345] Bernadette McSherry, 'Regulating seclusion and restraint in health care settings: The promise of the Convention on the Rights of Persons with Disabilities' (2017) 53 International Journal of Law and Psychiatry 39, 41.
[346] For the completeness of the picture: There are situations where persons with psychosocial disabilities are exposed to unliveable conditions outside of mental health institutions, either because they are homeless or live in a completely unliveable house. For their own protection, they are institutionalised, often against their will. This matter falls outside the scope of this subsection and is addressed in subsection 5.4.4.2 about the tension between protection and autonomy.
[347] See *A v United Kingdom*, App no 6840/74, 3 E.H.R.R. 131 (European Commission 1980).

violated the respect for human dignity and the prohibition against cruel, inhuman or degrading treatment, as contained in Article 5 AfChHPR.[348] Similarly, in the *Ximenes-Lopes v Brazil* judgment, the Inter-American Court concluded that a person with mental health conditions and psychosocial disabilities can be treated in an inhuman or degrading way because of the mere fact of having been admitted to an institution where the hospitalisation conditions, in and of themselves, violate the right to humane treatment.[349] *Stanev v Bulgaria* is recognised as the first case before the European Court in which living conditions in a social care institution were found to constitute inhuman and degrading treatment. The Court observed that, for a period of approximately seven years, the applicant had been exposed to concerning living conditions, which it enumerated in detail:

> [T]he food was insufficient and of poor quality. The building was inadequately heated and in winter the applicant had to sleep in his coat. He was able to have a shower once a week in an unhygienic and dilapidated bathroom. The toilets were in an execrable state and access to them was dangerous … In addition, the home did not return clothes to the same people after they were washed … which was likely to arouse a feeling of inferiority in the residents.[350]

The ECtHR found these conditions to constitute degrading treatment and, for this reason, the Court found a violation of Article 3 ECHR.[351]

In recent Concluding Observations, the CteeRPD has urged states to take measures to ensure that the living conditions of persons with disabilities in institutions respect the dignity of individuals and comply with the provisions of Article 15 CRPD.[352] In the report on Greece, for example, the Committee expressed its concerns about overcrowding, and the lack of specific measures to satisfy daily requirements to ensure respect for dignity, in mental healthcare institutions.[353]

5.4.3.4 *Controversial Issue: Justifications for Restrictive Interventions*

There seems to be agreement that involuntary treatment, when used to inflict severe pain or suffering, can constitute ill-treatment or torture, but when it comes to non-consensual treatment for the benefit of the patient and others, there are dissenting opinions. Especially when it comes to care for persons with mental health conditions and psychosocial disabilities, healthcare professionals frequently justify restrictive treatments without consent as being intended to benefit the patient, or as medically necessary. Based on laws, attitudes of stakeholders and practices which depend on the

---

[348] *Purohit and Moore v The Gambia*, Communication No. 241/2001, Sixteenth Activity report 2002–2003, Annex VII, paras 54–61.
[349] See *Ximenes-Lopes v Brazil* (n 326) para 113.
[350] *Stanev v Bulgaria*, App no 36760/06 (ECtHR, 17 January 2012) para 209.
[351] Ibid paras 201–213.
[352] See eg CteeRPD, 'Concluding observations on the initial report of Kuwait' (18 October 2019) UN Doc CRPD/C/KWT/CO/1, para 30(c); and CteeRPD, 'Concluding observations on the initial report of Greece' (29 October 2019) UN Doc CRPD/C/GRC/CO/1, para 24.
[353] CteeRPD, 'Concluding observations on the initial report of Greece' (n 352) para 24.

Chapter 5. A Human Rights Approach to Psychosocial Disability

idea that mental healthcare is largely about preventing dangerous behaviour,[354] human rights bodies have also justified restrictive interventions based on the notion of medical necessity, or persons with mental health conditions and psychosocial disabilities being perceived as dangerous to themselves or others. Despite claims of good intentions, and because of the widely acknowledged discriminatory character of psychiatric care, there are other scholars who critically view non-consensual mental health treatments as satisfying both the intent and purpose criteria of torture.[355] Thus, the notion of medical necessity has sparked a wide debate, mostly among the medical and legal professions, but also within the human rights discourse. This subsection addresses the controversy about so-called emergency situations.

In *Herczegfalvy v Austria* (1992), the ECtHR introduced the term 'medical necessity' as a possible justification for non-consensual psychiatric interventions. Concluding that the treatment was medically necessary, and in line with psychiatric care of the time, the Court found that continuously sedating and forcibly feeding a patient while they were tied to a bed for a period of two weeks did not lead to a violation of the right to be free from torture or cruel, inhuman or degrading treatment or punishment.[356] The Court further articulated that the use of force might be necessary and, thus, permissible in order 'to preserve the physical and mental health of patients who are entirely incapable of deciding for themselves and for whom [medical authorities] are therefore responsible'.[357] In the CPRD framework, such a standard cannot be seen as valid; since it is based on a premise of incapacity, it is incompatible with Article 12 CRPD. The Council of Europe CPT Standards agree with the idea that, as a matter of principle, treatment of persons admitted to psychiatric institutions should be based on their consent. However, the CPT Standards allow for derogations from this fundamental principle in clearly and strictly defined exceptional circumstances, if this is based on law.[358]

The World Psychiatric Association and American Psychiatric Association argue that, in situations where psychotic persons are dangerous and attempt to injure themselves or others, restraint may be the only way to prevent severe injury, to protect other patients and healthcare workers, and to save lives. These bodies agree that restraint must be closely monitored and applied humanely, including for the shortest time possible.[359] In *Bures v The Czech Republic*, the ECtHR reinforced that any form

---

[354] UNGA, 'Report of the Special Rapporteur on the right of everyone to the enjoyment of the highest attainable standard of physical and mental health, Dainius Pūras' (15 April 2020) UN Doc A/HRC/44/48, para 27.

[355] UNGA, 'Report of the Special Rapporteur on torture and other cruel, inhuman or degrading treatment or punishment, Juan E. Méndez' (n 61) para 32.

[356] *Herczegfalvy v Austria*, App no 10533/83 (ECtHR, 24 September 1992) paras 27, 83.

[357] Ibid para 82.

[358] Council of Europe, European Committee for the Prevention of Torture and Inhuman or Degrading Treatment or Punishment (n 305) para 41.

[359] Center for Human Rights and Humanitarian Law, *Torture in Healthcare Settings: Reflections on the Special Rapporteur on Torture's 2013 Thematic Report* (American University Washington College of Law 2014) 141–145.

of torture and ill-treatment must be prohibited, irrespective of the victim's behaviour or the circumstances.[360] It added that, in mental health institutions, where a person is deprived of one's liberty, recourse to physical force that is not necessary due to the person's conduct infringes upon the right to be free from torture and ill-treatment.[361] Nevertheless, the Court also found that, in exceptional circumstances, restraints can be used as a matter of last resort for persons with mental health conditions and psychosocial disabilities. It considered that 'using restraints is a serious measure which must always be justified by preventing imminent harm to the patient or the surroundings and must be proportionate to such an aim', and further declared that '[m]ere restlessness cannot therefore justify strapping a person to a bed for almost two hours'.[362] The HRCtee, which oversees the implementation of the ICCPR, also noted, in its General Comment 35, that non-consensual interventions may be justified under the following conditions:

> [It] must be necessary and proportionate, for the purpose of protecting the individual in question from serious harm or preventing injury to others. It must be applied only as a measure of last resort and for the shortest appropriate period of time, and must be accompanied by adequate procedural and substantive safeguards established by law.[363]

Former Special Rapporteur on Torture, Juan Méndez, rejects the validity of the 'medical necessity' doctrine in mental healthcare because it continues to be an obstacle to protecting against arbitrary abuses in mental healthcare settings. He notes that merely labelling practices as medically necessary or therapeutic, or as the result of good intentions or lack of resources, is not sufficient to justify ill-treatment.[364] The present Special Rapporteur on Torture, Nils Melzer, is of the same opinion. In a recent report, he stresses that involuntary psychiatric interventions on the grounds of 'the best interest of the patient' or 'medical necessity' usually involve highly discriminatory, and even coercive, attempts to control or correct the behaviour or choices of patients. Even when carried out with 'purportedly benevolent purposes', he concludes that such practices may amount to torture.[365] Furthermore, and reaffirming that disability is often wrongly characterised as a medical emergency, former Special Rapporteur on the Right to Health, Dainius Pūras, perceives that 'dangerousness' is a discriminatory approach, based mostly on prejudice instead of evidence, which reinforces the myth that persons with mental health conditions and psychosocial disabilities are

---

[360] *Bures v The Czech Republic* (n 335) para 83.
[361] Ibid para 86.
[362] Ibid para 96.
[363] HRCtee, 'General Comment No. 35: Article 9 (Liberty and security of person)' (General Comment No. 35) (16 December 2014) UN Doc CCPR/C/GC/35, para 19.
[364] UNGA, 'Report of the Special Rapporteur on torture and other cruel, inhuman or degrading treatment or punishment, Juan E. Méndez' (n 61) paras 35, 83.
[365] UNGA, 'Report of the Special Rapporteur on torture and other cruel, inhuman or degrading treatment or punishment, Nils Melzer' (n 300) para 37.

dangerous.[366] He further observes that justifying forced interventions because of subjective determinations of 'dangerousness' or 'medical necessity' by someone other than the person concerned requires better scrutiny, from a human rights perspective.[367] In particular, the criteria of being dangerous to oneself can be viewed as paternalistic justification, based on protectionist stereotypes, and in contradiction to respect for the interest of the person concerned.[368] Often, justifying coercive practices as medically necessary can be ascribed to a lack of resources for alternative treatment approaches and, thus, structural deficits.[369] Former Special Rapporteur on the Rights of Persons with Disabilities, Catalina Devandas-Aguilar, declares that standards or jurisprudence embracing the 'medical necessity' principle are, in principle, contrary to the CPRD, as the Convention prohibits 'all forms of coercion on the basis of actual or perceived impairment, even if additional factors or criteria are used to justify them'.[370]

This is where the old paradigm (medical approach to disability) and the new paradigm (human rights approach to disability), the latter of which was introduced by the CRPD, part ways. It can be concluded that situations where an agitated or violent patient poses a challenge must be met in an ethically appropriate manner. The challenge is to match these standards of psychiatry practice, the ECtHR, the CPT, and even the Human Rights Committee, which are based on actual crisis or emergency situations, and which represent compromise, with the uncompromising approach of the CRPD, as embraced by the CteeRPD and the Special Rapporteurs. The country study of Ghana in section 6.3 suggests a way of closing the gap between the real situation on the ground and what is mandated by the CRPD framework.

5.4.4 A BROADER PROTECTION AGAINST NON-CONSENSUAL TREATMENT: THE OPPORTUNITIES OF ARTICLE 16

Although Article 16 CRPD, the right to be free from exploitation, violence and abuse, has previously received little attention in general, the Article has the potential to prevent violence and abuse in specific situations of institutional mental healthcare, as well as in the private realm. Article 16 cannot be seen as duplicating rights contained in Articles 17 or 15 CRPD, Articles which were elaborated above. While these two other Articles already cover many situations, Article 16 contains a distinct set of rights. This

---

[366] UNGA, 'Report of the Special Rapporteur on the right of everyone to the enjoyment of the highest attainable standard of physical and mental health, Dainius Pūras' (n 6) para 64.
[367] UNGA, 'Report of the Special Rapporteur on the right of everyone to the enjoyment of the highest attainable standard of physical and mental health, Dainius Pūras' (n 354) para 32.
[368] Lecture of Laura Maria Serra on 'The CRPD & Tensions with other UN Sources of Law' at the 9th International Disability Law Summer School of the Centre for Disability Law & Policy National University of Ireland (Galway) on 19 June 2017.
[369] UNGA, 'Report of the Special Rapporteur on the right of everyone to the enjoyment of the highest attainable standard of physical and mental health, Dainius Pūras' (n 354) para 32.
[370] UNGA, 'Report of the Special Rapporteur on the right of everyone to the enjoyment of the highest attainable standard of physical and mental health, Dainius Pūras' (n 7) para 14.

offers the opportunity for a broader promotion and protection of mental health more generally, and protection against non-consensual treatment in particular.

5.4.4.1 The Scope of the Right to be Free from Exploitation, Violence and Abuse

At its core, Article 16 CRPD imposes obligations on states to protect persons with (psychosocial) disabilities 'both within and outside the home, from all forms of exploitation, violence and abuse'.[371] Notably, the conduct covered by the Article is violence and abuse against persons with psychosocial disabilities occurring within institutional care, public spaces and the family. Thus, the Article also includes violative conduct located beyond the usual limited realm of a state's relationship to individuals within its jurisdiction.[372] Scholars argue that the scope of Article 16 is intentionally broad, so as to cover all forms of exploitation, violence or abuse and not exclude any aspects by failing to mention them.[373] Drawing from the travaux préparatoire, the wording covers, at a minimum, 'physical or mental violence, injury or abuse, neglect or negligent treatment, maltreatment or exploitation, including sexual and economic exploitation and abuse, abandonment and harassment'.[374] Identifying specific behaviours to be violative, however, can be more complex, as it often depends on the context. 'Exploitation' is particularly used to describe forms of violence and abuse involving an economic or sexual aspect.[375] The WHO defines 'violence' in the context of health as 'the intentional use of physical force or power, threatened or actual ... against a group or community that either results in or has a high likelihood of resulting in injury, death, psychological harm, maldevelopment or deprivation.'[376] In the context of disability, the Council of Europe defines 'abuse' as '[a]ny act, or failure to act, which results in a breach of a vulnerable person's human rights, civil liberties, physical and mental integrity, dignity or general well-being, whether intended or through negligence.'[377] The use of the terms 'exploitation', 'violence' and 'abuse' indicates that only activities inflicted on persons with psychosocial disabilities by

---

[371] UNGA, CRPD (n 23) art 16(1).
[372] Frédéric Mégret, 'The Disabilities Convention: Human Rights of Persons with Disabilities or Disability Rights?' (2008) 30(2) Human Rights Quarterly 494, 508.
[373] See eg Peter Bartlett & Marianne Schulze, 'Urgently awaiting implementation: The right to be free from exploitation, violence and abuse in Article 16 of the Convention on the Rights of Persons with Disabilities (CRPD)' (2017) 53 International Journal of Law and Psychiatry 2, 5; or Marianne Schulze, *Understanding the UN Convention On The Rights Of Persons With Disabilities* (Handicap International 2010) 103.
[374] See UNGA, 'Report of the Ad Hoc Committee on a Comprehensive and Integral International Convention on the Protection and Promotion of the Rights and Dignity of Persons with Disabilities on its fifth session' (25 February 2005) UN Doc A/AC.265/2005/2.
[375] Marianne Schulze, *Freedom from exploitation, violence and abuse of persons with disabilities* (Council of Europe 2017) 8.
[376] WHO, 'Global status report on violence and prevention' (2014), <https://www.who.int/violence_injury_prevention/violence/status_report/2014/en/> accessed 14 November 2022, p 2.
[377] Council of Europe, Resolution ResAP(2005)1 on safeguarding adults and children with disabilities against abuse (2 February 2005), p 15.

others fall within the remit of the Article. Of course, this also includes situations in which third parties have the responsibility for persons with psychosocial disabilities but fail to exercise that duty, since failures of support, or wilful neglect, may amount to abuse.[378] Schulze provides a non-exhaustive list of examples of exploitation, violence and abuse in health- and care-related settings for persons with (psychosocial) disabilities, including:

- inappropriate doses of medication or deprivation of medication
- depriving of care and assistance
- refusal to conduct care as instructed
- threat not to provide care
- restraining
- emotional and social deprivation, loneliness
- disrespect for privacy[379]
- deprivation of independence and autonomy[380]
- creating undesired and unwarranted control(s) over a person's life
- gossip
- blaming a person for their impairment
- criticism for being ungrateful or not sufficiently grateful for support provided
- negative commentary about impairment.[381]

In considering how Article 16 interacts with Article 6 CRPD on the rights of women and girls with disabilities, the CteeRPD has also specified, in a non-exhaustive list, certain types of harm that fall within the scope of Article 16. These include, in addition to the above-mentioned types, physical force, inflicting fear or intimidation, exercising control, medical procedures or interventions performed without free and informed consent, administering electroshock treatment, and isolating or secluding.[382]

Up to this point, Article 16 seems to overlap significantly with Article 15 – the right to be free from torture or cruel, inhuman or degrading treatment – along with Article 17, the right to personal integrity. While much of the abusive or violent mental health treatment which falls within the scope of Article 16 may not amount to torture, due to the lack of a malevolent motive, it could still be considered inhuman or degrading treatment. Yet, unlike Article 15, the conduct covered by Article 16 does not have to reach a certain intensity. It embraces a wide range of lighter or subtler forms of harm, which puts it on an equal footing with Article 17. The characteristic that distinguishes Article 16 from Articles 15 and 17, and thus provides its added value for protection

---

[378] Peter Bartlett & Marianne Schulze (n 373) 7.
[379] An exception to this is situations where suicidal patients are – on a legal basis – monitored by camera.
[380] An exception to this could be situations where patients have to hand over their mobile phones because they keep on calling the emergency telephone numbers.
[381] Marianne Schulze (n 375) 14–15.
[382] CteeRPD, 'General comment No. 3 (2016) on women and girls with disabilities' (General Comment 3) (25 November 2016) UN Doc CRPD/C/GC/3, paras 31–32.

against non-consensual treatment, becomes especially apparent when analysing the state obligations as enshrined in the text of the Articles.

The obligation to protect persons with mental health conditions and psychosocial disabilities includes the duty to respond to cases where violence and abuse come to light, as well as adopting measures to prevent abuse. Under Article 15(2) CRPD, states are obliged to take 'all effective' legislative, administrative, judicial or other measures to prevent persons with (psychosocial) disabilities, 'on an equal basis with others', from being subject to violent or abusive conduct. Under Article 16(1), states must take 'all appropriate' legislative, administrative, social, educational and other measures to prevent such conduct. Besides Article 16 containing a longer list of measures, there is also a linguistic difference: the word 'appropriate' indicates a very broad scope of protective measures, not only confined to the criminal justice system, but also extending to other spheres of state responsibility, including social and educational measures.[383] Moreover, as Bartlett and Schulze observe, it is atypical for the CRPD not to have included a non-discrimination element, such as 'on an equal basis with others', in the wording of Article 16. In light of Article 5(4) CRPD, which expressly permits measures necessary to accelerate or achieve de facto equality, Bartlett and Schulze conclude that:

> the rights and state obligations established by Article 16 are not to be determined by reference to the rights of others under international law, nor are they dependent on establishing equality with the services provided to the remainder of the community in a given jurisdiction. 'Appropriate' protections from violence, exploitation and abuse are required for people with disabilities, even when the general population has no right to comparable protections.[384]

The CteeRPD has offered little guidance as to the extent of the obligations under Article 16(1). To date, its Concluding Observations focus primarily on legislative and administrative matters. The Committee has, for example, criticised a lack of legislative or policy frameworks aimed at protecting persons with disabilities against exploitation, violence or abuse, and a lack of sufficient funding for such measures.[385]

With Article 16(2), the obligations on states begin to expand beyond what is expressly required under Articles 15 and 17 CRPD. The importance of Paragraph 2 of Article 16, according to Keeling, is that prevention of all forms of exploitation, violence and abuse is outlined in the form of state obligations to provide support and assistance to enable persons with (psychosocial) disabilities to be safe, including

---

[383] Amanda Keeling, 'Article 16: Freedom from Exploitation, Violence, and Abuse' in Ilias Bantekas, Michael Ashley Stein & Dimitris Anastasiou (eds), *The UN Convention on the Rights of Persons with Disabilities: A Commentary* (Oxford University Press 2018) 479.

[384] Peter Bartlett & Marianne Schulze (n 373) 9.

[385] See eg CteeRPD, 'Concluding Observations on the initial Report of the Czech Republic' (n 341) para 35; 'Concluding Observations on the initial report of Kenya' (30 September 2015) UN Doc CRPD/C/KEN/ CO/1, para 32; 'Concluding Observations on the initial Report of Albania' (14 October 2019) UN Doc CRPD/C/ALB/CO/1, para 31; or 'Concluding Observations on the initial report of Myanmar' (n 66) para 29.

within communities, rather than to prevent harm by persons with (psychosocial) disabilities by segregating them from society.[386] Empowering individuals to safeguard themselves suggests a more contemporary protective approach. Preventive services under Article 16(2) include the state obligation to provide 'persons with [mental] disabilities and their families and caregivers [with] information and education on how to avoid, recognize and report instances of exploitation, violence and abuse'.[387] The CteeRPD's Concluding Observations reveal that states must make educational and informative services accessible, for instance through helplines.[388] In addition to educating affected individuals, their families and caregivers, the Committee has interpreted the regulation as also extending to the training of professionals, such as law enforcement officials, in order for them to identify and detect instances of violent and abusive conduct.[389]

A key mechanism to safeguard the right to be free from exploitation, violence and abuse[390] is the state obligation to ensure that all facilities and programmes designed to care for persons with (psychosocial) disabilities are monitored effectively by independent authorities, as enshrined in Article 16(3).[391] The case law of the IACtHR reflects this norm. In *Ximenes-Lopes v Brazil*, the Court declared that states have the duty to strictly supervise private and public psychiatric institutions to ensure that 'the patients' right to receive a worthy, human, and professional treatment be preserved and that said patients be protected against exploitation, abuse, and degradation'.[392] Under the Optional Protocol of the Convention Against Torture (OPCAT), states are already required to establish independent monitoring mechanisms for institutions where persons are detained. Yet, the remit of the duty under Article 16 stretches further into the wider public and private domain, as it extends beyond facilities and includes the monitoring of programmes as well.[393] However, neither the text of the Article, nor the CteeRPD, define what 'programmes' entail. Laing proposes that 'programmes' includes any community-based mental health service which is made available to persons with mental health conditions and psychosocial disabilities.[394] Such broad monitoring is desirable but poses obvious difficulties for state protection. For instance, how can carers be regulated? And how can private residences be monitored, since the collection of

---

[386] Amanda Keeling (n 383) 484.
[387] UNGA, CRPD (n 23) art 16(2).
[388] See eg CteeRPD, 'Concluding Observations on the initial Report of Gabon' (2 October 2015) UN Doc CRPD/C/GAB/CO/1, para 38; 'Concluding Observations on the initial Report of Kuwait (n 352) para 33.
[389] See eg CteeRPD, 'Concluding Observations on the initial Report of Gabon' (n 388) para 39; or 'Concluding Observations on the initial Report of Kuwait' (n 352) para 33.
[390] Judy Laing, 'Preventing violence, exploitation and abuse of persons with mental disabilities: Exploring the monitoring implications of Article 16 of the United Nations Convention on the Rights of Persons with Disabilities' (2017) 53 International Journal of Law and Psychiatry 27.
[391] UNGA, CRPD (n 23) art 16(3).
[392] *Ximenes-Lopes v Brazil* (n 326) para 108.
[393] Amanda Keeling (n 383) 487.
[394] Judy Laing (n 390) 32.

evidence might be problematic, given the right to respect for privacy and the right to respect for home and the family? Thus far, the CteeRPD has not addressed these issues around effective independent monitoring. The Committee's Concluding Observations have focused primarily on procedural matters, such as the lack of monitoring bodies which are independent from the government and institutions, and the lack of 'effective monitoring' where such mechanisms are in place, but exploitation, violence and abuse continue nevertheless.[395]

Given its focus on the recoveries of victims who have suffered abuse, Article 16(4) goes beyond Articles 15 and 17. It sets out detailed requirements for the state response to exploitation, violence and abuse, namely the promotion of physical, cognitive and psychological recovery, rehabilitation and social integration, and the provision of protection services.[396] However, what support for the reintegration of affected individuals should look like in instances where the abusive or violent treatment has occurred at home or in community-based services remains obscure. In general, the CteeRPD has criticised states for inadequate recovery services, insufficient rehabilitation services, ineffective complaint and redress mechanisms, and a lack of protection against reprisals.[397] Among other things, states are asked to provide emergency shelters, medical and psychological assistance, and redress in form of compensation.[398]

The last paragraph of Article 16 reveals that many instances of violence and abuse inflicted upon persons with (psychosocial) disabilities are not resolved. It obliges states to put in place effective legislation and policies to ensure that such instances are identified, investigated and prosecuted.[399] This obligation clearly goes hand in hand with the obligation to provide effective monitoring and the obligation to train professionals so that they can identify harm and investigate complaints. Several Concluding Observations have mentioned the lack of training. For example, Gabon was urged to provide training for 'police officers, justice personnel, staff providing custodial care in prisons or other places of detention, social workers, health professionals and other interlocutors' to counteract the reluctance to open investigations and to prosecute and sanction perpetrators.[400] In the context of psychiatric care, the Committee has especially criticised states for the lack of data on victims of violence and abuse, and the lack of records of the number of complaints reported.[401]

---

[395] See eg CteeRPD, 'Concluding Observations on the initial Report of Germany' (n 101) paras 35–36; or 'Concluding Observations on the initial Report of Turkey' (1 October 2019) UN Doc CRPD/C/TUR/CO/1, paras 34–35.
[396] UNGA, CRPD (n 23) art 16(4).
[397] See eg CteeRPD, 'Concluding Observations on the initial Report of El Salvador' (1 October 2019) UN Doc CRPD/C/SLV/CO/2–3, para 32; or 'Concluding Observations on the initial Report of Myanmar (n 66) para 29.
[398] See eg CteeRPD, 'Concluding Observations on the initial Report of El Salvador' (n 398) para 33; or 'Concluding Observations on the initial Report of Myanmar (n 66) para 30.
[399] UNGA, CRPD (n 23) art 16(5).
[400] CteeRPD, 'Concluding Observations on the initial Report of Gabon' (n 388) paras 38–39.
[401] CteeRPD, 'Concluding Observations on the initial Report of El Salvador' (n 388) para 33; or 'Concluding Observations on the initial Report of Kuwait' (n 352) para 32.

5.4.4.2　The Inherent Tension between Protection and Autonomy

Several scholars have argued that the most perceptible challenge for the effective implementation of Article 16 is achieving a balance between protecting individuals and safeguarding their personal autonomy and control. Lain suggests that the Article's protectionist approach 'seems incompatible with the ethos of autonomy and empowerment in the CRPD'.[402] As Bartlett proposes, Article 16 may 'provide a role for proactive state action of a sort that the person with disability may sometimes view as coercive'.[403] With regard to the relationship between Articles 16 and 12 CRPD, the question remains as to what actions states should take when a person with psychosocial disabilities appears to choose to live in objectively unhealthy conditions, and where protecting against such health hazards would require the compulsion to accept services the person concerned does not want? Neither the CRPD nor the CteeRPD has (yet) addressed this issue.

In considering this question, and what is particularly relevant for the discussion of non-consensual interferences, it is asserted here that the text of Article 16 does not allow persons to be forced into situations they do not want. Programmes to protect against abuse under the Article should not aim to control the person with disabilities in situations of potential abuse, justified on what is perceived to be in the person's best interest. In this regard, Bartlett and Schulze declare that, 'we do not achieve a human rights result by removing the human rights of the victim'.[404] Buttressed by the interpretation above, i.e. that Article 16 only covers activities that are inflicted by others, it is only logical that the protective measures under the Article focus on controlling the behaviour of the potential abuser. Thus, instead of the obligation to (forcefully) remove the person concerned from an abusive or violent situation, Article 16 obliges states to ensure the monitoring and inspection of services and care providers. The respective monitoring or inspection bodies then have the power to reduce or eliminate the risk of abuse and violence by making recommendations, taking enforcement action, or, if it is within the power of the body, using criminal or civil sanctions to prosecute providers.[405] Consequently, Article 16 can be understood to respond to the need for protection against external abuse, including abuse that takes place within the close social circle of persons, rather than limiting the autonomy or decision-making of the individual.[406]

---

[402]　Judy Laing (n 390) 32.
[403]　Peter Bartlett, 'The United Nations Convention on the Rights of Persons with Disabilities and Mental Health Law' (2012) 75(5) Modern Law Review 752, 760.
[404]　Peter Bartlett & Marianne Schulze (n 373) 13.
[405]　Judy Laing (n 390) 33.
[406]　Marie Fallon-Kund and others, 'Balancing autonomy and protection: A qualitative analysis of court hearings dealing with protective measures' (2017) 53 International Journal of Law and Psychiatry 69, 71.

5.4.5 OBLIGATIONS DERIVED FROM THE RIGHT TO BE FREE FROM NON-CONSENSUAL TREATMENT IN MENTAL HEALTHCARE

In the following paragraphs, the state obligations derived from Articles 15, 16 and 17 CRPD will be discussed, and it will be considered whether there are any particular obligations inherent in the right to personal integrity, the right to be free from torture or ill-treatment, and the right to be free from exploitation, violence and abuse, when the persons concerned are persons with mental health conditions and psychosocial disabilities and the applicable context is that of mental healthcare.

Following from the CteeRPD Guidelines and Concluding Observations, Article 17 CRPD obliges states to ensure measures that protect persons with psychosocial disabilities against medical or other mental health treatment given without their free and informed consent; such measures might include adequate counselling or making available efficient support mechanisms for decision-making.[407] To fulfil the obligations under Article 17, the CteeRPD urges states to adopt clear legislation that explicitly prohibits performing 'unnecessary, invasive and irreversible medical interventions'.[408] In recent reports, the CPT has highlighted that a patient's free and informed consent to (or refusal of) treatment must be actively sought, and relevant legislation must be revised so as to lay out the fundamental principle of free and informed consent. In addition, the CPT has called on states to clearly specify in their legislation the exceptional circumstances in which this principle may be derogated from. Firstly, if the patient does not agree with the proposed treatment, it can only be applied with a consenting external psychiatric opinion. Secondly, the law must give patients the opportunity to appeal against the treatment, to an independent external authority.[409] It is unclear whether this really contradicts the position of the CteeRPD, or whether the CteeRPD has a particular reason for simply not addressing such circumstances. Nevertheless, it is submitted here that it makes sense to include the CPT's proposal as a state obligation under Article 17 CRPD, to ensure that situations where treatment is contested but still carried out are dealt with in a human rights-compliant manner. After all, such situations occur in mental healthcare delivery for various reasons, and turning a blind eye to the matter, as done by the CteeRPD, does not ensure the best possible protection of persons with psychosocial disabilities. Ultimately, the CteeRPD

---

[407] See eg CteeRPD, 'Concluding Observations on the initial Report of Cyprus' (n 245) para 42.
[408] See eg CteeRPD, 'Concluding Observations on the combined second and third periodic reports of Australia' (15 October 2019) UN Doc CRPD/C/AUS/CO/2-3, para 34.
[409] See eg Council of Europe, 'Report to the Swedish Government on the visit to Sweden carried out by the European Committee for the Prevention of Torture and Inhuman or Degrading Treatment or Punishment (CPT),' (18–29 January 2021) Doc CPT/Inf (2021) 20, para 77; or 'Report to the Government of Ireland on the visit to Ireland carried out by the European Committee for the Prevention of Torture and Inhuman or Degrading Treatment or Punishment (CPT)' (23 September-4 October 2019) Doc CPT/Inf (2020) 37, para 123.

Chapter 5. A Human Rights Approach to Psychosocial Disability

also proposes that information on patients' rights must be made accessible in various formats, and that awareness must be raised of non-consensual treatments as harmful practices for which affected individuals can seek sufficient remedies.[410] Lastly, the obligations under Article 17 have been interpreted as putting in place programmes for independent review organisations that identify, investigate and follow up on cases in which a violation of the right to personal integrity has arisen.[411] This obligation is, further, directly enforced in the text of Article 16.

To comply with the obligation to respect under Article 15, states must ensure that their domestic laws on torture and inhuman or degrading treatment are applied and enforced in a non-discriminatory fashion, for example by criminally prosecuting violations in the mental healthcare context. The UN Committee against Torture has declared that the obligation to prohibit, prevent and redress torture and ill-treatment includes the contexts of mental health institutions, 'as well as contexts where the failure of the State to intervene encourages and enhances the danger of privately inflicted harm'.[412] In *Ximenes-Lopes v Brazil*, the Inter-American Court addressed state responsibility for the actions of private actors in mental healthcare delivery,[413] and confirmed that states have a heightened obligation to protect persons with mental health conditions and psychosocial disabilities from torture and ill-treatment by such third parties, because their conditions or situations put them more at risk of experiencing such treatment.[414] To fulfil Article 15, states are obliged to take all effective legislative, administrative, judicial or other measures to prevent persons with psychosocial disabilities, on an equal basis with others, from being subjected to torture or ill-treatment.[415] The reference to 'on an equal basis with others' may be understood as imposing the general obligations to adopt measures to prevent ill-treatment or torture, 'in such a manner as to take the special vulnerability of persons with disabilities properly into account'.[416] In *Mr X v Argentina*, the CteeRPD opined that the failure to adopt relevant measures and provide reasonable accommodation, if required by persons staying in institutions, might breach Article 15(2) CRPD.[417] This confirms that additional care may be required when protecting persons with psychosocial disabilities from torture and ill-treatment, especially in institutions. With regard to the main discussion points under Article 15, namely seclusion and

---

[410] See eg CteeRPD, 'Concluding Observations on the initial Report of Turkey' (n 395) para 37.
[411] See eg CteeRPD, 'Concluding Observations on the combined second and third periodic reports of Ecuador' (n 66), para 34; or CteeRPD, 'Guidelines on treaty-specific document to be submitted by states parties under article 35, paragraph 1, of the Convention on the Rights of Persons with Disabilities' (18 November 2009) UN Doc CRPD/C/2/3, p 11.
[412] Committee against Torture, 'General comment No. 2, Implementation of article 2 by States parties' (General Comment 2) (24 January 2008) UN Doc CAT/C/GC/2, para 15.
[413] *Ximenes-Lopes v Brazil* (n 326) paras 103, 150.
[414] Ibid para 103.
[415] UNGA, CRPD (n 23) art 15(2).
[416] Antonio Marchesi (n 278) 313.
[417] CteeRPD, *Mr X v Argentina*, Communication No 8/2012 (18 June 2014) UN Doc CRPD/C/11/D/8/2012, para 8.7.

restraints and their possible justification, the CPT urges states to regularly train all staff in psychiatric establishments in the appropriate ways of managing agitated patients.[418] To reduce the need to resort to seclusion or restraints, states should operationalise de-escalation rooms and relaxation rooms as alternatives.[419] To prevent imminent or immediate risk of harm to the individual or others, seclusion and restraint measures might be necessary as a last resort, if all other reasonable options have failed to contain the risk, as the discussion in subsection 5.4.3.4 showed. For that reason, even though the issue is (intentionally) not addressed within the CRPD framework, the author has chosen to include obligations with regard to these exceptional circumstances in this book. On the basis of CPT reports, states must comply with strict seclusion and restraint rules, which need to be enshrined in law, including that the measures should be applied for the shortest possible time (minutes rather than hours), that the equipment used is designed to limit discomfort or pain, that patients must receive full information on the reason for the measures, and that the measures must be recorded in institutions' records with details (see also subsection 6.3.3).[420] Not regulating such exceptional emergency situations would, it is submitted here, provide the opportunity for serious human rights violations. With strict and detailed regulations, human rights abuses can be minimised. Violations of Article 15 CRPD by state officials, non-state officials and private actors need to be investigated, prosecuted and punished;[421] especially with regard to wilful ill-treatment, the ECtHR has emphasised the need to set in place criminal sanctions.[422]

Under Article 16 CRPD, states have the obligation to protect against and prevent exploitation, violence and abuse. Persons with psychosocial disabilities, family members and caregivers, as well as doctors, judges, prosecutors and the police, must be informed and educated on situations amounting to abuse, as mentioned above. In addition to ensuring access to information and education, which is key for the prevention of violence and abuse, the CteeRPD urges states to appoint independent monitoring authorities to investigate violence and abuse effectively in all services and programmes designed to serve persons with disabilities.[423] Under Article 16, states are further obliged to provide accessible remedies and reparations to victims of non-consensual mental health treatment. Affected persons may require redress, adequate compensation, restitution, satisfaction, guarantees of non-repetition, and

---

[418] Council of Europe, 'Report to the Government of Ireland on the visit to Ireland carried out by the European Committee for the Prevention of Torture and Inhuman or Degrading Treatment or Punishment (CPT)' (n 409) para 111.
[419] Ibid para 115.
[420] See eg Council of Europe, 'Report to the Swedish Government on the visit to Sweden carried out by the European Committee for the Prevention of Torture and Inhuman or Degrading Treatment or Punishment (CPT),' (n 409); or 'Report to the Government of Ireland on the visit to Ireland carried out by the European Committee for the Prevention of Torture and Inhuman or Degrading Treatment or Punishment (CPT)' (n 409).
[421] Committee against Torture, General comment 2 (n 412) paras 15, 17, 18.
[422] *Bures v The Czech Republic* (n 335) para 81.
[423] CteeRPD, 'Concluding Observations on the initial Report of Germany' (n 101) para 35.

rehabilitation, including recovery and social reintegration services.[424] Peer support, for example, has been said to be an integral part of recovery-based services in the mental health context.[425] To make all this possible, access to complaint mechanisms must be ensured.[426] Recognising that persons with psychosocial disabilities may face legal, socio-economic or cultural barriers when accessing justice, or that they might be silenced or scared to file a complaint, the obligations under Article 16 are closely connected to Article 13 CRPD: the right to access to justice and the concomitant reasonable accommodation for support. To support victims, support services must be accessible to them, and resources need to be made available to the victims.[427] According to the CPT, state authorities must create an atmosphere that encourages the reporting of ill-treatment through appropriate channels, which includes that clear reporting lines must exist, as well as protective measures for individuals who disclose ill-treatment information.[428] Similarly to Article 15, Article 16 obliges states to put in place measures to identify, investigate and prosecute perpetrators, where appropriate. Pending the demise of mental health institutions (as set forth in Article 19 CRPD, see subsection 5.5.3), Article 16 can, in the particular context of institutional settings, be interpreted as requiring better resourcing for mental health institutions, addressing situations in which violence and abuse are most likely to occur, implementing programmes to minimise abuse, identifying and acting on abuse whenever it occurs, and supporting people affected by abuse with specific rehabilitation programmes.[429]

In general, the CteeRPD calls upon states to abolish policies and legislative provisions that allow or perpetrate non-consensual mental health treatment.[430] Instead of focusing on regulations allowing for non-consensual treatment, domestic mental health laws must focus on effectively safeguarding the relevant human rights. Articles 17, 15 and 16 reflect the nature of civil and political rights, and thus states have the immediate obligation to realise these rights. Aside from this, and what is

---

[424] See May Keys (n 246) 333; Tina Minkowitz, 'A Response to the Report by Juan E. Méndez, Special Rapporteur on Torture, Dealing with Torture in the Context of Health Care, as it Pertains to Nonconsensual Psychiatric Interventions' in Center for Human Rights and Humanitarian Law, *Torture in Healthcare Settings: Reflections on the Special Rapporteur on Torture's 2013 Thematic Report* (American University Washington College of Law 2014) 227, 238; and UNGA, CRPD (n 23) art 16.

[425] UNGA, 'Report of the Special Rapporteur on the right of everyone to the enjoyment of the highest attainable standard of physical and mental health, Dainius Pūras' (n 6) para 83.

[426] CteeRPD, 'Concluding Observations on the initial Report of Germany (n 101) para 35.

[427] CteeRPD, 'Guidelines on treaty-specific document to be submitted by states parties under article 35, paragraph 1, of the Convention on the Rights of Persons with Disabilities' (n 411) 11.

[428] Council of Europe, 'Report to the Bulgarian Government on the visit to Bulgaria carried out by the European Committee for the Prevention of Torture and Inhuman or Degrading Treatment or Punishment (CPT)' (10–21 August 2020) Doc CPT/Inf (2020) 39, para 18.

[429] Peter Bartlett & Marianne Schulze (n 373) 10.

[430] CteeRPD, General Comment 1 (n 125) para 42.

important to bear in mind, is the absolute and non-derogable nature of Article 15.[431] Examining coercion in mental healthcare settings from the perspective of a torture and ill-treatment protection framework consequently affords a strong legal protection against certain non-consensual treatment, and provides redress for affected individuals, thus going beyond the right to health norm mechanisms. The right to an adequate standard of mental healthcare, as part of the right to enjoy the highest attainable standard of health, determines state obligations towards persons suffering from mental health conditions and psychosocial disabilities. Conversely, the right to be free from torture and ill-treatment establishes objective restrictions on certain forms of mental health treatment.

5.4.6 SYNOPSIS

There is no doubt that Articles 17, 15 and 16 CRPD, protecting against non-consensual treatment, are aspirational in nature. The Articles open up new possibilities for a holistic human rights protection by fostering an appreciation of the lived experiences of persons with mental health conditions and psychosocial disabilities, including measures of satisfaction, strengthening the call for accountability and, lastly, calling for a repeal of inconsistent domestic legislation.[432] However, in light of their aspirational nature, the above analysis of the three CRPD norms has shown that there are considerable complexities and unresolved tensions.

Article 17 is the product of advocacy against non-consensual mental health treatment.[433] Respecting free and informed consent, as established in light of Article 17 CRPD, is a fundamental element of the treatment of persons with mental health conditions and psychosocial disabilities. Besides preventing various forms of violence, abuse, ill-treatment or even torture, informed consent can almost be interpreted as an integral safeguard for fully enjoying the right to mental health. The CRPD provides authoritative guidance on the rights of persons with psychosocial disabilities and prohibits non-consensual treatment on the grounds of psychosocial disability. This supersedes earlier standards, such as the often-referred-to 1991 Principles for the Protection of Persons with Mental Illness and for the Improvement of Mental Health Care. Notably, however, Articles 17, 15 and 16 do not particularly interdict all forms of compulsory interventions, such as least-restrictive measures in emergency situations. It seems that non-consensual treatment may be administered

---

[431] Leaned on the non-derogability of the prohibition of torture as outlined under Article 4(2) ICCPR and Article 2 CAT; as well as the fact that the absolute and non-derogable character of the prohibition of torture has become accepted as a matter of customary law, see Committee Against Torture, General comment 2 (n 412) para 1.
[432] See UNGA, 'Report of the Special Rapporteur on torture and other cruel, inhuman or degrading treatment or punishment, Juan E. Méndez' (n 61) para 84.
[433] Rosemary Kayess & Phillip French (n 265) pp 29–30.

Chapter 5. A Human Rights Approach to Psychosocial Disability

if the criteria that determine the grounds for such intervention do not make any distinction between persons with or without mental health conditions and psychosocial disabilities, and when the guiding principle for treatment is always to prevent (further) harm. After all, the lack of clarity as to how the Articles must be understood regarding exceptions to non-consensual treatment should not obscure some key points: Articles 17, 15 and 16 provide legal protection from various forms of non-consensual treatment. They offer a legal ground not to be arbitrarily exposed to such conduct, to file a complaint when a violation of these enshrined rights occurs, and to seek redress and recovery.

Former Special Rapporteur Pūras recognises that the reduction of non-consensual treatment and its eventual elimination is a challenging process, especially in countries where systems lack tools for non-coercive alternatives. Instead of justifying the existing conditions with ethical or legal explanations, immediate efforts should be set in motion to change what is no longer acceptable.[434] Concrete actions could include developing road maps to radically reduce coercive treatment practices, developing non-coercive alternatives to be used in practice, and mainstreaming alternatives to coercion in policies.[435] Non-coercive methods, including for emergency situations, include mental health crisis units, respite centres, response teams, empowerment psychiatry, the Personal Ombudsman model, family support conferencing, community development models for social inclusion, and different forms of peer support, such as peer support networks or peer-led crisis houses.[436] The Open Dialogue – the family and social network approach to care already mentioned in section 5.3 – is an example of a successful mental health system for acute mental health crisis, which can entirely replace emergency medicalised treatment, as has been proven in Lapland.[437]

Finally, effective protection from non-consensual mental health treatment demands more than ensuring the rights listed in this section. The conditions that give rise to these interventions must also be eliminated, such as depriving persons of their right to make their own decisions (Article 12 CRPD), their right to liberty (Article 14 CRPD), and their right to live independently and be included in the community (Article 19 CRPD). This leads to the next topic: the protection against institutionalisation.

To conclude the section on the protection from non-consensual mental health treatment, the following table provides an overview of the scope of, and obligations arising from, Articles 17, 15 and 17 CRPD, as analysed above:

---

[434] UNGA, 'Report of the Special Rapporteur on the right of everyone to the enjoyment of the highest attainable standard of physical and mental health, Dainius Pūras' (n 6) para 66.
[435] Ibid.
[436] Ibid para 83; or WHO (n 220) 36.
[437] UNGA, 'Report of the Special Rapporteur on the right of everyone to the enjoyment of the highest attainable standard of physical and mental health, Dainius Pūras' (n 6) para 83.

Table 5.4: Summary of the scope of, and obligations arising from, Articles 17, 15 and 16 CRPD

Scope	Article 17	– Respect for physical and mental integrity on an equal basis with others. – Recognition of the concept of free and informed consent as gatekeeper to personal integrity. – Possible limitations on the above in exceptional circumstances.
	Article 15	– Recognition that mental health treatment may amount to torture and ill-treatment if it fulfils the elements of: (i) severe physical or mental pain or suffering; (ii) an element of intent; (iii) a specific purpose; and (iv) state involvement or the acquiescence of a public official. – Acknowledgement that seclusion and restraints, as well as living conditions in institutions, may breach the right to be free from torture and ill-treatment. – Emergency situations as possible justifications for restrictive interventions.
	Article 16	– Protection from exploitation, violence and abuse within and outside the home. – Conduct covered by Article 16 does not have to reach a certain intensity (as is the case under Article 15). – Duty to adopt measures to prevent exploitation, violence and abuse (provision of information and training, as well as support and assistance). – Establishment of effective independent monitoring of facilities and programmes. – Duty to respond to cases of exploitation, violence and abuse.
Obligations	Article 17	– Ensuring respect for free and informed consent. – Ensuring access to information on the rights of patients.
	Article 15	– Reduction and eventual elimination of the use of force, seclusion and various forms of restraints. – Ensuring adequate living conditions in institutional care.
	Article 16	– Ensuring access to information and education on situations amounting to abuse and violence. – Monitoring mental health institutions and programmes. – Providing accessible remedies and reparations to victims of abuse and violence. – Putting in place measures to identify, investigate and prosecute perpetrators.

5.5 PROTECTION FROM INVOLUNTARY PLACEMENT IN AN INSTITUTION

Many domestic civil codes or mental health laws allow for persons with mental health conditions and psychosocial disabilities to be placed in an institution without their consent, based on an actual or perceived impairment. There are different forms of detention, including involuntary hospitalisation, institutionalisation in residential homes, or detention in line with the criminal justice system. Given the scope of this chapter, this book focuses only on involuntary hospitalisation and institutionalisation in mental healthcare facilities. Being detained in a mental health institution can be

Chapter 5. A Human Rights Approach to Psychosocial Disability

harmful, as it often deprives individuals of their liberty, places them under the control of others, and breaks their links to the community.

For reasons of clarity, the ways in which terms are used throughout this section are identified here. Based on the Oxford Dictionary, the term 'admission' is to be understood as 'the act of accepting somebody into an institution', hospitalisation as 'the fact of having to stay in a [mental] hospital for treatment', confinement as 'the state of being forced to stay in a closed space', and institutionalisation as 'the fact of being sent to live in an institution such as a prison or hospital for a period of time'.[438] Based thereon, involuntary admission may result in involuntary hospitalisation or confinement (and, thus, deprivation of liberty), which may lead to institutionalisation. Involuntary admission to a psychiatric institution therefore contributes to institutionalisation. When prohibiting involuntary hospitalisation in mental healthcare facilities (in line with Article 14 CRPD), institutionalisation would be prevented and community-based services would be promoted (in line with Article 19 CRPD).[439] At the same time, as Rosenthal and others comment, more resources for deinstitutionalisation, and better access to quality community-based services, would also enhance independent living (in line with Article 19 CRPD), and thus protect the right to liberty of persons with psychosocial disabilities (in line with Article 14 CRPD).[440] This shows how deeply intertwined the right to liberty (Article 14 CRPD) and the right to live independently and be included in the community (Article 19 CRPD) are, and why both rights are crucial for the promotion of mental health in general, and the protection from involuntary placement in mental health institutions in particular. Despite the wide approval of the CRPD, violations of Articles 14 and 19 CRPD against persons with psychosocial disabilities are largely ignored by states. This gives rise to the need for the ensuing analysis, which brings attention to various rights and safeguards needed to reduce human rights violations in the context of hospitalisation and institutionalisation in mental healthcare.

The paradigm shift embodied by the CRPD sheds light on the occurrence of arbitrary detention in mental healthcare facilities, and allows governments and mental healthcare providers to be questioned on a broad range of potential human rights violations, including involuntary hospitalisation, forced medical treatment, conditions inside medical facilities, and obstruction of independent living. The implicit human rights model of disability contained in the CRPD does not allow for the exclusion of persons with psychosocial disabilities from the enjoyment of their fundamental human rights, regardless of the amount of support services they might need.[441] The questions that will be answered throughout this section are: what does the right to be free from

---

[438] See Oxford Advanced Learner's Dictionary via https://www.oxfordlearnersdictionaries.com.
[439] WHO (n 220) 8.
[440] Eric Rosenthal & Leonard S Rubenstein, 'International human rights advocacy under the "Principles for the Protection of Persons with Mental Illness." (1993) 16(3–4) International Journal of Law and Psychiatry 257, 261.
[441] CteeRPD, 'General comment No. 5 (2017) on living independently and being included in the community' (General Comment 5) (27 October 2017) UN Doc CRPD/C/GC/5, para 60.

Intersentia 159

involuntary placement in mental health institutions state? And what measures do states have to take to respect, protect and fulfil that right? The aim of this section is to evaluate the roles of the right to liberty and security, as well as the right to living independently and being included in the community, for the realisation of the right to mental health.

This section begins by examining to what extent the right to the highest attainable standard of health norm addresses freedom from involuntary placement in institutions (subsection 5.5.1). Subsequently, the section turns to the normative analysis of the right to liberty (subsection 5.5.2), followed by an analysis of the right to live independently and be included in the community (subsection 5.5.3). To address a topical concern, both sections will also evaluate the interplay of involuntary placement and the right to life. Finally, the section maps an overview of the obligations deriving from Articles 14 and 19 CRPD (subsection 5.5.4).

5.5.1 INVOLUNTARY PLACEMENT AND THE RIGHT TO HEALTH NORM

The connection between deprivation of liberty and confinement in mental health institutions, and the right to the highest attainable standard of health, has been made by various authors.[442] Former Special Rapporteur on the Right to Health, Dainius Pūras, identified the intrinsic links between both rights by declaring that 'violations of the right to health emerge as both causes and consequences of confinement and deprivation of liberty'.[443]

In its interpretation of Article 12 ICESCR, the CteeESCR stated that every person who is detained must have access to healthcare services.[444] But does the Committee also address situations where persons are involuntarily hospitalised for the particular purpose of receiving mental health treatment? Because of the de facto deprivation of liberty, the issue of involuntary hospitalisation is considered mostly in the context of the right to liberty and security, and less frequently in relation to the right to health. Nevertheless, former Special Rapporteur Pūras categorised all forms of confinement in psychiatric facilities without free and informed consent as violations of the right to health.[445] Since the CteeESCR discussed informed consent as a fundamental element of the right to health norm extensively in its General Comment 14, it could be assumed that *involuntary* hospitalisation in mental healthcare institutions is indirectly addressed by the right to health norm.[446] The interpretation of the CRPD Committee is more

---

[442] See eg Brigit Toebes (n 25) 106; or Oddný Mjöll Arnardóttir (n 5) 258.
[443] UNGA, 'Report of the Special Rapporteur on the right of everyone to the enjoyment of the highest attainable standard of physical and mental health, Dainius Pūras' (n 133) para 18.
[444] CteeESCR, General Comment 14 (n 33) para 34; see also UNGA, 'Report of the Special Rapporteur on the right of everyone to the enjoyment of the highest attainable standard of physical and mental health, Dainius Pūras' (n 133) paras 34–39.
[445] UNGA, 'Report of the Special Rapporteur on the right of everyone to the enjoyment of the highest attainable standard of physical and mental health, Dainius Pūras' (n 133) para 6.
[446] Emphasis added.

straightforward in that regard: in its guideline on the right to liberty and security, the CteeRPD stated that involuntary hospitalisation in mental healthcare facilities contradicts the principle of free and informed consent of the person concerned for healthcare, under Article 25 CRPD.[447]

With regard to institutionalisation, both Article 12 ICESCR and Article 25 CPRD oblige states to provide mental health treatment and care in the community, and close to the affected person's home.[448] The CteeRPD stipulates, in particular, that it is a state obligation under Article 25 CRPD to provide available, accessible, adaptable and acceptable community-based health and support services required by persons with psychosocial disabilities. This includes the provision of nurses, physiotherapists, psychiatrists or psychologists, including for people staying at home.[449] To eliminate discrimination based on disability, the CteeESCR has imposed obligations on states to provide programmes which 'enable persons with disabilities to live an integrated, self-determined and independent life'.[450] Yet, the Committee of the ICESCR has not directly linked this obligation to mental health-related programmes or services.

It is concluded here that both right to health norms (Article 12 ICESCR and Article 25 CRPD) speak against involuntary placement in institutions, and for community-based mental health services. However, how this translates into changing practices remains unclear. To decrease involuntary placement in mental health institutions to an absolute minimum, and to end the practice of institutionalisation, the right to the highest attainable standard of health norm needs to be complemented with human rights that: (i) take into consideration the specific context of [mental] disability; and (ii) provide a set of obligations that states need to fulfil.

5.5.2 FREEDOM FROM INVOLUNTARY HOSPITALISATION (ARTICLE 14 CRPD)

> I suppose when you're involuntary, having that sort of label on you and knowing that you're trapped there [in the hospital] ... [you] feel very much like you've had your human rights taken away, you feel imprisoned, and you kind of feel, as I said before, a second-class citizen.[451]

As discussed in the previous section, involuntary hospitalisation is a common type of coercion in mental healthcare practice. As stated above, coercion does not have to be overt; it can also be subtle. For example, if individuals are pressured into accepting

---

[447] CteeRPD 'Guidelines on article 14 of the Convention on the Rights of Persons with Disabilities, The right to liberty and security of persons with disabilities' (2014) UN Doc CRPD/C/12/2, Annex IV, paras 10.
[448] CteeESCR, General Comment 14 (n 33) para 17; and UNGA, CRPD (n 23) art 25(c).
[449] CteeRPD, General Comment 5 (n 441) para 89.
[450] CteeESCR, General Comment 5 (n 34) para 16.
[451] Rebecca Murphy and others, 'Service Users' Experiences of Involuntary Hospital Admission Under the Mental Health Act 2001 in the Republic of Ireland' (2017) 68(11) Psychiatric Services 1127, 1130.

hospitalisation under the threat of involuntary admission if they do not, this would also be classified as involuntary hospitalisation. Even where they initially consent to be admitted to a mental healthcare institution, persons may be subject to de facto deprivation of liberty if they are not free to leave at will.[452] Hence, consent must be ongoing.[453] Case law further shows that persons who are placed in institutions because of a perceived mental incapacity to consent to hospital admission can subsequently be deprived of their liberty.[454] Lastly, mandatory outpatient treatment orders or community treatment orders, even if enforced in the community, with the treatment taking place outside of an institution, may also be considered as violating the right to liberty, since they are accompanied by a threat of detention if refused.[455] Altogether, persons are deprived of their liberty when: (i) they are either confined to a restricted space or placed in an institution, or are under continuous supervision and control; (ii) they are not free to leave; and (iii) they have not provided free and informed consent.[456] In general, deprivation of liberty is considered a more severe restriction than an interference with liberty of movement (Article 18 CRPD).[457]

The idea of liberty had been expressed in various human rights instruments before the enforcement of the CRPD. The right to liberty and security is, for example, enshrined in Article 3 Universal Declaration of Human Rights (UDHR), Article 9 ICCPR, Article 7 ACHR, Article 6 AfChHPR, and Article 5 ECHR. All of these expressions of the right are slightly different, but common elements are that the right to liberty can be restricted, provided that it is subject to a procedure prescribed by law, and that a deprivation of liberty which is arbitrary in nature violates one's human rights. In contrast to the other treaties, Article 5(1)(e) ECHR additionally, and precisely, allows for the lawful detention of persons of 'unsound mind'.[458] Although all the above-listed provisions emphasise that no one can be arbitrarily deprived of their liberty if this is not subject to a legal procedure, legal doctrine does not clearly clarify what arbitrariness means with regard to the right to liberty and security. Depending on the contemporary practice and culture of a country, detaining a person based on their mental health condition or psychosocial disability might be an acceptable exception to the right to liberty rather than being perceived as arbitrariness.[459] The CRPD dissolves such cultural assumptions and sets out clearly the right to liberty and security of persons

---

[452] UNGA, 'Report of the Working Group on Arbitrary Detention' (19 July 2017) UN Doc A/HRC/36/37, para 52.
[453] *Storck v Germany* (n 241) para 74.
[454] See *HL v The United Kingdom*, App no 45508/99 (ECtHR, 5 October 2004).
[455] UNGA, 'Mental health and human rights, Report of the United Nations High Commissioner for Human Rights' (n 32) para 30.
[456] Eilionóir Flynn and others, 'Report on disability-specific forms of deprivation of liberty' (2019), <https://www.nuigalway.ie/media/centrefordisabilitylawandpolicy/files/DoL-Report-Final.pdf> accessed 14 November 2022, p 13.
[457] HRCtee, General Comment No. 35 (n 363) para 5.
[458] See Council of Europe, European Convention for the Protection of Human Rights and Fundamental Freedoms (n 254) art 5(1)(e).
[459] Eilionóir Flynn and others (n 456) 11.

with (psychosocial) disabilities. Munro argues that, instead of understanding the right to liberty solely as offering guidance as to when it is permissible to deprive someone of their liberty, the CRPD framework considers why liberty matters for persons with psychosocial disabilities, and delineates how the law protects this right for this particular vulnerable group.[460]

5.5.2.1 The Scope of the Right to Liberty and Security

Article 14 CRPD does not explicitly refer to involuntary hospitalisation. Split into three parts, Paragraph 1(a) states the fundamental right to liberty and security; Paragraph 1(b) aims to ensure that any deprivation of liberty is lawful, systematic and non-discriminatory; and Paragraph 2 outlines protective provisions of deprivation.[461]

The Article provides, in the first part of Paragraph 1, that persons with psychosocial disabilities must, on an equal basis with others, enjoy the right to liberty and security.[462] Liberty and security can be described as two aspects of the same right, with liberty being the protection from unwarranted intrusions, and therefore the substantive aspect, and security protecting the procedural aspect.[463] The non-discrimination provision 'on an equal basis with others' stipulates that persons with psychosocial disabilities who pose a legitimate threat should be treated in the same way as any other person would be treated. The second part of Paragraph 1 sets out conditions under which the right to liberty and security may be restricted.[464] First, depriving someone of liberty must not be unlawful or arbitrary. The text of Article 14 is silent on whether this protection encompasses all forms of involuntary hospitalisation, or whether there might be exceptions under certain circumstances. Delineated from the CRPD case law, this section can be interpreted as reading the right to liberty in conjunction with Articles 5 and 12 CRPD, ensuring that persons with psychosocial disabilities are not detained in an institution against their will, i.e. without their informed consent, or with the consent of a substituted decision-maker.[465] The Committee has repeatedly interpreted Article 14 as requiring states to ensure that no one is detained against their will in any sort of mental health institution.[466] Second, the detention must be in accordance with the law. If a person is involuntarily admitted

---

[460] Lecture of Nell Munro on 'Deprivation of Liberty under the CRPD' at the 9th International Disability Law Summer School of the Centre for Disability Law & Policy National University of Ireland (Galway) on 21 June 2017.
[461] Michael Perlin & Eva Szeli, 'Article 14: Liberty and Security of the Person' in Ilias Bantekas, Michael Ashley Stein & Dimitris Anastasiou (eds), *The UN Convention on the Rights of Persons with Disabilities: A Commentary* (Oxford University Press 2018) 402.
[462] UNGA, CRPD (n 23) art 14(1)(a).
[463] Michael Perlin & Eva Szeli (n 461) 403.
[464] UNGA, CRPD (n 23) art 14(1)(b).
[465] Eilionóir Flynn and others (n 456) 31.
[466] See eg CteeRPD, 'Concluding Observations on the initial Report of Austria' (n 343) para 30; or 'Concluding Observations on the initial Report of Australia' (21 October 2013) UN Doc CRPD/C/AUS/CO/1, para 34.

to a locked ward, and the resulting deprivation of liberty is not in accordance with the procedure prescribed by national law, the confinement violates the right to liberty and security, as was, for instance, found in the ECtHR case *Storck v Germany*.[467] Third, the existence of a disability shall, under no circumstances, justify a deprivation of liberty. In *Noble v Australia*, the CteeRPD found that the applicant had been detained not because of a criminal conviction, but based on his mental and intellectual disability and the potential consequences thereof. Recalling that 'the existence of a disability shall in no case justify a deprivation of liberty',[468] the Committee considered Noble's detention to be a violation of Article 14(1)(b) CPRD.[469]

Based on Article 14(2), if persons with psychosocial disabilities are deprived of their liberty for other objectively justifiable reasons as opposed to unlawful or arbitrary reasons, they must be treated in accordance with the objectives of the Convention, including having access to reasonable accommodation.[470] This Paragraph can be understood as protecting certain guarantees and rights whenever liberty is denied. The Human Rights Committee emphasises that, in every lawful deprivation of liberty, effective remedies must be available to the person concerned. Without exception, involuntary hospitalised individuals must have the right to be brought before a judicial authority to ensure that the restriction of their liberty is subject to judicial control.[471] If, for instance, the circumstances justifying the detention have changed, the hospitalisation might be rendered unlawful. In such cases, the reviewing court must order immediate release and provide compensation.[472] With regard to the reasonable accommodation requirement under Article 14 CRPD, the Working Group on Arbitrary Detention (WGAD) proclaimed that this must include: (i) being treated with humanity, respect, and in a manner that takes into account the individual's special needs; (ii) being treated only on the basis of free and informed consent, and if needed with support for decision-making; (iii) having obstacles and barriers removed in order to have access to the physical environment, information and communication; (iv) being provided with legal or other appropriate support, including peer support, in order for the individual to be informed about the ways in which they might effectively and promptly secure their release; (v) being provided with free or affordable community-based services as alternatives; and (vi) being provided with compensation and other forms of reparations in the event of unlawful or arbitrary deprivation of liberty.[473] As a matter of fact, this proclamation by the WGAD resembles, to a large extent, Paragraph 2 of the draft

---

[467] *Storck v Germany* (n 241) para 112.
[468] UNGA, CRPD (n 23) art 14(1)(b).
[469] CteeRPD, Noble v Australia, Communication No 7/2012 (10 October 2016) UN Doc CRPD/C/16/D/7/2012, paras 8.7–8.8.
[470] UNGA, CRPD (n 23) art 14.
[471] HRCtee, General Comment No. 35 (n 363), paras 39–44.
[472] Ibid paras 41, 43.
[473] UNGA, 'Report of the Working Group on Arbitrary Detention, United Nations Basic Principles and Guidelines on Remedies and Procedures on the Right of Anyone Deprived of Their Liberty to Bring Proceedings Before a Court' (6 July 2015) UN Doc A/HRC/30/37, paras 103–107.

Article 14 CRPD, originally denominated as Article 10.[474] By way of example, in *Mr X v Argentina*, the CteeRPD concluded that Argentina had failed to meet its obligations under Article 14(2) CRPD. Despite making accommodations, the Committee considered that the state had not irrefutably demonstrated that these were sufficient for the requirements of persons with disabilities.[475]

Due to the absence, to date, of a fully elaborated authoritative interpretation of the guarantees under Article 14 CRPD, there is no definite interpretation of the scope of these guarantees. At the time of conducting this study, there were at least three pending cases before the CteeRPD that might shed more light on Article 14 in relation to mental healthcare.[476] Yet, the additional value of the CRPD norm for the mental health context is clear: it requires that no person can be deprived of their liberty on the grounds of a psychosocial disability, and that, if a person with psychosocial disability is deprived of liberty, access to reasonable accommodation must be ensured. With this, the CRPD profoundly challenges the understanding of the right to liberty, especially in the context of mental healthcare.

5.5.2.1.1 Deprivation of Liberty on the Basis of Psychosocial Disability

The CteeRPD Guidelines on Article 14, and the preparatory work on the Article, explain that Article 14 prohibits the deprivation of liberty on the basis of an actual or perceived psychosocial impairment, even if additional factors are used to justify the deprivation of liberty.[477] The Committee has asserted that this must be understood as providing an absolute prohibition on disability-specific deprivation of liberty.[478] It is incompatible with Article 14 and discriminatory in nature to allow for the detention of persons with actual or perceived psychosocial disabilities where the deprivation of liberty is grounded in the combination of a psychosocial disability and another element, such as being deemed dangerous to oneself or others, or needing care or treatment.[479] In various Concluding Observations, the CteeRPD has explicitly rejected

---

[474] See UNGA, 'Report of the Working Group to the Ad Hoc Committee on a Comprehensive and Integral International Convention on the Protection and Promotion of the Rights and Dignity of Persons with Disabilities' (n 281).

[475] CteeRPD, *Mr X v Argentina* (n 417) para 8.5.

[476] These pending Article 14 CRPD cases related to mental healthcare include issues such as institutionalization of persons with intellectual impairment (Australia), alleged forced hospitalisation and treatment including electroshock (Australia), and alleged hospitalisation in psychiatric hospital and appointment of guardian without consent (Germany), <https://www.ohchr.org/sites/default/files/Documents/HRBodies/CRPD/Tablependingcases.pdf> accessed 14 November 2022.

[477] CteeRPD 'Guidelines on article 14 of the Convention on the Rights of Persons with Disabilities, The right to liberty and security of persons with disabilities' (n 448) paras 6–7.

[478] See eg CteeRPD, General Comment 1 (n 125); or CteeRPD 'Guidelines on article 14 of the Convention on the Rights of Persons with Disabilities, The right to liberty and security of persons with disabilities' (n 447) para 6.

[479] See eg CteeRPD 'Guidelines on article 14 of the Convention on the Rights of Persons with Disabilities, The right to liberty and security of persons with disabilities' (n 447) para 13; and 'Concluding Observations on the Initial Report of Jordan' (15 May 2017) UN Doc CRPD/C/JOR/CO/1, para 29.

standards that attribute to psychosocial disability the possibility of causing harm, or the need for treatment and care, which then lead to hospitalisation.[480] Yet, so far, the Committee has not commented on disability-neutral situations, which are, for example, linked to the preservation of public order.[481] The CteeRPD's position is supported by different bodies and stakeholders, including the WGAD, which endorsed the CteeRPD's interpretation in one of its reports,[482] as well as in the recent case of *Mr. N*. Here, the WGAD affirmed that Mr N's involuntary admission to a mental hospital constituted a deprivation of liberty contrary to Article 14 CRPD. The WGAD established that the Japanese government had not followed the national legal provision when involuntarily hospitalising Mr N and, thus, it could not be invoked to justify the detention.[483] Moreover, it found that Mr N had first been arrested for a minor criminal offence, but then, without any connection to the initial incident, he had been placed in a psychiatric hospital against his will. Therefore, the WGAD concluded that his detention and subsequent internment in the hospital had been purely on the basis of his psychosocial disability, and therefore constituted a deprivation of liberty in a discriminatory manner.[484] Former Special Rapporteur on Torture, Manfred Nowak, also affirmed the CRPD standards in one of his reports on protecting persons with disabilities,[485] as did the former Special Rapporteur on the Right to Health, Anand Grover.[486] Likewise, in its Concluding Observations, the Committee on the Elimination of All Forms of Discrimination against Women has urged states to prohibit 'disability-based detention of women, including involuntary hospitalization and forced institutionalization'.[487] Of course, detention for treatment and care, or preventive detention, may be lawful, but former High Commissioner for Human Rights, Navanethem Pillay, has emphasised that they are only lawful if 'de-linked from the disability and neutrally defined so as to apply to all persons on an equal basis'.[488] Certainly, the right to liberty is not an absolute right, as it can be restricted in accordance with the law, for reasons of public health or

---

[480] See eg CteeRPD, 'Concluding Observations on the initial Report of Kuwait' (n 352) para 28; 'Concluding Observations on the initial Report of Turkey' (n 395) para 29; or 'Concluding Observations on the initial Report of Cuba' (10 May 2019) UN Doc CRPD/C/CUB/CO/1, para 29.

[481] European Union Agency for Fundamental Rights (FRA), *Involuntary placement and involuntary treatment of persons with mental health problems* (Publications Office of the European Union 2012) 16.

[482] UNGA, 'Report of the Working Group on Arbitrary Detention' (n 452) para 55.

[483] Working Group on Arbitrary Detention (WGAD), Opinion No. 8/2018 concerning Mr. N (Japan) (23 May 2018) UN Doc A/HRC/WGAD/2018/8, para 36.

[484] Ibid para 46.

[485] UNGA, 'Interim report of the Special Rapporteur on torture and other cruel, inhuman or degrading treatment or punishment, Manfred Nowak' (n 278) para 64.

[486] UNGA, 'Report of the Special Rapporteur on the right of everyone to the enjoyment of the highest attainable standard of physical and mental health, Anand Grover' (n 135) para 72.

[487] See eg Committee on the Elimination of Discrimination against Women, 'Concluding observations on the combined fourth and fifth periodic reports of India' (24 July 2014) UN Doc CEDAW/C/IND/CO/4–5, para 37.

[488] UNGA, 'Annual Report of the United Nations High Commissioner for Human Rights: Thematic Study on enhancing awareness and understanding of the Convention on the Rights of Persons with Disabilities' (26 January 2009) UN Doc A/HRC/10/48, para 49.

safety. However, the restriction must be necessary, proportionate and justified;[489] this is where opinions differ.

Irrespective of their strong support for Article 14 CRPD, neither international human rights bodies nor national legislators have embraced an absolute ban on disability-specific detention; this is grounded in the idea that, in certain instances, persons with psychosocial disabilities should be detained because of their actual or perceived impairments, provided there are additional factors. Among these bodies and individuals are the HRCtee, the Committee against Torture,[490] the Subcommittee on the Prevention of Torture and Other Cruel, Inhuman or Degrading Treatment or Punishment,[491] and former Special Rapporteur on Torture, Juan Méndez. Their interpretations of the right to liberty are in clear contrast to the interpretation standards of the CRPD Committee. According to the HCTee, for example, the right to liberty may imply that, under specific circumstances, involuntary admission to psychiatric facilities could constitute a form of deprivation of liberty that is compatible with human rights law. According to the Human Rights Committee's interpretation in General Comment 35, involuntary admission cannot simply be based on the existence of a disability, but must be carried out only for the purposes of protecting the individual in question from serious harm or preventing injury to others.[492] On this basis, the Committee ruled, in the case of *A v New Zealand*, that detaining A for nine years because of his paranoia and the danger he posed to himself and others was neither arbitrary nor unlawful (under Article 9 ICCPR).[493] Various scholars support this approach. For example, Freeman and others highlight the benefit of involuntarily hospitalising persons with psychosocial disabilities by observing that 'not admitting a person because of [psychosocial] disability could in some circumstances result in the long-term deprivation of liberty – possibly in a prison – rather than a potentially much short(er)-term "deprivation" in a hospital.'[494]

Former Special Rapporteur Méndez confirmed the risk that deprivation of liberty based on the grounds of psychosocial disability may lead to the infliction of severe pain and suffering, which could amount to ill-treatment and torture. Yet, in one of his reports, he also supported the detention of persons with psychosocial disabilities, if necessary to protect the safety of the person concerned or others. Besides such

---

[489] Eilionóir Flynn and others (n 456) 23.
[490] See eg Committee Against Torture, 'Concluding observations on the seventh periodic report of Finland' (20 January 2017) UN Doc CAT/C/FIN/CO/7, paras 22–23; 'Concluding observations on the seventh periodic report of France' (10 June 2016) UN Doc CAT/C/FRA/CO/7, paras 29–30; and 'Concluding observations on the fourth periodic report of Azerbaijan' (27 January 2016) UN Doc CAT/C/AZE/CO/4, paras 26–27.
[491] See Subcommittee on Prevention of Torture and Other Cruel, Inhuman or Degrading Treatment or Punishment (SPT), 'Approach of the Subcommittee on Prevention of Torture and Other Cruel, Inhuman or Degrading Treatment or Punishment regarding the rights of persons institutionalized and treated medically without informed consent' (26 January 2016) UN Doc CAT/OP/27/2.
[492] HRCtee, General Comment No. 35 (n 363) para 19.
[493] See *A v New Zealand*, Communication No 754/1997 (HRCtee, 3 August 1999).
[494] Melvyn Freeman and others (n 13) 846.

emergency cases, Méndez added that an individual might, further, be deprived of his liberty if 'he has been reliably shown to be of "unsound mind"',[495] directly referring to what are known as the 'Winterwerp criteria'. Before clarifying these criteria, it is important to note that, in a statement to the Human Rights Council shortly after the publication of his report, Méndez reconsidered his position, saying that '[d]eprivation of liberty on grounds of mental illness is unjustified ... I believe that the severity of the mental illness cannot justify detention nor can it be justified by a motivation to protect the safety of the person or of others.'[496] This statement has been disseminated less widely than the report. Despite the statement being welcomed by CRPD supporters, it is not sufficient to reduce the confusion that the inconsistency caused.[497]

In its landmark judgment of *Winterwerp v The Netherlands* (1979),[498] the ECtHR identified what were later called the Winterwerp criteria: a framework consisting of three procedural tests to assess the lawfulness of detaining persons with mental health conditions and psychosocial disabilities in a psychiatric facility, under the ECHR. The three minimum conditions that must be satisfied under the Winterwerp criteria are: (i) a competent national authority must demonstrate, based on sufficiently recent objective medical expertise,[499] that the person concerned suffers from a true mental disorder; (ii) the degree of the mental disorder must warrant compulsory confinement; and (iii) the continued confinement must be justified based upon the persistence of such mental disorder.[500] To summarise, a certain severity of psychosocial disability may justify detention. The Court found that the confinement of Winterwerp, who suffered from schizophrenia, constituted a lawful detention of a person of unsound mind. Adding that the detention was in accordance with the law, the Court concluded that the right to liberty had not been violated.[501] In subsequent jurisprudence, the Winterwerp criteria were often recapitulated.[502] In the landmark judgment of *Stanev v Bulgaria*,[503] the ECtHR developed the case law around the right to liberty further. After establishing that the applicant had been deprived of his liberty within the meaning of the ECHR, the Court assessed the lawfulness of the detention. It reaffirmed that the right to liberty must protect persons from arbitrariness, and in addition to being in conformity with national law, the detention must be necessary to safeguard the individual or public interest.[504] With regard to the second Winterwerp criterion,

---

[495] UNGA, 'Report of the Special Rapporteur on torture and other cruel, inhuman or degrading treatment or punishment, Juan E. Méndez' (n 61) para 69.
[496] Human Rights Council, 'Special Rapporteur on torture and other cruel, inhuman or degrading treatment or punishment, Statement by Mr. Juan E. Méndez' (4 March 2013), <www.madinamerica.com/wp-content/uploads/2013/03/torture.pdf> accessed 14 November 2022, p 5.
[497] See Tina Minkowitz (n 424) 231.
[498] *Winterwerp v The Netherlands*, App no 6301/73 (ECtHR, 24 October 1979).
[499] The component that the 'objective medical expertise' must be *sufficiently recent* (emphasis added) was added by the judgement of *PW v Austria*, App no 10425/19 (ECtHR, 21 June 2022) para 53.
[500] *Winterwerp v The Netherlands* (n 498) para 39.
[501] Ibid paras 41–43, 44–50, 52.
[502] *DD v Lithuania*, App no 13469/06 (ECtHR, 14 February 2012) para 157.
[503] *Stanev v Bulgaria* (n 350).
[504] Ibid para 143.

the Court reiterated that it may be necessary to detain persons with mental health conditions and psychosocial disabilities 'not only where the person needs therapy, medication or other clinical treatment to cure or alleviate his condition, but also where the person needs control and supervision to prevent him, for example, causing harm to himself or other persons.'[505] It further added that the place of detention must be a hospital, clinic or another appropriate institution to treat persons with mental health conditions and psychosocial disabilities.[506] In its assessment, the Court found that Stanev's indefinite and involuntary placement in the social care institution had neither been ordered in accordance with a procedure prescribed by law, nor justified in line with any of the Winterwerp criteria. Therefore, it concluded that the involuntary placement was an arbitrary and unlawful deprivation of liberty and, thus, a violation of the right to liberty.[507] Notably in this case, the Court set out additional safeguards for protecting the right to liberty. By recognising that the welfare of the person concerned should be taken into account, it insisted that the objective need for hospitalisation must not automatically lead to the imposition of measures that deprive the person of liberty. Moreover, the Court stated that protective measures must, as far as possible, reflect the wishes and preferences of persons who are capable of expressing them.[508] These safeguards reaffirm the Council of Europe Committee of Ministers Recommendation Rec(2004)10, which defined criteria that must be met for involuntary hospitalisation: a mental health condition that represents a significant risk of severe harm, the non-availability of less restrictive means of providing appropriate care, consideration of the affected person's opinion, and a therapeutic purpose behind the placement.[509]

In consideration thereof, in *DD v Lithuania*,[510] the ECtHR found that the involuntary admission and the subsequent deprivation of liberty were not unlawful. Firstly, the applicant suffered from a psychosocial disability of a degree that met all Winterwerp minimum conditions. Secondly, the applicant had run away after being removed from institutional care and taken home, making the involuntary admission necessary. Lastly, there were no appropriate alternative measures for the applicant's case.[511] In a more recent judgment from 2019, the ECtHR asserted that 'Article 5 [ECHR], as currently interpreted, does not contain a prohibition on detention on the basis of impairment, in contrast to what is proposed by the UN Committee on the Rights of Persons with Disabilities … concerning Article 14 of the CRPD.'[512] The Court highlighted that Article 5(1)(e) ECHR embraces a therapeutic aim that recognises the state obligation to 'ensure appropriate and individualised therapy, based on the specific

---

[505] Ibid para 146.
[506] Ibid para 147.
[507] Ibid paras 159–160.
[508] Ibid para 153.
[509] Council or Europe, 'Committee of Ministers Recommendation No Rec(2004)10' (22 September 2004), art 17.
[510] *DD v Lithuania* (n 502).
[511] Ibid para 157.
[512] *Rooman v Belgium*, App no 18052/11 (ECtHR, 31 January 2019) para 205.

features of the compulsory confinement'.[513] Various scholars have stressed the need to develop a clear notion of 'a person of unsound mind' within the ECHR context, to ensure that Article 5(1)(e) does not become a convenient catch-all, but instead urges states to ensure appropriate treatment for the people in need. Among these scholars is Szwed, who argues that, as a supplement to the criteria currently used by the ECtHR (such as posing danger to oneself or others, and the unavailability of less restrictive means to remedy the threat), it must be proven that 'persons of unsound mind' are individuals affected by disorders that 'exclude or significantly reduce their ability to make informed decisions about their own health and/or to control their own behaviour and recognise the meaning of their own actions'.[514] These supplementary criteria refer to the profound impact of the disorder on a person's decision-making capacity and ability to self-control. Yet, even such a narrower interpretation of the norm would collide with the standard set forth in the CRPD.

Although the ECHR is the only regional human rights instrument to include an exception to the right to liberty based on mental health conditions and psychosocial disabilities in its normative text, the other regional human rights bodies have also accepted such exceptions in the past. In *Purohit and Moore v The Gambia*,[515] the African Commission dismissed the claim that the authorised detention of persons considered to have mental health conditions and psychosocial disabilities violates the prohibition on arbitrary detention in Article 6 AfChHPR (the right to liberty). The Commission reasoned that the protection of the right to liberty does not apply to persons with mental health conditions and psychosocial disabilities who are hospitalised because of the need for medical assistance.[516] Nevertheless, in the recently published Protocol on the Rights of Persons with Disabilities in Africa, language similar to that contained in the CRPD is used. Under the Protocol, the right to liberty includes that '[t]he existence of a disability or perceived disability shall in no case justify deprivation of liberty'.[517] The Inter-American Commission has also previously allowed for depriving someone of their liberty in a psychiatric hospital or other institution, as a measure of last resort, when there is a serious likelihood of immediate or imminent danger to the person concerned or others.[518] In more recent reports, however, the Inter-American human rights bodies have built on the interpretation of the CRPD Committee. In *Luis Eduardo Guachalá Chimbó v Ecuador*, the Inter-American Commission relied heavily on the CteeRPD's interpretation when delineating the right to liberty of persons with mental health conditions and psychosocial disabilities.[519]

---

[513] Ibid.
[514] Marcin Szwed, 'The notion of 'a person of unsound mind' under Article 5 §1(e) of the European Convention on Human Rights' (2020) 38(4) Netherlands Quarterly of Human Rights 283, 299.
[515] *Purohit and Moore v The Gambia* (n 348).
[516] Ibid para 68.
[517] African Union, Protocol to the African Charter on Human and Peoples' Rights on the Rights of Persons with Disabilities in Africa (adopted 29 January 2018), art 9(5).
[518] Organization of American States, Principles and Best Practices on the Protection of Persons Deprived of Liberty in the Americas (2008), principle III, 3.
[519] See *Luis Eduardo Guachalá Chimbó v Ecuador* (n 75) paras 133–139.

Chapter 5. A Human Rights Approach to Psychosocial Disability

The Commission observed that Guachalá had been hospitalised without his informed consent, and that the state had failed to provide him with the support needed to decide on his own about admission to the psychiatric hospital.[520] For that reason, the IACHR considered Guachalá's hospitalisation to be disability-based discrimination constituting an arbitrary deprivation of liberty incompatible with Article 7 ACHR (the right to liberty), among other violations found by the Court.[521] While the African and American human rights bodies have recently moved towards a CRPD understanding of the right to liberty, it is not yet clear whether change is under way within the ECHR framework. Although an Additional Protocol to the Convention on Human Rights and Biomedicine, concerning the protection of human rights and dignity of persons with mental health conditions and psychosocial disabilities regarding involuntary placement and involuntary treatment, is currently being drafted, it has already been widely criticised for not being CRPD compliant.[522] And the narrower interpretation of 'persons with unsound mind' proposed by Szwed,[523] which would at least set stronger limits on the permissible scope of involuntary psychiatric hospitalisation, has not yet been considered or applied by the ECtHR. Aside from regional human rights bodies, many countries have also undertaken legislative reforms concerning the deprivation of liberty. Most of the recent reforms, however, do not acknowledge the discriminatory nature of depriving a person with mental health conditions and psychosocial disabilities of their liberty,[524] but instead strengthen the procedural safeguards.[525] Other countries have changed their laws from allowing compulsory admission to allowing compulsory treatment instead.[526] Irrespective of the legislative changes, many scholars still consider involuntary hospitalisation of persons with mental health conditions and psychosocial disabilities to be necessary[527] for reasons such as those elaborated above, including medical necessity, dangerousness, and protection from further harm.

In *Luis Eduardo Guachalá Chimbó v Ecuador*, the Inter-American Commission further emphasised that detaining persons with mental health conditions and psychosocial disabilities in psychiatric institutions cannot be considered adequate for treatment, 'as [the institutions] make it difficult to establish non-violent, respectful, and healthy relationships, and because they have a negative impact on the basic and social determinants of mental health'.[528] It is the lack of community services that encourages

---

[520] Ibid para 178.
[521] Ibid para 179.
[522] See eg Statement of the European Network of National Human Rights Institutions (ENNHRI) on the Draft Additional Protocol to the Oviedo Convention available at: <http://ennhri.org/wp-content/uploads/2019/09/Statement-on-the-Draft-Additional-Protocol-to-the-Oviedo-Convention.pdf> accessed 14 November 2022.
[523] See Marcin Szwed (n 514) 299.
[524] See eg Ghana's new mental health law (Mental Health Act 2012).
[525] The United Kingdom amended its Mental Capacity Act by creating the Deprivation of Liberty Safeguards.
[526] This will be elaborated further in subsection 5.5.2.3.
[527] Eilionóir Flynn and others (n 456) 40.
[528] *Luis Eduardo Guachalá Chimbó v Ecuador* (n 75) para 177.

deprivation of liberty and institutionalisation.[529] Being able to enjoy the right to liberty is, therefore, central to the implementation of Article 19 CRPD: the right to live independently and be included in the community – and vice versa.

5.5.2.2 Controversial issue: Suicide Prevention versus the Right to Liberty

While the scope of the fundamental right to liberty and security seems clear, the CRPD framework does not provide any guidelines on the conditions under which involuntary hospitalisation in mental healthcare institutions is considered legitimate. Therefore, it remains unresolved whether, and to what extent, Article 14 CRPD can be restricted. Some scholars suggest that involuntary placement in a mental health institution cannot always be deemed a breach of Article 14.[530] In the particular context of mental health, several human rights bodies have asserted that states have the positive obligation to prevent suicide or self-harm by providing mental healthcare. The following questions therefore arise: what is the scope of this positive obligation under the right to life? And how does it relate to the autonomy-related right to liberty? Or, in other words, can a person's liberty be restricted to preserve their right to life?

The recent ECtHR case of *Fernandes de Oliveira v Portugal* may shed light on this matter, as it considered in depth the duty of the state to protect the right to life of mental healthcare patients. The applicant's son, AJ, suffered from a range of severe mental disorders, and was hospitalised on a voluntary basis eight times over a period of sixteen years. After an attempted suicide, he was voluntarily admitted with temporary restrictions to his movement, which were later lifted, allowing him to walk around the institution grounds again. A few weeks later, he left the institution without notifying staff and died by jumping in front of a train before his absence was noticed.[531] In its judgment, the Court identified two positive obligations under the right to life: the regulatory duty and the operational duty. The first of these obliges states to regulate institutions to protect the lives of the patients, for example through the provision of an adequate quality of personnel. In the instant case of AJ's voluntary admission to the hospital, this might involve checking the patient's attendance seven times per day while still respecting their privacy.[532] The majority decision held that, with regard to voluntary admission, the regulatory duty had been sufficiently met. The second – operational – duty requires states to take more direct measures to prevent harm or minimise risk, in cases where individuals are identified as being in risk of harm to themselves or others. Factors that give rise to this duty in the context of mental healthcare include: (i) a history of mental health problems; (ii) the gravity of the mental condition; (iii) previous attempts to commit suicide or self-harm; (iv) suicidal thoughts or threats; and (v) signs of physical or mental distress.[533] The questions raised in the

---

[529] Ibid para 134.
[530] See eg Francesco Seatzu (n 236) 299.
[531] *Fernandes de Oliveira v Portugal*, App no 78103/14 (ECtHR, 31 January 2019) paras 10–28.
[532] Ibid paras 116–123.
[533] Ibid paras 108–115.

case were whether the authorities knew, or ought to have known, that the victim posed a real and immediate risk of suicide (based on the five outlined factors), and if so, whether they put in place restrictive measures to avert the risk. At this point, the Court acknowledged that the overzealous application of the operational duty raises issues with regard to personal liberty and privacy rights. The majority of judges concluded that there was insufficient evidence of real and immediate risk of self-harm in the first place, making the assessment of whether reasonable measures were taken to prevent harm irrelevant.[534] Consequently, the majority decision of the Grand Chamber found no violation of the substantive limb of the right to life (Article 2 ECHR).[535] Prior to the case of *Fernandes de Oliveira v Portugal*, the operational duty had only applied to involuntary patients. Key in the present case is, therefore, that the Court established that there is a difference between voluntary and involuntary admitted patients. While the operational duty to take reasonable measures to prevent persons from self-harm also exists in cases of voluntary admission, standards of scrutiny should be applied more strictly in cases of involuntary admission.[536] In a dissenting judgment, joined by Judge Harutyunyan, Judge Pinto de Albuquerque argued that:

> [t]he right to life prevails over the right to liberty, especially when the psychopathological condition of the individual limits his or her capacity for self-determination. It is nothing but pure hypocrisy to argue that the State should leave vulnerable suicidal inpatients in State-run psychiatric hospitals free to put an end to their lives merely in order to respect their right to freedom.[537]

To this he added that it is particularly relevant to consider that AJ was said to be an especially vulnerable person, even when treated on a voluntary basis.[538] Judge Pinto de Albuquerque claimed that not seeing his diagnosed psychosocial disability as involving a foreseeable risk of suicide was inconsistent with previous court judgments.[539] Even in the absence of a known risk, the lack of basic surveillance in the hospital was pointed out by the judge, including a gap of 16 hours without supervision prior to AJ's suicide, as well as a gap of more than 24 hours in medication, which should have been identified by hospital staff as basic risk indicators.[540]

In his analysis of the judgment, and especially the dissenting opinion, Barlett critically points out that widening the scope of the protective measures under the right to life could be used to support the practice over-institutionalisation and coercion for

---

[534] Ibid paras 130–132.
[535] Ibid para 133.
[536] Ibid para 124.
[537] *Fernandes de Oliveira v Portugal*, App no 78103/14 (ECtHR, 31 January 2019), Partly Concurring, Partly Dissenting Opinion of Judge Pinto de Albuquerque joined by Judge Harutyunyan, para 21.
[538] Ibid para 22; see also Paragraph 124 of the judgement.
[539] *Fernandes de Oliveira v Portugal*, App no 78103/14 (ECtHR, 31 January 2019), Partly Concurring, Partly Dissenting Opinion of Judge Pinto de Albuquerque joined by Judge Harutyunyan, para 23.
[540] Ibid paras 35–36.

convenience.[541] He suggests that, when supportive services within hospitals to prevent suicide or self-harm are addressed under the right to life, one must also consider the right to live in the community, and thus offer such supportive services in the community as well. This approach is much in line with the CteeESCR's approach to the matter. To prevent suicide and preserve the right to life of persons with mental health issues, the CteeESCR has urged states to increase access to mental health services. Instead of institutionalising affected individuals, the Committee suggests scaling up community-based services and alternatives to the medical model, such as peer support.[542] As such, the positive obligation to prevent suicide or self-harm is acknowledged, but not to the extent of restricting a person's liberty.

5.5.2.3 Involuntary Treatment as an Alternative to Involuntary Hospitalisation?

Coercion in mental healthcare, whether it is involuntary treatment or involuntary hospitalisation, should be eliminated. This was elaborated in detail in section 5.4, and earlier in this subsection 5.5.2 about Article 14. However, in light of this ambitious goal, it has also been pointed out in this book that there are different opinions about emergency situations where there is a risk of harm to self or others (subsections 5.4.2.2 and 5.4.3.4). Since such situations exist, concrete solutions are needed. While the author strongly believes that non-coercive alternatives (such as those presented in this book) should always take precedence, and that mental healthcare should be designed in such a way that coercion is no longer necessary, there is still a long way to go.

There seems to be a trend in some countries towards changing legislation to allow involuntary treatment in the community as an alternative to forced admission.[543] For instance, under the new mental health law of the Netherlands, involuntary hospitalisation (if necessary, with treatment carried out in the hospital) only takes place if persons with mental health conditions and psychosocial disabilities cannot be treated – by force if necessary – in the community.[544] As the example of suicide prevention shows, the restriction of liberty, even to save a life, is highly controversial. Could it, therefore, be better to treat persons with mental health conditions and psychosocial disabilities involuntarily in ambulant care instead of depriving them of their liberty by

---

[541] Peter Barlett, 'The Right to Life and the Scope of Control: Fernandes de Oliveira v Portugal' (18 March 2019), <https://strasbourgobservers.com/2019/03/18/the-right-to-life-and-the-scope-of-control-fernandes-de-oliveira-v-portugal/> accessed 14 November 2022.

[542] Committee on Economic, Social and Cultural Rights, 'Concluding observations on the second periodic report of Lithuania' (24 June 2014) UN Doc E/C.12/LTU/CO/2, para 20.

[543] Mental Health Europe & Mental Health Initiative of the Open Society Foundations, 'Mapping Exclusion: Institutional and community-based services in the mental health field in Europe' (November 2012), <https://mhe-sme.org/wp-content/uploads/2017/11/mapping_exclusion_-_final_report_with_cover.pdf> accessed 14 November 2022, p 13.

[544] See Nikita V Alexandrov & Natalie Schuck, 'Coercive interventions under the new Dutch mental health law: Towards a CRPD-compliant law?' (2021) 76(59) International Journal of Law and Psychiatry.

admitting them to an institution against their will? Without going into detail, this topic will briefly be addressed here.

Under the CRPD framework, involuntary treatment with the least restrictive measures is not explicitly prohibited in emergency situations (as established in subsection 5.4.6), whereas Article 14 CRPD prohibits the deprivation of liberty based on psychosocial disability, even where the deprivation of liberty is grounded in the combination of a psychosocial disability and another element, such as posing a risk of harming oneself or others. Several scholars argue that involuntary treatment in the outpatient setting offers advantages. First, affected individuals are not removed from their own environment, and close friends and family can offer support, which facilitates the affected individual's return to civil life.[545] Second, it provides a less restrictive environment compared to being forcibly admitted to an institution, and avoids the possibility of readmissions because of relapses.[546] Third, some argue that treating affected individuals at an earlier stage (requiring them to take medication at home) prevents more far-reaching measures down the road (such as involuntary hospitalisation).[547] However, the disadvantage of involuntary treatment in the community over involuntary admission is that it reduces the possibility of finding a consensus with the patient about their treatment.[548] In other words, even when they are involuntarily admitted to hospital, a patient might still become a voluntary patient and consent to the treatment being offered.

Irrespective of the advantages and disadvantages, it should be noted that involuntary treatment (even in the community) is contradictory to the very essence of access to community-based mental health services that promote the human rights of persons with mental health conditions and psychosocial disabilities, as will be analysed subsequently. Yet, with the aim of deinstitutionalisation, as analysed in the following section, involuntary treatment in the community might very well become the 'necessary evil' for emergency situations.

5.5.3 DEINSTITUTIONALISATION AND INDEPENDENT LIVING ARRANGEMENTS (ARTICLE 19 CRPD)

I just felt I hadn't any control of what was going to happen with me, how long I was going to stay in [the hospital] or anything. I think [the treatment team] had the decision made up

---

[545] See Henk JJ Leenen and others, *Handboek gezondheidsrecht* (Boom Uitgevers Den Haag 2020).
[546] Álvaro Moleón Ruiz & José Carlos Fuertes Rocañín, 'Psychiatrists' opinion about involuntary outpatient treatment' (2020) 20(1) Revista Española de Sanidad Penitenciaria 39.
[547] Tweede Kamer der Staten-Generaal, 32 399 Regels voor het kunnen verlenen van verplichte zorg aan een persoon met een psychische stoornis Wet verplichte geestelijke gezondheidszorg, Nr. 3, Memorie van Toelichting (2010), <https://zoek.officielebekendmakingen.nl/kst-32399-3.html> accessed 14 November 2022.
[548] Álvaro Moleón Ruiz & José Carlos Fuertes Rocañín (n 546).

already beforehand and that was it. Even if I was progressing in my health as the days went on, they wouldn't release me.[549]

Around the world, thousands of people with psychosocial disabilities languish in mental health institutions, often under poor conditions, including overcrowding, lack of hygiene, and violence and abuse. Such practices emerge from the stigma associated with mental health conditions, cultures of segregated and institutional care, the lack of appropriate alternative community-based support services, and inherent power asymmetries in policy and clinical practice that recognise patients as passive recipients of healthcare instead of active rights-holders.[550] The historical background of such institutions goes back to the 1800s, when large asylums were established, out of the social welfare movement, to care for the 'weak'. Asylums were built to provide basic care in locations far away from the Industrial Revolution, which was perceived to be increasing mental health problems. At the same time, locating persons with psychosocial disabilities in remote areas, thus making them less visible, also maintained strict moral codes. Lack of funding and increased admissions then led to the deterioration of what was initially designed to provide good living conditions.[551] Nowadays, there is broad consensus on the need to transition from large psychiatric institutions to comprehensive mental health services based in the community. Nevertheless, many states still invest mental health resources in institutions instead of developing the services necessary to enable persons with psychosocial disabilities to live independently, and in the community.[552]

Often, institutions symbolise isolation and segregation from society. Patients may be subject to rules and routines, be disciplined and controlled by staff, may have limited or no access to the outside world, and may have difficulties in accessing complaint procedures.[553] The European Committee for the Prevention of Torture is among the human rights bodies that have expressed concerns regarding the inadequacy of community-based services, which forces affected individuals to remain in psychiatric institutions. For the CPT, such institutions pose a significant risk of institutionalisation, and often have a detrimental effect on mental health treatment.[554] Former Special Rapporteur on the Right to Health, Dainius Pūras, articulates that social exclusion is 'a

---

[549] Rebecca Murphy and others (n 451) 1130.
[550] See Human Rights Watch (n 27) 273; and UNGA, 'Report of the Special Rapporteur on the right of everyone to the enjoyment of the highest attainable standard of physical and mental health, Dainius Pūras' (n 355) para 59.
[551] See European Joint Action on Mental Health and Well-being, 'Towards community-based and socially inclusive mental health care' (2017), <https://ec.europa.eu/health/sites/default/files/mental_health/docs/2017_towardsmhcare_en.pdf> accessed 14 November 2022, p 11.
[552] CteeRPD, General Comment 5 (n 441) para 1.
[553] Oliver Lewis & Ann Campbell, 'Violence and abuse against people with disabilities: A comparison of the approaches of the European Court of Human Rights and the United Nations Committee on the Rights of Persons with Disabilities' (2017) 53 International Journal of Law and Psychiatry 45, 48.
[554] Council of Europe, 'The CPT standards' (n 269) paras 57–58.

core obstacle to recovery and the full enjoyment of [patients'] right to mental health'.[555] He describes securing interpersonal, community and broader connections as 'essential psychosocial determinant[s] of mental health', and as 'vital to the promotion and protection of the right to mental health'.[556] With the coming into force of the CRPD, community living and access to mental health (support) services in the community are no longer just favourable policy developments, but are instead internationally recognised human rights.[557] Article 19 CRPD codifies the right to live independently and be included in the community. The provision reflects the essence of the Convention, as it puts full inclusion and effective participation into normative terms.

Although the CRPD contains its most developed articulation, the right to live independently and be included in the community has its roots in other international human rights treaties. Article 29(1) UDHR recognises that the free and full development of a person is only possible within the community,[558] and Article 12 of the ICCPR provides a right to liberty of movement and freedom to choose one's residence, a right which can also be found in Article 15 CEDAW.[559] Furthermore, Article 11 ICESCR provides the right to an adequate standard of living,[560] and Article 23(1) Convention on the Rights of the Child (CRC) implies that the state has an obligation to develop deinstitutionalisation programmes and support to enable life within the community.[561] Preceding provisions that vaguely resemble Article 19 CRPD can also be found in regional human rights treaties.[562] The 1999 Inter-American Convention on the Elimination of All Forms of Discrimination against Persons with Disabilities urges states to develop effective 'means and resources designed to facilitate or promote the independence, self-sufficiency, and total integration into society of persons with

---

[555] UNGA, 'Report of the Special Rapporteur on the right of everyone to the enjoyment of the highest attainable standard of physical and mental health, Dainius Pūras' (n 354) para 59.
[556] Ibid.
[557] See eg CteeRPD, 'Concluding Observations on the initial Report of Iraq' (23 October 2019) UN Doc CRPD/C/IRQ/CO/1, para 36; CteeRPD, 'Concluding Observations on the initial Report of Malta' (17 October 2018) UN Doc CRPD/C/MLT/CO/1, para 29; or CteeRPD, 'Concluding Observations on the initial Report of the Philippines' (n 66) para 34.
[558] UNGA, Universal Declaration of Human Rights (UDHR) (10 December 1948) UNGA RES 217A (III), art 29(1).
[559] See UNGA, International Covenant on Civil and Political Rights (ICCPR) (adopted 16 December 1966, entered into force 23 March 1976) 999 UNTS 171, art 12; and UNGA, Convention on the Elimination of All Forms of Discrimination against Women (CEDAW) (adopted 18 December 1979, entered into force 3 September 1981) 1249 UNTS 13, art 15.
[560] UNGA, International Covenant on Economic, Social and Cultural Rights (ICESCR) (adopted 16 December 1966, entered into force 3 January 1976) 993 UNTS 3, art 11.
[561] See UNGA, Convention on the Rights of the Child (CRC) (adopted 20 November 1989, entered into force 2 September 1990) 1577 UNTS 3, art 23(1); and Committee on the Rights of the Child, 'General Comment No. 9 (2006): The rights of children with disabilities' (27 February 2007) UN Doc CRC/C/GC/9, para 47.
[562] As a matter of completeness, it should be highlighted that the African human rights system also includes a resembling provision, however, it was drafted after the coming into force of the CRPD. Article 14 of the 2018 Protocol to the African Charter on Human and Peoples' Rights on the Rights of Persons with Disabilities in Africa not only corresponds with Article 19 CRPD, but further sets out in detail what the 'right to life in the community' entails.

disabilities'.[563] More similar to Article 19 CRPD is the provision in the 1996 European Social Charter (revised) which establishes the right of persons with disabilities to 'independence, social integration and participation in the life of the community'.[564]

Two main themes that emerge from Article 19 CRPD are deinstitutionalisation and the development of community-based services to support independent living, and thus the establishment of independent living arrangements.[565] Independent living arrangements are in direct contradiction to institutionalisation. Drawing from Goffman's concept of 'total institution',[566] and the subsequently developed definitions of 'institution' based thereon, institutionalisation can be defined as:

> any place in which people who have been labeled as having a disability are isolated, segregated and/or compelled to live together. [It] is also any place in which people do not have, or are not allowed to exercise control over their lives and their day-to-day decisions. An institution is not defined merely by its size.[567]

In the 2022 Guidelines on deinstitutionalization, including in emergencies, the CteeRPD describes institutionalisation as 'discriminatory practice against persons with [mental] disabilities' (contrary to Article 5 CRPD), involving 'de facto denial of the legal capacity' of affected individuals (breaching Article 12 CRPD), and 'constituting detention and deprivation of liberty based on impairment' (contrary to Article 14 CRPD).[568] The Committee further points out that institutionalisation 'exposes persons with [mental] disabilities to forced medical intervention with psychotropic medications, such as sedatives, mood stabilizers, electro-convulsive treatment, and conversion therapy, infringing articles 15, 16 and 17 [CRPD].'[569] Institutionalisation is not only limited to segregation in large psychiatric institutions. It may also apply if persons are placed within the community but are still isolated at home, in group homes, sheltered or protected living homes, in rehabilitation centres, or in psychiatric hospitals, or where the community-based services that are provided inhibit choice and control.[570] The CteeRPD

---

[563] Organization of American States, Inter-American Convention on the Elimination of All Forms of Discrimination Against Persons with Disabilities, AG/RES. 1608 (XXIX-O/99) (adopted 7 June 1999, entered into force 4 September 2001), art 4(2)(b).
[564] Council of Europe, European Social Charter (revised) (adopted 3 May 1996, entered into force 1 July 1999) ETS 163, art 15.
[565] Lecture of Noelin Fox on 'Meaning of Article 19 of the CRPD' at the 9th International Disability Law Summer School of the Centre for Disability Law & Policy National University of Ireland (Galway) on 21 June 2017.
[566] Erving Goffman & William B Helmreich, 'On the Characteristics of Total Institutions' in Erving Goffman (ed), *Asylum* (Anchor Books 1961) 1–124.
[567] Definition by European Network on Independent Living, available at Center for Policy Studies: <https://cps.ceu.edu/research/eccl/> accessed 14 November 2022.
[568] CteeRPD, 'Guidelines on deinstitutionalization, including in emergencies' (10 October 2022) UN Doc CRPD/C/5, para 6.
[569] Ibid.
[570] János Fiala-Butora and others, 'Article 19: Living Independently and Being Included in the Community' in Ilias Bantekas, Michael Ashley Stein & Dimitris Anastasiou (eds), *The UN Convention on the Rights of Persons with Disabilities: A Commentary* (Oxford University Press 2018) 530–558, 549.

considers all mental health settings where a person 'can be deprived of their liberty for purposes such as observation, care or treatment and/or preventive detention',[571] as form of institutionalisation. Thus, the term 'independent living arrangements' refers to settings in which persons do not lose their personal choice and autonomy as a result of the imposition of certain life and living arrangements, irrespective of whether they live in large-scale institutions, smaller group homes or individual homes. Consequently, deinstitutionalisation and the establishment of independent living arrangements need to be evaluated beyond the closure or downsizing of psychiatric institutions, as will be analysed in more detail in the following subsection.

5.5.3.1 The Scope of the Right to Live Independently and be Included in the Community

Article 19 CRPD plays a distinct role within the CRPD framework. It is one of the broadest and most intersectional Articles of the Convention, and the CteeRPD considers it to be a precondition for the full implementation of the Convention.[572] Article 19 entails civil and political rights (the right to liberty of movement and freedom to choose one's residence: see Article 12 ICCPR), as well as economic, social and cultural rights (the right to an adequate standard of living, including adequate clothing, food and housing: see Article 11 ICESCR). Article 19 CRPD reflects two distinct dimensions: the right to independent living and the right to be included in the community. By recognising Article 19 as the 'equal right of all persons with disabilities',[573] the affected individual's level of intellectual capacity or self-functioning, or the level of support they require, cannot limit or deny the enjoyment of the right.[574]

5.5.3.1.1 The Right to Live Independently

Article 19(a) requires states to ensure that persons with psychosocial disabilities 'have the opportunity to choose their place of residence and where and with whom they live on an equal basis with others and are not obliged to live in a particular living arrangement.'[575] The provision entails an individual dimension that is central to the enjoyment of the whole right: the individual choice of how, where and with whom to live.[576] This choice is not limited to the place of residence, but also includes all aspects of a person's living arrangements, including the daily routine and way of life, among others.[577] There are two issues at stake concerning measures to ensure

---

[571] CteeRPD, 'Guidelines on deinstitutionalization, including in emergencies' (n 568) para 15.
[572] CteeRPD, General Comment 5 (n 441) para 6.
[573] UNGA, CRPD (n 23) art 19.
[574] CteeRPD, General Comment 5 (n 441) para 20.
[575] UNGA, CRPD (n 23) art 19(a).
[576] Ibid.
[577] CteeRPD, General Comment 5 (n 441) para 24.

the choice of residence and living arrangements, namely individual choice and deinstitutionalisation.[578]

Individual choice implies that the will and preferences of the person concerned are taken in consideration, and are respected. In this regard, living independently does not mean that persons with psychosocial disabilities must live a 'highly individual and self-sufficient life' at a distance from other people. Rather, it indicates that they can choose and control their living arrangements with the same level of independence and interdependence within society as others.[579] The most common reasons for persons with psychosocial disabilities being unable to exercise their individual choices are the lack of alternatives to choose from, the lack of available information regarding their range of options, and their being prevented from exercising choices due to legal restrictions deriving from guardianship regulations.[580] Individual choice, therefore, links Article 19 to the recognition and exercise of legal capacity as provided by Article 12 CRPD. Ensuring individual choice for patients is often interwoven with challenging the legitimacy and use of guardianship or other substituted decision-making regimes, as the landmark ECtHR cases of *Shtukaturov v Russia* and *Stanev v Bulgaria* show. In both cases, the applicants were placed in closed psychiatric institutions by guardians, and were not able to directly challenge their placements. In *Shtukaturov v Russia*, violations of the right to private and family life (Article 8 ECHR) and the right to liberty (Article 5 ECHR) were found on account of the applicant's incapacitation and his confinement in, and inability to obtain release from, the psychiatric institution.[581] In *Stanev v Bulgaria*, the Court also discussed the applicant's distance and isolation from the community, his lack of choice, and the institution's regimented daily schedule, among other factors, and thereby found a violation of Article 5 ECHR. However, Stanev's claim relating to respect for his private and home life (Article 8 ECHR), and thus his right to live in the community, was rejected.[582] In the more recent case of *AMV v Finland*, the Court also dismissed the applicant's ability to choose on where and with whom to live. The ECtHR rejected the applicant's claims under Article 8 ECHR, arguing that, due to his disability, he was not able to understand the consequences of a move. Moreover, the interference with his right to private life was declared proportionate, based on the need to protect the individual concerned.[583] This judgment once more shows the ECtHR's approach of articulating concerns for protection as trumping the fundamental rights of persons with disabilities. In line with the CRPD, persons with psychosocial disabilities

---

[578] See Giuseppe Palmisano, 'Article 19 [Living Independently and Being Included in the Community]' in Valentina Della Fina, Rachele Cera & Giuseppe Palmisano (eds), *The United Nations Convention on the Rights of Persons with Disabilities* (Springer International Publishing 2017) 364–367.

[579] Commissioner for Human Rights & Council of Europe, 'The right of people with disabilities to live independently and be included in the community' (2012), <https://rm.coe.int/the-right-of-people-with-disabilities-to-live-independently-and-be-inc/16806da8a9> accessed 14 November 2022, p 16.

[580] CteeRPD, General Comment 5 (n 441) paras 25–26.

[581] *Shtukaturov v Russia* (n 145).

[582] *Stanev v Bulgaria* (n 350) paras 249–252.

[583] *AMV v Finland*, App no 53251/13 (ECtHR, 23 March 2017) paras 69–92.

who allegedly do not understand the consequences of the choices they make must be provided access to support that enables them to exercise choice and control.[584]

The other crucial issue under Article 19(a) concerns deinstitutionalisation. Although the provision does not explicitly prohibit forced institutionalisation, the CteeRPD interprets Article 19(a) as such.[585] In the original Draft Elements of the CRPD, the then-titled 'right to live and be part of the community' entailed the 'right not to reside in an institutional facility' and the state obligation to take all necessary measures to ensure that 'no person with disability is institutionalised'.[586] Opting for a less demanding approach, the Working Group developed the text so as to require states to ensure that '[p]ersons with disabilities are not obliged to live in an institution'.[587] Some members of the Working Group nonetheless insisted that the provision was too demanding, while others voted for a clear prohibition against forced institutionalisation and a stronger provision obliging states to eliminate institutional care. The final text of what is now Article 19(a) represents a more positive approach of reinforcing inclusion and offering an alternative to institutionalisation.[588] As Palmisano notes, Article 19(a) implies that persons with psychosocial disabilities cannot be obliged to live in a particular living arrangement. After all, community living seems to be at the core of Article 19. Past CteeRPD Concluding Observations, and the recent Guidelines on deinstitutionalization, including in emergencies, demonstrate that isolating and segregating persons – in private and public spheres – is not in conformity with Article 19.[589] The CteeRPD clearly states in its Guidelines that to realise the right of persons with psychosocial disabilities to live independently and be included in the community (Article 19 CRPD), institutionalisation needs to be prevented and deinstitutionalisation processes need to be planned.[590] The Committee urges states to 'abolish all forms of institutionalization, end new placements in institutions and refrain from investing in institutions', and it calls practices, such as 'renovating settings, adding more beds, replacing large institutions with smaller ones, [or] renaming institutions' a violation of Article 19.[591]

---

[584] See eg CteeRPD, 'Concluding Observations on the initial Report of Nepal' (16 April 2018) UN Doc CRPD/C/NPL/CO/1, para 29.

[585] CteeRPD, 'Guidelines on deinstitutionalization, including in emergencies' (n 568) paras 4–13.

[586] See Working Group of the Ad hoc Committee on a Comprehensive and Integral International Convention on Protection and Promotion of the Rights and Dignity of Persons with Disabilities, Chair's Draft text (I-IV) Elements (December 2003), <https://www.un.org/esa/socdev/enable/rights/wgcontrib-chair1.htm> accessed 14 November 2022.

[587] UNGA, 'Report of the Working Group to the Ad Hoc Committee' (27 January 2004) UN Doc A/AC.265/2004/WG/1, Annex I, art 15(b).

[588] Giuseppe Palmisano (n 578) 357–358.

[589] See eg the criticism of transferring residents from large-scale institutions into psychiatric hospital units or small group homes instead of independent living arrangements, see eg CteeRPD, 'Concluding Observations on the combined second and third periodic reports of the former Yugoslav Republic of Macedonia' (n 66) para 31; or the criticism of investing public resources in residential institutions, or misusing the funds given for deinstitutionalisation, see eg CteeRPD, 'Concluding Observations on the combined second and third periodic reports of Spain' (13 May 2019) UN Doc CRPD/C/ESP/CO/2–3, para 37; CteeRPD, 'Guidelines on deinstitutionalization, including in emergencies' (n 568) para 11.

[590] CteeRPD, 'Guidelines on deinstitutionalization, including in emergencies' (n 568) para 1.

[591] Ibid paras 8, 20.

The Committee further clarifies that institutionalisation can never be considered a form of protecting persons with psychosocial disabilities, and poverty or lack of support services in the community cannot be used to justify maintenance of institutions or delays in their closure.[592]

To gradually deinstitutionalise persons with psychosocial disabilities, alternative service models must be offered that enable an 'integrated, continuing, preventative, participatory, and community-based psychiatric care and health system'.[593] Ultimately, deinstitutionalisation is only possible if sufficient support services are accessible within the community, leading the analysis to Paragraph (b) of Article 19.

5.5.3.1.2 The Right to be Included in the Community

The right to be included in the community, enshrined in Article 19(b) CRPD,[594] relates to the principles of full and effective inclusion and participation, and thus refers to a social dimension of the right.[595] It requires states to ensure access to a range of high-quality, individualised in-home, residential and other community support services, as well as inclusive mainstream services in the community; services which support living and inclusion in the community, and which prevent isolation or segregation from the community.'[596] This includes the right for persons with psychosocial disabilities to have access to the health and support services they need in order to be fully included and participate in society.[597] Therein, the CRPD recognises access to such individualised support services as a right rather than just medical, social or charity care. Access to support services is a precondition for independent living. The services must be designed in a way that prevents isolation and segregation, and which fosters living in the community. This aspect of Article 19 was specifically addressed in the decision of the individual communication *HM v Sweden*. In this case, the CteeRPD found that providing the complainant with the requested in-home support service was the only option to support her living inclusively in the community, and to prevent her from having to enter a specialised healthcare institution. The Committee concluded that the state depriving the complainant of such an individualised support service violated Article 19(b).[598] To reiterate the interdependence of the CRPD norms once more, access to individualised support services is a type of reasonable accommodation under Article 5 CRPD, as explained in section 5.2.

---

[592] Ibid paras 8–9.
[593] See eg Organization of American States, Principles and Best Practices on the Protection of Persons Deprived of Liberty in the Americas (n 518).
[594] For the purpose of this book, Article 19(c) CRPD will not further be analysed, although it makes up another part of the right to be included in the community.
[595] CteeRPD, General Comment 5 (n 441) paras 16(b), 19.
[596] UNGA, CRPD (n 23) art 19(b); and CteeRPD, 'Guidelines on deinstitutionalization, including in emergencies' (n 568) para 22.
[597] UNGA, CRPD (n 23) art 19(b).
[598] See CteeRPD, *HM v Sweden* (n 68).

Chapter 5. A Human Rights Approach to Psychosocial Disability

Central to support service provision is that the person with psychosocial disability can freely choose and decide on the service providers according to their own preferences. Support must be 'individualized, personalized and offered through a variety of options',[599] encompassing a wide range of formal and informal community-based assistance. Only then can inclusion and participation, and independent living, be fulfilled.[600] Support services, according to the CteeRPD, include 'personal assistance, peer support, supportive caregivers for children in family settings, crisis support, support for communication, support for mobility, the provision of assistive technology, support in securing housing and household help, and other community-based services.'[601] Personal assistance, as explicitly referenced in Article 19(b), must be 'individualized, based on individual needs, and controlled by the user'.[602] The CteeRPD highlights that personal assistance is key for independent living, and must be available for everyone who needs it.[603] To be in conformity with Article 19, personal assistance must always guarantee the full self-determination and self-control of the person with psychosocial disabilities. For persons with psychosocial disabilities, being able to access personal assistance connotes a move from a medical to a social approach concerning mental healthcare, where their personal autonomy is respected.[604] The CteeRPD has been very explicit in declaring that national schemes that exclude persons with psychosocial disabilities from being able to access personal assistance are not compliant with the CRPD.[605]

But what if these community-based alternatives to institutionalisation do not exist? The CteeRPD has, in fact, expressed its concerns regarding the lack of individualised support services, including personal assistance, that would enable persons with psychosocial disabilities to be included in the community, especially in rural areas.[606] It strongly recommends that states implement community support services, across the country, that are available, accessible, affordable and of high quality.[607] Some of the barriers faced when developing community mental health services, say Fiala-Butora and others, are the lack of adequate mental health legislation or policies, the lack of integration of mental health services into the general health system, and insufficient budgets.[608] Indeed, resources are needed to create, strengthen and maintain

---

[599] CteeRPD, 'Guidelines on deinstitutionalization, including in emergencies' (n 568) para 23.
[600] CteeRPD, General Comment 5 (n 441) paras 28–31.
[601] CteeRPD, 'Guidelines on deinstitutionalization, including in emergencies' (n 568) para 26.
[602] Ibid para 27.
[603] CteeRPD, General Comment 5 (n 441) para 16(d).
[604] János Fiala-Butora and others (n 570) 557.
[605] See eg CteeRPD, 'Concluding Observations on the initial Report of Austria' (n 466) para 38.
[606] See eg CteeRPD, 'Concluding Observations on the initial Report of the Philippines' (n 66) para 34; 'Concluding Observations on the initial Report of Poland' (29 October 2018), UN Doc CRPD/C/POL/CO/1, para 32; 'Concluding Observations on the initial Report of Myanmar' (n 66) para 37; or 'Concluding Observations on the initial Report of Albania' (n 385) para 33.
[607] See eg CteeRPD, 'Concluding Observations on the initial Report of the Philippines' (n 66) para 35; or 'Concluding Observations on the initial Report of Myanmar' (n 66) para 38.
[608] János Fiala-Butora and others (n 570) 553.

community-based services. The Council of Europe Commissioner of Human Rights explains that:

> there may be a need for additional resources, particularly during the process of phasing out residential institutions and replacing them with community-based services and supports. When this process is completed, however, studies have shown that there can be cost savings once services and supports are transferred to the community and institutions are phased out.[609]

Hence, costs cannot serve as an excuse for maintaining institutionalised mental healthcare, and for continuously isolating and segregating people in psychiatric institutions. Regarding the allocation of funding and resources, the CteeRPD also urges states to 'stop using public funds for the construction and renovation of institutions [and instead] allocate them… to ensure the sustainability of inclusive community support systems and inclusive mainstream services'.[610]

5.5.3.2 Institutionalisation as a Threat to Life

As can be derived from the Common European Guidelines on the Transition from Institutional to Community-Based Care, which reference the Explanatory Note to Rec (2004)10 on the protection of human rights and dignity of persons with psychosocial disabilities:

> the continuing failure to provide adequate care to people in psychiatric institutions, highlight[s] the absence of 'fundamental means necessary to support life (food, warmth, shelter) … as a result of which patients have been reported to have died from malnutrition and hypothermia'.[611]

An example of where institutionalisation resulted in death is the landmark case of *Câmpeanu v Romania*, brought before the ECtHR in 2011. It has been described as the first case detailing various human rights abuses inflicted upon persons residing in long-term psychiatric institutions.[612] After having lived his whole life in the hands of the domestic authorities, Câmpeanu, who suffered from severe psychosocial disabilities and was infected with HIV, was transferred to a psychiatric hospital where he was placed

---

[609] Council of Europe Commissioner for Human Rights, *The right of people with disabilities to live independently and be included in the community* (Council of Europe Publishing 2012) 32.
[610] CteeRPD, 'Guidelines on deinstitutionalization, including in emergencies' (n 568) para 30.
[611] See European Expert Group on the Transition from Institutional to Community-based Care, *Common European Guidelines on the Transition from Institutional to Community-based Care* (Brussels 2012) 44; council of Europe, 'Explanatory Memorandum to Recommendation Rec (2004)10 of the committee of Minister to member states concerning the protection of human rights and dignity of persons with mental disorders' (22 September 2004) CM/Rec(2004)10, para 65.
[612] INTERIGHTS, 'The Centre for Legal Resources On Behalf of Valentin Câmpeanu v Romania' (nd), <www.interights.org/campeanu/index.html> accessed 14 November 2022.

in a department without psychiatrists. There, he was only treated with sedatives and vitamins, and no medical investigation was conducted. His state of health deteriorated, and he died one week after admission; the real cause of his death was never investigated. In addition to the lack of care, the Court noted the generally appalling living conditions in the institution, with deficiencies in the heating and water systems; the sanitary conditions; the provision of appropriate food; and in medical assistance, including both medical staff, and medical resources such as medication.[613] Given the hospital conditions and his heightened state of vulnerability, the ECtHR found that, by placing Câmpeanu into that psychiatric institution, the domestic authorities had unreasonably put his life in danger. Consequently, the Court found a violation of the right to life (Article 2 ECHR).[614] In a third-party intervention to the case, the former Council of Europe Commissioner for Human Rights, Thomas Hammarberg, asserted that states and institutions often fail to respect the right of persons with psychosocial disabilities, so that isolating them in institutions leads to severe detrimental consequences,[615] and that, for this reason, psychiatric institutions should be open to independent public scrutiny, and be visited regularly by independent inspection mechanisms.[616] The Commissioner concluded that the ECHR provisions regarding the human rights of persons with (psychosocial) disabilities should be interpreted in the light of the CRPD, and in keeping with its main object and purpose,[617] leading back to the importance of recognising and guaranteeing the right to live independently and be included in the community.

5.5.4 OBLIGATIONS DERIVED FROM THE RIGHT TO BE FREE FROM INVOLUNTARY PLACEMENT IN A MENTAL HEALTHCARE INSTITUTION

The following paragraphs discuss the states' obligations derived from Articles 14 and 19 CRPD with respect to the obligations to respect, protect and fulfil the right to liberty and security and the right to live independently and be included in the community.

To respect the right to liberty as enshrined in Article 14 CRPD, states must refrain from engaging in any act that interferes with or curtails the enjoyment of the right to liberty, and from authorising such practices under domestic laws or policies.[618] Under Article 14, states have the positive duty to protect the right to liberty and security

---

[613] The Centre for Legal Resources On Behalf of *Valentin Câmpeanu v Romania*, App no 47848/08 (ECtHR, 17 July 2014) paras 134–141.
[614] Ibid paras 143–144.
[615] Council of Europe Commissioner for Human Rights, 'Third party intervention, Application No. 47848/08 The Centre for Legal Resources on behalf of Valentin Câmpeanu v. Romania' (14 October 2011) CommDH(2011)37, para 12.
[616] Ibid para 35.
[617] Ibid para 42.
[618] Lecture of Laura Maria Serra (n 368).

against practices by third parties, including private actors such as health or mental health professionals outside of hospital settings, or other caregivers. States are obliged to facilitate that persons with mental health conditions and psychosocial disabilities can enjoy the right to liberty.[619] In this regard, the CteeRPD has repeatedly urged states to repeal legislation that allows for involuntary admission to mental healthcare facilities based on actual or perceived impairments, including the imposition of such admission as a threat.[620] This encompasses hospitalising persons with mental health conditions and psychosocial disabilities for their treatment and care without their free and informed consent, as well as preventive detention on the grounds of a likelihood of them posing danger to themselves or others, if linked to an apparent or diagnosed psychosocial disability.[621] In fact, states are obliged to take all necessary legal, administrative and judicial measures not only to prevent involuntary admissions and hospitalisations based on psychosocial disability, but also to provide adequate and effective remedies allowing those who are institutionalised to challenge their deprivation of liberty.[622] The ECtHR and the Working Group on Arbitrary Detention further urge states, in line with the right to liberty, to establish mechanisms to undertake periodic judicial reviews of cases where persons with psychosocial disabilities are institutionalised.[623] Moreover, under Article 14, the CteeRPD obliges states to develop deinstitutionalisation strategies and offer sufficient community-based outpatient mental health services, drawing a link to Article 19.[624]

The obligations under Article 19 CRPD can be split into two types. Given the nature of civil and political rights, states have the immediate implementation obligation to ensure individual choice under Article 19(a) (the right to live independently). Deinstitutionalisation and Article 19(b) – the right to access individualised support services – entail a progressive realisation obligation, as this is an economic, social and cultural right. The CteeRPD nevertheless points out that this progressive realisation also involves the immediate obligation to design and adopt concrete strategies, action plans and resources to develop independent living support services to replace institutional

---

[619] Ibid.
[620] See eg CteeRPD, 'Concluding Observations on the initial Report of Greece' (n 352) para 22; 'Concluding Observations on the initial Report of India' (n 189) para 31; 'Concluding Observations on the initial Report of Kuwait' (n 353) paras 28–29; or 'Concluding Observations on the initial Report of Cuba' (n 480) paras 29–30; and UNGA, 'Mental health and human rights, Report of the United Nations High Commissioner for Human Rights' (n 32) para 31.
[621] UNGA, 'Annual Report of the United Nations High Commissioner for Human Rights: Thematic Study on enhancing awareness and understanding of the Convention on the Rights of Persons with Disabilities' (n 488) para 49.
[622] See UNGA, 'Report of the Working Group on Arbitrary Detention, United Nations Basic Principles and Guidelines on Remedies and Procedures on the Right of Anyone Deprived of Their Liberty to Bring Proceedings Before a Court' (n 473) para 103; or *Stanev v Bulgaria* (n 350) para 190.
[623] See UNGA, 'Report of the Working Group on Arbitrary Detention, United Nations Basic Principles and Guidelines on Remedies and Procedures on the Right of Anyone Deprived of Their Liberty to Bring Proceedings Before a Court' (n 473) para 105; and *Stanev v Bulgaria* (n 350) para 172.
[624] See eg CteeRPD, 'Guidelines on deinstitutionalization, including in emergencies' (n 569) paras 1, 13; and CteeRPD, 'Concluding Observations on the initial Report of Austria' (n 466) paras 30–31.

Chapter 5. A Human Rights Approach to Psychosocial Disability

settings, including those run and controlled by non-state actors.[625] Article 19 requires states to refrain from directly or indirectly interfering with, or limiting the enjoyment of, the right to live independently and be included in the community.[626] The CteeRPD calls on states to 'immediately provide individuals with opportunities to leave institutions', as well as 'immediately halt new placements in institutions, adopt moratoriums on new admissions and on the construction of new institutions and wards, and … refrain from refurbishing or renovating existing institutions'.[627] Old institutions should only be renovated insofar as necessary to safeguard physical safety.[628] Thus respecting the rights under Article 19 means that institutionalisation must be phased out. In order to enable access to community-based support services, laws, policies or structures that create barriers to living independently and being included in the community must be repealed, individuals who are confined against their will must be released, and all forms of guardianship regulations must be replaced with supported decision-making alternatives.[629] In order to protect the rights under Article 19, states are obliged to take measures to prevent family members or other private entities (such as privately run psychiatric institutions) from directly or indirectly interfering with these rights. The Committee proposes that monitoring mechanisms, as outlined under Article 16 CRPD, be set up to protect affected individuals from being isolated and abandoned in institutions, including private institutions. The obligation to protect the right to living independently and being included in the community also includes the duty to prevent the use of private or public funds for establishing or maintaining any form of institutionalisation.[630] The obligation to fulfil the rights enshrined in Article 19 requires states to promote, facilitate and provide appropriate legislative, administrative, budgetary, judicial, programmatic, promotional and other measures to ensure the full realisation of Article 19. Legal and policy frameworks should be set up to 'enable the development of inclusive community support systems and mainstream services and the creation of a reparations mechanism, and guarantee the availability, accessibility and effectiveness of remedies for survivors of institutionalization.'[631] High-quality and structured deinstitutionalisation strategies should be adopted, which contain 'a detailed action plan with timelines, benchmarks and an overview of the necessary and allocated human, technical and financial resources.'[632] As long ago as 1978, the Italian Mental Health Act established a ban on building new psychiatric hospitals, and on admitting new patients to existing ones.[633] This type of forward-looking provision can also be found in more recent legislation. The Mental Health Acts of Argentina (2010) and

---

[625] CteeRPD, General Comment 5 (n 441) para 39; and CteeRPD, 'Guidelines on deinstitutionalization, including in emergencies' (n 568) para 16.
[626] CteeRPD General Comment 5 (n 441) paras 40, 47.
[627] CteeRPD, 'Guidelines on deinstitutionalization, including in emergencies' (n 568) para 13.
[628] Ibid para 49.
[629] Ibid para 48.
[630] Ibid paras 50–52.
[631] CteeRPD, 'Guidelines on deinstitutionalization, including in emergencies' (n 568) para 53.
[632] Ibid para 67.
[633] Italy, Basaglia Law, Law 180 of 1978, 13 May 1978.

Uruguay (2017) both prohibit the creation of new mental hospitals, to step up efforts towards community-based mental healthcare.[634] To achieve deinstitutionalisation, a wide range of community-based individualised support services need to be established (including functioning and responsive community mental health teams), and states should invest in self-advocacy, peer support, circles of support and other community-based support services.[635] In addition, inpatient psychiatric institutions need to be replaced with outpatient psychiatric care in the community.[636] Former Special Rapporteur on the Rights of Persons with Disabilities, Catalina Devandas-Aguilar, stresses the importance of ensuring timely access to community services and support, as well as of substantive and procedural safeguards for the health and safety of patients before deinstitutionalisation takes place. Ill-conceived and under-resourced deinstitutionalisation initiatives may be counterproductive and detrimental to the rights of persons with psychosocial disabilities.[637] After all, persons with psychosocial disabilities must also be informed about their right to live independently and be included in the community. Recognising that system transformation takes time, former Special Rapporteur Pūras calls on states to work towards improving the situation by ensuring humane conditions for those living within existing mental health institutions. At the same time, he urges states to 'strongly asserting the legal case for large-scale systems reform and community transformation'.[638] Palmisano also interprets the state's legal obligation as being to adopt measures aiming at, and being capable of, facilitating the achievement of the goals under Article 19, rather than the actual and complete achievement of these goals.[639] Deinstitutionalisation and establishing independent living arrangements cannot happen overnight. In the words of former UN High Commissioner for Human Rights, Zeid al-Hussein:

> Effective deinstitutionalization requires a systemic approach, in which the transformation of residential institutional services is only one element of a wider change in areas such as health care, rehabilitation, support services, education and employment, as well as in the societal perception of disability.[640]

---

[634] See Argentina, Ministry of Health, Ley Nacional de Salud Mental. Ley N° 26.657 y su Decreto Reglamentario N° 603/13, 2 December 2010, sec 27; and Uruguay, General Assembly, Salud Mental, Ley N° 19.529 (adopted 2017), sec 38.

[635] CteeRPD, 'Guidelines on deinstitutionalization, including in emergencies' (n 568) paras 70–71.

[636] See CteeRPD, General Comment 5 (n 441) paras 54–58; and Council of Europe, 'Report to the Bulgarian Government on the visit to Bulgaria carried out by the European Committee for the Prevention of Torture and Inhuman or Degrading Treatment or Punishment (CPT)' (n 428) para 15.

[637] UNGA, 'Report of the Special Rapporteur on the rights of persons with disabilities, Catalina Devandas-Aguilar, Rights of persons with disabilities' (11 January 2019) UN Doc A/HRC/40/54, para 67.

[638] UNGA, 'Report of the Special Rapporteur on the right of everyone to the enjoyment of the highest attainable standard of physical and mental health, Dainius Pūras' (n 354) para 68.

[639] Giuseppe Palmisano (n 578) 362.

[640] UNGA, 'Thematic study on the right of persons with disabilities to live independently and be included in the community, Report of the Office of the United Nations High Commissioner for Human Rights' (12 December 2014) UN Doc A/HRC/28/37, para 25.

5.6. CONCLUDING SUMMARY

If all of the rights analysed within Chapter 5 were to be captured under 'the right to access mental healthcare', this right could be described as the right of persons with mental health conditions and psychosocial disabilities to exercise freedom of choice and control over decisions affecting their mental health treatment and care, with the maximum level of self-determination and interdependence within the community, with support if needed, and without being discriminated against based on their mental health conditions and psychosocial disabilities.[641] Adopting a holistic, preventive, responsive and, in particular, person-centred approach in mental healthcare is an important component of realising the human right to mental health. The CRPD has enormous potential, particularly because the Committee can under the Optional Protocol to the Convention receive and consider complaints from, or on behalf of, individuals or groups who claim to be victims of a violation. Furthermore, the CRPD has been used as an interpretative tool for judgments by regional human rights bodies, as has been pointed out throughout this chapter. The CRPD offers a framework with detailed principles and rights protecting persons with psychosocial disabilities, and it imposes various obligations relevant for the promotion of mental health, the provision of humane and dignified mental healthcare, and the protection of the rights of patients. A summary of these obligations is offered in the following table:

Table 5.5: Mapping of the right to access mental healthcare obligations derived from the CRPD

Rights	Obligations
Equality and non-discrimination (Article 5)	– Providing reasonable accommodation (when required) and specific measures. – Taking measures to raise awareness about rights of persons with psychosocial disabilities.
Equal recognition before the law (Article 12)	– Abolishing regimes of substituted decision-making. – Providing access to supported decision-making. – Creating safeguards for support.
Protecting the integrity of the person (Article 17)	– Ensuring respect for free and informed consent. – Ensuring access to information on the rights of patients.
Freedom from torture or cruel, inhuman or degrading treatment or punishment (Article 15)	– Reduction and eventual elimination of the use of force, seclusion and various forms of restraints. – Ensuring adequate living conditions in institutional care.

---

[641] See CteeRPD, General Comment 5 (n 441) para 8.

Rights	Obligations
Freedom from exploitation, violence and abuse (Article 16)	– Ensuring access to information and education on situations amounting to abuse and violence. – Monitoring mental health institutions and programmes. – Providing accessible remedies and reparations to victims of abuse and violence. – Putting in place measures to identify, investigate and prosecute perpetrators.
Liberty and Security (Article 14)	– Preventing involuntary admission and hospitalisation based on psychosocial disability, or based on another factor which is linked to psychosocial disability. – Guaranteeing access to justice and access to reasonable accommodation in case of deprivation of liberty for other objectively justifiable reasons.
Living independently and being included in the community (Article 19)	– Ensuring choice and control by persons with psychosocial disabilities regarding their living arrangements. – Establishing access to community-based individualised services. – Developing deinstitutionalisation strategies.

The Articles enumerated above are almost all civil and political human rights. In line with Article 4(2) CRPD, civil and political rights are subject to immediate compliance rather than progressive realisation depending on available resources.[642] The right to the highest attainable standard of health, on the other hand, falls under the ambit of economic, social and cultural rights, and is, therefore, subject to progressive realisation. Hence, while resource constraints may justify only partial fulfilment of the right to access mental healthcare as part of the right to enjoy the highest attainable standard of mental health (see section 4.2), system inadequacies and a lack of resources or services cannot justify a state's non-compliance with the obligations derived from most rights analysed in this chapter,[643] especially obligations derived from the absolute prohibition of torture and ill-treatment.[644] This can be seen as one key benefit of delineating such a comprehensive right to mental health(care) framework.

As mentioned throughout this chapter, states have the obligation to prevent third parties, such as private mental healthcare providers, from interfering with the enjoyment of the rights detailed above. But to what extent do private actors have human right responsibilities? There are various documents that codify patients' rights with the aim of eliminating human rights abuses in healthcare settings, among them the 2005 Declaration of Lisbon on the Rights of the Patient, which stipulates that '[p]hysicians

---

[642] Here, it needs to be noted that economic, social and cultural rights may also impose obligations which are of immediate effect, including the guarantee that the rights are exercised without discrimination, as well as the undertaking to take steps for the right's realization within a reasonably short time after states became party to the treaty, see CteeESCR, 'General Comment No. 3: The Nature of States Parties' Obligations (Art. 2, Para. 1, of the Covenant)' (14 December 1990) UN Doc E/1991/23.
[643] Unless otherwise noted within the respective sections.
[644] See UNGA, 'Report of the Special Rapporteur on torture and other cruel, inhuman or degrading treatment or punishment, Juan E. Méndez' (n 61) paras 81–84.

and other persons or bodies involved in the provision of health care have a joint responsibility to recognize and uphold' rights,[645] including the rights to medical care of good quality, and to freedom of choice and self-determination. Cohen and Ezer define 'patients' rights' as consumer rights with fundamental limitations because the patient is seen as a recipient of care rather than a human being, and therefore call for the 'human rights in patient care' concept as an alternative. Under this concept, providers have obligations vis-à-vis the patients that go beyond providing care, with a focus on the nature and quality of the service, namely on good-quality care that also respects, protects and fosters the dignity and freedom of the patients. Additionally, the 'human rights in patient care' concept also recognises that healthcare providers enjoy human rights, such as the right to decent working conditions, which Cohen and Ezer describe as 'essential to nurturing a culture of respect for human rights within health care delivery systems'.[646] Consequently, to ensure that private healthcare providers adhere to these 'human rights in patient care', the state's duty to protect the rights of persons with mental health conditions and psychosocial disabilities implies the obligation to amend or establish appropriate policies and regulations, ensure appropriate training, monitor services and enforce standards, create opportunities for complaints and redress, and ensure investigation and accountability procedures where warranted.[647]

The CRPD lays the foundation for a paradigm shift that aims to eliminate human rights violations from contemporary mental healthcare. The human rights approach to disability, as outlined in this chapter, considers intersecting human rights holistically to promote and protect humane and dignified care for persons with mental health and psychosocial disabilities. Once again, however, it is important to emphasise that mental healthcare services cannot be transformed without attention to the structural causes of poor mental health. As Chapman and others emphasise, '[r]ights-based … approaches to mental health promotion are those that have moved health systems beyond individualized responses toward action on a range of structural barriers and inequalities (social determinants) that negatively affect mental health.'[648] Therefore, the author would like to reiterate that it is essential to combine the right to access mental healthcare (as analysed in this chapter) with the previously analysed right to underlying determinants of mental health (see section 4.2.1.1) under the comprehensive right to mental health framework (as established in this book).

The CRPD, and especially the CteeRPD's approach, can both be characterised as aspirational. Nevertheless, the shortcomings of the Convention also need to be

---

[645] World Medical Association, Declaration of Lisbon on the Rights of the Patient (revised) of 2005, preamble.
[646] Jonathan Cohen & Tamar Ezer, 'Human rights in patient care: A theoretical and practical framework' (2013) 15(2) Health and Human Rights Journal 7.
[647] See Ibid; and Ximena Andión Ibañez & Tamar Dekanosidze, 'The State's obligation to regulate and monitor private health care facilities: the Alyne da Silva Pimentel and the Dzebniauri cases' (2017) 38(17) Public Health Reviews 1.
[648] Audrey Chapman and others, 'Reimagining the Mental Health Paradigm for Our Collective Well-Being' (2020) 22(1) Health and Human Rights Journal 1, 3.

highlighted. The issues and barriers that people with physical disabilities face are different to those faced by people with psychosocial disabilities. Some Articles of the CRPD, such as the right to accessibility in Article 9, or the right to personal mobility in Article 20, are worded to particularly address circumstances to which persons with physical disabilities are exposed. On the other hand, no Article has been explicitly drafted to protect persons with psychosocial disabilities. Article 19 CRPD, the right to live independently and be included in the community (as analysed in subsection 5.5.3), and especially its related General Comment, more elaborately explain the provision's implication for persons affected by physical disabilities. Delineating the elements of the norm that are relevant for people with psychosocial disabilities poses challenges. Despite being an important treaty for advancing the rights of people with mental health and psychosocial disabilities, not all Articles of the CRPD are responsive to psychosocial disability in the same way as they are to physical disability.

Moreover, the often-absolutist pronouncements of the CRPD framework remain theoretical, and lack a specific focus that would allow for direct application of the regulations to concrete, individual situations. As a consequence, governments are left without a feasible road map to guide their (radical) domestic law reforms. The fact that the CRPD has been ratified by 181 states and regional integration organisations shows the overall agreement with, and support for, the Convention. Yet, the CteeRPD's view of mental healthcare practice is barely reflected in domestic law. As Fallon-Kund and others rightfully proclaim, '[t]he CRPD provides us with a moral compass but it does not, in any concrete way, inform us what procedural or legislative changes should be made to achieve results that impact on individuals in a rights-enhancing manner.'[649]

To strengthen mental healthcare and, thus, the promotion and protection of mental health, the CteeRPD could strengthen its recommendations and provide a comprehensive set of guidelines for law- and policy-makers aimed at bridging the implementation gap between human rights rhetoric and the reality lived by persons with mental health conditions and psychosocial disabilities. The paradigm shift introduced by the CRPD surely raises important legal and ethical issues that deserve further scrutiny. It remains to be seen how human rights courts will use the CRPD in the future, in light of their established case law on mental health. To find out the extent to which the approach set out in the CRPD has sparked debate in public policy and the practice of psychiatry, the following part of this book will scrutinise the impact and implementation of the delineated mental healthcare-related CRPD regulations, using the examples of Ghana and Germany as case studies.

---

[649] Marie Fallon-Kund and others (n 406) 76.

PART 3
COUNTRY STUDY ANALYSIS

CHAPTER 6
BRIDGING THEORY AND PRACTICE THROUGH COUNTRY STUDIES

6.1 INTRODUCTION

States take different approaches when it comes to giving effect to the right to mental health in the domestic legal order. While some states adopt concrete laws, policies or practices on the rights of persons with mental health conditions and psychosocial disabilities, others seek to regulate rights and obligations under general (health) laws, policies and practices, which are not always specifically targeted at persons with mental health conditions and psychosocial disabilities. According to the Committee on Economic, Social and Cultural Rights (CteeESCR), legislation which outlines rights and obligations with regard to mental health is highly desirable, and may even be indispensable for ensuring the effective promotion and protection of the right to mental health.[1] An important and necessary feature of the right to mental health framework delineated from international law, as described in Part 2 of this book, is that it provides a comprehensive but also objective framework of rights (or international standards), which can be applied in any country. Therefore, for the process of domestication, such an international framework should take account of domestic particularities.

Without this study being primarily concerned with the universality or cultural relativity of human rights theories per se, these theories indicate the need for contextual approaches in human rights research. As Donnelly observes, '[t]he global human rights regime relies on national implementation of internationally recognized human rights'.[2] Without this, the enjoyment of human rights is contingent and relative. Moreover, how exactly these rights are interpreted in national laws, policies and practices can ensure or hinder their effective implementation.[3] From a governance

---

[1] Committee on Economic, Social and Cultural Rights (CteeESCR), 'General Comment No. 3: The Nature of States Parties' Obligations (Art. 2, Para. 1, of the Covenant)' (14 December 1990) UN Doc E/1991/123, para 3; and CteeESCR, 'General Comment No. 14: The Right to the Highest Attainable Standard of Health (Art. 12)' (General Comment 14) (11 August 2000) UN Doc E/C.12/2000/4, para 53.

[2] Jack Donnelly, 'The Relative Universality of Human Rights' (2007) 29(2) Human Rights Quarterly 281, 283.

[3] Jill Stavert & Rebecca McGregor, 'Domestic legislation and international human rights standards: the case of mental health and incapacity' (2018) 22(1) The International Journal of Human Rights 70, 70–71.

perspective, considering local realities is, therefore, vital. It takes into account the national priority given to the rights and the ability of a country to put in place a working structure. Studying domestic legislation is also helpful because of its practical relevance.

It is for this reason that Part 3 of this book presents two country studies, namely that of Ghana and Germany, to explore the interplay between human rights and mental health frameworks in practice, and to further amplify the understanding of the right to mental health framework adopted by this research study. Ultimately, this chapter will draw attention to the interaction between the international and domestic levels, and how the two can mutually influence each other. Thus, the purpose of this chapter is not merely to inform about how the right to mental health is given effect to in Ghana and Germany; it also aims to draw a broader conclusion. Can general lessons be learnt from the two case studies? Could a country guide best practice based on its own established rules that do not strictly follow international standards, and by doing so, advance the right to mental health framework? As Sally Engle Merry articulates, '[h]uman rights offer local communities new ways of defining problems and seeing solutions through various kinds of cultural appropriation.'[4] But implementing global human rights views into the national legal system does not only lead to a redefinition of local practices, but it also influences the global human rights system itself. Merry describes this 'process of cultural appropriation' as a dynamic negotiation that drives the global human rights system to change.[5]

Chapter 6 commences with an introductory section providing information on the research approach and methodology of the country studies (section 6.2). Following this is the analysis of how Ghana (section 6.3) and Germany (section 6.4) have enacted laws and regulations to provide solid legal grounds for the promotion and protection of the right to mental health, and to what extent this is compatible with the obligations derived from international human rights law as established in Part 2 of this book.

6.2 DESIGN

6.2.1 RESEARCH APPROACH

The purpose of the country study analysis is twofold. First, it seeks to assess how international human rights law, in the context of mental health, influences domestic settings by itself, as well as through domestic legislation, i.e. the implementation and application of respective human rights standards in national legislation and mental healthcare practice. Second, it aims to explore the localisation of human rights (in other words, the need to make human rights more locally relevant by interpreting international norms in the light of local needs), and how, if at all, best practices in

---

[4] Sally Engle Merry, 'Changing rights, changing culture' in Jane Cowan, Marie-Bénédicte Dembour and Richard Wilson (eds), *Culture and Rights: Anthropological Perspectives* (Cambridge University Press 2012) 50.
[5] Ibid.

domestic settings may advance the understanding and application of the right to mental health. Drawing on the findings of Chapters 4 and 5, the central questions for this chapter are: to what extent has mental health as a human right been given effect to in Ghana and Germany through legislative or policy measures? And how, if at all, can the chosen case studies serve as examples to advance the understanding of the right to mental health, and the right to accessing mental healthcare in particular?

As a point of departure, it is crucial to generate an in-depth understanding of the mental health context in which the human rights standards need to be applied. The local realities of Ghana's and Germany's mental health service provision will be assessed in light of the AAAQ analysis, as developed in General Comment 14 of the CteeESCR, which was explained in more detail in section 4.2.1.2.[6] After a general overview of the countries' backgrounds, the country studies will turn to a normative analysis. As indicated by the questions outlined above, the normative analysis has two components. In addition to examining the domestic mental health legislative framework as a whole, key challenges persisting in each country will be highlighted. It is precisely in these subsections that the applicability of the Convention on the Rights of Persons with Disabilities (CRPD) approach will be put to the test.

At this point, it is important to clarify that, by studying the domestic mental health policies of the two countries, the focus of the case studies is not purely on the right to mental healthcare, as other components of the broader right to mental health might also be discussed, to enrich the analysis of a human rights approach to accessing mental healthcare. Nonetheless, as will be apparent throughout the chapter, the focus is always on the healthcare components of the countries' respective mental health policies and programmes. Other rights regarding education, employment, family life and more, which are of no less importance for persons with mental health conditions and psychosocial disabilities, will not be discussed, as these remain largely unrelated to the main topic of this book.

6.2.2 METHODOLOGY

As outlined in Chapter 1, this chapter adopts both descriptive and empirical approaches. At the outset, the methodology for both case studies is congruent: the author carried out desktop research in the English language for both countries, searching for and analysing relevant laws, policies and academic literature. The data collection method was then expanded to encompass different approaches, which enrich the case studies in their own ways. For the case study on Germany, the author searched not only for English-language academic literature or the English-language versions of legislation, but also for documents in the German language. To prevent errors in the translation of legal norms, the author chose the official versions published by government authorities. Where no official English-language version was available (for legislation or academic

---

[6]   CteeESCR, General Comment 14 (n 1).

literature), the author referenced the original German-language version. In such cases, the author provided the translation herself. Due to the limited available academic, and particularly legal, research, the case study on Ghana was enriched by data obtained through interviews with key mental health stakeholders during a field study in Ghana in April/May 2018 (see methods of data collection below). These included officials from the (mental) health sector, policy-makers, human rights lawyers, and members of civil society organisations. The results of these interviews feed directly into the discussion and analysis in section 6.3.

6.2.2.1   Rationale for Country Selection

As mentioned earlier in this book, many countries around the world have updated their mental health laws in line with international and regional human rights treaties.[7] Ghana and Germany are among these countries. Based on a number of criteria, Ghana and Germany are considered as suitable case studies for this book.

Firstly, both countries are so-called best-practice countries in the field of mental health legislation. Ghana has gone through a substantial legislative reform process to reverse its previously rather paternalistic stance on mental health. With the aim of promoting the human rights of persons with mental health conditions and psychosocial disabilities, and improving access to mental healthcare services, the World Health Organization (WHO) endorsed Ghana's new mental health law as an example for best-practice legislation, a very progressive mental health law which can serve as role model for other low- and middle-income countries wishing to develop or reform their mental health legislative frameworks.[8] Germany's mental health efforts were acknowledged specifically in respect of implementing advanced planning models as early as the late 2000s, making the country a pioneer in this field. In Germany, every person can develop advance directives, including in the context of mental healthcare, which are binding by law. Thereby, a person can appoint a supporter who will communicate that person's will to a mental healthcare practitioner; or the person can predefine which kinds of mental healthcare treatment they would like, or not like, to receive. Once they have been completed by a person, both documents have the potential to diminish coercion in psychiatry.[9] Being considered best-practice countries was an important factor in choosing these countries for the study of the practical implications of international standards and a human-rights compliant access to mental healthcare. Besides the fact that this status implies an elevated awareness of, and priority given to, the topic, choosing best-practice countries might make it easier to filter out the potential gaps and

---

[7]   See section 3.4; or World Health Organization (WHO), 'Mental Health Atlas 2020' (2021), <https://www.who.int/publications/i/item/9789240036703> accessed 14 November 2022, p 3.

[8]   See WHO, 'Ghana' (nd), <https://www.who.int/mental_health/policy/country/ghana/en/> accessed 14 November 2022; and George Hudson Walker & Akwasi Osei, 'Mental health law in Ghana' (2017) 14(2) British Journal of Psychiatry International 38.

[9]   See eg WHO, 'Supported decision-making and advance planning: WHO QualityRights Specialized training: course guide' (2019), <https://apps.who.int/iris/handle/10665/329609> accessed 14 November 2022.

complications that exist between international law and domestic law, as well as in the implementation of these laws in practice.

Secondly, suitable local research opportunities were available in both countries. The author worked for a well-respected local human rights organisation in Ghana.[10] For almost a year, the author was part of their human rights and mental health project, and was responsible for the project's (legal) research activities. The author participated in various policy drafting activities, established connections to stakeholders throughout the country, and conducted field visits, all of which were to the benefit of this book. The author is German by birth, and studied international human rights law in Germany, and thus in a German context. With German as the author's mother tongue, documents and discussions in the German language could be interpreted and included to enrich the findings of this book.

Thirdly, and perhaps most importantly, this book is concerned with improving access to mental healthcare in all regions of the world. Various criteria were considered with regard to the localisation of the right to mental health framework. A lack of adequate mental healthcare cannot simply be attributed to resource-constrained countries only. Ghana, a country of the Global South, is ranked as a lower middle-income country, according to the Human Development Index and World Bank classification, and therefore represents a low- and middle-income country (LMIC). Germany, a country in the Global North, is ranked towards the top of the high-income countries (HICs), and thus represents this category.[11] Besides their rankings, Ghana and Germany are further interesting as counterparts due to their dissimilar political, legal and social backgrounds.

Despite the fact that some comparisons could be drawn between Ghana and Germany, it is important to emphasise that the country studies have not been set up to be comparative.

6.2.2.2   Methods of Data Collection for the Case Study on Ghana

Because of its particularity, the data collection process and analysis demand further clarification. The empirical study was conducted in four successive phases: (i) preparations for in-depth interviews as a data collection tool, based on findings of the preceding desk research; (ii) preparation of field work; (iii) data collection; and (iv) data analysis. In the initial stage, relevant stakeholders for interviews were identified before the actual data collection process was prepared. Possible interviewees were selected in consultation with a local expert. After receiving ethical clearance from the Scientific and Ethics Committee of the Faculty of Law of the University of Groningen,[12] on-site data

---

[10]   Human Rights Advocacy Centre (HRAC) in Accra, Ghana.
[11]   See United Nations Development Programme (UNDP), *Human Development Report 2020. The next frontier: Human development and the Anthropocene* (UNDP 2020); and the World Bank, 'Countries and Economies' (nd), <https://data.worldbank.org/country> accessed 14 November 2022.
[12]   According to local authorities, an ethical approval by the respective board in Ghana was not necessary as the interviews did not include any patients.

collection was carried out. Table 6.1 provides an overview of respondents, specifying their positions (where relevant) and sectors, with the dates when the interviews were carried out.

Table 6.1: Overview of interviewees (case study on Ghana)

Interviewee	Position	Sector	Date
Ghana Association of Faith Healers (interviewee 1)	General Secretary	NGO/CSO	17/04/2018
Ministry of Health (interviewee 2)	Representative	Government agency	19/04/2018
BasicNeeds Ghana (interviewee 3)	Representative	NGO/CSO	20/04/2018
Psychiatry Department of the Korle-Bu Teaching Hospital (interviewee 4)	Psychologist	Healthcare	23/04/2018
Human Rights Advocacy Centre (interviewee 5)	Executive Director	NGO/CSO	24/04/2018
Ghana Federation of Disability Organizations (interviewee 6)	Representative	NGO/CSO	02/05/2018
Ghana Federation of Traditional Medicine Practitioners Associations (interviewee 7)	Representative	NGO/CSO	04/05/2018
Pantang Hospital (interviewee 8)	Psychiatrist	Healthcare	04/05/2018
Ghana Federation of Traditional Medicine Practitioners Associations (interviewee 9)	National Organiser	NGO/CSO	08/05/2018
Commission on Human Rights and Administrative Justice (interviewee 10)	Director of Human Rights	Government agency	10/05/2018
Christian Health Association of Ghana (interviewee 11)	Representative	NGO/CSO	14/05/2018
Mental Health Authority (interviewee 12)	Deputy Director	Government agency	21/05/2018
National Council for Persons with Disability (interviewee 13)	Executive Director	Government agency	21/05/2018
MindFreedom Ghana (interviewee 14)	Executive Director	NGO/CSO	22/05/2018
Mental Health Society of Ghana (interviewee 15)	Executive Director	NGO/CSO	29/05/2018

In total, 15 one-on-one in-depth interviews were conducted. A list of questions was developed, and the focus of the open-ended questions was altered, based on each interviewee. The topics included:

- The interviewee's understanding of the right to mental health.
- The interviewee's views on challenges in mental healthcare provision.
- The interviewee's views on the current status of available mental health laws, policies and programmes.

- The interviewee's views on challenges in the implementation of available laws, policies and programmes.
- The interviewee's views on the practices of, and collaboration with, the informal mental health sector.
- The interviewee's views on the way forward to promote the right to mental health in Ghana.

All interviews followed the same procedure. The purpose of the interview was explained, and the interviewee was familiarised with the informed consent form. After consent was given, the interview started, and it was recorded, with the participant's permission. The interviewees were able to ask questions before, during and after the interviews. They also had the option to revoke any information given, during or after the interview. The author transcribed the interviews verbatim, and the information was analysed by establishing a coding system. As far as possible, the author cross-checked statistical information and objectified data mentioned by the interviewees.

As is the case with any qualitative case-study research, various limitations existed. While it is an asset to this study that English is the official language of Ghana, and all interviewees had fluent English language proficiency, language might nevertheless have been a barrier for some. Despite objectifying the observations as much as possible, the findings represent the personal opinions of the interviewees, and cannot, therefore, be generalised upon. Lastly, the selection of stakeholders interviewed was limited and, thus, the opinions of a narrow, while still carefully selected, circle of interviewees formed the basis of the country study. Ultimately, the empirical findings enhanced the country study on Ghana, but a more structural analysis of the specific issues would be necessary to draw more generalised conclusions.

6.3 COUNTRY STUDY I: GHANA

As detailed in the Introduction, the objective of this chapter is to explore the interplay of human rights standards and mental health(care) frameworks in practice. The present section reveals whether Ghana is implementing mental health regulations grounded in international human rights law. This section, moreover, attempts to further the understanding of interventions amounting to ill-treatment, an important challenge in Ghana, which has also been discussed internationally in recent years. First, this section elaborates on the background information on Ghana, to ensure that readers can contextualise the findings and have an overview of the local mental healthcare system (subsection 6.3.1). Next is an examination of Ghana's mental health legislative framework (subsection 6.3.2). Subsequently, the country's regulations regarding interventions that amount to ill-treatment will be analysed and discussed in detail (subsection 6.3.3). The question addressed in this section is: does the Ghanaian mental health law domesticate the provisions of the CRPD successfully, or are there specific situations in mental healthcare practice where this is not even appropriate?

Part 3. Country Study Analysis

6.3.1 BACKGROUND OF GHANA

6.3.1.1   Geographic, Demographic and Economic Characteristics

Ghana is a coastal country in sub-Saharan West Africa a few degrees north of the equator, extending to roughly 238,000 square kilometres. The country is home to a variety of ethnic, linguistic, and religious groups, and has a population of approximately 30 million. Life expectancy at birth is 64 years for women and 62 for men, the infant mortality rate is 37 per 1,000 live births, and the median age of Ghanaian citizens is 30 years.[13] Ghana is considered a lower middle-income country, and has a per capita gross national income of 4,099 USD, and a gross domestic product per capita of 4,212 USD. The country's poverty rates show that 30.1 per cent of the population live in multidimensional poverty (taking into account deprivations faced in health, education and standard of living), and 13.3 per cent of the population live on less than 1.90 USD a day, which the World Bank classifies as extreme poverty.[14]

6.3.1.2   Legal and Administrative Context

Ghana inherited its common law system from the British colonial rule that was in place until 1957. In common law, court decisions are based on prior judicial pronouncements according to the stare decisis principle, meaning that similar scenarios and facts should be approached in the same way. This is especially the case where parties disagree on what the existing statutes and written rules of law say. Thus, the body of law is created by judges and quasi-judicial tribunals.[15] 'The common law of Ghana', as defined in the country's constitution, also includes the rules of customary law, meaning that issues in customary law are recognised as questions of law (rather than questions of fact). The legal landscape of Ghana, nevertheless, continues to modify customary law to meet a formal legal standard. Therefore, customary law is still considered subordinate to decisions by the superior court(s), which most often rules in accordance with common law.[16] Ghana, like many other common law states, adopted a dualist legal structure. The dualist approach posits that international law instruments that are ratified by Ghana must be incorporated or transformed into domestic legislation for them to have effects in the national legal order. Unlike the constitutions of other African countries,[17] the Constitution of Ghana does not explicitly include international law as a source of

---

[13]   Centers for Disease Control and Prevention, 'CDC in Ghana' (nd), <https://www.cdc.gov/globalhealth/countries/ghana/pdf/Ghana_Factsheet.pdf> accessed 14 November 2022.
[14]   See UNDP, *Human Development Report 2019, Beyond income, beyond averages, beyond today: Inequalities in human development in the 21st century* (UNDP 2019).
[15]   Christian N Okeke, 'The use of international law in the domestic courts of Ghana and Nigeria' (2015) 32 Arizona Journal of International and Comparative Law 372, 381–384.
[16]   Ibid.
[17]   See eg the Constitution of Kenya (adopted 2010) and the Constitution of the Republic of South Africa (adopted 1996).

law. Thus, for international norms to have legal effect, they must be incorporated in other legislation.

Many African countries revised their constitutions after becoming state parties to the International Covenant on Economic, Social and Cultural Rights (ICESCR).[18] While other African countries offer an exposition of the right to health amongst other fundamental human rights, either as a highest attainable standard of health norm, or as a right to have access to healthcare services,[19] the Constitution of Ghana lists only 'the right to good healthcare' as a directive principle.[20] To strengthen the legal status of economic, social and cultural rights in Ghana, however, the Supreme Court decided in *Ghana Lotto Operators Association v National Lottery Authority* (2007–2008) that Articles falling under the directive principles are enforceable rights.[21] Therefore, the right to good healthcare can be argued to be justiciable in principle. Lastly, it is also worthwhile pointing out Section 33(5) of the Constitution, which indicates that the enjoyment of all human rights considered to secure the dignity of the person must be ensured, even if they are not explicitly mentioned among the fundamental human rights.[22] This could be interpreted as protecting the right to (mental) health, which encompasses the right to access humane and dignified mental healthcare.[23]

Administratively, Ghana is divided into 16 regions, and further into 260 districts. In line with the decentralised structure of local governance, the Ghana Health Services and Teaching Hospitals Act of 1996 (Act 525) also enforced the decentralisation of the health sector to improve healthcare delivery at local levels. The Mental Health Act of 2012 (Act 846) specifically aims at creating a new mental health system with community-based care and a stronger protection of human rights. As part of the efforts to increase access to mental healthcare at a local level, the Mental Health Authority, an agency under the Ministry of Health, published the 2018 *Guidelines for integrating mental health into the general health care system*. The Guidelines promulgate the establishment of psychiatric departments in all teaching hospitals (tertiary level), psychiatric wings in all regional hospitals (secondary level), and beds in all district hospitals and polyclinics (primary level). Additionally, mental health assessment and first aid is being made accessible in all health centres and Community-based Health Planning and Services (CHPS) compounds, as a further component of the primary health care delivery.[24] While the Mental Health Authority is responsible for proposing and implementing mental

---

[18] Manisuli Ssenyonjo, 'The influence of the International Covenant on Economic, Social and Cultural Rights in Africa' (2017) 64 Netherlands International Law Review 259, 269.
[19] See eg the Constitution of Kenya (adopted 2010), art 43; or the Constitution of the Republic of South Africa (adopted 1996), sec 27(1)(a).
[20] The Constitution of the Republic of Ghana (adopted 1992, amended 1996), sec 34(2).
[21] *Ghana Lotto Operators Association v National Lottery Authority* [2007–2008] SCGLR 1089.
[22] The Constitution of the Republic of Ghana (n 20) sec 33(5).
[23] Natalie Schuck, 'Mental health and exploitation, violence and abuse: the domestication of articles 5 and 16 of the African Charter on Human and Peoples' Rights in Ghana and its implication for conventional and traditional mental healthcare' (2019) 3 African Human Rights Yearbook 179, 188.
[24] See Republic of Ghana, Mental Health Authority, 'Guidelines for integrating mental health into general health care system including child and adolescent health care' (2018).

health policies, and for promoting accessible, affordable and culturally appropriate mental healthcare, the Regional and District Sub-Committees and Coordinators are responsible for the execution and coordination of mental healthcare at the regional and district levels.

6.3.1.3   Mental Health Service Provision

In Ghana, mental healthcare is provided by public and private bodies in specialised, general, and scientific herbal facilities, as well as by private bodies in traditional or alternative health facilities. As indicated in section 6.1, Ghana's mental health service provision will be illustrated based on the AAAQ.

Ghana has three public psychiatric hospitals with a total of 1,322 beds, three teaching hospitals with smaller psychiatric departments, five regional hospitals with psychiatric units, two general public hospitals, and six private clinics that provide psychiatric services.[25] All of these consist of inpatient and outpatient departments. In large parts of the country, community-based psychiatric services are offered by community psychiatric nurses who are connected with district hospitals, but mostly operate from CHPS compounds. Aside from the formal mental healthcare sector, a large number of persons with mental health conditions and psychosocial disabilities make use of so-called informal traditional and faith-based healers. In total, Ghana has 33 practising specialist psychiatrists (0.1 per 100,000 population),[26] and roughly 100 clinical psychologists (0.3 per 100,000 population).[27] Only a small percentage of the estimated 650,000 persons with severe mental disorders, and more than 2 million with moderate to mild mental disorders, receive treatment.[28] Data collected by the Mental Health Authority shows that, in 2017, a total of 142,210 persons were treated in outpatient departments, and a total of 5,560 persons were admitted to a hospital for treatment.[29] While these numbers have increased significantly over recent years, the treatment gap for mental health conditions and psychosocial disabilities in Ghana is still estimated to be more than 98 per cent.[30] In the interviews conducted, nine stakeholders raised serious concerns about the lack of available resources, especially with regard to facilities and human resources.[31] Two stakeholders explained, however,

---

[25] See Republic of Ghana, Ministry of Health, 'The mental health system in Ghana' (2013); Julian Eaton & Sammy Ohene, 'Providing Sustainable Mental Health Care in Ghana: A Demonstration Project' in Sheena Posey Norris, Erin Hammers Forstag & Bruce M Altevogt (eds), *Providing Sustainable Mental and Neurological Health Care in Ghana and Kenya* (National Academies Press 2016) 183–232; Republic of Ghana, Mental Health Authority, 'Psychiatrists in Ghana as at 2nd December, 2019' (2019), <https://mhaghana.com/publications/> accessed 14 November 2022.
[26] Republic of Ghana, Mental Health Authority (n 25).
[27] Julian Eaton & Sammy Ohene (n 25) 194.
[28] WHO, 'Ghana, a very progressive mental health law' (2007), <https://www.who.int/mental_health/policy/country/GhanaCoutrySummary_Oct2007.pdf> accessed 14 November 2022, p 15.
[29] See Republic of Ghana, Mental Health Authority, 'Annual Report, Mental Health Data' (2017).
[30] WHO (n 28) 15.
[31] See interviewees 2, 3, 4, 5, 9, 10, 11, 13 and 15, see Table 6.1.

that increasing decentralisation, and integration of mental health in primary healthcare facilities, would eventually provide for an adequate number of available facilities and personnel.[32] While the availability of psychotropic medication has been scarce in the past, the more pressing current issue is the high cost of the medication,[33] leading to the assessment of accessibility below.

Accessibility issues are aggravated by high levels of stigma and discrimination surrounding mental health conditions. Deeply rooted in traditional beliefs, many Ghanaians do not perceive mental health conditions and psychosocial disabilities as a medical condition, but rather as supernatural, as being possessed by demons, as having to do with a curse on the family, or with being punished for some wrongdoing.[34] Hence, people are afraid of mental health conditions and psychosocial disabilities, which also leads to de facto discrimination in mental health service provision. Interviewee 8 described that, even in the healthcare sector, persons with psychosocial disability are called 'abodong': crazy people who cannot be cured.[35] Besides the non-discrimination component of accessibility, geographical accessibility is a major issue. The three psychiatric hospitals that provide almost half of the psychiatric services in the country (with 61,341 outpatient treatments and 2,356 admissions in 2017)[36] are all located in the far south. In the northern regions, and in rural areas, there are no clinical psychiatrists and almost no clinical psychologists.[37] Many people from remote communities must travel hours to seek any kind of psychiatric service at all. The intended decentralisation of mental healthcare, integration into primary healthcare, and expansion of community-based services would solve the issue of geographical inaccessibility.[38] Community psychiatric nurses operating from district hospitals already play an integral role in community-based psychiatric services,[39] most of which are currently outpatient services, including clinic-based follow-ups. Despite the facilitation of mental health services in more rural areas, however, most medication is still only accessible in pharmacies in urban areas, or in specialist psychiatric facilities.[40] The third component of accessibility of mental health services – economic accessibility – is of no less concern.[41] As a matter of policy, mental health services, including consultations, admissions and all medication, are – at least in theory –

---

[32] See interviewees 12 and 15, see Table 6.1.
[33] WHO, 'WHO-AIMS Report on mental health system in Ghana' (2011), p 11.
[34] Julian Eaton & Sammy Ohene (n 25) 189; Human Rights Watch, 'Like a death sentence: Abuses against persons with mental disabilities in Ghana' (2012) < https://www.hrw.org/report/2012/10/02/death-sentence/abuses-against-persons-mental-disabilities-ghana> accessed 14 November 2022; and interviewees 1, 2, 8, 10, 14, see Table 6.1.
[35] Interviewee 8, see Table 6.1.
[36] See Republic of Ghana, Mental Health Authority (n 29).
[37] Republic of Ghana, Ministry of Health, 'Ten Year Mental Health Policy 2018–2027: Ensuring a mentally healthy population' (2018), p 20.
[38] See interviewees 3, 5, 11, 13, 14, 15, see Table 6.1.
[39] Julian Eaton & Sammy Ohene (n 25) 188.
[40] See Republic of Ghana, Ministry of Health (n 25) 21; or Julian Eaton & Sammy Ohene (n 25) 190.
[41] See interviewees 2, 3, 4, 6, 11, 14, 15, see Table 6.1.

available at no cost from the public sector. For that reason, when the National Health Insurance Scheme (NHIS) was introduced, there was no need to cover mental health conditions and their treatment under the scheme. In reality, affected individuals and their families often cannot afford to travel long distances to hospitals that offer free care. Furthermore, mental healthcare, and thus the public psychiatric hospitals, are highly underfunded, leading to insufficient free essential medication for patients. Consequently, the financial burden is, after all, placed on patients, who have to purchase relatively expensive medicine out of pocket without any refund.[42] Interviewee 3 highlighted that persons with mental health conditions and psychosocial disabilities indicate not being able to access medication as a main concern:

> They need treatment, and that is medication … Because without the medication they cannot even come to you and talk to you. They can't even do anything. I have been part of consultations and I can bring reports. You would see … medication comes first.[43]

Although the new mental health law obliges the government to support the psychiatric hospitals financially,[44] there has been a continuous lack of government subventions.[45] And while some psychotropic medications are now covered by the NHIS, efforts are still ongoing to fully include psychiatric services under the scheme.[46] With regard to information accessibility, many interviewees raised the concern that there is a widespread lack of understanding of what mental health really is. Interviewee 11 explained that their organisation creates awareness in the community by going from house to house:

> We educate them on what mental health is, who it can affect, and the signs and symptoms … when someone is having a mental health issue. Then afterwards … we go into the conditions, the general conditions, we educate them on it. If it is depression, how can you tell, if somebody is having depression, early signs … We go in all those details. Usually, it is interesting because at the end of such awareness creation, a lot of people come out [as suffering from a mental health condition].[47]

Raising awareness, advocating, and educating the public on mental health, according to various stakeholders, is an integral step for ensuring access to mental health services.[48]

---

[42] See Republic of Ghana, Ministry of Health (n 25) 19; Julian Eaton & Sammy Ohene (n 25) 194; or OHCHR, 'Report of the Special Rapporteur on torture and other cruel, inhuman or degrading treatment or punishment' (5 March 2014) UN Doc A/HRC/25/60/Add.1, para 70.
[43] Interviewee 3, see Table 6.1.
[44] Republic of Ghana, Mental Health Act (Act 846) of 2012, sec 81.
[45] Mark Boye, 'Inside Accra Psychiatric Hospital: The good, the bad, the ugly!' (7 September 2017), GhanaWeb, <https://www.ghanaweb.com/GhanaHomePage/health/Inside-Accra-Psychiatric-Hospital-The-good-the-bad-the-ugly-578188> accessed 14 November 2022.
[46] See Julian Eaton & Sammy Ohene (n 25) 194; and Interviewees 2, 6, 14 and 15, see Table 6.1.
[47] Interviewee 11, see Table 6.1.
[48] See interviewees 1, 4, 6, 11, 12, and 14, see Table 6.1.

Acceptability is an interesting element within the Ghanaian context. Acceptable mental healthcare signifies that the cultural traditions of the people, such as traditional healing practices and medication, need to be respected.[49] The issue of acceptable mental healthcare that may violate the principle of quality will be discussed below in this country study. Due to the cultural conception of mental health and ill health, traditional healthcare plays a particular role in the treatment of mental health conditions and psychosocial disabilities. It is believed that around 80 per cent of the population turn to traditional healthcare, either alone or in combination with so-called Western medicine.[50] As evaluated in subsection 2.3, understanding the causative factors or ways of managing conditions are not the only decisive factors when choosing the type of care; also decisive is the availability of other sources of healthcare in the surrounding area. When discussing the accessibility of mental health services, interviewee 15 explained that it is:

> difficult for people with this condition to even access health care … the [formal] orthodox medicine is not there. So what option am I left with? … I would rather go to the prayer camp.[51]

Despite being widely accepted amongst the population, Ghana's traditional healthcare has been in the spotlight for various human rights infringements, including people being chained or shackled, flogged, or being forced to fast, or to take herbal concoctions.[52] Traditional practitioners describe these methods as necessary for an effective and holistic healing process, as the herbal drinks contain spiritual healing powers, the flogging shoos away the demons, and the forced fasting starves the evil spirits.[53] While the practices might be culturally appropriate and acceptable, they raise concerns in light of medical ethics (another component of acceptability), which includes the principles of 'do no harm', choice, control, autonomy and dignity.[54] Furthermore, such practices may undermine the last of the AAAQ elements, namely quality.

To be of (good) quality, mental health services require the use of evidence-based practices for the purposes of prevention, promotion, treatment and recovery.

---

[49] Maite San Giorgi, The Human Right to Equal Access to Health Care (Intersentia 2012) 60.
[50] Nah Dove, 'A Return to traditional healthcare practices; A Ghanaian study' (2010) 40(5) Journal of Black Studies 823, 823.
[51] Prayer camps are among the informal (mental) healthcare institutions to which persons go/are brought to receive spiritual and/or religious healing for their health condition; Interviewee 15, see Table 6.1.
[52] Republic of Ghana, Ministry of Health (n 37); and Committee for the Prevention of Torture in Africa, 'Intersession Activity Report' (2016), <https://www.achpr.org/public/Document/file/English/59os_inter_session_report_comm_mute_eng.pdf> accessed 14 November 2022.
[53] Lilly NA Kpobi and others, 'Traditional herbalists' methods of treating mental disorders in Ghana' (2018) 56(1) Transcultural Psychiatry 250, 259.
[54] United Nations General Assembly (UNGA), 'Report of the Special Rapporteur on the right of everyone to the enjoyment of the highest attainable standard of physical and mental health, Dainius Pūras' (15 April 2020) UN Doc A/HRC/44/48, para 65.

Especially in the informal traditional healthcare sector, the evidence basis of applied practices may be questionable. Different interviewees had reservations about the use of herbal medicine, which is commonly administered by traditional practitioners. While interviewee 4 explained that a specific herb might aid in the treatment of some mental health conditions because 'it reduces electrolyte activity', or because it 'increases levels of serotonin',[55] others pointed out the danger of unregulated herbal medication where the source of ingredients, or even the ingredients themselves, are unknown. Such medication could contain an overdose of a toxin that can harm the liver or kidneys, or there might be side effects when mixing it with psychotropic medication.[56] For health facilities, goods and services to be of good quality, patients must be seen not only as users of care services, but as active rights-holders. In its Concluding Observation on Ghana, the Human Rights Committee expressed its concern about inadequate treatment in public psychiatric institutions, as well as in unregistered private facilities. The report outlined that forced medication, confinement and inhumane practices constitute violations of Article 7 (the right to be free from torture or cruel, inhuman or degrading treatment or punishment), Article 9 (the right to liberty and security) and Article 10 (the right of persons deprived of their liberty to be treated with humanity and with respect for their inherent dignity) of the International Covenant on Civil and Political Rights (ICCPR).[57] Furthermore, after his last visit to Ghana, former Special Rapporteur on Torture, Juan Méndez, called Ghana's mental health practices and services 'dreadfully inadequate'.[58] In his report, he articulated that the existing deplorable conditions, both in psychiatric institutions and in traditional healthcare facilities, give rise to human rights abuses, especially inhumane treatment, against patients.[59] His findings demonstrate that ill-treatment also occurs in the formal psychiatric hospitals. Méndez reported poor sanitation, overcrowding, and the administration of electroshock therapy with the use of restraints, and without anaesthesia. He further doubted that consent to treatment is always truly free and informed in practice, despite hospital files documenting patients' consent.[60] Thus, ill-treatment in mental health service provision in Ghana continues to pose a challenge.[61] For this reason, the author will, in subsection 6.3.3, evaluate the domestic legal provisions protecting against involuntary interventions amounting

---

[55] Interviewee 4, see Table 6.1.
[56] See interviewees 3, 6, 8 and 14, see Table 6.1.
[57] Human Rights Committee (HRC), 'Concluding observations on the initial reports of Ghana' (9 August 2016) UN Doc CCPR/C/GHA/CO/1, paras 27–28.
[58] UNGA, 'Follow up report of the Special Rapporteur on torture and other cruel, inhuman or degrading treatment or punishment on his follow-up visit to the Republic of Ghana, Juan Méndez' (25 February 2015) UN Doc A/HRC/31/57/Add.2, para 62.
[59] Ibid paras 68–75.
[60] UNGA 'Report of the Special Rapporteur on torture and other cruel, inhuman or degrading treatment or punishment, Juan E. Méndez, Mission to Ghana' (n 42) paras 68–71.
[61] See Republic of Ghana, Ministry of Health (n 37); or Human Rights Watch, 'Ghana should implement commitments on mental health issues' (2018), <https://www.hrw.org/news/2018/03/15/ghana-should-implement-commitments-mental-health-issues> accessed 14 November 2022.

to inhumane treatment and abuse. Ultimately, poor quality care might be an even bigger barrier than insufficient accessibility of care.[62]

6.3.2 GHANA'S MENTAL HEALTH LEGISLATIVE FRAMEWORK

By ratifying the CRPD in July 2012, Ghana indicated its consent to be bound by this treaty. Pursuant to Article 4 CRPD, the state became obliged to adopt appropriate legislation, policies and practices for the implementation of the rights recognised in the CRPD, and to modify or abolish existing laws that discriminated against persons with mental health conditions and psychosocial disabilities. The following subsections will give an overview of Ghana's mental health regulations for protecting and promoting the right to mental health(care).

6.3.2.1 Relevant Legislation

In March 2012, Ghana passed its new Mental Health Act (Act 846), replacing the unimplemented 1972 Mental Health Decree (NRCD 30). The adoption of this new law was perceived as a major milestone for addressing mental health as a public health concern, and for protecting the human rights of persons with mental health conditions and psychosocial disabilities in Ghana.[63] The Mental Health Act spells out the rights of persons with mental health conditions and psychosocial disabilities in relation to accessing care, and regulates the protection of vulnerable groups in healthcare settings. It reflects international human rights standards and best practices, while taking into consideration local conditions, requirements and customs. The overall aim of the Act is to create a new and modern community-based mental health system for the protection of persons with mental health conditions and psychosocial disabilities. It provides a legal framework for the safe and qualitative treatment of persons with mental health conditions and psychosocial disabilities (as well as other rights for such people, such as marriage, employment, accommodation and voting rights), and it stipulates changes to the organisation and provision of mental health services. The Act also outlines specific ways of funding such services, and establishes an authority to govern mental health services.[64]

The Mental Health Act applies to any public or private licensed mental health facility where persons with mental disorders are hospitalised (and, thus, not to ambulant care), and covers every person with any degree of mental disorder.[65] A mental disorder is defined as:

---

[62] Presentation of Regien Biesma-Blanco, Maternal & Child Health: A Global Perspective, Aletta Research Meet-Up 5th April 2019 Groningen.
[63] Victor Doku and others, 'Implementing the Mental Health Act in Ghana: Any Challenges Ahead?' (2012) 46(4) Ghana Medical Journal 241.
[64] See eg Akwasi Osei and others, 'The new Ghana mental health bill' (2011) 8(1) Psychiatry International 8; George Hudson Walker & Akwasi Osei (n 8) 38–39.
[65] Republic of Ghana, Mental Health Act (n 44) sec 95.

[a] condition of the mind in which there is a clinically significant disturbance of mental or behaviour functioning associated with distress or interference of daily life and manifesting as disturbance of speech, perception, mood, thought, volition, orientation or other cognitive functions to such degree as to be considered pathological but [excluding] social deviance without personal dysfunction.[66]

The Act applies to all licensed facilities for mental healthcare provision, including private mental health hospitals, and traditional and faith-based centres.[67] Yet, it specifically distinguishes between the public and private, as well as formal and informal, sectors, in light of specific service provision. For instance, only accredited institutions are allowed to admit persons against their will, or for involuntary care. Traditional or faith-based centres are not considered accredited institutions.[68] Walker and Osei explain that the main reason for this regulation is the reduction of human rights abuses, as the informal sector commonly keeps involuntary persons shackled in chains or otherwise secluded.[69] The same applies to private mental health hospitals without psychiatrists. If no psychiatrist is available, a private facility is also not allowed to admit persons involuntarily.[70]

In addition to provisions against discrimination in everyday life, the Act identifies clear rules for the admission and treatment of persons with mental health conditions and psychosocial disabilities. As general rule, it provides the right of 'humane and dignified treatment at any time with respect to personal dignity and privacy', and the right to be 'informed of the relevant information pertaining to admission including [the patient's] rights'.[71] In cases where, due to a mental health condition, persons cannot give consent, their right to medical treatment cannot be denied.[72] Section 57 defines the right to the highest attainable standard of mental healthcare, and entitles affected individuals to 'the same standard of care as a person with physical health problems and [they] shall be treated on an equitable basis including quality of in-patient food, bedding, sanitation, buildings, levels and qualifications of staff, medical and related services and access to essential medicines.'[73] This section further encompasses the right to have access to psychotropic drugs and other psychosocial rehabilitative interventions as needed. Moreover, the standard of treatment in section 57 includes a prohibition on the use of intrusive and irreversible treatment in emergency cases, as well as a prohibition on subjecting patients to any form of inhumane treatment. The Legislative Instrument to the Act, the Mental Health Regulations of 2019 (L.I. 2385)

---

[66] See Republic of Ghana, Mental Health Act (n 44) sec 97. According to section 95, persons with mental retardation are included in the definition and persons with personality disorders are excluded.
[67] As they can obtain a licence from the Traditional Medicine Practice Council pursuant to the Traditional Medicine Practice Act 2000 (Act 575).
[68] Republic of Ghana, Mental Health Act (n 44) sec 51.
[69] George Hudson Walker & Akwasi Osei (n 8) 38.
[70] Republic of Ghana, Ministry of Health, Mental Health Regulation (L.I. 2385) of 2019, sec 42.
[71] Republic of Ghana, Mental Health Act (n 44) sec 55(2)(5).
[72] Ibid sec 56.
[73] Ibid sec 57(2).

(hereinafter referred to as the 'Legislative Instrument' or the 'Regulations'), further details the standards in mental healthcare delivery as including evidence-based, clinically accepted and ready medication, equipment and supplies; the establishment of quality assurance teams for quality assurance and improvement activities; appropriately trained personnel; supportive services, for patients, that are necessary for care and rapid improvement; recreational activities and rehabilitative areas.[74] As a general rule, each patient, no matter whether voluntary or involuntary, must have a treatment plan. At all times, patients have the right to free and full information pertaining to their treatment plan and mental health condition. Access to such information can be denied, however, when the information is considered harmful to the well-being of the patient. Information should also be accessible to primary caregivers. Yet, unless information is 'absolutely essential' to the patient's interests, or for the safety of the caregiver, patients can object to this information being shared with caregivers. And where patients are incapable of understanding the information, their representative should be given access to it.[75] While this seems practicable, using the term 'representative' also gives rise to the highly contested question of guardianship regulation within domestic mental health legislation.

A closer look at section 68, which regulates competence, capacity and guardianship, clarifies the guardianship regime within Ghana's legislation. The section states that, when a person is found to lack the mental capacity, upon examination by mental health professionals, including a psychiatrist, the court can appoint a guardian for 'the personal protection of that person', a decision which the court must review annually. Family members or social welfare institutions can apply to the court for such appointments. According to the law, guardianship can be limited to a specific area, while for other areas the person retains capacity.[76] One of the areas in which a person could be represented by a guardian is 'the right to treatment of choice'. One might argue that a representative deciding the 'treatment of choice' for a patient, by 'taking treatment … decisions on behalf of the incapacitated person' is inherently contradictory.[77] However, the law seems to substantiate the substituted decision-making regime by stating that: (i) guardianship for persons with psychosocial disabilities should always be the last resort; (ii) the guardian must consult with the incapacitated person as far as possible; and (iii) a high standard of substituted judgement must be used.[78] After all, an incapacitated person has the right to contest the application for guardianship, or to appeal against the court decision, personally or with the help of a representative.[79] Consequently, section 68 gives the impression that the Mental Health Act recognises a person's capacity to hold rights and duties, and to exercise these rights and duties. Thus, the law acknowledges the understanding of legal capacity and its distinction from the

---

[74] Republic of Ghana, Mental Health Regulation (n 70) secs 36–38.
[75] Republic of Ghana, Mental Health Act (n 44) sec 62.
[76] Ibid sec 69.
[77] Ibid, sec 69(6).
[78] Ibid sec 68.
[79] Ibid sees 68(5), 70.

concept of mental capacity, as articulated by the Committee on the Rights of Persons with Disabilities (CteeRPD) (see subsection 5.3.2.1). However, the Act defines 'capacity' as a 'functional ability to understand or form an intention with regard to an act', and persons with mental health conditions and psychosocial disabilities are 'presumed to have capacity until reliably proven otherwise'.[80] The term 'functional ability' could be characterised as what the CteeRPD identifies as the 'functional approach': the restriction of a person's legal capacity based on the process by which they make a decision. The functional approach is criticised by the CteeRPD. After all, the Act fails to provide more details, such as the reasons for declaring a person incompetent in the first place, or what a high standard of substituted judgement by a guardian actually requires. The question that remains is: why is the Act not in favour of supported decision-making as defined within the CRPD framework (Article 12)? One reason could be that, at the time the law was adopted, the term 'supported decision-making' was not commonly used with regard to the scope of the right to legal capacity. The CteeRPD's General Comment No. 1, which highlights the need to shift from a substituted decision-making paradigm to so-called 'supported decision-making', and which explains in depth what 'supported decision-making' entails, was indeed published two years after the coming into force of the Mental Health Act. Thus, although it does not use the (later introduced) terminology of 'supported decision-making', the provisions of the Mental Health Act (and the intentions of its drafters) may well be in conformity with the very essence of a 'supported decision-making regime', as already analysed above. Another reason could be that the Act does not actually endorse supported decision-making, or favour a complete shift to supported decision-making, as intended by the CRPD framework. It is plausible that the drafters intended to recognise that some people lack the capacity to be involved in a (supported) decision-making process, such as persons with severe dementia, who fall under the Act. This would also clarify why the Act refers to the 'functional ability approach'. Due to the unavailability of insights into the drafting history of the Act, this question remains open.

Another worthwhile dimension of the Act is the possibility of filing a complaint, as will be demonstrated in more detail in subsection 6.3.3.2. A Mental Health Review Tribunal, which is to be established according to the law, is to be specifically mandated to hear and investigate complaints, as one of its functions.[81] Additionally, Visiting Committees are to be established, to visit and inspect all mental health institutions, in order to ensure that the rights of persons with mental health conditions and psychosocial disabilities are being protected.[82] Yet, at the time of writing, neither the Tribunal nor the Visiting Committees have been operationalised.

In addition to the 2012 Mental Health Act, Ghana passed the Persons with Disability Act in 2006 (Act 715), and the Traditional Medicine Practice Act in 2000 (Act 575), both of which are relevant for promoting and protecting mental health.

---

[80] Ibid sec 97.
[81] Ibid sec 26.
[82] Ibid sec 36.

Chapter 6. Bridging Theory and Practice through Country Studies

Although persons with psychosocial disabilities are, by definition, protected by the Persons with Disability Act, and despite references to the provision of free general and specialist medical treatment and rehabilitative care, the Persons with Disability Act does not regulate (mental) healthcare, or the access to related services, in more detail than the Mental Health Act. Such specific regulations have to be derived from the new Mental Health Act, according to the Executive Director of the National Council of Persons with Disabilities (NCPD). He has further disclosed that the responsibility for programmes and interventions on mental health matters lies solely with the Mental Health Authority, not with the Council.[83] The second piece of legislation mentioned above – the Traditional Medicine Practice Act – focuses mainly on the registration and licensing of practitioners, but not on the practices themselves. Its examination would, therefore, go beyond the scope of this book.

6.3.2.2 Relevant Policies, Guidelines and Programmes

In recent years, Ghana has published a new policy and a number of new guidelines. The *Mental Health Policy 2018–2027* guides the implementation of the Mental Health Act, and the establishment of the Tribunal and Visiting Committees, which are essential mechanisms for human rights protection in line with the Act. Upholding the dignity and autonomy of persons with mental health conditions and psychosocial disabilities, and ensuring their freedom from discrimination, are among the guiding principles of the Policy.[84] Calling human rights abuses one of the greatest challenges of mental healthcare in Ghana, the Policy aims to ensure, protect and promote human rights as follows:

- guaranteeing the rights of persons with mental health conditions and psychosocial disabilities
- strengthening the Mental Health Review Tribunal and Visiting Committees
- collaborating with ministries and government agencies, NGOs, traditional rulers and civil society
- engaging the informal mental healthcare sector to respect the human rights of persons under their care.[85]

However, the Policy fails to explain how the Tribunal and Visiting Committees should be established and operated. And besides referring to particular stakeholders as responsible actors in the collaboration to protect human rights, the Policy lacks any details with regard to their specific roles. The document that intends to foster the human rights protection of persons with mental health conditions and psychosocial

---

[83] See interviewee 13, see Table 6.1.
[84] Republic of Ghana, Ministry of Health (n 37) 12.
[85] Republic of Ghana, Ministry of Health (n 37) 30.

disabilities can, therefore, be criticised for failing to specify the precise strategies that would outline clear action steps and responsibilities.[86]

In 2018, the Mental Health Authority also launched a set of guidelines to protect against human rights abuses in mental healthcare settings. The *Guidelines for Traditional Healers* aim specifically to strengthen the monitoring of human rights activities in traditional and faith-based centres. They regulate matters like appropriate housing, and adequate provision of water, clothing and food, as well as safety and security, and other human rights guarantees. The Guidelines explicitly prescribe freedom from discrimination; freedom from cruel, inhuman and degrading treatment, such as flogging, restraint in chains, shackles and other such forms of treatment; freedom from forced or unremunerated labour; freedom from sexual harassment, rape and indecent assault; and freedom from forced confession; as well as respecting the right to belief (not forcing a client to adapt a certain religious belief), and the right to confidentiality.[87] Because of the prevalence of these forms of treatment in practice, the Guidelines specifically lay out that patients cannot be restrained using chains, shackles, logs, ropes or cages. In emergency cases where there is a high risk or imminent danger to self or others, an aggressive or violent person can be restrained with a soft cloth, bedsheet or blanket, but must then be transferred to a formal mental health facility.[88]

To improve the availability and accessibility of mental health services, the *Guidelines for Integrating Mental Health into General Health Care System Including Child and Adolescent Health Care* were developed. These provide direction on integrating mental health into general healthcare effectively and efficiently. They further stipulate that community-based mental health services must encompass a recovery-based approach that supports affected individuals to achieve what they aspire for themselves. Thus, the providers of the services offered must ensure that they: (i) listen and respond to the individual's understanding of their mental health condition and what would help them recover; (ii) work with individuals as equal partners in their own care; and (iii) offer individuals a choice of treatment and therapies.[89] These requirements implicitly link to Article 12 CRPD – the right to legal capacity and to be able to exercise one's own rights – as well as to Article 17 CRPD: the right to respect for personal integrity. The last of the three new sets of guidelines are the *Guidelines for Conducting Peer Reviews at Psychiatric Hospitals*, which seek to improve the standard of service delivery in Ghana's three psychiatric hospitals, through a detailed peer-review procedure. The overall aim is to ensure the provision of humane and high-quality care in these hospitals.[90]

---

[86] Natalie Schuck (n 23) 191.
[87] Republic of Ghana, Mental Health Authority, 'Guidelines for Traditional and Faith-based Healers in Mental Health' (2018), p 7.
[88] Ibid.
[89] Republic of Ghana, Mental Health Authority (n 24) 9.
[90] Republic of Ghana, Mental Health Authority, 'Guidelines for Conducting Peer Reviews at Psychiatric Hospitals' (2018).

Since many persons with mental health conditions and psychosocial disabilities seek treatment in the informal sector, it is also valuable to examine whether and how practices are regulated in these settings. While the Traditional Medicine Practice Act does not shed light on this matter, the 2006 *Code of Ethics and Standards of Practice for Alternative Medicine Practitioners in Ghana* provides specific regulations for traditional and faith-based healers, including regulations on treatment. For instance, practitioners are prohibited from discriminating against patients on the grounds of the nature of their illnesses or disabilities, must show a high sense of integrity, and must respect patients' decisions not to accept a certain kind of treatment.[91] Practitioners are asked not to persuade individuals to come and receive treatment other than by their own free will, and patients must be informed about their conditions, and the management and treatment of their conditions, including risks, with the exception of emergency situations where practitioners have to act quickly.[92] During consultation, examination and treatment, the patient's privacy must be respected, and only traditional or religious rites that are acceptable to the patient may be used as part of therapy.[93] In light of this document,[94] human rights standards might seem to be valued and upheld in traditional and faith-based mental healthcare practice. Yet, the question is whether practitioners know about these regulations and understand their implications; and if they do, to what extent do they adhere to what is enshrined in their Code of Ethics and Standards?

In February 2019, the Mental Health Authority, in partnership with the WHO, launched the QualityRights initiative in Ghana. Over the course of three years, this e-training programme with online coaching aimed to train at least 5,000 people on mental health, human rights and recovery. The ultimate goal was to foster attitudes and practices that respect dignity and human rights, and to promote holistic, person-centred and recovery-oriented care and support.[95] At the time of writing, the effects of this training had not yet been analysed. Together with various sensitisation activities on human rights in mental healthcare, carried out by different NGOs throughout the country, the WHO programme tries to tackle one persisting challenge: eliminating interventions that amount to coercion, violence and abuse, by improving the quality of care in the formal and informal mental healthcare delivery system.

---

[91] Republic of Ghana, Ministry of Health, 'Code of Ethics and Standards of Practice for Alternative Medicine Practitioners in Ghana' (2006), arts 27, 28.
[92] Ibid arts 25, 33.
[93] Ibid arts 24, 30, 35.
[94] The reason why this document is important is that it is specifically written for traditional and faith-based healthcare practitioners by the Traditional and Alternative Medicine Practice Council. As for the whole regulatory framework as presented above, especially the Mental Health Act, stakeholders from the traditional and faith-based healthcare context have strongly voiced the failure of including them in the drafting process.
[95] See Human Rights Watch, 'Not everyone is celebrating on Independence Day in Ghana' (2019), <https://www.hrw.org/news/2019/03/13/not-everyone-celebrating-independence-day-ghana> accessed 14 November 2022; and QualityRights in Mental Health – Ghana Project (nd), <http://qualityrightsgh.com/> accessed 14 November 2022.

6.3.3 PERSISTING KEY CHALLENGE: INTERVENTIONS AMOUNTING TO ILL-TREATMENT

According to data collected during the year before the coming into force of the Mental Health Act, 2 per cent of all admissions to mental health hospitals and 8 per cent of all admissions to general hospital psychiatric inpatient units were 'legally sanctioned involuntary admissions'. The remaining admissions where either voluntary, or against the will of the individual but with the proxy consent of their relative, which was still considered voluntary. While involuntary admissions are not ill-treatment per se, Chapter 5 illustrated how they are often a precursor to the use of seclusion and restraints. Although no hospitals kept records on the use of seclusion and restraints, the Ministry of Health estimated that around 20 per cent of all patients had been subject to seclusion or restraint measures.[96] The following subsections will illustrate how the new and promising mental health law not only regulates involuntary admission and treatment, but also protects against interventions that may amount to ill-treatment.

6.3.3.1 The Legal Framework regarding Voluntary and Involuntary Interventions

As explained in subsection 5.4.3.1, ill-treatment is a circumstance or procedure in the context of mental healthcare provision to which a patient has not consented.[97] Therefore, as a point of departure, this section will first discuss whether, and to what extent, Ghana's mental health legislation addresses voluntary and involuntary interventions.

The Mental Health Act provides that persons in need of treatment for their mental health condition can choose to contact mental health facilities for outpatient or inpatient treatment. The Act clearly outlines that voluntary patients must give consent, and that their right to refuse treatment must be respected. Cases of long-term stay voluntary patients must be reported to the Mental Health Review Tribunal, and when being admitted, persons must be informed about all necessary things pertaining to their admission.[98] The Mental Health Regulations of 2019 (L.I. 2385) set out in more detail that patients must sign a consent form for voluntary admission, and that they must be given detailed information and education on all relevant information, including, but not limited to, the nature of medication, available alternative medication(s), consent to medication, the right to refuse medication, and the implications of refusing medication. Moreover, they must sign a separate consent form for medication.[99] As stipulated in the Act, they must be informed that a request for discharge cannot be granted in the event that they meet the requirements for involuntary admission at that later time. Yet,

---

[96] The Republic of Ghana, Ministry of Health (n 25) 25.
[97] However, as discussed in section 5.4, not offering treatment to persons with mental health conditions and psychosocial disabilities who is in need (because he or she refuses treatment) may also amount to ill-treatment according to some jurisdictions and scholars.
[98] Republic of Ghana, Mental Health Act (n 44) sees 39–40.
[99] Republic of Ghana, Mental Health Regulation (n 70) sec 21.

the Regulations add that, in such cases, patients must be informed about their right of appeal to the Mental Health Review Tribunal. Nevertheless, this shows that, besides recognising voluntary interventions, the law explicitly acknowledges the need for involuntary interventions. In fact, a large section of the Act is dedicated to involuntary treatment procedures.

There are two criteria for non-consensual interventions under the Mental Health Act: under a certificate of urgency, or based on another person's/entity's recommendation to court for temporary involuntary treatment.[100] In both cases, the person does not consent to being admitted, and will be forcibly brought to a mental health facility. Whenever it is expedient for the welfare of persons suspected to have a mental health condition or psychosocial disability, or for public safety because of their condition, such persons can be taken to a mental health facility by the police, a relative or any other person. If, upon examination, a registered medical practitioner is convinced that the person requires urgent treatment, and thus meets the criteria for treatment as an emergency case, a certificate of urgency is issued, and the person can be placed under care, observation and treatment. The Regulations further specify that a person cannot be admitted unless the certificate of urgency form is countersigned by a second practitioner, who is also convinced that emergency care is needed.[101] The Act and Regulations are silent on whether the medical or health practitioners must be independent. In cases where an immediate admission to a facility or mental health facility is impracticable, persons can be detained at any other place of safe custody for up to 48 hours before being transferred to such a facility.[102] 'Any other place of safe custody' includes all private mental health clinics without psychiatrists; informal mental health centres, such as traditional or faith-based facilities; police cells; or other placements within a community. The Act strictly regulates that detention in a mental health facility under the certificate of urgency cannot exceed a period of 72 hours. After 72 hours, a person admitted as an emergency case must either have opted to become a voluntary patient or be discharged, or a court order for temporary treatment must have been obtained.[103] The limited duration of admission for urgent cases can be interpreted as a safeguard, but the provisions fail to clarify the requirements for meeting the criteria of an emergency case in the first place. Do persons, for example, have to show aggressive behaviour or be violent? Only when examining a form in an appendix to the Regulation can a vague justification for emergency care be inferred, this being that the treatment is required because the psychosocial disability 'seriously impairs the person's ability to react appropriately to his or her environment or to associate with others', so that care, supervision and control is required to 'prevent his/her substantial mental or physical deterioration or for the protection

---

[100] The term involuntary treatment in the Mental Health Act refers to both involuntary admission and treatment and can therefore be seen as equivalent to 'involuntary interventions'.
[101] Republic of Ghana, Mental Health Regulation (n 70) sec 29(5).
[102] Republic of Ghana, Mental Health Act (n 44) sec 48.
[103] Ibid sec 49.

of the person or for the protection of others'.[104] This means that agitated or violent behaviour is not even especially necessary as a justification for emergency care, since calmness or absent-mindedness could, in some circumstances, also be classified as an 'inappropriate reaction to the environment'. Besides the lack of clarity, a study by Anokye and others reveals that one of the biggest challenges with this provision is the lack of knowledge about the certificate of urgency among healthcare workers, including the issuance and usage of the certificate. Many respondents to their study did not know about the 48- and 72-hour time limits for detention, were unaware of the places from where the certificate could be obtained, and out of all the reasons given for when a certificate of urgency can be issued, most respondents answered that this was when the person concerned showed 'signs of having a mental illness'.[105] Although adequate knowledge about the certificate of urgency was higher among psychiatrists than other healthcare workers, Anokye and others nevertheless point out that there is a need for adequate training on the mental health legislation, in order to ensure that its provisions are being followed.

Requirements for temporary involuntary treatment, i.e. the other criteria for non-consensual interventions, are clearly outlined in the Act. Any person, whether a relative or an unrelated person, can apply to a court for the involuntary admission or treatment of a person believed to have a severe mental disorder, if the person concerned is either at personal risk or poses a risk to others, or where there is a substantial risk that the disorder will seriously deteriorate. The recommendation to court, which must be supported by one medical and one mental health practitioner, must fulfil four criteria for temporary involuntary treatment. Firstly, it must set out in detail the reasons why the person should be under care, observation and treatment. Secondly, facts supporting this opinion must be shown. Thirdly, the person must be suspected to lack the capacity to make their own informed treatment decisions. And, lastly, the treatment must be necessary to improve the person's condition, to restore their capacity to make treatment decisions, to prevent serious deterioration, or to prevent harm to themselves or to others.[106] Subsequently, the Mental Health Review Tribunal has 48 hours to examine these facts. If the Tribunal is satisfied, it can order the placement of that person under care, observation or treatment in a psychiatric hospital for a maximum period of one month.[107] However, if a psychiatrist or head of a facility is of the opinion that the severity of the mental health condition warrants prolonged treatment for the welfare of the person and the safety of the public, and the likelihood of a partial or complete recovery can be specified, a recommendation can be made to the Tribunal. If the Tribunal is satisfied, it can order prolonged treatment for up to twelve months, which

---

[104] See Republic of Ghana, Mental Health Regulation (n 70), Appendix, Form Eight, Involuntary Admission of Patient under Certificate of Urgency.
[105] Reindolf Anokye and others, 'Knowledge of mental health legislation in Ghana: a case of the use of certificate of urgency in mental health care' (2018) 12(37) International Journal of Mental Health Systems.
[106] Republic of Ghana, Mental Health Act (n 44) sec 42.
[107] Ibid sec 43.

must be reviewed after six months.[108] During the period specified on admission, an involuntary patient is not allowed to leave the hospital without the consent of a psychiatrist or head of facility. These persons of authority can, however, allow a temporary discharge for a maximum period of 30 days.[109]

Several mental health stakeholders in Ghana are critical of the involuntary intervention procedures laid out in the Act.[110] While the court application for temporary involuntary treatment is clearly intended as a safeguard, interviewee 3 argued that the long and complicated application process is not feasible for the mental health practitioner. This interviewee supports a procedure whereby anyone who brings a person to mental health facilities must fill in a form, and if anything comes up, the person who filled in the form would be held responsible.[111] Interviewee 8 also pointed out that the application to court is more of an obstacle than an asset, especially for families who would usually bring people for treatment to a mental health facility without the necessary court recommendation. It is then up to the practitioner to take a decision. With sometimes more than 50 people waiting to be seen, there is often no time to conduct a proper examination, as decisions need to be made quickly. Even if there is not enough reason for an involuntary admission, to what extent does the practitioner need to take into account the family's information about the deterioration in the individual's condition and the possible danger to the individual or others? The best thing to do, according to interviewee 8, is to admit the person for further observation under the certificate of urgency, even if this is unlawful. And knowing that the earlier the treatment starts the better, it is also very likely that persons will not only be admitted against their will, but also treated against their will.[112] Instead of highlighting the impracticability of the involuntary treatment provisions, some pointed out that the challenge is the controversial nature of the provisions. Interviewee 6 highlighted the contradiction between declaring that nobody can be forced into a facility, but forcing people to be admitted against their will because they are perceived as dangerous or aggressive, and argued that the Act fails to address this. This interviewee agreed that, in extreme situations, such as being unconscious, specific measures must be taken. Any other circumstance, however, must be approached with more communication and engagement.[113] Adding to this point, interviewee 10 suggested that the right not to be involuntarily admitted and treated is not absolute, and, as such, it is unclear in which situations the right would be violated. According to interviewee 10, the legal justifications for abandoning the affected human rights need to be made clear, and it needs to be ensured that these exceptions are not misused for any forcible intervention.[114]

---

[108] Ibid secs 46–47.
[109] Ibid secs 50, 52.
[110] See interviewees 3, 4, 5, 6, 8, 9 14 and 15, see Table 6.1.
[111] See interviewee 3, see Table 6.1.
[112] See interviewee 8, see Table 6.1.
[113] See interviewee 6, see Table 6.1.
[114] See interviewee 10, see Table 6.1.

In light of the CRPD, many of these provisions regarding involuntary interventions can be criticised, something also particularly mentioned by interviewees 14 and 15, both of whom referred explicitly to the CRPD.[115] For example, Article 14 CRPD prohibits deprivation of liberty based on psychosocial disabilities, even if treatment has been found to be necessary for various reasons. Hence, the very requirements for temporary involuntary admission and treatment under Ghana's mental health law are in tension with the CRPD framework. With regard to persons who lack the capacity to make informed treatment decisions, Article 12 CRPD identifies the need to set up supported decision-making mechanisms. The Mental Health Act, on the other hand, rather presumes the incapacity of persons with psychosocial disabilities, and does not specify support for decision-making in any way. These findings are supported by the former Special Rapporteur on Torture, Juan Méndez, who declared in his report on Ghana that the provisions of the Mental Health Act regarding involuntary admission and treatment are not in line with the international human rights standards as outlined in the CRPD. He asserted that involuntary admission should not take place 'unless strictly required'. If so, it must be guaranteed that patients have access to actual healthcare services, certain safeguards 'to secure patient's rights' must be established, all mental health facilities must be independently monitored, 'effective judicial review' of the admission must be available, and 'access to legal aid' as well as 'a remedy for cruel, inhuman and degrading treatment' occurring in any mental health institution must be provided.[116]

As pointed out in Chapter 5, involuntary treatment does not necessarily equate to ill-treatment, as, for the latter, a certain threshold of severity must be reached. Yet, taken from the extensive analysis in Chapter 5, procedures such as emergency sedation or injecting tranquilisers against a person's will, and non-consensual electroconvulsive treatment, seclusion and restraint measures, as well as living conditions in mental health institutions, may amount to ill-treatment (see subsection 5.4.3.1).[117] How does the Mental Health Act regulate such interventions?

6.3.3.2 *The Legal Framework to Protect against Ill-treatment*

As argued before, allowing for involuntary interventions may open the door to ill-treatment in mental healthcare. Both the Ghanaian Mental Health Act and its Legislative Instrument prescribe that patients must be free from torture or any cruel,

---

[115] See interviewees 14 and 15, see Table 6.1.
[116] UNGA, 'Report of the Special Rapporteur on torture and other cruel, inhuman or degrading treatment or punishment, Juan E. Méndez, Mission to Ghana' (n 42) para 104; and UNGA, 'Follow up report of the Special Rapporteur on torture and other cruel, inhuman or degrading treatment or punishment on his follow-up visit to the Republic of Ghana' (n 58) para 64.
[117] This is not to diminish the argument that involuntary treatment, as discussed under subsection 5.4.3.4 in terms of justification for restrictive interventions, may unfortunately be necessary under certain circumstances to protect a person from himself or herself and/or the environment, for instance in case of an acute psychosis.

inhuman or degrading treatment.[118] In order to preserve a person's dignity, being free from ill-treatment includes not being subject to unauthorised seclusion, practices such as flogging and restraining in chains or shackles, or living conditions that inhibit personal hygiene.[119] Based thereon, and grounded in the normative analysis in subsection 5.4.3, this subsection will explore how Ghana's legal framework protects against ill-treatment in the form of inhumane living conditions, or seclusion and restraint procedures.

With regard to living conditions to preserve welfare, the Mental Health Act merely states, in section 57, that patients are entitled to quality inpatient food, bedding and sanitation.[120] Further details, however, are set out in the Legislative Instrument. Accommodation in mental health facilities must be hygienic; adequately aired and illuminated; free from congestion; free from rodents, reptiles and insects; free from offensive smells; and clean, with storage and laundry facilities. Each person must also have a bed with a mattress and clean sheets.[121] For sanitation, the facility must provide potable water for patients, a borehole if necessary, Veronica buckets in case of water shortages, and an adequate number of clean toilet facilities that guarantee privacy.[122] Furthermore, patients should not only be provided with well-fitting clothes, but also with three nutritious meals a day, and a special diet where necessary. Under no circumstances should a person be forced to fast.[123] Ghana's legal framework regarding living conditions, in fact, mirrors the provisions as expounded in the normative analysis in subsection 5.4.3.

Seclusion and restraints are regulated in section 58 of the Mental Health Act. Seclusion is defined as the confinement of the person, which is the same definition as elaborated in the normative analysis in subsection 5.4.3. Restraint is defined as the immobilisation of a person through mostly 'physical measures', to prevent harm; for transfer to a place of seclusion, or to another mental health facility; or to administer medication.[124] This interpretation differs from the findings in subsection 5.4.3.2. The Act specifies that involuntary seclusion or 'minimal mechanical restraints' can only be applied when there is imminent danger to the patient or others, and when tranquilisation is not readily available or deemed appropriate. Shortly after the coming into force of the Act, former Special Rapporteur on Torture, Juan Méndez, criticised the Act for allowing coercive measures, especially seclusion and restraints, should tranquilisation not be readily available or deemed appropriate.[125] According to section 58 of the Act, seclusion or restraints cannot be used as punishment, or for the

---

[118] Republic of Ghana, Mental Health Act (n 44) sec 57(3); and Republic of Ghana, Mental Health Regulation (n 70) sec 35(i).
[119] Republic of Ghana, Mental Health Regulation (n 70) sec 35(c)(d).
[120] See Republic of Ghana, Mental Health Act (n 44) sec 57(2).
[121] Republic of Ghana, Mental Health Regulation (n 70) sec 30.
[122] Ibid sec 31.
[123] Ibid sees 32, 33.
[124] See Republic of Ghana, Mental Health Act (n 44) sec 97.
[125] See UNGA, 'Follow up report of the Special Rapporteur on torture and other cruel, inhuman or degrading treatment or punishment on his follow-up visit to the Republic of Ghana' (n 58) para 72.

convenience for staff, and to safeguard this, seclusion and restraint measures must be authorised by the head of the facility or the senior nurse in charge, and the process must be documented. In addition to the Act, the Legislative Instrument regulates seclusion and restraint procedures in more detail, to prevent any abuse, and to limit the procedures as much as necessary. To be secluded, a specific Seclusion Authorisation Form must be filled out, and the seclusion itself cannot exceed a total of four hours within a 24-hour period, where the patient under seclusion must be reviewed every 15 minutes. Further, the seclusion room must only be occupied by one person at a time, and must be designed to prevent injury to the person.[126] In the Seclusion Authorisation Form, the responsible staff have to fill out, among other things, the reason for seclusion; whether the person is on sedation, and the medication and dosage used; the date and time of seclusion; and observation notes.[127] For restraints, the Legislative Instrument sets out regulations for specifically mechanical restraints. Where mechanical restraints are needed, the use of handcuffs, chains, ropes, logs or other items likely to cause bruises is prohibited. The document proposes the use of soft materials or items that do not cause injury. When being restrained, patients must be reviewed every 15 minutes, and cannot be restrained for more than 48 hours. If restraints are needed for more than 48 hours, the person must be transferred to a 'capable health facility' where 'alternative arrangements for security' can be made.[128] Such 'alternative arrangements' could be interpreted as administering tranquilisation, which – according to the Act's definition of restraints – would not fall under the scope of restraining measures. What at first seems a peculiar provision only makes sense when it is considered that the Legislative Instrument also regulates informal mental health facilities which do not administer medication.[129] If an informal mental health practitioner restrains an agitated or violent person to prevent self-harm or harm to others, and if none of the informal procedures applied ease the mental episode within 48 hours, it only makes sense that the affected person must then be transferred to a public mental health facility which offers other forms of treatment to help them.[130] Similarly to seclusion, the restraint procedure is safeguarded through the use of a Restraint Authorisation Form. Amongst other things, the form must record the reason for restraint, the method of restraint, any medication used, and the date and time of restraint.[131] The Legislative Instrument further stipulates that a patient cannot be secluded and mechanically restrained at the same time.[132]

There have been recent landmark legal reforms in other jurisdictions that are said to respect, protect and fulfil the rights of people with mental health conditions and

---

[126] Republic of Ghana, Mental Health Regulation (n 70) sec 25(1)-(5).
[127] Ibid Appendix, Form Three, Seclusion Authorisation Form.
[128] Ibid sees 25(6)-(8)(10) and 43(f).
[129] While the informal practice may use herbs or other plant-based sedatives, they are often not evidence-based and/or not administered in regulated doses.
[130] Republic of Ghana, Mental Health Regulation (n 70) sec 43(f).
[131] Ibid Appendix, Form Four, Restraint Authorisation Form.
[132] Ibid sec 25(9).

psychosocial disabilities in line with CRPD standards, and are thus considered as best-practice examples for regulating seclusion and restrains.[133] One of these landmark reforms is India's Mental Healthcare Act of 2017. Very similarly to the Ghanaian legislation, India's Act stipulates that physical restraint measures can only be used where they are the only means available to prevent imminent and immediate harm to the person concerned and others; that they must be authorised by a psychiatrist in charge of the person's treatment; that they must not be used for longer than is absolutely necessary to prevent risk of significant harm; that they must be recorded in detail in a report; and that they cannot be used as form of punishment, or due to a shortage in staff.[134] Likewise, Peru's 2020 Mental Health Act also allows for restraint measures only in emergency situations that pose imminent and immediate danger to the life or health of the patient or others.[135] The comparison of India's and Peru's 'best-practice' mental health legislation to the Ghanaian legislation underlines that Ghana's mental health law is already aligned with the CRPD. The only difference is that the Indian and Peruvian laws outlaw the use of seclusion and solitary confinement in psychiatric care completely, which the Ghanaian law does not.[136]

It can be concluded that sections 57 and 58 of the Mental Health Act incorporate a human rights approach to disability. The influence of international human rights standards drawn from the CRPD on the domestic law-making is obvious. But can the domestic legislation also help to advance the understanding of the right to mental health, and possibly close gaps that the CRPD has left open? The normative analysis in subsection 5.4.3 shows that seclusion and restraint measures are seen as critical within the CPRD framework. Yet, neither the text of the CRPD nor the interpretation by the CteeRPD offer clear guidelines as to the specific (emergency) cases when seclusion or restraint can, exceptionally, be used. Here, the detailed regulations within Ghana's mental health law can provide guidance. In addition to the regulations as detailed above, Ghana's mental health legislation also offers protection against violations of seclusion and restraint, or inhumane living conditions, through different procedures that can be interpreted as safeguards. The following text illustrates four procedures drawn from the Ghanaian law: a treatment plan, regular audits, complaint procedures, and the possibility of appeal.

Based on the Legislative Instrument, each patient must have a written treatment plan based on an assessment, and this must include a discharge plan, a continuing

---

[133] See WHO, 'Guidance on community mental health services: Promoting person-centred and rights-based approaches' (2021), <https://www.who.int/publications/i/item/9789240025707> accessed 14 November 2022, p 186.

[134] India, Ministry of Law and Justice, Mental Healthcare Act, Law No 10 of 2017 (adopted 2017).

[135] Peru, Decreto Supremo que aprueba el Reglamento de la Ley N° 30947, Ley de Salud Mental, Decreto Supremo No 007–2020-SA, 5 March 2020, <https://busquedas.elperuano.pe/normaslegales/decreto-supremo-que-aprueba-el-reglamento-de-la-ley-n-30947-decreto-supremo-n-007–2020-sa-1861796–1/> accessed 14 November 2022, arts 3(5), 28.

[136] See India, Ministry of Law and Justice, Mental Healthcare Act (n 134), sec 97(1); and Peru, Decreto Supremo que aprueba el Reglamento de la Ley N° 30947 (n 135) art 28.

care plan and a review plan.[137] The treatment plan is to be reviewed regularly, and revised when necessary. Patients and their caregivers must be involved in the treatment plan,[138] which could be interpreted as alluding to Articles 12 and 17 CRPD. Although details about the involvement of the patients and caregivers are not given, it can be assumed that such a treatment plan would considers a patient's will and preferences.

All formal mental health facilities must undergo regular audits conducted by Mental Health Authority staff, to ensure that their activities comply with the statutory requirements, policies and procedures.[139] In addition to these regular audits, the above-mentioned Visiting Committees are tasked with inspecting all mental health institutions at least once a year without prior notice. Various interviewees specifically expressed their concerns regarding the lack of monitoring of informal mental health centres such as prayer camps.[140] Thus, the mandate to inspect informal as well as formal mental health facilities is important. Among the duties of the Visiting Committees are interviewing patients without the presence of facility staff, and receiving and enquiring into complaints against staff.[141] These audits and inspections could be understood as independent monitoring procedures as laid out by Article 16 CRPD. Although, at the time of conducting this study, there are still no Visiting Committees in operation, their task nevertheless seems promising for the future of protecting human rights in mental health. As interviewee 13 expressed, 'because monitoring and supervision does not go on properly, that is why these abuses go on'.[142] Aside from the duties and responsibilities of the Visiting Committees, their membership is also worth noting. Each Committee is to consist of one psychiatrist or other mental health personnel member who holds no direct service role in the region, one experienced legal practitioner, one representative of the local social service and Regional Health Management team, two community representatives, and one Regional Council representative.[143] While bringing together local as well as non-local members with different professional backgrounds can be considered as a strength of the Visiting Committees, it might also impede their efforts because of existing or newly arising conflicts of interest.[144] Which of these two factors will ultimately dictate the work of the Visiting Committees remains to be seen.

As stated above, the Mental Health Act also introduces a complaint procedure. The head of any mental health facility must ensure that a written complaints policy, outlining the procedure for complaints and how to respond to complaints, is set up, and that the complaints procedure is complied with. Patients, or their relatives or caregivers, must be informed about the available complaints procedure by receiving a written copy

---

[137] Republic of Ghana, Mental Health Regulation (n 70) sec 15(b).
[138] Republic of Ghana, Mental Health Act (n 44) sec 45(1)(4).
[139] Republic of Ghana, Mental Health Regulation (n 70) sec 20.
[140] See interviewees 3, 10, 13 and 15, see Table 6.1.
[141] Republic of Ghana, Mental Health Act (n 44) sec 36.
[142] Interviewee 13, see Table 6.1.
[143] Republic of Ghana, Mental Health Act (n 44) sec 35.
[144] Natalie Schuck (n 23) 191.

of it.[145] If either the patients or their relatives or caregivers are dissatisfied with the management of the patient's mental health condition, they can file a complaint to one of the facility's senior mental health personnel, who then has to report it to the head of the facility.[146] If the head of the facility does not take appropriate or satisfactory action within 48 hours, the aggrieved parties can make an appeal to the Mental Health Review Tribunal, which then has to respond within 21 days.[147]

In general, each patient or their relative or caregiver has the right to appeal against the patient's involuntary admission and treatment, including ill-treatment, and can seek counsel or be represented in an appeal. As part of the appeal, a patient also has the right to seek an independent medical opinion.[148] However, the Legislative Instrument specifically states that persons who have been involuntarily admitted based on a court order cannot appeal against their admission.[149] While this seems arbitrary at first, it only makes sense, given that the institution that issued the court order, after careful inspection, in the first place is the same institution as the one hearing the appeals. Persons with mental health conditions and psychosocial disabilities must be able to enjoy their right to access legal advice and legal counsel whenever they request it, or when the staff of a mental health facility is of the opinion that the affected individual requires it.[150] This can be considered as the ultimate safeguard for the protection against ill-treatment in the mental health sector.

The positive implications that Ghana's Mental Health Act can have for mental healthcare practice are clear. Nevertheless, various scholars have, in particular, expressed their concerns with regard to the informal mental health sector. Special Rapporteur Méndez has urged the enactment of laws that prohibit the admission and treatment of children in informal mental health centres, such as prayer camps, and has advised the enactment of laws that specifically ban inhumane practices in such mental health facilities, including mandatory fasting, chaining or any other prolonged restraints. While the ban inhumane practices is already regulated in the above-mentioned *Guidelines for Traditional Healers*, the legal force behind legislation would of course be stronger. Méndez recalls that ill-treatment in informal mental health institutions 'unequivocally amount[s] to torture even if committed by non-State actors under conditions in which the State knows or ought to know about them',[151] and claims that reasons for chaining or shackling, such as preventing aggressive behaviour or escape, do not fall within the scope of exceptions for temporary restraint measures recognised by international standards. Besides regulating, controlling and supervising the practices of mental health facilities to prevent any form of ill-treatment, he has

---

[145] Republic of Ghana, Mental Health Regulation (n 70) sec 18.
[146] Republic of Ghana, Mental Health Act (n 44) sec 59(1).
[147] Ibid sec 59(2).
[148] Ibid sec 44; and Republic of Ghana, Mental Health Regulation (n 70) sec 24(10).
[149] Ibid sec 24(10).
[150] Ibid sec 55.
[151] UNGA, 'Follow up report of the Special Rapporteur on torture and other cruel, inhuman or degrading treatment or punishment on his follow-up visit to the Republic of Ghana' (n 58) para 72.

called upon the government of Ghana to investigate and prosecute cases of alleged ill-treatment, especially in informal mental healthcare practice, under the criminal law.[152] This has also been stressed by both the Human Rights Committee and the Committee on the Rights of the Child in their reports on Ghana.[153] Mfoafo-M'Carthy and Grishow also question whether the Act will really achieve the ideals of the CRPD in practice, highlighting, in particular, the significant challenges of regulating Ghana's informal mental healthcare system.[154] In this system, cruel, inhuman and degrading practices, such as physically inflicting pain as punishment, prolonged seclusion, chaining, dire living conditions, and the denial of access to adequate healthcare, still remain common.[155]

When everything is taken together, what is the way forward when it comes to addressing practices amounting to ill-treatment in places such as faith-based and traditional centres? The underlying challenge, according to Read and others, is the perception that ill-treatment in traditional healthcare may, in fact, be accepted as necessary under moral beliefs, as many Ghanaians place community integrity above individual rights.[156] Hence, the real questions are: what is, through a human rights lens, the role of traditional healthcare in providing access to mental healthcare? Should it be perceived as a challenge, or rather as a pathway, to such access?

6.3.3.3   *The Role of Traditional Healthcare: A Pathway or a Challenge?*

Ghana's Mental Health Act endorses community-based care rather than institutional care, and acknowledges the significant role of traditional and faith-based healers in mental health care provision. The Act specifically states that, for the Mental Health Authority to achieve its objectives, a collaboration with the Traditional and Alternative Medicine Council and other providers of informal mental health care is necessary, 'to ensure the best interest of persons with mental disorders'.[157] Yet, how can informal mental health facilities be regulated so as to ensure culturally acceptable care, on the one hand, but safeguards against human rights violations, on the other?

---

[152]   UNGA, 'Report of the Special Rapporteur on torture and other cruel, inhuman or degrading treatment or punishment, Juan E. Méndez, Mission to Ghana' (n 42) para 105; and UNGA, 'Follow up report of the Special Rapporteur on torture and other cruel, inhuman or degrading treatment or punishment on his follow-up visit to the Republic of Ghana' (n 58) para 68.

[153]   HRC, 'Concluding observations on the initial reports of Ghana' (n 57) paras 27–28; and Committee on the Rights of the Child (CteeRC), 'Concluding observations on the combined third to fifth periodic reports of Ghana' (13 July 2015) UN Doc CRC/C/GHA/CO/3–5, paras 47–48.

[154]   Magnus Mfoafo-M'Carthy & Jeff D Grishow, 'Mental illness, stigma and disability rights in Ghana' (2017) 5 African Disability Rights Yearbook 84, 97.

[155]   See Human Rights Watch (n 34); and Human Rights Watch, 'Living in Chains: Shackling of People with Psychosocial Disabilities Worldwide' (2020).

[156]   Ursula M Read and others, 'Local suffering and the global discourse of mental health and human rights: An ethnographic study of responses to mental illness in rural Ghana' (2009) 5 Globalization and Health, 12.

[157]   Republic of Ghana, Mental Health Act (n 44) sec 3(m).

As early as 1991, the WHO recognised the important contribution of traditional medicine to the provision of healthcare, especially amongst populations with limited access to formal healthcare systems, and urged collaboration between informal and formal providers to ensure the use of 'scientifically proven, safe and effective traditional remedies'.[158] Ultimately, collaboration with the formal healthcare sector could also improve the quality of informal treatment.[159] Particularly in light of big treatment gaps, as are present in Ghana, the potential of traditional and faith-based practitioners as key players in mental healthcare provision is being promoted,[160] at least until sufficient formal mental health services are made available.[161] Informal care providers often have more time for patients, and the 'healing procedures' may even include unscientific procedures such as music and dance therapy, or a form of psychotherapy through prayer.[162] Some interviewees, notably also professionals in the formal mental health system, pointed at the placebo effects that persons with mild mental health conditions and psychosocial disabilities may experience when turning to traditional or faith-based healers who they strongly believe can cure their illnesses.[163]

Allowing traditional and faith-based practitioners to provide mental healthcare can also be viewed as respecting people's rights to choose the treatment they like or prefer, and, in a broader sense, as a way of respecting their right to freedom of religion or freedom of assembly.[164] While this is widely accepted, the issue of inhumane and degrading treatment practices within the informal mental health context needs to be discussed. Among the different informal treatment methods, which also include the use of herbal remedies, ritual objects and prayer, prescribed behaviours for preventive purposes raise particular concerns over ill-treatment. As illustrated earlier in this book, such ill-treatment includes isolation, restraints and dietary restrictions.[165] What needs to be explored at this point is: when assessing ill-treatment in informal mental healthcare, could the right to freedom of religion or assembly prevail over the right to health, or specifically the right to be free from inhumane or degrading treatment? This is an interesting question, especially where individuals freely choose to be treated in traditional or faith-based centres, or prefer informal over formal mental healthcare. Research conducted in Ghana shows that, with the passing of the Mental Health Act, many informal providers now ask patients to fill out so-called letters of undertaking,

---

[158] See WHO 'Executive Board Resolution EB87.R24 (1991) Traditional medicine and modern health care', eighty-seventh session, 14–25 January 1991.

[159] Quality, as analysed above, includes evidence-based practices. Through collaboration, evidence-based medicine could be administered by formal healthcare practitioners while informal practitioners might still make use of traditional or faith-based procedures (such as prayer or dancing) which do not violate human rights (as fasting or flogging would).

[160] Ursula Read, 'Rights as Relationships: Collaborating with Faith Healers in Community Mental Health in Ghana' (2019) 43 Culture, Medicine and Psychiatry 613, 619.

[161] See Interviewees 1, 4 and 8, see Table 6.1.

[162] See Interviewees 1 and 12, see Table 6.1.

[163] See Interviewees 4, 6, 7, 8 and 13, see Table 6.1.

[164] See Interviewees 5, 8 and 15, see Table 6.1.

[165] Lily NA Kpobi and others (n 53) 256, 258.

which indicate their consent to the treatment practices to be performed.[166] Can such 'inhumane and degrading methods' then really amount to a violation of patients' human rights to be free from torture or cruel, inhumane or degrading treatment or punishment? Can one consent to ill-treatment? Scholars, among them Okyerefo, argue that religion is often viewed as a higher-order morality that prevails over professional ethics, or even national legislation.[167] Regardless, the implications of Ghana's mental health law are clear: traditional and faith-based mental healthcare is an accepted form of mental healthcare, including when it is carried out without any supporting scientific or medical evidence, but only when it is carried out in a humane and non-degrading manner in accordance with legal standards. This implies that certain practices must be discontinued, even if the termination of such practices affects the very essence of the treatment, and even if this is questionable under the right to enjoy freedom of religion or assembly.[168] Bearing in mind that freedom of religion and assembly are not absolute rights, they can be limited on grounds justified under international human rights law.

After his follow-up visit to Ghana, former Special Rapporteur Méndez expressed the opinion that:

> [n]either ... traditional practices [nor] the fact that families tend to approach prayer camps voluntarily, may be invoked to excuse the perpetuation of practices amounting to torture and other ill-treatment, and the State has an urgent obligation to address these practices and replace them with an approach informed by science and the principles of free and informed consent, dignity ... and right to be free from torture and other ill-treatment.[169]

In his final report, former Special Rapporteur on the Right to Health, Dainius Pūras, endorsed the availability of alternatives to formal mental healthcare, but also underlined the necessity for rights-based support, specifically acceptable and high-quality responses to mental healthcare needs. In his opinion, acceptable care is not only about being culturally appropriate, and about respect and trust between the provider and user, or about respect for medical ethics, but must also empower individuals to control their lives and well-being.[170] He stated that 'the use of coercion ... compromises the right to quality care'.[171] To guarantee quality rights-based care, treatment requires the use of evidence-based practices, and collaboration between service providers must be effective. Yet, how can formal and informal mental healthcare providers collaborate to promote psychiatric alternatives for what could be described as inhumane practices, and will this ultimately solve the existing problems?

---

[166] Ursula Read (n 160) 628.
[167] Michael PK Okyerefo, 'The gospel of public image in Ghana' in H Englund (ed), *Christianity and Public Culture in Africa* (Ohio University Press 2011) 204–216.
[168] Natalie Schuck (n 23) 195.
[169] UNGA, 'Follow up report of the Special Rapporteur on torture and other cruel, inhuman or degrading treatment or punishment on his follow-up visit to the Republic of Ghana, Juan Méndez' (n 58) para 74.
[170] UNGA, 'Report of the Special Rapporteur on the right of everyone to the enjoyment of the highest attainable standard of physical and mental health, Dainius Pūras' (n 54) para 65.
[171] Ibid para 66.

Read articulates that, when promoting collaboration between the formal and informal sectors, 'there is little acknowledgement of the potential irony of transferring persons from one form of coercion to another'.[172] According to Ghana's mental health law, but also in the global mental health discourse more generally, psychopharmaceuticals are presented as the modern and more humane alternative to mechanical restraints. In plain language, while the forced application of strong sedatives to calm aggressive or agitated patients and restore their 'right mind' is generally accepted in mental healthcare practice worldwide, the use by traditional practitioners of mechanical restraints, such as chains, for the same ends, is contested. In other words: intervening procedures performed by informal providers are said to contravene human rights, while psychotropics (commonly used in formal mental health delivery) are said to fulfil the right to humane treatment.[173] These differing positions on how to regulate aggressive patients is just one of the disparate regulations within Ghana's new mental health framework, which explains why many informal mental healthcare actors are hostile towards collaborating with the formal sector. The language of the Mental Health Act suggests that the decision whether to collaborate lies in the hands of the formal mental health professionals. Read argues, however, that it may be the formal mental health worker who lays out the terms for collaboration, but it is ultimately up to the traditional practitioner who accepts help to manage the aggressive or agitated individuals or refuses collaboration.[174] Interviewees working closely with the informal care sector stated that, once informal care providers realise that the medication formal mental health workers use to calm patients is effective, they often welcome the help, or even want to be trained on how to administer the medication themselves.[175] To avoid enmity, and to build a good relationship between the sectors to ensure that formal mental healthcare workers are accepted within informal care facilities, it is important to engage informal practitioners in meetings and discussions regarding mental healthcare in Ghana, to officially recognise their authority and competence, and thus officially acknowledge the integral role they play in service delivery. It is important for informal providers to know that the formal mental health workers do not aim to close their facilities or force them to do certain things, but to work with them to improve the services provided in such facilities.[176] Ideally, according to some of the interviewees, collaboration ensures that patients receive evidence-based medication from the formal mental health sector to help manage their conditions, while still participating in prayer, ritual dances or singing in the informal facilities.[177] Adding to this, interviewee 7 commented that aggressive or agitated persons should always be managed and calmed by the formal mental healthcare sector before traditional or faith-

---

[172] Ursula Read (n 160) 629.
[173] Ibid 627–628.
[174] Ibid p 629.
[175] See interviewees 1, 3 and 4, see Table 6.1.
[176] See interviewees 1, 3 and 15, see Table 6.1.
[177] See interviewees 2, 3 and 11, see Table 6.1.

based practitioners start their healing.[178] There should be a form of mutual respect.[179] This form of collaboration has been put into practice throughout Ghana. Nonetheless, to really raise the standard of care provided, fully eradicating what is recognised as ill-treatment and replacing it with more humane alternatives such as administering psychopharmaceuticals, more time must be invested in sensitising and educating informal mental health practitioners.

Almost all interviewees expressed the view that it is the informal mental health providers' lack of education on mental health and human rights in general, as well as the Mental Health Act in particular, which leads to ill-treatment and unintentional human rights abuses.[180] Interviewee 7 explained that:

> health workers ... have been trained on how to handle some of these aggressive patients, but the faith healers don't have that know-how. So in their own mind, they find ways and means to control or put some of these aggressive patients under control. So if there is a norm or there is a standard on how to control such persons, it is left to the Government to make the standard available to the faith healer.[181]

Notably, it is not just government agencies,[182] non-governmental organisations[183] and the formal mental health sector that are educating and sensitising traditional practitioners on the Mental Health Act and the rights of patients, but also the traditional practitioners themselves.[184] At first, according to interviewee 11, traditional and faith-based practitioners:

> don't know that what they are doing is against the rights of the people. They don't know that chaining them is against [their rights], they don't know that forcing them to fast when they can't even think for themselves it is against their rights.[185]

But after educative programmes, this interviewee and their organisation have witnessed improvements with regard to the treatment of people in informal mental health facilities, collaboration between informal practitioners and community psychiatric nurses or local formal healthcare services for administering psychopharmaceuticals, and referrals of violent persons to the nearest formal mental health services.

With all of the efforts that have been put in place to establish good collaboration between the formal and informal sectors to eliminate ill-treatment from mental healthcare, one question remains: could it be that these efforts in fact serve to mask

---

[178] See interviewee 7, see Table 6.1.
[179] See interviewee 14, see Table 6.1.
[180] See interviewees 1, 2, 3, 4, 6, 7, 9, 11, 13, 14 and 15, see Table 6.1.
[181] Interviewee 7, see Table 6.1.
[182] Such as Mental Health Authority or Ghana Health Services.
[183] Such as BasicNeeds Ghana and the Christian Health Association of Ghana (CHAG).
[184] Such as the Traditional Medicine Practice Council, the Ghana Federation of Traditional Medicine Practitioners Associations (GHAFTRAM) or the Ghana Association of Faith Healers (GAFH).
[185] Interviewee 11, see Table 6.1.

the greater need to adequately fund mental healthcare services? It does not hurt to ask whether investing more money in mental healthcare delivery might prove to be the most effective way of reducing ill-treatment and improving mental healthcare. Some human rights workers claim that Ghana's government is taking an 'escapist approach' by allowing informal mental healthcare to continue, rather than investing in good-quality formal mental healthcare delivery.[186]

6.3.4 CONCLUDING SUMMARY

The preceding analysis has shown that the new Ghanaian discourse on mental health is promising. It incorporates a human rights approach to disability, which is also visible in the specific provisions regulating seclusion, restraints and living conditions (the focus of this country study). As mentioned above, the CPRD framework lacks guidance on whether, when and how seclusion and restraints may be used, which can be considered a shortcoming of the treaty. The text of the CRPD does not specifically outlaw seclusion and restraint measures. Rather, it is the CteeRPD that has condemned seclusion and restraint. And while not even the Committee has taken a stand on its exceptional use in emergency situations, former Special Rapporteur on the Rights of Persons with Disabilities, Catalina Devandas-Aguilar, has criticised the 'medical necessity' justification, but not forced interventions based on 'dangerousness' (see subsection 5.4.3.4). As Szmukler argues, the problem lies in people with psychosocial disabilities being stereotypically considered intrinsically dangerous, although dangerousness as consequence of a psychosocial disability is only found in a minority of cases. It is, therefore, difficult to justify why a law should allow for persons with mental health conditions and psychosocial disabilities to be preventively secluded and restrained on account of their (perceived) risk to themselves or others, when such regulation is not in place for persons without mental health conditions and psychosocial disabilities.[187] At the same time, Szmukler and others argue that the CRPD approach is most likely not excluding involuntary treatment in all cases, especially in emergency cases.[188] It is reasonable to assume that some degree of coercion can be justified, in order to protect patients, or where there is risk not only to these patients, but to others as well. Hence, in such circumstances, interferences would not amount to ill-treatment.

Through the detailed regulation of seclusion and restraints, and the four specific procedures established throughout the Mental Health Act, which can be seen as safeguards for the protection against ill-treatment, Ghana's mental health legislation can, therefore, serve as an example to further advance the understanding of the right to mental health in general, and a human rights approach to accessing (quality) mental

---

[186] See Ursula Read (n 160) 631.
[187] See George Szmukler, 'Coercion in Psychiatric Treatment and Its Justification' in D Moseley & G Gala (eds), *Philosophy and Psychiatry* (Routledge 2016) 125–146.
[188] George Szmukler and others, 'Mental health law and the UN Convention on the rights of persons with disabilities' (2014) 37(3) International Journal of Law and Psychiatry 245, 250.

healthcare in particular, especially regarding emergency situations. Furthermore, Ghana's mental health law considers both the important role the traditional and faith-based health sector plays for society, and the danger that this sector poses in terms of human rights infringements. Various regulations, especially those referring directly to the informal sector, aim to safeguard human rights in informal mental healthcare practice. Hence, besides serving as an example for promoting the right to mental health(care) in general, Ghana's legislation can also act as a best-practice example for other countries where the informal mental healthcare sector plays a similarly important role.

To some extent, the author supports the regulation regarding time-limited seclusion and restraint measures with soft materials, as outlined in the Mental Health Act, and particularly the Legislative Instrument, for situations of imminent and immediate danger. Nevertheless, the author would like to draw attention to three shortcomings in the Ghanaian legal framework, and make some recommendations regarding these. Firstly, the Act does not recognise chemical restraints (restraining through medication) within its category of restraints. In fact, the Act seems to propose that applying mechanical and physical restraints might be necessary for administering medication (forcefully). Consequently, this could imply that the (over)use of tranquilisation would not raise concerns under the Act. The author would, therefore, recommend that the law recognises the involuntary use of sedation or psychotropic drugs as a form of restraint, and not simply as an acceptable alternative to physical restraint. Ideally, the law should contain appropriate safeguards to protect against the inappropriate use of tranquilisers. In light of the fact that the use of chemical restraints can amount to ill-treatment, they need to be restricted and controlled. Secondly, the author believes that allowing for the use of seclusion and restraints should be further curtailed, so that these restrictive measures cannot be justified by considering tranquilisation as 'inappropriate' (see section 58 of the Act). In fact, the use of seclusion and restraints should be limited to situations where there is a risk of imminent and immediate harm to patients or others, and only where other methods have not been successful.[189] Such other methods, which should be identified in a mental health policy document, could include the development of individualised plans to explore sensitivities and signs of distress (in advance of an emergency situation), the use of comfort rooms (when experiencing distress), or, for situations of extreme distress, the use of de-escalation techniques to divert, distract, or withdraw the patient, and breakaway techniques for staff safety, as well as the use of response teams in 'unmanageable' situations.[190] Of course, the author acknowledges that there are cases in which a person suddenly becomes aggressive and immediate action is needed. In such cases, the proposed alternatives would possibly not be successful in avoiding harm to the person concerned, or to the

---

[189] In cases where persons become suddenly aggressive and immediate action is needed, the proposed alternatives might not be possible/successful.

[190] See eg WHO, 'Strategies to end seclusion and restraint: WHO QualityRights Specialized training: course slides' (2019), <https://apps.who.int/iris/handle/10665/329747> accessed 14 November 2022.

surrounding environment. Thirdly, the author wants to address the complexity of regulating the traditional healthcare sector. As described above, there is a clash between culturally appropriate care and quality care. The author would recommend drafting a new guideline specifically targeted at strengthening the collaboration between the formal and informal sectors, to eliminate inhumane practices in informal mental healthcare delivery. Such collaboration should include educating and training informal practitioners on mental health and human rights, and having formal practitioners work together with informal practitioners in treating patients in traditional and faith-based healthcare centres. The initial sensitisation programmes that have been carried out successfully throughout the country could be stepped up, and used as an example for drafting a strategy with clear action steps connected to responsible actors. At all times, the informal mental healthcare providers should be included in decision-making.

Interviewee 14, who also elaborated on the Act's shortcomings during the interview, nevertheless concluded with a Ghanaian proverb, saying that 'it is better to have one [than] not to have anything at all'.[191] Indeed, Ghana's new mental health law marks a big step forward, even if some provisions could be amended to strengthen the protection of persons with mental health conditions and psychosocial disabilities.

Before amendments to the legislation are proposed, it is important that the Act first be fully implemented, in order to see its actual positive effects, and side effects. As explored above, essential mechanisms, such as the Mental Health Review Tribunal and Visiting Committees, are still not operating fully. Different stakeholders have voiced their doubts about the government's level of commitment to this implementation, and have called the slow implementation a clear lack of prioritisation of advancing mental healthcare.[192] Interviewee 15 expressed the opinion that '[w]e cannot implement every bit at a go, but we will need to start from somewhere. And in doing that, we need to start with proper prioritization of what has to happen.'[193]

Other scholars have highlighted the inadequate allocation of resources as a major challenge for the implementation of the Act, and have framed securing finance as a top priority for its implementation.[194] Walker has established that the lack of funding has impeded matters such as improvements to training facilities, hiring more staff, creating mental health units at the secondary level in regional and district hospitals, and even setting up treatment plans. Ways to source and sustain funding seem to be a major challenge: one that has not been adequately addressed by either the Act or the Legislative Instrument.[195] Although the importance of financing mental health services for a successful implementation of the Act cannot be downplayed, further analysing this

---

[191] See interviewee 14, see Table 6.1.
[192] See interviewees 5 and 15, see Table 6.1.
[193] Interviewee 15, see Table 6.1.
[194] See Victor Doku and others (n 63); and Daniel A Awenva and others, 'From Mental Health Policy Development in Ghana to Implementation: What are the Barriers?' (2010) 13(3) African Journal of Psychiatry 184, 184.
[195] Georg Walker, 'Ghana Mental Health Act 846 2012: a qualitative study of the challenges and priorities for implementation' (2015) 49(4) Ghana Medical Journal, 268, 270.

Part 3. Country Study Analysis

issue, or suggesting a way forward, lies beyond the scope of this book. Ultimately, it is the responsibility of the government to protect people with mental health conditions and psychosocial disabilities from human rights abuses. Until the government fully meets this obligation, the promotion of human rights protection remains in the hands of civil society organisations.

6.4 COUNTRY STUDY II: GERMANY

This section investigates whether Germany is implementing the right to mental health and access to mental healthcare in a human rights-compliant manner. Similarly to the country study on Ghana, it deals more specifically with one key issue, namely the much-disputed guardianship regulation. This section commences by providing background information on Germany, to contextualise the findings, and to give on overview of the local mental healthcare system (subsection 6.4.1). The following subsection is an examination of Germany's mental health legislative framework as it exists today (subsection 6.4.2). Subsequently, the country's guardianship regulation will be analysed and discussed in detail (subsection 6.4.3). The overarching question addressed in section 6.4 is: to what extent is the domestic law in compliance with the CRPD, and is this even desirable?

6.4.1 BACKGROUND OF GERMANY

6.4.1.1 Geographic, Demographic and Economic characteristics

Germany is a country in Western Europe covering roughly 357,000 square kilometres. It is the most populous country in the European Union, with a population of approximately 83 million. Life expectancy at birth is 84 years for women and 79 years for men, the infant mortality rate is 3.1 per 1,000 live births, and the median age of German citizens is 47.4 years,[196] making it the third-oldest population in the world. Germany is considered very highly developed, and has a per capita gross national income of 46,946 USD, and a gross domestic product per capita of 45,959 USD.[197] The 2019 Poverty Report ranks 15.5 per cent of Germany's population as poor, meaning that they live in households with an entire net income of less than 60 per cent of the average income.[198] This percentage, however, does not include persons living in care homes or

---

[196] See UNDP (n 14); and UNDP, 'Germany' (nd), <http://hdr.undp.org/en/countries/profiles/DEU> accessed 14 November 2022.
[197] See UNDP (n 14).
[198] The poverty line for single households is for example €1,035 per month, for a couple in a household €1,553; see Deutscher Paritätischer Wohlfahrtsverband (Joint Welfare Association), *30 Jahre Mauerfall – Ein viergeteiltes Deutschland. Der Paritätische Armutsbericht 2019* (Der Paritätische Gesamtverband 2019) 6.

in refugee centres, or homeless people, suggesting that the actual poverty rate is much higher.[199]

6.4.1.2 Legal and Administrative Context

The German legal system is a civil law system and has its core principles codified in its constitution, which is called the Basic Law (Grundgesetz). Traditionally, as is the case in Germany, a civil law system is divided into public law and private law. Each division contains various important laws, which regulate relations between the state and private legal entities, and between two private legal entities, respectively. In contrast to the common law system, case law is subordinated to statutory law or written rules of law. With regard to international law, the Basic Law prescribes neither a monistic approach, nor a dualistic approach in its pure form. The principle of openness to international law (Völkerrechtsfreundlichkeit), as enshrined in the preamble to the Basic Law, refers mainly to general rules of international law and customary international law, which should be considered as part of the German legal system.[200] As far as international treaties are concerned, scholars agree that Germany's legal system follows a dualistic approach.[201] For international law instruments to become effective at the domestic level, the international regulations first have to be adopted in national legislation.

Despite Germany being referred to as a welfare state, the catalogue of the Basic Law enshrining fundamental human rights is almost silent on the matter of economic, social and cultural rights.[202] Plausible reasons for this are, firstly, that the constitution was meant to be dissociated specifically from its predecessor, the Weimar Constitution, which included various social rights, but which led to dramatic historical events. Secondly, civil and political rights, in particular, were much at threat during the National Socialist tyranny, and thus it was of utmost importance to assert civil and political rights in the Basic Law. And, thirdly, it is claimed that the Basic Law was not meant to design what life should look like, especially because fulfilling economic, social and cultural rights promises would pose difficulties.[203] Altogether, despite some constitutional rights containing 'social content',[204] references to the right to health or access to care are absent.

---

[199] Ibid.
[200] See Federal Republic of Germany, Grundgesetz (adopted 1949, amended 2020), art 25: 'The general rules of international law shall be an integral part of federal law. They shall take precedence over the laws and directly create rights and duties for inhabitants of the federal territory.'; and Rüdiger Wolfrum and others, 'The reception of international law in the German legal order: An introduction' in Erika de Wet, Holger Hestermeyer & Rüdiger Wolfrum (eds), *The implementation of international law in Germany and South Africa* (Pretoria University Law Press 2015) 4–5, 17–18.
[201] Rüdiger Wolfrum and others (n 200) 13.
[202] Mirja Trilsch, *Die Justiziabilität wirtschaftlicher, sozialer und kultureller Rechte im innerstaatlichen Recht* (Springer 2012) 506.
[203] Ibid 73–77.
[204] See, eg the special protection of marriage and family life in Article 6(1); or the equal right of persons with disabilities in Article 3(3).

Germany is a federal country composed of 16 states (Länder). Each state has its own government, legislature, judiciary and constitution, all of which are subject to the overall constitutional framework determined by the Basic Law. Despite various different regulations on the rights to work, education, housing and social security, one looks in vain for the right to health(care) in the various provincial constitutions. Nevertheless, federal legislation, and laws adopted by the various Länder (hereinafter referred to as Länder laws) regulate various components of health(care), and specifically mental health(care). Like the structure of governance, the public healthcare system is also highly decentralised. Actual mental health service provision is a local responsibility. In all 16 Länder, the Länder Ministry of Health has a unit in charge of mental health affairs, and there are additional Länder mental health advisory boards (Landesbeirat für psychische Gesundheit), with representatives from the psychiatric, medical, social care and social welfare sectors, and from patient families or patients themselves, as well as permanent local boards for the coordination of mental health services at the levels of municipalities and counties.[205]

6.4.1.3   Mental Health Service Provision

Throughout Germany, mental healthcare is provided by public and private institutions in specialist or general healthcare facilities, as well as in non-hospital, community-based facilities (including, to some extent, general practitioners). Just as in the Ghana case study, Germany's mental health service provision will be explained by reference to the AAAQ.

In Germany, 274 mental hospitals and 401 psychiatric units in general hospitals, with a total of 56,671 beds, offer inpatient care.[206] Despite not being explored further in this study, there are also specialised facilities for children and adolescents (a total of 144), forensic inpatient units (a total of 77), and residential care facilities (a total of 1,283), which provide mental healthcare. Hospital-based settings almost exclusively provide intensive psychiatric care. The majority of people are treated in the more integrated general hospital settings (1,009 per 100,000 population), rather than in any of the types of segregated specialist hospitals (766 per 100,000 population).[207] Besides inpatient facilities, there are outpatient services attached to hospitals, particularly for individuals with severe mental disorders and ongoing psychotic disorders, and an increasingly large range of different forms of non-hospital, community-based mental

---

[205] Anke Bramesfeld and others, 'Managing Mental Health Service Provision in the Decentralized, Multi-layered Health and Social Care System of Germany' (2004) 7(1) The Journal of Mental Health Policy and Economics 3.

[206] See WHO, 'Mental Health Atlas 2017 Member State Profile; Germany' (2018), <https://www.who.int/publications/m/item/mental-health-atlas-2017-country-profile-germany> accessed 14 November 2022; and Deutsche Gesellschaft für Psychiatrie und Psychotherapie, Psychosomatik und Nervenheilkunde e. V. (DGPPN), 'DGPPN-Faktenblatt: Aktuelle Zahlen und Fakten der Psychiatrie und Psychotherapie' (2020), <https://www.dgppn.de/_Resources/Persistent/a2e357dac62be19b5050a1d89ffd8603cfdb8ef9/20201008_Factsheet.pdf> accessed 14 November 2022.

[207] WHO (n 206).

health facilities and services all over the country. For instance, each of Germany's over 400 municipal authorities (local governments) offer public social psychiatric services (Sozialpsychiatrischer Dienst), with a wide range of care and support for individuals and their families, including consultations, preventive care, crisis intervention, aftercare, home visits and more.[208] Additionally, there are outpatient medical doctors (in office practice) in psychiatry, psychosomatic medicine, or psychotherapy; psychologists; psychological psychotherapists (psychologische Psychotherapeuten); non-medical practitioners of psychotherapy (Heilpraktiker für Psychotherapie); coaches and counsellors with private practices; and also pastoral care by telephone (Telefonseelsorge).[209] Registered mental health professionals working in governmental and non-governmental settings include 14,230 specialist psychiatrists (17.14 per 100,000 population), 48,265 psychologists (58.14 per 100,000 population) and 16,482 other specialist doctors with additional qualifications in mental health (19.85 per 100,000).[210] Despite these seemingly high numbers, German mental healthcare services lack the human resources to meet the demand. Out of the 27.8 per cent of the adult population (17.8 million people) that will have a mental disorder each year, only 18.9 per cent of the total adult population receive treatment.[211]

Stigma and discrimination also play a role in the accessibility of mental health services in Germany. Although discriminatory attitudes towards people with mental health conditions and psychosocial disabilities have decreased considerably in recent years, former mental health patients are still believed to be devalued and rejected by the public to some extent.[212] Being ashamed of their illnesses, and afraid of the stigma that accompanies mental health treatment, many affected Germans do not seek help. Moreover, people are still critical of mental health treatment options, and believe that it is the affected person's own responsibility to get well again. This phenomenon is not only found within the public, but also amongst staff within the healthcare system. Patients complain that not all doctors take them and their problems seriously, leading to even more self-stigmatisation.[213] In terms of physical accessibility, mental

---

[208] Hermann Elgeti, 'Sozialpsychiatrische Dienste in Deutschland: Ein großes Versprechen' (2019) 43(2) Soziale Psychiatrie 16.

[209] See eg Hans Joachim Salize and others, 'Mental health care in Germany' (2007) 257 European Archives of Psychiatry and Clinical Neuroscience 92; and Jan Kaspers, 'Germany's mental health system in a nutshell. Shedding light on the confusing German therapy system' (2016), <www.jan-kaspers.de/articles/download/german_mental_health_nutshell.pdf> accessed 14 November 2022.

[210] DGGPN (n 206).

[211] Ibid.

[212] Matthias C Angermeyera and others, 'Changes in the perception of mental illness stigma in Germany over the last two decades' (2014) 29(6) European Psychiatry 390, 393.

[213] See Irmgard Vogt, 'Gesundheitsberufe und stigmatisierende Tendenzen gegenüber psychisch Kranken: Ein systematischer Überblick' (2018) as part of the dgvt congress presentations on *Stigmatisierung von Menschen mit psychiatrischen Diagnosen: Beständigkeit und Wandel*, <https://www.dgvt-kongress.de/rueckblick/programm/programmuebersicht-2018/samstag-03-maerz-2018/stigmatisierung-von-menschen-mit-psychiatrischen-diagnosen-bestaendigkeit-und-wandel/> accessed 14 November 2022; and Wolfgang Gaebel and others, 'Psychisch Kranke: Stigma erschwert Behandlung und Integration' (2004) 48 Deutsches Ärzteblatt 553.

healthcare services are accessible throughout the country. However, there are regional differences. The service provision of community-based mental healthcare in private facilities with approved licenses (Zulassung zur vertragsärztlichen Versorgung, also called Kassenzulassung) is much lower in rural settings, leading to long waiting times for therapies.[214] As for economic accessibility, all private and public health insurances cover care and treatment (including medication) costs in inpatient facilities, psychiatric outpatient departments, and most community-based mental healthcare services, for individuals who are diagnosed as mentally ill.[215] Health insurance is mandatory for all private persons residing in Germany. Based on the solidarity principle, all persons, no matter whether they are employed, self-employed or unemployed, are enrolled in either the private or public health insurance scheme, and thus receive cost-free mental healthcare. However, in order to circumvent long waiting times in community-based services, more and more affected individuals choose to pay for therapy themselves. With out-of-pocket payments, affected individuals do not have to go through the lengthy bureaucratic process of having their health insurance approve their therapy first, and can usually start therapy right away. Furthermore, self-payment gives more freedom when it comes to choosing psychotherapists or therapy methods, as neither of these need to be approved by the health insurance system.[216] Conversely, this also cuts waiting times. In recent years, the accessibility of information about mental health and mental healthcare has increased profoundly. There are various awareness-raising campaigns, with the biggest being the anti-stigma initiative by the German Alliance for Mental Health (Aktionsbündnis Seelische Gesundheit). Together with over 90 alliance partners, including experts from psychiatry, and health promotion and self-help groups, it implements and supports awareness campaigns and prevention programmes, organises workshops, conducts trainings, and promotes the interests of people with mental health conditions and psychosocial disabilities and their families.[217] Gaebel is amongst the German scholars advocating for such awareness-raising initiatives, in order to increase knowledge, decrease public stigma – and, thus, self-stigma – and, as a result, to (amongst other things) increase the numbers of affected individuals accessing help.[218]

---

[214] Petra Bührung, 'Psychotherpaeutische Versorgung: Die Frage der Gerechigkeit' (2021) 2 Deutsches Ärzteblatt 55.

[215] For instance, any person with a mental health condition can obtain therapy by a community-based psychotherapist who has an approved license (*Kassenzulassung*) for a period that the respective psychotherapist declares as suitable for the diagnoses, with standard treatment times of one year; see Jan Kaspers (n 209).

[216] Which is required for cost-coverage by the health insurance.

[217] See German Alliance for Mental Health (nd), <https://www.seelischegesundheit.net/> accessed 14 November 2022; or Aktionsbündnis Seelische Gesundheit, 'Together for mental health against stigma' (nd), <https://www.seelischegesundheit.net/images/stories/buendnis/ABSG_FL_2017_en-web.pdf> accessed 14 November 2022.

[218] See eg Wolfgang Gaebel, 'Pro und Kontra: Machen Antistigmakampagnen Sinn? [For and Against: Do Anti-Stigma Campaigns Make Sense?]' (2005) 32(5) Psychiatrische Praxis 218.

According to CteeESCR General Comment 14, the acceptability of mental healthcare services includes factors such as them being culturally appropriate and respectful to medical ethics.[219] While the first of these factors was particularly relevant for the discussion in the Ghanaian context, the author wants to focus specifically on the latter, in the context of Germany. Medical ethics, as stated previously, include, amongst other things, the principles of choice, control, autonomy, will, preference and dignity.[220] This implies that the principles of individual autonomy and interdependence, which encompass the freedom for people to make their own choices, must be respected.[221] The principles of medical ethics listed above also directly point to Article 12 CRPD – the right to equal recognition before the law – which, derived from the normative analysis in section 5.3, includes the right to legal capacity, as well as the right to access supported decision-making. It is particularly the system of guardianship within Germany's mental health legislation that has raised concerns before the CteeRPD.[222] In light of ongoing discussions about the non-compliance of Germany's guardianship regulation with the CRPD, and recent efforts to reform this guardianship law, the intention here is to specifically examine (in subsection 6.4.3) the legislation around the question of incompetence and the system of representation.

The fourth element o the AAAQ is (i) high quality mental healthcare based on (ii) scientifically approved and evidence-based standards. The latter is uncontested in Germany. More controversial is the definition and assessment of 'high-quality', especially in psychiatry, and in relation to respect for autonomy and protection of inherent dignity. Germany has not been of concern to UN agencies or international organisations regarding the use of questionable drugs, lack of hospital equipment, or sanitary conditions in mental health facilities. However, in 2015, the CteeRPD criticised ongoing and widespread coercive interventions in psychiatric institutions, which compromise the quality of care. In its Concluding Observation on Germany, the Committee called upon the German government to prohibit involuntary placement in institutions, and to have this reflected in legislation; and to recognise the use of physical and chemical restraints, as well as solitary confinement, as acts of torture, and formally abolish these.[223] Considering the continuous use of involuntary treatment of persons with mental health conditions and psychosocial disabilities, the CteeRPD recommended that the necessary measures be taken to ensure that mental healthcare is 'always delivered with the free and informed consent of the individual concerned'.[224] Marschner has presented an international comparison which shows that the number

---

[219] CteeESCR, General Comment 14 (n 1) para 12(c).
[220] UNGA, 'Report of the Special Rapporteur on the right of everyone to the enjoyment of the highest attainable standard of physical and mental health, Dainius Pūras' (n 54) para 65.
[221] See UNGA, Convention on the Rights of Persons with Disabilities (CRPD) (adopted 13 December 2006, entered into force 3 May 2008) 2515 UNTS 3, preamble, para 14.
[222] See Committee on the Rights of Persons with Disabilities (CteeRPD), 'Concluding observations on the initial report of Germany' (13 May 2015) UN Doc CRPD/C/DEU/CO/1, paras 25–26.
[223] Ibid paras 30(a), 33.
[224] Ibid, paras 37, 38(b).

of involuntary admissions in Germany is relatively high, at 15.9 per cent of all mental health patients.[225] He further estimated that roughly 10 per cent of all inpatient patients are subject to coercive treatment, including isolation or mechanical or chemical restraints. While this percentage might seem low, Marschner argues that this is still a significant number, given the level of seriousness of the interference with a person's fundamental rights.[226] Although the provisions regarding coercive interventions have already been amended, back in 2013, to set stricter criteria, Zinkler points out that, in particular, coercive medication, e.g. involuntary treatment with antipsychotic drugs, is still commonly used in mainstream psychiatry.[227] To improve the quality of mental healthcare in Germany, precautionary measures and access to support have become imperative. Both topics will be discussed in the subsequent analysis.

6.4.2 GERMANY'S MENTAL HEALTH LEGISLATIVE FRAMEWORK

Germany ratified the CRPD in March 2009, without any reservation being entered by the government. Thereby, the CRPD became binding law under Germany's constitution, which must be applied by all state entities, including at the Länder level. Due to the German approach to international law, the normative content of the CRPD was formally validated, but the treaty retains the status of international law by its nature.[228] This means that, for the rights recognised in the CRPD to become directly applicable and not just to be used as interpretative aid by federal and Länder courts, the legislature must formally approve them in form of a federal law.[229] In line with Article 4 CPRD, the following will give an overview of whether, and to what extent, Germany has adopted appropriate legislation or modified and abolished existing laws that discriminate against persons with mental health conditions and psychosocial disabilities. How does Germany's mental health legislative framework protect and promote the right to mental health(care)?

---

[225] Compared to 2.8 percent in Portugal, 4.3 percent in Denmark, 10.9 percent in Ireland or 13.6 percent in England.
[226] Rolf Marschner, 'Menschen in Krisen: Unterbringung und Zwangsbehandlung in der Psychiatrie', in Valentin Aichele (ed), *Das Menschenrecht auf gleiche Anerkennung vor dem Recht: Artikel 12 der UN-Behindertenrechtskonvention* (Nomos 2013) 204–5.
[227] See eg Martin Zinkler, 'Germany without Coercive Treatment in Psychiatry – A 15 Month Real World Experience' (2016) 5(1) Laws, 15.
[228] See Valentin Aichele, 'Germany' in Lisa Waddington & Anna Lawson (eds), *The UN Convention on the Rights of Persons with Disabilities in Practice: A Comparative Analysis of the Role of Courts* (Oxford University Press 2018) 155, 157.
[229] See Article 59(2) of the Basic Law: 'Treaties that regulate the political relations of the Federation or relate to subjects of federal legislation shall require the consent or participation, in the form of a federal law, of the bodies responsible in such a case for the enactment of federal law. In the case of executive agreements the provisions concerning the federal administration shall apply mutatis mutandis'.

6.4.2.1   Relevant Legislation

Unlike Ghana, there is no single comprehensive mental health law in Germany. Nor is there a generally recognised definition of 'mental health', 'mental disorder,' 'psychosocial disability', or 'mental health facilities'. Important components of mental health laws that promote mental health and protect persons with mental health conditions and psychosocial disabilities can, nevertheless, be found in a range of federal laws and Länder laws. After giving an overview of applicable norms within various federal laws, the following paragraphs will analyse the more comprehensive Länder laws regarding their provisions on involuntary admission and treatment, complaint procedures and community-based care.

On the federal level, the Basic Law lists, among the fundamental human rights, the prohibition of discrimination on various grounds, including disability. It specifically states that 'no person shall be disfavoured because of disability'.[230] Book IX of the Social Code (Sozialgesetzbuch – Neuntes Buch), regarding the rehabilitation and participation of persons with disabilities, includes provisions on the rights of persons with psychosocial disabilities to, inter alia, live independently and be included in the community and, connected to the non-discrimination norm, ensures that persons with disabilities have the right to receive benefits to avoid or avert disadvantages and strengthen their self-determination.[231] Book IX further provides the right to have one's wishes and preferences respected.[232] Moreover, one section of the Civil Code (Bürgerliches Gesetzbuch) covers all guardianship regulations (rechtliche Betreuung) for, inter alia, persons with psychosocial disabilities,[233] which will be examined in more detail later in this chapter. This section includes provisions on non-acute care, specifically for persons deemed unable to care for themselves. The Federal Penal Code (Strafgesetzbuch) norms regulating forensic psychiatric care will not be examined further in this book.

Besides federal legislation, which always takes precedence over Länder law, each of the 16 states in Germany has its own mental health law (Psychisch-Kranken-Gesetz). Many Länder refer to these as laws adopted to 'protect' and 'support' the persons concerned.[234] The state laws regulate mental healthcare services in general, and provide – depending on the state law in question – norms regarding specific aspects of the mental healthcare system. These include norms on:

- budgets and costs of (the organisation of) mental healthcare services
- the coordination of support services

---

[230]   Federal Republic of Germany, Grundgesetz (n 200) art 3.
[231]   See Federal Republic of Germany, Sozialgesetzbuch (SGB IX) Neuntes Buch (adopted 2001, amended 2020), art 1.
[232]   Ibid art 8.
[233]   See Federal Republic of Germany, German Civil Code (adopted 1896, amended 2023), arts 1814–1881.
[234]   The states Baden-Württemberg, Berlin, Bremen, Hamburg, Mecklenburg-Western Pomerania, Lower Saxony, North Rhine-Westphalia, and Saxony-Anhalt call it the *Gesetz über Hilfen und Schutzmaßnahmen bei psychischen Krankheiten*.

Part 3. Country Study Analysis

- the responsibilities of the public social psychiatric services (Sozialpsychiatrischer Dienst) regarding outpatient support and care
- the organisation of inpatient care (including keeping personal belongings, personal correspondence, receiving visits, leave of absence, leisure activities, a range of schooling or vocational training lessons, and the freedom of religion)
- the right to make informed decisions about one's treatment
- the application of treatment plans
- the appointment of voluntary patient advocates (Patientenfürsprecher) for inpatient care, who consider the wishes and preferences of the persons concerned and advise them accordingly. Patient advocates can also report instances of significant deficiencies in the care and treatment of affected individuals.

Irrespective of their differences, all Länder laws focus in particular on the involuntary admission and treatment of persons with acute mental health conditions and psychosocial disabilities or acute exacerbations of chronic psychosocial disabilities.

6.4.2.1.1 Involuntary Admission

Despite considerable differences in the details of each Länder law, there are two necessary conditions for involuntary admissions common to all of these state laws: firstly, the person must have a mental disorder; and, secondly, due to the disorder, the person must be an acute danger to themselves or to others. The procedure for involuntary admission always includes either a municipal authority or the police ruling that acute psychiatric care is necessary, a medical doctor testifying that danger is caused by the mental disorder, and a local or regional court confirming the rightfulness of the admission, based on expert psychiatric testimony within a short time of the admission.[235] Since deprivation of liberty is seen as a strong interference with human rights, federal law in Germany stipulates that detained persons must be released by the end of the following day, at the latest, if no court order has been obtained.[236] Building on this, the Länder laws of 15 states set a limit of 24 hours after involuntary admission to a closed institution if no court order has been obtained. One Länder law specifies that persons admitted on Friday may be detained without court order until midday on Monday.[237] Upon obtaining a court order, the maximum detention times vary greatly between the different Länder laws, ranging from days to weeks.[238] Different regulations also apply with regard to the detention facilities. Ten states require that involuntary

---

[235] See Federal Republic of Germany, Act on Proceedings in Family Matters and in Matters of Non-contentious Jurisdiction (adopted 2008, amended 2020), arts 312ff; and Jürgen Zielasek & Wolfgang Gaebel, 'Mental health law in Germany' (2015) 12(1) British Journal of Psychiatry International 14, 15.
[236] See Federal Republic of Germany, Grundgesetz (n 200) art 104(2).
[237] Deutsches Institut für Menschenrechte, 'Entwicklung der Menschenrechtssituation in Deutschland Juli 2017-Juni 2018. Bericht an den Deutschen Bundestag gemäß §2 Absatz 5 DIMRG' (2018), pp 66–67.
[238] Jürgen Zielasek & Wolfgang Gaebel (n 235) 15.

admission must be to a hospital, of which nine states specifically state that it must be a psychiatric hospital or a psychiatric unit of a general hospital. The other six states also allow for admission into different types of facilities for the elderly, for people with (physical and mental) disabilities, and for psychosocial support. Involuntary admission to such institutions can be viewed critically from a human rights perspective, as these institutions offer long-term care (which is not always needed) behind closed doors, and not necessarily under the supervision of doctors. This opens the door for a wide range of human rights infringements in mental healthcare, such as unregulated involuntary and inhumane treatment.[239]

Where persons with chronic psychosocial disabilities already have a legal guardian (based on the Civil Code's guardianship regulations), they can also be involuntarily admitted to an institution under the auspices of the Civil Code. This is limited to cases in which, due to deteriorating psychosocial disability, (i) there is a risk of suicide or serious self-harm, or (ii) where medical intervention is required to avert imminent serious harm to health and the intervention can only be carried out after admission and the person is unable to recognise the need for admission due to their psychosocial disability. Involuntary admission is only possible following a court order. In acute cases, the court order may be issued promptly in retrospect.[240] However, no particular time limit on what constitutes 'promptly' is defined by law. Importantly, the Civil Code regulates only involuntary admission to avoid imminent self-harm, rather than harm to others, due to a mental health condition. Under the Civil Code, detention is limited to four to six weeks, and can only be extended with a renewed court hearing. For periods exceeding 12 weeks, an independent expert psychiatric witness is required.[241]

The regulations on involuntary admission based on a person's mental health condition or psychosocial disability (and additional factors) in the Länder laws and Civil Code are in tension with the provisions of the CRPD framework and the related regulations for non-discriminatory deprivation of liberty, as analysed in subsection 5.5.2. Despite the non-discrimination provision in the German Basic Law, the German Supreme Court does not support the CteeRPD's interpretation of the restriction of liberty.[242] The Court has found that the absence in German law of a mechanism which allowed persons with (psychosocial) disabilities to be admitted to a hospital, without their consent, to receive life-saving treatment would be unconstitutional. The Court held that this would be contrary to the state's duty to protect its citizens, and that, in its view, such a measure is not inconsistent with the CRPD.[243] This tension between the German Supreme Court and the CRPD is representative of the position in many states around the world, where governments have the duty to preserve the life and health of individuals (see subsections 5.4.2.2 and 5.5.2.2).

---

[239] Deutsches Institut für Menschenrechte (n 237) 67.
[240] See Federal Republic of Germany, German Civil Code (n 233) art 1831.
[241] Jürgen Zielasek & Wolfgang Gaebel (n 235).
[242] Deutsches Institut für Menschenrechte (n 237) 66.
[243] See Bundesverfassungsgericht (2016): Order of 26 July 2016, 1 BvL 8/15.

6.4.2.1.2 Involuntary Treatment

Germany's Supreme Court has found in several instances that persons with mental health conditions and psychosocial disabilities can choose not to be treated.[244] In a milestone judgement in 2011, the Court nevertheless held that involuntary treatment may be justified where: (i) persons lack the capacity to recognise the need for treatment because of their psychosocial disabilities; and (ii) where the benefits of the proposed procedure outweigh the potential dangers posed by the procedure. Moreover, according to the Court, the measures must be necessary to avoid serious and imminent damage to the health of the affected person, and can only be applied if no alternatives are available, as ultima ratio.[245] The Court further provided strict requirements for involuntary treatment. Firstly, medical personnel must always try to receive the free and informed consent of the patient regarding the treatment. Staff must also share all necessary information pertaining to the treatment with patients: even those who are allegedly incompetent. Apart from in emergency cases, this information must be shared on a timely basis to enable judicial protection to be obtained. When carried out, involuntary treatment must be supervised and documented, and an external independent body, which can be a judge, ombudsman or other authority, must be involved when deciding on the necessity of such treatment. In emergency cases, the external body requirement ceases to apply.[246] When implementing this judgment, each Länder law set out the details of these requirements differently. Two Länder laws do not specify that information pertaining to the treatment must be shared, eight do not specify that information must be shared in a timely manner, three are silent on the need to supervise involuntary treatment, and three do not include a documentation practice. Furthermore, two Länder laws do not provide that an involuntary treatment procedure must be examined by an independent body. Adding to the requirements derived from the Supreme Court's judgment, some states grant even more safeguards, by ordering that a debriefing must follow an involuntary treatment, or that the head of a facility must authorise involuntary treatment procedures.[247]

Under the Civil Code, when it comes to persons with psychosocial disabilities who are under guardianship, until 2012 only a guardian's agreement to involuntary treatment sufficed. Following rulings from the Supreme Court,[248] legal disputes about a guardian's permissions led to amendments to this part of the law. Since 2013, therefore, persons with psychosocial disabilities under guardianship can only be subjected to involuntary treatment by permission of the legal guardian if all requirements for involuntary treatment (as specified in the 2011 Supreme Court judgement above) have been met and a special court ruling for the planned procedure has been obtained. Since

---

[244] See eg Bundesverfassungsgericht (1998): Order of 23 March1998, 2 Bvr 2270/96, para 15; or Bundesverfassungsgericht (2015): Order of 02 June 2015, 2 Bvr 2236/14, para 18.
[245] Bundesverfassungsgericht (2011): Order of 23 March 2011, 2 Bvr 882/09.
[246] Ibid paras 56–71.
[247] See Deutsches Institut für Menschenrechte (n 237) 69.
[248] Especially the milestone decision of 2011 as outlined above.

2023, the law also stipulates that the involuntary treatment must correspond to the presumed will and preference of the person concerned.[249]

Besides the regulations of the Länder laws and the Civil Code, involuntary interventions can also be justified under the Federal Penal Code, in cases of self-defence and necessity (Notwehr und Notstand).[250] These are situations in which persons with mental health conditions and psychosocial disabilities represent an extreme and acute danger to themselves or to others, and other persons, including medical or mental health personnel, provide 'acute help' (referring to assistance/care). In fact, studies have shown that some hospitals justify involuntary treatment more often as self-defence or necessity according to the Federal Penal Code than they do under the regulations outlined in the Länder laws or the Civil Code.[251]

With regard to seclusion and restraint – specific measures of involuntary treatment – the German Supreme Court considers these to be strong interferences with the rights of affected individuals, but does not impose an absolute prohibition. In a recent court decision, stronger safeguards for the use of seclusion and restraint measures were defined. The federal and state legislators were asked to implement these in their respective laws, or to modify existing regulations accordingly.[252] For mechanical restraints persisting for longer than 30 minutes, a court order must be obtained. As is the case with other involuntary treatment procedures, restraint measures must be supervised and documented in detail. For restraints, the Supreme Court also specifically orders personal one-on-one supervision, and a regular reassessment of their necessity.[253]

To conclude, under German legislation, involuntary treatment (with strong safeguards) is permitted to avoid serious and imminent damage to the health of an affected individual, or where an affected individual poses extreme and acute danger to others. Allowing involuntary treatment – even in such emergency situations – is seen as unacceptable within the CRPD framework, as elaborated in more detail in section 5.4.3.4.

6.4.2.1.3 Complaint Procedures

Generally, any court order concerning a mental healthcare practice can be appealed by the patient. Furthermore, Visiting Committees (Besuchskommissionen) are tasked with reviewing specialised psychiatric institutions (but not any other institutions), and investigating whether legal standards have generally been complied with. Their focus is not necessarily on receiving individual complaints. Either way, Visiting Committees cannot act upon human rights infringements, and only report back to

---

[249] See Federal Republic of Germany, German Civil Code (n 233) art 1832; and Jürgen Zielasek & Wolfgang Gaebel (n 235) 16.
[250] See Federal Republic of Germany, Strafgesetzbuch (adopted 1872, amended 2020), arts 32, 34.
[251] See Deutsches Institut für Menschenrechte (n 237) 65–66.
[252] Bundesverfassungsgericht (2018): Order of 24 July 2018, 2 Bvr 309/15, Bvr 502/16.
[253] Ibid paras 81–92, 95.

the ministry responsible for the respective facilities.[254] The specific mandates of the Committees are, once again, regulated in the Länder laws, which offer various different regulations. In some states, the mandate includes investigations of standards based on the guardianship regulations (Betreuungsrecht) of the Civil Code, while others allow only for the investigation of standards in line with the Länder laws. The state laws further differ in terms of the frequency of the Committees' visits, whether visits must be announced, and whether persons with lived experiences should form part of the Committees.[255] Despite being an important mechanism for ensuring human rights in mental healthcare, there are clear legal gaps regarding Visiting Committees: what about reviewing other non-specialised psychiatric institutions that offer mental healthcare services? Or infringements based on the Civil Code regulations, or other federal law norms? And notwithstanding that there are regulations establishing Visiting Committees in all but one state, these Committees have not yet commenced work in all of these states.

An additional promising complaint procedure mechanism is, therefore, offered by complaint offices (Beschwerdestellen). Integrated in some Länder laws, and established in some states,[256] these independent offices receive individual complaints and offer consultations to affected persons. Complaint offices are considered to be an important interface with judicial protection, as they share relevant information about patient's rights and legal protection, and can link to lawyers.[257]

6.4.2.1.4 Community-based Care

Despite its relevance for the right to mental health, up until now federal and Länder mental health legislation has barely considered community-based mental healthcare. As Zielasek and Gaebel point out, the Civil Code addresses mental healthcare almost exclusively with regard to involuntary interventions that must always be carried out in inpatient mental healthcare units.[258] As for the Länder laws, their focus is mainly on acute danger situations that are, traditionally, taken care of in an inpatient environment. However, the latest amendments to some Länder mental health laws strengthen community-based mental healthcare, including preventive care and clinical follow-up support. States are tasked with establishing and promoting community-based mental healthcare, in the form of self-help groups and organisations, easily accessible counselling centres, crises services that offer psychosocial help in mental crises, and sufficient outpatient emergency care.[259] Furthermore, some laws outline detailed

---

[254] See Deutsches Institut für Menschenrechte (n 237) 84.
[255] Ibid 85.
[256] See an up-to-date list of available complaint offices throughout Germany: <www.beschwerde-psychiatrie.de/liste.html> accessed 14 November 2022.
[257] See Deutsches Institut für Menschenrechte (n 237) 85.
[258] Jürgen Zielasek & Wolfgang Gaebel (n 235) 15.
[259] See eg the mental health laws of Bavaria, Berlin, Brandenburg, Hesse, Mecklenburg-Western Pomerania, and Rhineland-Palatinate.

procedures of follow-up support after (involuntary) inpatient care. The aims are to help affected individuals, through medical and psychosocial care, to reintegrate into society and become independent and autonomous, as well as to prevent future inpatient care. Some legislation also encompasses support in finding housing and employment.[260]

6.4.2.2   Relevant Strategies, Plans and Programmes

Although there is no recent German mental health policy, there are various relevant mental-health related strategies and plans. Germany's 2020 Global Health Strategy focuses on achieving the health targets of the 2030 Sustainable Development Goals agenda.[261] The promotion of mental health is included in different parts of the strategy. Yet, details regarding a mental health action plan have not been included. The latest national mental health strategy, entitled *Depressive disorders: prevention, early detection, sustainable treatment*, was published in 2006. It offers innovative ways of intervening meaningfully to promote mental health and prevent depression. The strategy defines goals and subgoals regarding education; prevention; diagnosis; treatment; respect for the affected individuals' decisions regarding their treatment; rehabilitation; and the care structure, and formulates actions to be taken to achieve each of the subgoals. Each action step is assigned to a responsible actor.[262] As this national strategy focuses purely on depressive disorders, it is worthwhile also looking at Germany's national disability strategy and plan, which applies to all forms of psychosocial disabilities. In line with the understanding and definition of disability outlined in the CRPD, the 2016 *Second National Action Plan for the Implementation of the CRPD* aims to further promote the inclusion of persons with (psychosocial) disabilities, through 175 specific targeted measures across 13 areas with defined responsible actors.[263] As part of the action field 'construction and living' in connection with measures for inclusion, the Action Plan states that the new Federal Participation Act must outline that care is offered outside institutions, and that services are person-centred, respecting the wishes and preferences of affected individuals regarding their choices of residence (drawing a connection with Article 19(a) CRPD).[264] This measure has already been implemented. The Action Plan also outlines, as part of the action field 'privacy rights', two research projects to

---

[260] See eg the mental health laws of Brandenburg, Bremen, Hamburg, Mecklenburg-Western Pomerania, North Rhine-Westphalia, Saxony-Anhalt, and Thuringia.

[261] See Federal Republic of Germany, 'Strategie der Bundesregierung zur globalen Gesundheit' [Global Health Strategy] (2020), <https://www.bundesgesundheitsministerium.de/fileadmin/Dateien/5_Publikationen/Gesundheit/Broschueren/GlobaleGesundheitsstrategie_Web.pdf> accessed 14 November 2022.

[262] See Federal Republic of Germany, 'Depressive Erkrankungen: verhindern, früh erkennen, nachhaltig behandeln' (2006), <https://gesundheitsziele.de/cms/medium/261/Gesundheitsziele_Depression_BMG_01-03-06.pdf> accessed 14 November 2022.

[263] See Federal Republic of Germany, 'Nationaler Aktionsplan 2.0 der Bundesregierung zur UN-Behindertenrechtskonvention (UN-BRK)' (2016), <https://www.bmas.de/DE/Soziales/Teilhabe-und-Inklusion/Nationaler-Aktionsplan/nationaler-aktionsplan-2-0.html> accessed 14 November 2022.

[264] Ibid 119, 128.

evaluate the guardianship regulation: one focusing on the quality and deficits of the guardianship concept (drawing a connection with Article 12(3) CRPD), and the other focusing on alternatives to guardianship and the promotion thereof (drawing a connection with Article 12(2) CRPD).[265] Another research project within the same action field is to evaluate the necessity of coercive measures, and possibilities for preventing coercion through the use of alternative voluntary treatment methods, in mental healthcare facilities (drawing a connection with Article 17 CRPD).[266] The first two research projects have already published their results in extensive reports,[267] which certainly influenced recent discussions on reforming the guardianship regulations, as will be elaborated shortly. Besides the aforementioned national strategies and plans, various states in Germany have their own general health, mental health or disability strategies and guidelines.[268] Due to their limited scope of application, this book does not examine these in detail.

Two recent mental health programmes to promote mental health and prevent mental ill health are especially worth pointing out. From 2016 to 2019, Germany took part in the six-country project 'e-Mental Health Innovation and Transnational Implementation Platform North-West Europe', aiming to improve the quality and uptake of e-mental health. With the overarching goal of promoting mental health and reducing treatment gaps in mental healthcare, the objectives of the project were promoting more affordable, accessible, effective and empowering mental healthcare through activities in research, product development, policy and communication. After implementing the initial results in urban settings, the project was extended in 2020 to capitalise on the results, and to implement specific activities to introduce e-mental health technology to service providers in more rural areas as well.[269] The other programme worth mentioning was initiated in October 2020 by the German Ministries of Labour and Social Affairs, Health, and Family Affairs, called Mental Health (Offensive Psychische Gesundheit). It encourages an open dialogue about psychological stress factors, and aims to strengthen the network of prevention and support services, and cooperation between these services. The approach spans all life stages and social environments that affect people's mental health, including

---

[265] Ibid 186, 199.

[266] Ibid 187, 200.

[267] See Federal Ministry of Justice and Consumer Protection, *Qualität in der rechtlichen Betreuung. Abschlussbericht* (Bundesanzeiger Verlag 2018); and Federal Ministry of Justice and Consumer Protection, *Umsetzung des Erforderlichkeitsgrundsatzes in der betreuungsrechtlichen Praxis im Hinblick auf vorgelagerte „andere Hilfen"* (Bundesanzeiger Verlag 2018).

[268] See WHO, 'MiNDbank: More Inclusiveness Needed in Disability and Development; Country Resources: Germany' (nd), <www.mindbank.info/collection/country/germany> accessed 14 November 2022.

[269] See Aktionsbündnis Seelische Gesundheit, 'EU project Interreg eMEN' (nd), <https://www.seelischegesundheit.net/themen/e-mental-health> accessed 14 November 2022; and Interreg North-West-Europe eMEN, 'Project Summary' (nd), <https://www.nweurope.eu/projects/project-search/e-mental-health-innovation-and-transnational-implementation-platform-north-west-europe-emen/> accessed 14 November 2022.

the workplace, school and university, as well as family and friends, and specifically recognises the added burden of the COVID-19 pandemic.[270]

6.4.3 PERSISTING KEY CHALLENGE: GUARDIANSHIP REGULATION (BETREUUNGSRECHT)

According to the Federal Office of Justice, there are approximately 1.3 million ongoing guardianship proceedings in Germany.[271] In its 2015 Concluding Observation on Germany, the CteeRPD found the legal instrument of guardianship (rechtliche Betreuung) to be incompatible with the CRPD, especially Article 12. It called for the development of professional quality standards for supported decision-making, and the elimination of all forms of substituted decision-making mechanisms.[272] To eliminate the shortfalls in relation to Article 12 CPRD, the German Federal Government passed reforms of the guardianship regulation in March 2021 which came into force in January 2023. The following will illustrate how Germany's currently applicable mental health legislation regulates the question of incompetence and the system of representation, and to what extent this complies with the approach envisioned by the CRPD.

6.4.3.1 *The Legal Framework regarding the Question of Incompetence*

Most European judicial systems have adopted the approach of presuming the capacity of adult individuals, and consider them to be competent unless the opposite is proven. Thus, no person with mental health condition or psychosocial disability is ipso facto incompetent.[273] Likewise, in accordance with Article 1 of the German Civil Code, Germany recognises that all living people have legal capacity. However, German law differentiates between the capacity to hold rights (Rechtsfähigkeit), as enshrined in Article 1 of the Civil Code, and the capacity to act on these rights (rechtliche Handlungsfähigkeit).[274] Articles 104, 827 and 828 of the Civil Code specify that adults are regarded as having the capacity to act, including the capability to enter into legal transactions or commit crimes, which presumes that they have the necessary insight

---

[270] See Federal Ministry of Labour and Social Affairs, 'Aktionswoche der Offensive Psychische Gesundheit' (nd), <https://inqa.de/DE/vernetzen/offensive-psychische-gesundheit/aktionswoche.html> accessed 14 November 2022.
[271] See Federal Office of Justice, 'Verfahren nach dem Betreuungsgesetz 1992 bis 2017' (nd), <https://www.bundesjustizamt.de/DE/Themen/Buergerdienste/Justizstatistik/Betreuung/Betreuung_node.html> accessed 14 November 2022.
[272] CteeRPD, 'Concluding observations on the initial report of Germany' (n 222) paras 25–26.
[273] Herman Nys and others, 'Patient Capacity in Mental Health Care: Legal Overview' (2005) 12(4) Health Care Analysis 329, 331.
[274] Jana Offergeld, *Unterstützung der Selbstbestimmung oder fremdbestimmende Stellvertretung? Rechtliche Betreuung aus der Perspektive von Menschen mit Lernschwierigkeiten* (Beltz Juventa 2021) 29–30.

and decision-making capacity to do so.[275] Nevertheless, exceptional circumstances may restrict major-age persons' capacity to act, and deem them incompetent. Here, the Civil Code differentiates between a declaration of incompetence and a declaration of intent presumed to be void.[276]

6.4.3.1.1 Restriction of the Capacity to Act

Firstly, according to the law, a person is declared mentally incompetent or 'incapable of contracting' if 'he is in a state of pathological mental disturbance, which prevents the free exercise of will, unless the state by its nature is a temporary one'.[277] Although the Civil Code does not define the term 'state of pathological mental disturbance', a decision of Bavaria's Higher Regional Court brings clarity. According to the Court, a mental disturbance that prevents the exercise of free will exists if an affected person is unable to use and understand information to make a particular decision and communicate that decision. Conversely, a person can only exercise free will if their decision-making process is not subject to the influence of the will of others, or influenced by uncontrollable urges and ideas.[278]

Secondly, in addition to the declaration of incompetence of persons suffering from long-lasting mental disturbances, a declaration of intent is presumed to be void when a person is in a state of temporary mental disturbance or unconsciousness.[279] In other words, even when experiencing a mental disturbance which is only temporary, persons may be considered unable to give their informed consent, and may be precluded from freely exercising their will.

In the most prominent Federal Constitutional Court decision regarding the question of incompetence of persons with mental health conditions and psychosocial disabilities, in accordance with Article 12 CPRD, the Court evaluated the constitutionality of a Länder law allowing the treatment of persons in psychiatric institutions with medication against their will, after having been assessed as being incapable of taking their own decisions. Considering the constitutional right to personal integrity, and the significance of Article 12 CRPD, the Court stated that the right to exercise legal capacity is not absolute. While it generally considered mental health treatment against the will of the affected person to be unconstitutional, it ruled that the right to autonomy can be restricted in cases of lack of capacity caused by illness.[280] As can be seen from the report on this case, there are mechanisms used in mental healthcare settings to assess the decision-making capacities of persons having mental health problems. However, there are no official guidelines enshrined in law or policy for the assessment of capacity.

---

[275] Federal Republic of Germany, German Civil Code (n 233) arts 104, 827–828.
[276] The author chooses to use the word 'void' in this context instead of invalid, because the official English translation of the German Civil Code uses the term 'void'.
[277] Federal Republic of Germany, German Civil Code (n 233) art 104(2).
[278] See BayOlG NJW 1992, 2100.
[279] Federal Republic of Germany, German Civil Code (n 233) art 105(2).
[280] See Bundesverfassungsgericht (n 245) paras 52, 53; and see Valentin Aichele (n 228) 172–3.

Could the Civil Code regulations which declare persons incompetent then be classified as incompatible with Article 12(1) and (2) of the CRPD? At this point, it is important to recall that legal capacity, in line with Article 12 CPRD, includes both the capacity to hold rights and the capacity to exercise and act upon these rights, both of which are distinct from the concept of mental capacity (see subsection 5.3.2.1). At the outset, it seems as though the Civil Code regulations arbitrarily regard persons with psychosocial disabilities as lacking the capacity to act, based on their psychosocial disabilities. However, Articles 104 and 827 of the Civil Code apply equally to persons without disabilities, as their scope of application is not restricted in this regard. The concept of 'pathological mental disturbance' may cover persons whose psychosocial impairment might lead to a disability, as well as unconscious persons or persons having other illnesses that preclude their free exercise of will.[281] As Brosey explains, legal incapacity as a status has been abolished in German law. As for the capacity to act, whether or not a person is mentally competent to do so will depend on the specific circumstances in which they are seeking to act.[282] Thus, rather than questioning (and restricting) a person's legal capacity, which would be incompatible with Article 12(2) CRPD, the provisions of the Civil Code can be understood as addressing a person's mental capacity, and thus their ability to make decisions. In its initial report to the CteeRPD, the German government declared that, instead of restricting the right to legal capacity, the Civil Code regulations outlined above aim to protect persons who lack mental capacity; to protect against disadvantageous consequences from undesirable legal transaction obligations entered into by people while in a state precluding their free exercise of will; and to protect against such people incurring liability for damage towards another person, with regard to which they should not be held responsible.[283] However, whether Germany fulfils its obligation under Article 12(3) CRPD, namely ensuring that persons who lack mental capacity to make a decision have access to support for decision-making, needs to be analysed next.

6.4.3.1.2 Avoidance of Heteronomy in Situations of Impaired Decision-making Skills

As elaborated in subsection 5.3.2.1, the CRPD framework acknowledges that a person may have impaired decision-making skills (or, in other words, lack mental capacity) because of a mental health condition or psychosocial disability. Instead of denying legal capacity to such an individual and appointing a legal guardian, the individual should be entitled to access support for decision-making, according to Article 12(3) CRPD. For

---

[281] See UNGA, 'Consideration of reports submitted by States parties under article 35 of the Convention, Initial reports of States parties, Germany' (7 May 2013) UN Doc CRPD/C/DEU/1.
[282] Dagmar Brosey, 'Supported Decision-making and the German Law of Betreuung. A legal perspective on supported and substitute decision-making regarding Art. 12 CRPD' in Dagmar Coester-Waltjen, Volker Lipp & Donovan WM Waters (eds), *Liber Amicorum Makoto Arai* (Nomos 2015) 133.
[283] See UNGA, 'Consideration of reports submitted by States parties under article 35 of the Convention, Initial reports of States parties, Germany' (n 281).

situations in which persons with mental health conditions and psychosocial disabilities cannot express their informed consent (or are declared incompetent to do so), the German legislation provides for three guardianship-avoiding 'other assistances'. Over recent years, these precautionary measures have become established as alternatives to guardianship, with the aim of strengthening the right to self-determination. This is where the German legal framework forges new ground. The three mechanisms outlined below appear to be part of the category of measures to support decision-making. In some ways, however, the mechanisms render support for decision-making, in situations where a person lacks the ability to make their own decisions, unnecessary.

In 2007, the power of attorney (Vorsorgevollmacht) was established under the Civil Code.[284] It is a legal action that involves a competent adult appointing a proxy – a person they trust – to act as their guardian, and to deal with legal transactions whenever the grantor of power of attorney is no longer able or willing to look after their own affairs.[285] A person in possession of the authorisation form may act at any time with immediate effect, including with regard to health matters, once the grantor becomes unwilling or unable to look after their own affairs. More far-reaching measures, including admission to, and seclusion within, psychiatric institutions, need a judge's approval.[286] It is important to note that, in Germany, a spouse or other family member cannot automatically act as a proxy. Although a power of attorney does not have to be documented in a particular form or be certified, certification by a notary guarantees its recognition. Either way, the person granted power of attorney must store the original document and present it when the need to act upon it arises. In general, with the power of attorney, the need to appoint a guardian can be prevented.[287]

The advance directive on care (Betreuungsverfügung) was established as a new instrument under the Civil Code in 2009. Through the advance directive, a person still capable of making decisions can choose which person(s) of trust should be appointed as their guardian by a court in due course. To some extent, this can further regulate a person's wishes and preferences concerning the guardianship procedure, including areas of responsibility, instructions regarding medical procedures or financial matters, or their place of residence. While several different people can be named for different areas of responsibility, the advance directive can also state which people should under no circumstances be appointed as guardian.[288] The advance directive must be submitted to the local district court. For the advance directive to come into force, guardianship must be set up by means of a court order. If the local district court is aware of such an advance directive when setting up guardianship for an affected individual, it must take the advance directive of the individual into consideration

---

[284] Federal Republic of Germany, German Civil Code (n 233) art 1820.
[285] Institut für transkulturelle Betreuung e.V., 'German Guardianship Law' (2010), pp 16–17.
[286] Tanja Bratan and others, 'Implementation of the UN Convention on the Rights of Persons with Disabilities: A Comparison of Four European Countries with Regards to Assistive Technologies' (2020) 10(74) Societies, 8.
[287] Federal Republic of Germany, German Civil Code (n 233) art 1815.
[288] See Tanja Bratan (n 286) 8–9; or Institut für transkulturelle Betreuung e.V., (n 285) 15.

when reaching a decision regarding who to appoint as guardian. The final decision on whether to appoint the suggested person(s) as guardian(s) lies with the court. If he or she fulfils the requirements to be a guardian, and is then appointed, such a guardian will always be monitored by the court in the same way as it would monitor any other appointed guardian. Although the two precautionary measures – the power of attorney and the advance directive – seem alike, their application is different. The power of attorney instrument itself authorises a third person to act as proxy once it has been signed by the person concerned. The advance directive, on the other hand, is an instrument that merely suggests the preferred guardianship procedure (which must then be considered) to the court, and the persons listed within the advance directive only start acting on behalf of the person concerned once they have officially been appointed by court.

The living will (Patientenverfügung) was introduced in 2009 as yet another instrument to preserve a person's self-determination.[289] The two previously mentioned types of documents appoint a trusted person to make decisions on behalf of individuals who are no longer capable of doing so on their own. Instead of passing on their decision-making power to a trusted person, the living will enables an individual to make decisions regarding medical measures, such as diagnosis and therapy, on a precautionary basis. The living will lays out a person's own wishes regarding future medical treatment. The document usually includes very precise information, naming possible illnesses and health conditions, and which treatment measures the person would choose or reject. For mental health-related needs, a person can specify which types of treatment, care and support they want, and which they do not want. Such advance planning could also be useful for drafting recovery plans, and helping to guide affected individuals and caretakers through crisis situations in mental healthcare. Besides having to be in written form, there are no rules regarding the form of the living will. Guardians, attorneys and attendant doctors must observe the living will and act accordingly, once they know of its existence.[290]

The common objective shared by the power of attorney, the advance directive and the living will is to protect and promote an individual's self-determination in the event of their future incapacity. In some way, these advance plans guarantee that an affected individual's will and preferences will be respected in a situation where they lack decision-making capacity, even if that means a trusted person will be nominated (as proxy or guardian) to communicate the best interpretation of their will and preferences. Importantly, all of these German advance plans are only available if a person had full capacity when they were issued. Do these legal advancements indicate that the institution of supported decision-making, in line with Article 12(3) CRPD, has been implemented in the Civil Code?

Recently, the legislative reforms of some countries have been recognised internationally as best-practice examples for removing barriers to the exercise of legal

---

[289] Federal Republic of Germany, German Civil Code (n 233) art 1827.
[290] See Institut für transkulturelle Betreuung e.V. (n 285) 18.

capacity, enhancing the role of supported decision-making in mental healthcare, and ending civil guardianship for persons with psychosocial disabilities.[291] Among these is the 2019 law reform in Colombia, which introduced, among other things, two informal support mechanisms as support measures for people with low-level support needs, namely drafting advance directives (to outline wishes and preferences regarding certain areas of life in advance), and support agreements (to appoint a trusted person who will assist in making decisions).[292] In view of the similarity of the Colombian reforms to the German provisions, it can be assumed that the German advance plans were a source of inspiration. This similarity means that the German regulations can also be classified as removing barriers to the exercise of legal capacity and promoting supported decision-making, in the spirit of the CRPD framework. The support agreement in Colombia, which is very similar to both the German power of attorney and the advance directive on care, differs in one aspect: the Colombian law does not provide that such an agreement must be drafted in advance, while the affected person still has full decision-making capacity. Canada takes a similar approach. According to the British Columbia Representation Agreement Act of 1996, a person with a psychosocial disability can initiate a 'representation agreement', in which they assign a trusted person or support network to support them in exercising their rights according to their wishes and preferences; and such representation agreement can also be initiated by someone who is already considered mentally incapacitated, as long as only low-level support is needed.[293]

Allowing advance plans only in advance (as the name suggests) is a shortcoming of the German law. In cases where no advance plan is available and a person with psychosocial disabilities needs low-level support, the system of guardianship comes into effect. Many people in Germany with psychosocial disabilities are subject to a system of representation, as addressed in the CteeRPD Concluding Observation, and as will be illustrated next.

6.4.3.2   The Legal Framework regarding the System of Representation

This subsection will analyse how the German system of representation is set up, and to what extent it is compatible with human rights. It will examine whether it may be considered a form of support for decision-making (based on Article 12(3) CRPD), and

---

[291]   See WHO (n 133) 186; and Legislative Assembly of the Republic of Costa Rica, Law No 9379, Ley para la promoción de la autonomía personal de las personas con discapacidad (adopted 2016); Congress of Colombia, Law No 1996 of 2019, Por medio de la cual se establece el régimen para el ejercicio de la capacidad legal de las personas con discapacidad mayores de edad (adopted 2019); Peru, Decreto Supremo que aprueba el Reglamento de la Ley N° 30947 (n 135); India, Ministry of Law and Justice, Mental Healthcare Act (n 134) sees 5–17; or Congress of the Philippines, Republic Act No 11036 (adopted 2017).
[292]   Congress of Colombia, Law No 1996 of 2019 (n 291).
[293]   See Ministry of Attorney General and Legislative Assembly of British Colombia, Representation Agreement Act [RSBC 1996] CHAPTER 405 (adopted in 1996), sec 7.

what safeguards the German law puts in place to prevent abusive measures relating to the exercise of legal capacity (based on Article 12(4) CRPD).[294]

In 1992, Germany officially replaced the system of guardianship (Vormundschaft) with the system of custodianship (Betreuung), the latter being described as a system of care and support in which a person under custodianship maintains their right to self-determination as far as possible, and in which a person's free will is better taken into account than under guardianship.[295] It is for this reason that, within the German context, this study will refer to a system of custodianship, instead of a system of guardianship, from hereon forward. Mammeri-Latzel, a German judge, explains that the German adult custodianship law is characterised by three principles. The principle of necessity implies that a custodian should not be appointed as long as a person can manage their affairs independently, or with the help of a trusted person. The principle of self-determination or autonomy ensures that an individual under custodianship is given the possibility of leading a self-determined life by making their own decisions. A custodian only becomes involved if the affected person is unable to make such decisions. And, lastly, the principle of preservation of rights sets the rule that, regardless of a (psychosocial) disability, an adult under custodianship continues to hold fundamental rights.[296] The statutory basis for legal custodianship is laid down in Article 1814 of the Civil Code. It states that if a person of full age cannot manage his or her affairs in whole or in part and this is due to an illness or disability, the custodianship court shall appoint a custodian for him or her, however, a custodian may not be appointed against the free will of the person of full age.[297]

While, in most countries, guardianship is accompanied by the deprivation of legal capacity, the German Civil Code provision underscores what many legal scholars have been arguing for years: a person's legal capacity and contractual ability is not revoked under the German custodianship law, or through the appointment of a custodian.[298]

---

[294] The aim of this section is to assess the system of guardianship as mechanism to ensure the enjoyment of Article 12 CRPD, the right to equality before the law. The section will examine whether the German guardianship system can be considered a form of supported decision-making. This section does not aim to critically analyse every single provision of German guardianship law. The author acknowledges that some provisions, such as Article 1831 (custodial commitment and custodial measures) and Article 1832 (medical coercion), are central legal norms of the guardianship law. However, the German country study does not focus on involuntary treatment and hospitalisation, so that a more detailed analysis of these articles than undertaken in subchapter 6.4.2.1 would go beyond the scope of this country study in general, and this subsection in particular.

[295] European Union Agency for Fundamental Rights (FRA), *Legal capacity of persons with intellectual disabilities and persons with mental health problems* (FRA 2013) 31, 36.

[296] Maria Mammeri-Latzel, 'Overview of German Adult Guardianship Law from the Perspective of a German Judge (1st instance)' in Makoto Arai, Ulrich Becker, Volker Lipp (eds), *Adult Guardianship Law for the 21st Century* (Nomos 2013) 121.

[297] Federal Republic of Germany, German Civil Code (n 233) art 1814(1) and (2).

[298] See Dagmar Brosey (n 282) 129. It is only one specific occasion when the custodianship law overtly limits the legal capacity of the person under custodianship to the extent where the substituted decision of the custodian prevails. This is where a person under custodianship (or their property) is exposed to substantial danger or risk of serious harm and in which the person concerned lacks the ability to respond accordingly; see Federal Republic of Germany, German Civil Code (n 233) art 1825. Since

Rather, individuals have the power to apply for a custodian on their own, even if they are, allegedly, mentally incompetent. Also, the legal representative may only be appointed for groups of tasks for which the custodianship is necessary. Furthermore, an affected individual has the power to refuse the appointment of a custodian if this is against their free will. This, once more, highlights the right to self-determination within the custodianship law, and shows that the system of custodianship is rather a measure of last resort. Yet, this second part of Article 1814 of the Civil Code also shows the limitations on a person's right to self-determination. Based on a psychiatrist's opinion, the court may find that a person has no free will regarding the necessity of a custodian, and in such cases, the law obliges the court to support and protect an affected person by appointing a custodian, even if the affected individual disagrees.[299]

Aichele and Degener and other scholars have argued that the German system of legal representation cannot be seen as a measure of support for decision-making as envisioned by Article 12(3) CRPD, as it carries an element of heteronomy.[300] Others, including Brosey or Lipp, raise the point that custodians must comply with the will and preferences of the person under custodianship and support them in expressing these. They claim, therefore, that the custodian's decision-making process follows that of a supporting and not substituting decision-maker. Thus, the custodianship can be classified as a measure of supported decision-making.[301] Since the legislative reform that came into force in January 2023, the custodianship regulations include a separate Article addressing the will and preferences of persons under custodianship and the duties of the custodian; Article 1821 of the Civil Code. The content of the Article largely reflects what the CteeRPD envisages in the context of supported decision-making: custodians *support* individuals in managing their *own* affairs; custodians must attend to the affairs of individuals in such a way as to enable the individuals to live their lives according to their *will and preferences*; custodians must *ascertain the will and preferences* of the persons under custodianship and take actions *accordingly,* the latter also applying to will and preferences expressed prior to custodianship, unless it is evident that individuals no longer wish to comply with them.[302] However, Article 1821(3) adds that custodians should not comply with the will and preferences of individuals for two reasons. First, if individuals (or their property) would be considerably endangered by the will and preferences and the individuals cannot recognise this danger due to their illness or disability. Second, if the individuals' will and preferences is unreasonable

---

this norm applies only for law of property, it is therefore less relevant for the discussion on mental healthcare and will therefore not be elaborated further.

[299] See Dagmar Brosey (n 282) 133; and Federal Republic of Germany, Act on Proceedings in Family Matters and in Matters of Non-contentious Jurisdiction (n 235) art 276.

[300] Valentin Aichele & Theresia Degener, 'Frei und gleich im rechtlichen Handeln – Eine völkerrechtliche Einführung zu Artikel 12 UN-BRK' in Valentin Aichele (ed), *Das Menschenrecht auf gleiche Anerkennung vor dem Recht: Artikel 12 der UN-Behindertenrechtskonvention* (Nomos 2013) 49.

[301] See eg Dagmar Brosey (n 282); or Volker Lipp, 'Legal Protection of Adults in Germany – An Overview' (2016), <https://www.bgt-ev.de/fileadmin/Mediendatenbank/Themen/Einzelbeitraege/Lipp/Lipp_Legal_Protection_Adults.pdf> accessed 14 November 2022.

[302] Emphasis added; Federal Republic of Germany, German Civil Code (n 233) art 1821(1) and (2).

for custodians.³⁰³ Lipp argues that protective measures (to avoid harm to the person concerned) contain an element of heteronomy, which cannot be defined as support.³⁰⁴ While it remains unclear what can be considered 'unreasonable for custodians', this formulation indicates heteronomy. Yet, and this is again compatible with the supported decision-making regime as analysed in subsection 5.3.2.2, Article 1821(4) of the Civil Code states that if custodians cannot ascertain the will and preferences of individuals, or if they do not comply with the will and preferences because it would harm the person concerned, then custodians must act in line with the best interpretation of the will and preferences. To ascertain the presumed will and preferences, custodians must take into account concrete indicators, such as previous statements, ethical or religious convictions and other personal values. Close relatives and other trusted persons should be consulted to determine the presumed will and preferences.³⁰⁵

Despite the advancements of the German custodianship regulations towards a system of supported decision-making through the recent law reform, the exceptions for when custodians should not comply with the will and preferences of persons under their care do not fully correspond to what the CRPD framework defines as support for decision-making. But what rules should apply in situations of imminent harm? The CteeRPD does not address such situations as possible exceptions to its opposition to 'best interest' determination. Furthermore, neither does the CteeRPD address how to deal with situations where persons have never been able to express their will or preferences (for instance, children with psychosocial disabilities), or where persons constantly change their opinions. Scholten and others criticise the reservations of the CteeRPD, and argue that not acting in a person's best interest in such exceptional situations cannot be justified ethically or medically.³⁰⁶ Could the German custodianship regulation, despite – or precisely because of – its element of heteronomy in such exceptional circumstances, be a welcome solution?

Considering internationally recognised best-practice examples, it is worth noting that the highly regarded Colombian law also provides for exceptional formal support through judicial adjudication, meaning that a person is appointed to provide support by court order in cases of high-level support needs.³⁰⁷ Likewise, Costa Rica's Law No. 9379 of 2016 established the system of personal assistance, where the assisting person acts as guarantor for equality before the law. One key provision in Costa Rica's law is that the foundation of a personal assistant's work is a personal assistance plan, drafted together with the person concerned, and outlining in detail all of the support the

---

303   Ibid art 1821(3).
304   Volker Lipp, 'Erwachsenenschutz, gesetzliche Vertretung und Artikel 12 UN-BRK', in: Valentin Aichele (ed), *Das Menschenrecht auf gleiche Anerkennung vor dem Recht: Artikel 12 der UN-Behindertenrechtskonvention* (Nomos 2013) 341.
305   Federal Republic of Germany, German Civil Code (n 233) art 1821(4).
306   Matthé Scholten and others, 'Equality in the informed consent process: competence to consent, substitute decision-making, and discrimination of persons with mental disorders' (2021) 46(1) Journal of Medicine and Philosophy 108.
307   See Congress of Colombia, Law No 1996 of 2019 (n 291).

affected individual wants to receive.[308] In conclusion, it seems important to analyse whether the German custodianship system follows a human rights approach, rather than simply condemning the fact that such a system exists at all.

What seems to be in line with the supported decision-making regime as outlined by the CteeRPD is the specific Civil Code provision on medical treatment.[309] It declares that a patient's will and preferences must be considered, regarding their overall health condition and prognosis. Thereby, a patient's will, as expressed in their living will (Patientenverfügung), must form the basis for any decision, and if a living will is not available, the custodian must determine the will and preferences with regard to treatment or the presumed will (in line with Article 1827 of the Civil Code), and decide on this basis whether the patient consents to or prohibits a medical treatment.[310] The value of the will and preferences of persons with (psychosocial) disabilities, in terms of Article 12 CRPD, has also been considered by the German Federal Social Court. It ruled that the obligation of appointed representatives should not only be to act on the basis of what they consider to be in the best interest of the person under custodianship, 'but rather – as far as possible and reasonable – to support the latter in exercising his or her legal and other capacity to act'.[311]

Either way, there is a risk of substituted decision-making through the invocation of a custodian and the accompanying power of legal representation in general. For this reason, the Civil Code offers a range of safeguards to protect persons under custodianship (based on Article 12(4) CRPD). First, the court considers family members or other trusted persons from the affected individual's close circle as possible custodians if the individual has not already suggested anyone under the advance directive (Betreuungsverfügung). Only if no suitable person is available should a person conducting custodianship as an occupation or profession be appointed.[312] Prior to the appointment of a custodian, the court will conduct an in-person hearing with the person with psychosocial disability, to obtain a personal impression of the individual's circumstances.[313] In addition to this, the court must obtain a medical report, by a psychiatrist or a physician experienced in psychiatry, which covers the medical condition, abilities and disabilities of the person concerned.[314] Lastly, the court must consider alternatives to the custodianship, as suggested by a competent public authority (Betreuungsbehörde).[315] Based on all this information, the custodianship court will decide whether appointing a custodian is necessary. At all times, the custodianship court will supervise the custodian's activities, including their compliance with the

---

[308] See Legislative Assembly of the Republic of Costa Rica, Law No 9379 (n 291) arts 12–15.
[309] This section only relates to medical interventions in general, and does not address involuntary treatment or medical coercion regulated in Article 1832 of the Civil Code.
[310] Federal Republic of Germany, German Civil Code (n 233) art 1827(2).
[311] Bundessozialgericht (2013): Order of 14 November 2013, B 9 SB 84/12 B. 113, para 9.
[312] Federal Republic of Germany, German Civil Code (n 233) art 1816(3), (5).
[313] Federal Republic of Germany, Act on Proceedings in Family Matters and in Matters of Non-contentious Jurisdiction (n 235) art 278.
[314] Ibid art 280.
[315] Ibid art 279(2).

requirements to maintain regular personal contact and discuss important matters with the person under care. If necessary, the court will intervene against breaches of a custodian's duties through instructions or prohibitions.[316] The custodianship court must approve to any consent or non-consent to medical treatment which the custodian expresses, if there is a justified risk that the person under custodianship will die as a result of the intervention or suffer serious and prolonged damage to their health.[317] Yet, court approval is not necessary if the medical measure corresponds to the living will (Patientenverfügung) of the person concerned.[318] Generally, and this needs to be highlighted in the context of psychosocial disability, the custodian should help prevent the deterioration of the person under custodianship's condition, and work to remove or improve the illness that led to custodianship in the first place. If the custodian is a professional (rather than a trusted person appointed on the basis of an advance directive), measures planned to achieve this must be outlined in the custodianship plan.[319] Here, too, the German regulation seems to be in line with what is defined as best practice in Costa Rican law, namely the personal assistance plan mentioned above. Once the circumstances enable the cancellation of custodianship, the custodianship must be terminated.[320] If the person under custodianship appointed a custodian themselves, the custodianship can also be cancelled on the application of that person.[321] In other cases, the custodianship will be terminated, at the latest, seven years after the measures were ordered.[322] At any time, the person under custodianship can request a review of the custodianship by a court.[323] Family members or persons of trust can also file a complaint, on behalf of the person under custodianship, against a decision made in the interest of that person, and a competent public agency has the right to file a complaint against decisions regarding the custodian's appointment in general, or the scope, substance or status of a measure taken by the custodian after they have been appointed.[324] The safeguards relating to the custodianship procedure could be interpreted as being in line with the safeguarding requirements under Article 12(4) CRPD. They contain components such as being proportional to the person's circumstances, being applicable for the shortest time possible, and being subject to review by a judicial body. Whether these measures are enough to ensure respect for the will and preferences of the person, and that there is no conflict of interest or undue influence on the part of the custodian, is debatable.

In a study undertaken by the EU Agency for Fundamental Rights, respondents under custodianship (including, but not limited to, Germans) expressed the view that

---

[316] See Federal Republic of Germany, German Civil Code (n 233) arts 1816, 1861–1867.
[317] Ibid art 1829.
[318] Ibid art 1827.
[319] Ibid art 1863.
[320] Ibid art 1871.
[321] Ibid art 1871(2).
[322] Federal Republic of Germany, Act on Proceedings in Family Matters and in Matters of Non-contentious Jurisdiction (n 235) art 294(3).
[323] Ibid art 291.
[324] Ibid art 303.

the system is generally satisfactory to them.[325] However, a study published in 2017 by the German Federal Ministry of Justice and Consumer Protection, on the quality of the custodianship system, provides further insights. Findings suggest that custodians should spend more time building stronger relationships with, and supporting the decision-making of, the individuals under their care. Especially when the situations of people with psychosocial disabilities worsen, and the need for mental healthcare arises, those affected often feel that their right to make their own decisions is not being respected.[326] Situations of concern include increasing the dosage of medication, ordering inpatient instead of outpatient care, and coercive interventions in actual crisis situations. For this reason, there should always be binding written agreements between the custodian and the person under custodianship, in relation to outpatient and inpatient care, and a specific crisis plan and crisis aid should be elaborated in advance. Commissioned as an independent monitoring mechanism under Article 33 CPRD, the German Institute for Human Rights found that certain quality standards for the custodians themselves and their work, especially regarding sensitive areas such as mental healthcare, should be established, and that the (legal) supervision of the courts should be improved, in order to guarantee these standards.[327] The law reform that came into force in January 2023 certainly introduces new quality standards. It is still uncertain, however, how these will be implemented in practice.

Finally, the principle of subsidiarity of custodianship, as envisioned by the German legislator, needs to be emphasised. To ensure adherence to this principle, and that mental healthcare is as free as possible from heteronomy, the importance of sufficient access to concrete support for persons with psychosocial disabilities to make their own decisions deserves a closer look.

6.4.3.3   Accessible Supportive Measures as Alternatives

Various scholars hold the opinion that Germany needs to further enhance the availability of alternative support measures, to ensure their precedence over the appointment of a custodian.[328] Indeed, the law obliges the custodianship court to examine whether an affected individual can resort to accessible supportive measures that would render the appointment of a custodian redundant.[329] This raises the

---

[325] FRA (n 295) 44.
[326] See Vanita Matta and others, *Qualität in der rechtlichen Betreuung* (Bundesanzeiger Verlag 2018).
[327] See Staatliche Koordinierungsstelle, 'Das deutsche Betreuungsrecht im Lichte der UN-Behindertenrechtskonvention: Positionspapier der Staatlichen Koordinierungsstelle nach Art. 33 UN-BRK (Fachausschuss Freiheits- und Schutzrechte)' (2017).
[328] See Volker Lipp, 'Kritik und Reform des Betreuungsrechts' (2017), <https://docplayer.org/124708824-Kritik-und-reform-des-betreuungsrechts.html accessed 12 April 2021> accessed 14 November 2022; Klaus Lachwitz, 'Funktion und Anwendungsbereich der"Unterstützung"("support") bei der Ausübung der Rechts- und Handlungsfähigkeit gemäß Artikel 12 UN-BRK – Anforderungen aus der Perspektive von Menschen mit geistiger Behinderung', in: Valentin Aichele (ed) *Das Menschenrecht auf gleiche Anerkennung vor dem Recht: Artikel 12 der UN-Behindertenrechtskonvention* (Nomos 2013) 85–88; or Dagmar Brosey (n 282) 129.
[329] See Federal Republic of Germany, German Civil Code (n 233) art 1814(3).

question of how exactly alternative support measures are regulated and put into practice.

One could refer to the three types of precautionary measures or advance plans, as outlined in subsection 6.4.3.1, which, however, come with their own limitations. Another example from the German law is the so-called benefits for participation (Leistungen zur Teilhabe), to support an independent and self-determined life. Benefits for participation can be arranged through means other than monetary means, or in the form of personal budgets, with the latter giving the individual concerned more choice regarding the arrangement of the benefit. Across various chapters, Book IX of the Social Code provides for benefits for participation in relation to living arrangements, working life, community life, education and medical rehabilitation. The legislator formulated the provisions by describing the aim of the benefits rather than the actual benefits. For medical rehabilitation, the provision includes 'psychotherapy' as one of the benefits a person may use, and generally sets out other useful alternatives to custodianship, such as measures to help a person activate self-help capabilities or develop social skills, or to make connections with local self-help groups or consultation centres.[330] The law provides that the person concerned can choose from a catalogue of different benefits, according to their own will and preferences. Yet, an authority has the power to approve or reject their selections.[331] In practice, authorities often balance the benefits chosen by an affected person against other, possibly more cost-effective alternatives, which may lead to the requested benefit being denied.[332] Furthermore, as Lachwitz points out, affected individuals may be hindered in filing applications regarding their personal budgets if they are found to be incapable of contracting, according to Articles 104 or 105 of the Civil Code.[333] In such cases, applying for a personal budget will only possible be through the appointment of a custodian. Both examples show the limitations of 'benefits for participation' as a support measure. Essentially, 'benefits for participation' may not appropriately fulfil the requirements of Article 12(3) CRPD to provide access to support.

6.4.4 CONCLUDING SUMMARY

The assessment of the German mental health legislative framework is that it reflects a human rights approach to disability. This also holds true for the norms regarding the question of incompetence, and the supported decision-making regime in line with Article 12 CRPD, which were the focus of this country study. As for the question of incompetence, Germany unquestionably provides guidance as a best-practice example for other countries regarding the establishment of advance plan mechanisms. Whether

---

[330] See Federal Republic of Germany, Sozialgesetzbuch (SGB IX) Neuntes Buch (n 231) art 42.
[331] Ibid arts 1–89.
[332] Klaus Lachwitz (n 328) 95.
[333] Ibid 92–93.

and how Germany fulfils the requirements of a supported decision-making regime deserves a closer look. Clearly, legal representation by a guardian does not fall within the CteeRPD's definition of support, as elaborated in various sections of this book. Yet, neither does the right to equal recognition before the law, as outlined in the Convention, strictly abolish any form of legal representation, especially in exceptional circumstances. Rather, the CteeRPD merely speaks against any form of substituted decision-making. But can Germany's custodianship regulation be classified as enforcing a substituted decision-making regime? Germany's custodianship regime would certainly be contradictory to Article 12 CRPD if it revoked a person with psychosocial disabilities' legal capacity, or if it allowed for medical research, sterilisation or other intrusive and irreversible interventions against the will of that person. None of this is the case under Germany's legislation. Under the law, custodians are tasked with: (i) supporting individuals in exercising their will and preferences; and (ii) ensuring that they are protected against harm, even if that requires action contrary to their expressed or presumed will and preferences. As elaborated above, in the specific context of medical treatment, the will and preferences of the person concerned (be it through a living will, or as otherwise expressed or determined) must be respected. By definition, this should include all mental healthcare treatment received while being under custodianship. In light of the continuing use of involuntary admission and treatment in mental healthcare, to avert the threat of death or substantial damage to health (see section 5.3.2.1), will and preferences can, nevertheless, evidently be limited. Clearly, this system of representation mirrors what is described as a safeguard within the Yokohama Declaration (see section 5.3.2.2): support by a legal representative to protect against human rights infringements, and to take action when rights are threatened.

The CRPD obliges states to ensure access to support for a person with psychosocial disabilities who may require support in exercising their legal capacity. It further stipulates that safeguards relating to a person's exercise of legal capacity should be proportional to the degree to which the measures affect the person's rights and interests in accordance with international human rights law. What if a state did everything possible to ensure that an individual maintained the capacity to act and make decisions on their own (for instance, through advance plans)? Clearly, the CRPD does not oblige states to establish a system of legal representation. However, if all efforts to offer access to support for autonomous decision-making were not sufficient to safeguard the enjoyment of legal capacity, could legal representation be justified as last resort? And if the life or health of a person under custodianship was at risk, could acting in their best interest really be contradictory to the overall aim of the CRPD? States have to ensure that measures relating to the exercise of legal capacity are 'proportional and tailored to the person's circumstances, apply for the shortest time possible and are subject to regular review by a competent, independent and impartial authority or judicial body'.[334] Clearly, the burden of proof would be on the state to justify why other support mechanisms were not available or sufficient in each individual case, and why legal

---

[334] UNGA, CRPD (n 221) art 12(4).

representation was necessary as a last resort. This burden of proof also comes into play where persons under custodianship are subjected to mental health interventions against their will or preferences.

There are scholars who advocate the abolition of legal representation altogether. However, the author endorses the position of Aichele and Degener, who hold that legal representation is an interference with the right to equal recognition before the law which can be justified if proportional to the degree to which it affects a person's rights and interests.[335] Unlike legislation in some other countries, Germany's custodianship regulation does not revoke or limit the enjoyment of fundamental human rights: quite the contrary. As analysed above, its provisions are in no way discriminatory towards persons with (psychosocial) disabilities. They include norms on respecting a person's will and preferences, and on the best interpretation of will and preferences. In addition to implementing mental health as a human right in Germany through legislative measures, Germany's law further advances the understanding of the right to mental health. The German custodianship law displays a solution for people who require high-level support, and who have not taken any of the precautionary measures described in this section. With the various safeguards enshrined in the regulations, aiming also to protect persons under custodianship from abuse and undue influence, it is even questionable whether Germany's custodianship regulation falls within the category of a substituted decision-making regime, as condemned by the CteeRPD.

In order to close the gaps between guardianship law and Article 12 CPRD, the legislative reform, which came into force in January 2023, clearly defines legal representation as support for the person concerned, with the need for substitution only if necessary. The will and preferences of the person under custodianship became central to all processes under the custodianship regulation, whether with regard to the specific tasks of the custodian, or the acceptance or rejection of a potential custodian before their appointment. It is therefore uncertain which parts of Germany's custodianship regulation, if any, will once more be criticised by the CteeRPD in light of Article 12 CRPD.

In summary, the German custodianship regime for persons with psychosocial disabilities and high-level support needs cannot be seen as problematic in itself. But what about the alternative support measures provided by law, which can be considered as integral components of the broader custodianship system?[336] For advance plans (as found in the Civil Code) to become more effective tools for persons with psychosocial disabilities in general, and for their mental healthcare in particular, it is recommended here that their existence be promoted more strongly, to ensure that more persons fill out these documents while still being considered competent to do so. Extending educational programmes on the benefits of advance plans to the wider community, and also considering different inclusive forms of communication, could reach even more persons.

---

[335] Valentin Aichele & Theresia Degener (n 300) 56–58.

[336] Considering that the custodianship can only be effectively subsidiary if appropriate supportive measures are accessible.

Based on the examples of Colombia and Canada, as mentioned above, the power of attorney (Vorsorgevollmacht) and advance directive on care (Betreuungsverfügung) should also be able to be drafted by persons with psychosocial disabilities who already require low-level support. Following the Colombian example, in situations where a person has already been declared to need low-level support, a notary can be tasked with verifying whether the agreement is truly in accordance with what the person concerned has expressed as their will and preferences.[337] Using the example of the Canadian representation agreement, the German advance plans should also regulate more forms of support, such as life planning (taking into consideration the wishes of the person regarding their life ahead), representational support (expressing the wishes of the supported person in a way that can be understood by others), relationship-building support (establishing trustworthy relationships between persons who feel, or are, isolated), and administrative support (connecting the person to service providers that take care of administrative work). Ultimately, the goal is to establish an individualised network that recognises the person with a psychosocial disability as an individual who can take their own decisions based on their own will and preferences.[338]

To ensure a higher degree of self-determination within the existing regulatory framework of 'benefits for participation' (as found in Book IX of the Social Code), two further developments are recommended here. First, the individuals concerned must be able to choose from a bigger variety of benefits according to their own preferences, and not simply be required to accept what is approved by an authority. Second, instead of offering a general catalogue of benefits, authorities should offer each individual a qualitative consultation with regard to individualised benefits that are suitable for their needs. Such a qualitative and personalised consultation could also render the involvement of a custodian redundant in the event that a person is declared to be incapable of contracting. Given that both of these advancements may add to the costs associated with the alternative measures of support, it is important to establish regulations so that, in practice, the German system does not turn its back on such alternative measures, and simply make use of the possibly less time-consuming and cheaper option of appointing a custodian.

In addition to these formally regulated support measures, it is advised here that informal and community-based support systems be strengthened and implemented. Inspiration for such support systems can, for instance, be drawn from the Swedish Personal Ombudsman (PO) model, as briefly mentioned in section 5.3. This system is also widely recognised as a good example of a supported decision-making model for persons with severe psychosocial disabilities. Being available throughout the country, an independent PO, with no commitments or responsibilities vis-à-vis another authority, supports individuals in their decision-making processes, based purely on the wishes of the client. Areas that a PO can help with include family matters, finances, and accessing support, housing, healthcare and much more. There is no fixed format

---

[337] See Congress of Colombia, Law No 1996 of 2019 (n 291) art 16.
[338] See Klaus Lachwitz (n 328) 86–87.

Chapter 6. Bridging Theory and Practice through Country Studies

or formal procedure, which makes the PO model easily accessible for everyone. The PO has no fixed working hours or office, but instead works wherever and whenever the client wants them to. The system is based completely on trust, and is therefore often described as a professional friendship involving long-term engagement. Clients are not asked to adjust to a system; POs are instead tasked with finding creative ways to work with the client, and to support the client in gaining better control over their affairs.[339]

It is concluded here that, in addition to the widely welcomed and anticipated reform of the custodianship regulation which came into force in 2023, the German government should implement structural reforms to enhance the variety of available, effective and appropriate support measures of which persons with psychosocial disabilities can make use, both when exercising their legal capacity in general, and specifically with regard to mental healthcare services.

The German legal framework, with its advance plans, alternative support measures and custodianship regulation for high-level support needs, already serves as a great example for advancing the understanding of the right to mental health in this highly contested area of persons lacking decision-making competence. The above recommendations would further strengthen the human rights approach and, it is submitted here, provide even stronger legal protection for persons with psychosocial disabilities when accessing mental healthcare.

---

[339] WHO (n 133) 107–111.

PART 4

ADVANCING THE RIGHT TO MENTAL HEALTH: CONCLUSIONS AND RECOMMENDATIONS

CHAPTER 7
CONCLUSIONS AND RECOMMENDATIONS

7.1 INTRODUCTION

The rationale for this book was to utilise and understand the existing law, in order to guide legislation, policies and strategies for the comprehensive promotion of mental health at the international, regional, and domestic levels. The COVID-19 pandemic has once again demonstrated how important it is to promote and protect the right to mental health. The purpose of this book was to explore the central research questions, namely *which rights and obligations exist for the protection of mental health under international human rights law?*, and *how should access to mental healthcare services be regulated from a human rights perspective?* Through a systematic examination of international, regional and national legislation, this book has demonstrated that the 'right to mental health' encompasses multiple rights and state obligations. In this way, it has established a framework for the right to mental health, consisting of key norms for the promotion and protection of mental health (first central research question). With particular attention to the issue of access to mental healthcare services, the right to mental health framework has been enriched by identifying existing shortcomings and addressing remaining challenges (second central research question). Through the inclusion of country studies and domestic legislation, regional peculiarities and traditions have been considered, to ensure a comprehensive human rights approach when formulating the right to mental health. On this basis, this book offers recommendations for implementing the right to mental health and advancing rights-based and person-centred access to mental healthcare, through regional and domestic legislative frameworks.

In the words of Smith, human rights-based research can make a tangible difference, not only by influencing governments, but also by 'strengthening the capacities and understanding of rights holders whose rights may be compromised'.[1] Given that, around the globe, mental health laws, policies and strategies are being drafted or reformed to be more human rights-compliant, and to offer better protection for persons with mental health conditions and psychosocial disabilities, this book may be of great value.

The findings of this book are summarised in section 7.2, followed by a set of recommendations for different actors (section 7.3), and final remarks (section 7.4).

---

[1] Rhona Smith, 'Human rights based approaches to research' in Lee McConnell and Rhona Smith (eds), *Research Methods in Human Rights* (Routledge 2018) 22.

7.2. CONCLUSIONS

This section presents the main findings of this book. The following paragraphs will first reflect on the answers to the subquestions listed in Chapter 1. Finally, a table will present the content of the right to mental health framework, in response to the central research questions.

In contemplating the first subquestion – *what is meant, in this study, by 'mental health', 'psychosocial disability' and 'mental healthcare'?* – 'persons with mental health conditions and psychosocial disabilities' was identified as suitable term for this book, to ensure the promotion, protection, and inclusion of all persons with mental health problems who have been neglected and segregated for far too long. Besides defining various different pieces of terminology, the book demonstrated the strong influence of culture on accessing mental healthcare. Culture influences perceptions of mental health conditions and psychosocial disabilities, health-seeking behaviour and the therapeutic relationship. It further defines the different approaches to mental healthcare, namely conventional mental healthcare, traditional mental healthcare or a combination of both. This shows the significance of culture in connection with mental healthcare, and the need for it to be considered when developing legislation, policies and strategies to promote and protect mental health. In answering the question, *what are the human rights challenges that persons with mental disorders face in the mental healthcare context?*, it became clear that the human rights challenges are multifaceted. There are barriers to accessing mental healthcare services, as well as specific human rights violations in the provision of mental healthcare. As a result, the book chose to address these challenges by focusing on a human rights approach to accessing mental healthcare.

The book's main normative analysis systematically examined the right to mental health and the applicable human rights framework. To answer the following three subquestions, the book synthesised the concepts of the right to the highest attainable standard of health (based on the International Covenant on Economic, Social and Cultural Rights (ICESCR)) and disability law (based on the Convention on the Rights of Persons with Disabilities (CRPD)), and integrated these into an analytical right to mental health framework:

- *What does the right to mental health entail?*
- *To what extent does the right to the highest attainable standard of physical and mental health, in particular Article 12 ICESCR, respect, protect and fulfil mental health as a stand-alone norm?*
- *Which additional human rights are relevant for guaranteeing access to mental healthcare, and what are the derived obligations?*

Thus, the 'right to mental health', as set forth in this book, is a combination of the right to the highest attainable standard of health, derived from the ICESCR, and other rights provided in the CRPD. From the right to the highest attainable standard of health emerges the right to underlying determinants of (mental) health, and also the right to mental health facilities, goods and services. The latter can also be understood as the right to access mental healthcare. In addition, the highest attainable standard of health norm gives rise to the state obligations to respect, protect and fulfil mental health as a human right. Despite being a key norm, the book has illustrated that the right to the highest attainable standard of health is insufficient to fully protect and promote the right to mental health. Human rights in mental health go beyond the right to the highest attainable standard of health norm. To ensure human rights-based access to mental healthcare (in response to the second central research question), it is necessary to include more human rights to complement the right to mental health framework. These additional human rights address persistent human rights challenges in mental healthcare provision, which inhibit the enjoyment of the right to mental health generally, and access to mental healthcare specifically. Because the CRPD addresses the specific needs of persons with (psychosocial) disabilities, the additional human rights have been taken from the CRPD framework. As the analysis in this book has shown, the CRPD promotes transformative equality and introduces a paradigm shift in mental healthcare, recognising patients as active rights-holders rather than simply recipients of care. The CRPD challenges existing rights frameworks in several ways, which gives rise to various controversial debates. It is submitted here that the CRPD framework fails to sufficiently strengthen the human rights protection of persons with mental health conditions and psychosocial disabilities. This is particularly evident in the absolutistic approach to regulating appropriate interventions in mental health crisis situations. Contrary to the position of the Committee on the Rights of Persons with Disabilities (CteeRPD), emergency situations may justify involuntary treatment (including hospitalisation) as a last resort to prevent serious danger to patients or others. It is of paramount importance to ensure that such situations are handled in a human rights-compliant manner. The CRPD's aspirational nature underlines existing complexities and leaves unresolved tensions. The challenge is to find practical solutions that are in conformity with the human rights of affected individuals.

Thus, after examining the relevant CRPD provisions, there were still unanswered questions. The country studies aimed to provide answers by analysing *to what extent has mental health as a human right been given effect to in Ghana and Germany?*, and *how, if at all, can the chosen case studies serve as examples to advance the understanding of the right to mental health, and the right to accessing mental healthcare in particular?* (subquestions specific to the country study analyses). In each country study, one persisting key challenge within the national context was addressed. The two key challenges that were addressed – interventions amounting to ill-treatment (Ghana), and the guardianship regulation (Germany) – are among the complexities for which the CRPD framework does not provide straight answers. Derived from domestic legislation and other best-practice country examples, the study on Ghana provided guidance on how to regulate seclusion and restraints in a human rights-compliant manner. This includes various safeguards to protect against ill-treatment. The analysis of Ghana also advanced the right to mental health, by proposing regulations for informal mental healthcare provision. It proposed that humane and dignified care be ensured in the informal sector, through an effective collaboration between formal and informal mental healthcare providers. The German country study analysis focused on the guardianship regulation, and studied the legal context of incompetence and supported decision-making. For situations in which a person's capacity to make decisions is lacking, the German law has established three different advance plan mechanisms. These render legal representation unnecessary. Derived from other best-practice countries, these mechanisms could also be strengthened by extending their use so that they can also be utilised by persons with low-level support needs. The German country study also drew attention to formal and informal community-based support services, as welcome alternatives to legal representation. If no advance plan or community-based support is available, the German country study showed that legal representation, based on human rights standards, for high-level support needs can be a solution. German law offers various safeguards for this. Both country studies thus provide practical legislative and policy solutions to close some of the gaps in the CRPD and, as such, support the framing of a comprehensive right to mental health.

However, can the CRPD shortcomings, in terms of providing practical solutions to specific difficult situations, really be seen as a failure of the overall paradigm shift contained in the CRPD, which is to utilise a human rights approach to promote mental health(care)? A lot of the controversy centres around how involuntary interventions have been addressed, especially the full respect for legal capacity and the abolition of coercive practices such as forced treatment (including seclusion and restraint) and hospitalisation. As this book has elaborated, these areas are where most human rights violations of people with mental health conditions and psychosocial disabilities occur. For this reason, it is paramount to strengthen the protection in these areas. It is conceded that, because of limitations in current mental healthcare practice, and the difficult context of emergency situations, involuntary practices (forced treatment and hospitalisation) may be needed as a means of last resort. This applies to situations where alternatives that align with the CRPD, such as advance directives (if available) or supported decision-making, are insufficient to prevent harm. The value in adopting the CRPD paradigm is that any involuntary intervention is seen as an opportunity to review, learn and devise alternative measures that can be put in place for persons with mental health conditions and psychosocial disabilities, to avoid coercive practices in the future. Applying this CRPD approach, even in the most difficult scenarios, strengthens the possibilities for non-coercive practices in the future: something that is not enabled by the old paradigm (medical approach to disability), in which coercive practices are seen as necessary and justified.

The main outcome of this book is a holistic definition of the right to mental health that encompasses a set of underlying determinants of mental health, and several rights guaranteeing access to humane and dignified mental healthcare with a range of safeguards. This is not to suggest that a new right to mental health needs to be

Chapter 7. Conclusions and Recommendations

elaborated, but rather to give an indication of how existing human rights norms should be interpreted. The central research questions were:

- *Which rights and obligations exist for the protection of mental health under international human rights law?*
- *How should access to mental healthcare services be regulated from a human rights perspective?*

To answer these questions, all human rights norms underlying the right to mental health framework, including their specific components and safeguards, are summarised in Table 7.1 below. While all of the rights listed in the table form the answer to the first central research question, it is particularly the following rights that clarify how access to mental healthcare services should be regulated from a human rights perspective (second central research question): (i) the right to equality and non-discrimination; (ii) the right to equal recognition before the law; (iii) the right to protection for the integrity of the person; (iv) the right to be free from torture or cruel, inhuman or degrading treatment or punishment; (v) the right to be free from exploitation, violence and abuse; (vi) the right to liberty and security of person; and (vii) the right to live independently and be included in the community.

Table 7.1: The right to mental health in detail

Human Right	Components and safeguards (if available)
The right to the highest attainable standard of mental health	– Right to underlying determinants of mental health. • Physical environment determinants (e.g. drinking water, food, housing, sanitation). • Psychosocial determinants (e.g. supportive relationships, community identity). • Structural determinants (e.g. structures of power and governance). • Political determinants (e.g. laws and policies). – Right to access mental healthcare and support. • Including preventive, medical, social and rehabilitative services. • Mental health care and support must be available, accessible, acceptable and of good quality. • If informal mental healthcare is prevalent in a state, mental healthcare and support must be made up of a collaboration of the formal and informal mental healthcare sectors.
The right to equality and non-discrimination	– Protection against direct or indirect discrimination on the basis of psychosocial disability, in practice or in law. – Elimination of discrimination through reasonable accommodation or specific measures.

Intersentia 273

Part 4. Advancing the Right to Mental Health: Conclusions and Recommendations

Human Right	Components and safeguards (if available)

The right to equal recognition before the law	– Right to legal capacity (to hold rights and duties, and to exercise and act upon these rights and duties), and mental capacity to consent.
	– Right to supported decision-making.
	  • Access to support in exercising legal capacity/making decisions.
	  • Safeguards for support mechanisms, to ensure protection against conflicts of interest, exploitation, abuse and undue influence, consisting of:
	    – Ensuring respect for a person's will and preferences, if needed, acting according to the best interpretation of the will and preferences.
	    – Prohibiting consent on behalf of an individual.
	    – Setting up monitoring systems to ensure that rights, will and preferences are always respected.
	    – Ensuring assessment of support needs, time limits for support measures, and access to judicial review.
	    – Setting up complaint and redress mechanisms.
	  • Making advance planning available to persons with full capacity and low-level support needs.
	  • Setting up formal support for persons with high-level support needs, if advance plans do not exist, with the following safeguards (additional to the ones listed above):
	    – Drafting of support plan together with the person concerned.
	    – Support to be proportional to the person's circumstances.
	    – Formal support for the shortest possible time.
	    – Subject to review by a judicial body.

The right to protection for the integrity of the person	– Right to express prior, free and informed consent to treatment, or to refuse treatment.
	– If consent cannot be given (e.g. in emergency situations), the situation must be handled as it would be in a context where the affected person does not have a mental health condition or psychosocial disability.
	– Safeguards to ensure protection of integrity:
	  • If needed, access to support for expressing consent.
	  • The opportunity to appeal against unwanted treatment.
	  • Setting in place programmes for independent review organisations to identify, investigate, and follow up on cases in which a violation of the right to personal integrity has arisen.

The right to be free from torture or cruel, inhuman or degrading treatment or punishment	– The right to living conditions, in mental healthcare facilities, that are respectful to the dignity of the patients.
	– The right to not be secluded or (physically, mechanically or chemically) restrained, unless there is a therapeutic justification for this, such as treatment in situations that pose an immediate or imminent risk or danger to the life or health of the affected person or others.
	– The right to access non-coercive support in mental health crises (emergency situations).
	  • Drafting of a treatment plan that also outlines possible crisis interventions.
	  • Making use of alternatives to seclusion or restraints, such as de-escalation techniques, or the development of comfort rooms and relaxation rooms.
	  • The use of seclusion and restraint only as last resorts, and for the shortest possible time, by regulating various safeguards, including that:
	    – The procedure must be authorised by authoritative personnel.
	    – The equipment used must be designed to limit discomfort or pain.
	    – Patients must receive full information on the reasons for the measure.
	    – Measures must be supervised, and their details recorded.

Chapter 7. Conclusions and Recommendations

Human Right	Components and safeguards (if available)
	– Safeguards to prevent against torture and ill-treatment, including: • Regular audits of mental health facilities. • Available and accessible complaint mechanisms, and the sharing of information about complaint procedures. • Opportunities to appeal against coercive interventions. • Available redress mechanisms, including the investigation, prosecution and punishment of violations by state officials, non-state officials and private actors (including informal mental healthcare providers).
The right to be free from exploitation, violence and abuse	– Right to protection within and outside the home. – Right to access support and assistance to enable persons with mental health conditions and psychosocial disabilities to be safe, including within communities, including: • Information and education for the public. • Training for professionals on how to avoid, recognise and report instances of violence and abuse. – Safeguards to prevent exploitation, violence and abuse. • Effective monitoring, by independent authorities, of all facilities and programmes designed to care for persons with mental health conditions and psychosocial disabilities. • Available redress mechanisms, including the investigation, prosecution and punishment of violations by state officials, non-state officials and private actors (including informal mental healthcare providers). – A state obligation to promote physical, cognitive and psychological recovery, rehabilitation and social integration, including through peer support and the provision of protection services as response to exploitation, violence, and abuse.
The right to liberty and security of person	– Right not to be involuntarily hospitalised. – All deprivations of liberty must be lawful, systematic and non-discriminatory. • Deprivation of liberty on the grounds of psychosocial disabilities, or a combination of a psychosocial disability and another element (such as medical necessity), is considered discriminatory. – Safeguards for situations where liberty is deprived. • Access to legal or other appropriate support, including peer support. • Access to a judicial authority. • Having access to the physical environment, information and communication. • Being provided with free or affordable community-based services, as alternatives to institutionalisation. • Being provided with compensation and other forms of reparation, in the event of violations of this right.
The right to live independently and be included in the community	– Right to individual choice on how, where and with whom to live. – State obligation to link institutionalisation to strict criteria. • Prohibition of the creation of new segregated institutions (with integration of mental healthcare in existing general healthcare settings instead). • Implementation of policy for deinstitutionalisation. – Right for a person to access community health and support services in accordance with their own wishes and preferences. – Safeguard to prevent institutionalisation: • Timely access to health and support services in the community.

7.3 RECOMMENDATIONS

In light of the preceding analysis, it has become clear that structural deficiencies have hampered efforts to guarantee the right to mental health. Although health economics, health care administration, public health and medicine are key areas influencing (mental) healthcare reforms,[2] the protection of the rights of persons with mental health conditions and psychosocial disabilities must not be neglected in the ongoing debates. The advantage of a rights-based approach to mental health is that it highlights a state's legal obligations to ensure the right to mental health, and encourages rights-holders to claim their mental health-related rights. For this reason, this section provides a set of recommendations on how a human rights approach to mental health can, in reality, help advance the realisation of the right to mental health. The following recommendations are for states (and state actors), the CteeRPD, and non-governmental organisations (NGOs).

7.3.1 STATES (AND STATE ACTORS)

The first, and most important, recommendation for states (and state actors) is to explicitly recognise the right to mental health in domestic legislation. It does not necessarily have to be recognised in specific new mental health laws (if these do not already exist), but could also be included in general health or disability laws.[3] Moreover, domestic legislation should grant individuals the right to mental health, to ensure that rights-holders can seek redress for violations in domestic courts, which would result in better protection for the right to mental health. Based on the analysis in Chapter 4, it is argued here that legislation must include at least the core obligations of the right to mental health as identified in this book, which must be fulfilled regardless of resource constraints. States should pay particular attention to mental health promotion and protection (by ensuring underlying determinants of mental health), to proactively protect against psychosocial disability. In addition, states should ensure available, accessible, acceptable and good-quality mental healthcare, including the provision of services in rural areas, as well as care that does not cause financial hardship (ideally, free care). It would be beneficial if domestic legislation provided for additional state obligations, and defined and elaborated more precisely on the scope of the right to mental health, as described in Chapter 5, and partly in Chapter 6. Ideally, the law should provide for the exercise of legal capacity, the promotion of alternatives to coercion in mental healthcare, a transition towards community-based mental healthcare and support, regular inspections by an independent authority, and the establishment of complaint and redress mechanisms. In countries where the informal mental healthcare

---

[2] See Yi Zhang, Advancing the Right to Health Care in China towards Accountability (Intersentia 2019) 18.
[3] It falls outside the scope of this book to examine the advantages or disadvantages of a stand-alone law or mental health legislation integrated into general health/disability law.

sector is prominent, as in Ghana, informal mental healthcare should also be regulated by law, with the goal of fostering collaboration between formal and informal mental healthcare providers, and informal mental healthcare providers should be involved when drafting such legislation.

Second, states (and state actors) should adopt and implement domestic policy directives with precise instructions for implementing the right to mental health, including plans of action, and the responsibilities of different actors. The policies should cover six areas. First, they should outline action steps and responsibilities for mental health promotion and prevention in society, to raise awareness and eliminate discrimination. The goals of initiatives to promote mental health should be to maintain or enhance mental well-being, as well as to increase resilience. Mental health prevention efforts should reduce incidences of events that can cause mental ill health. Second, the policies should offer guidance on service delivery, including the organisation and development of preventive, curative and rehabilitative mental health services by the public and private sectors. This should include efforts to deinstitutionalise services, integrate mental healthcare into primary healthcare, and create community-based networks of services. Care options should be scaled up and diversified. If traditional forms of mental healthcare are offered domestically, this section of the policy must also address details about possible collaborations between formal and informal care providers. Third, the policies must consider the development of an adequate mental health workforce. Besides ensuring adequate staffing, and adequate distribution of staff across the country, as well as the right skill mix, specific training on human rights, and explicitly on the right to mental health (including duties, safeguards, etc.), is an important aspect. The training should not be limited only to healthcare providers (formal and informal), but should also be offered to members of all other professions that interact with people with mental health conditions and psychosocial disabilities, such as law enforcement or the judiciary. Fourth, the policies should also promote human rights-based, person-centred, recovery-oriented and evidence-based care, including psychotherapeutic and psychotropic drug interventions. In this context, alternatives to coercive interventions in mental health crisis situations need to be outlined (including responsibilities and steps for implementing these), as well as specific safeguards for situations requiring short-term seclusion or restraint. Fifth, the policies must outline how independent monitoring systems will be established and operationalised, to protect against any violations of the right to mental health. Sixth, the policies must clarify the details of funding and budgeting for the mental health system. Mental healthcare must be affordable and accessible for everyone. Besides engaging people with lived experiences of psychosocial disabilities in decision-making processes, informal mental healthcare providers must also be included (in countries with informal mental healthcare provision) in discussions when developing mental health policies.

Lastly, states should take their responsibilities to draft reports on the implementation of the right to mental health, and their reporting obligations vis-à-vis UN treaty bodies, seriously. Their assessments should provide reliable and adequate information, including on challenges faced, and on measures taken to improve the situation.

7.3.2 THE COMMITTEE ON THE RIGHTS OF PERSONS WITH DISABILITIES (CTEERPD)

The human rights treaty body of independent experts which monitors the implementation of the Convention has an important role to play in the protection of the right to mental health. Its mandate includes the provision of recommendations to support the implementation of the norms enshrined in the CRPD. The CteeRPD should better explain practical solutions to issues that have generated controversial debates. Instead of simply prohibiting certain measures (such as involuntary admission and treatment, including seclusion and restraints), the Committee should inform states precisely how they can handle situations where rights must be balanced, and situations where there is imminent risk or danger to the affected person or others. Neglecting the fact that such situations demand practical actions does not solve the problem. The CteeRPD should address such solutions in Concluding Observations, or possibly in a general comment on the right to health (Article 25 CRPD).

7.3.3 NON-GOVERNMENTAL ORGANISATIONS (NGOS)

NGOs should be aware of the technical and substantive implications of the right to mental health, and should invoke the right to mental health in their activities. The scope and content of the right to mental health should be addressed in national policies, and NGOs should provide guidance to decision-makers in this regard. Additionally, they should address injustices by, for example, providing shadow reports to the UN human rights treaty monitoring bodies, and supporting individuals in filing complaints of human rights violations.

Further, NGOs should share information on, and increase public awareness of, the right to mental health. Through human rights education, NGOs should encourage individuals to uphold the right to mental health, for themselves and others. Ultimately, it is everyone's shared responsibility to realise the right to mental health in society.

7.4 FINAL REMARKS

This book has addressed one of the most timely but under-studied issues in public health. The full enjoyment of the right to mental health remains a distant goal worldwide. The intention of this book is to get one step closer to that goal: it offers a blueprint for how states should ensure the right to mental health in a manner consistent with human rights.

Although much has been addressed in this book, the important topic of accountability has fallen outside of its scope. More studies need to be conducted to determine how best to monitor, supervise and regulate state actors' compliance with their obligations, and how to redress violations of these. Accountability can be

Chapter 7. Conclusions and Recommendations

considered a cornerstone of human rights, and establishing effective accountability mechanisms is essential for the full realisation of the right to mental health.

Moreover, additional and practical guidance is needed on how exactly domestic laws should be drafted to comprehensively ensure the right to mental health. At the time of writing, the World Health Organization (WHO), together with the Office of the High Commissioner for Human Rights (OHCHR), were in the process of developing a joint publication, titled *Guidance on Mental Health, Human Rights and Legislation*. According to the OHCHR website, '[t]he publication aims to be a resource for countries when considering legislative measures to support the transformation of mental health systems, in line with international human rights law'.[4] The WHO/OHCHR publication therefore seems a promising tool for law- and policy-makers to bridge the gap between theory and practice.

Lastly, some human rights dimensions concerning persons with mental health conditions and psychosocial disabilities fell outside the scope of this book, although they are no less important in providing full human rights protection to this vulnerable group and, as such, promoting and protecting their mental health.

---

[4] Office of the High Commissioner for Human Rights (OHCHR), 'Call for inputs: Draft guidance on Mental Health, Human Rights, and Legislation published jointly by WHO and OHCHR' (nd), <https://www.ohchr.org/en/calls-for-input/calls-input/draft-guidance-mental-health-human-rights-legislation-who-ohchr> accessed 14 November 2022.

LIST OF INSTRUMENTS

INTERNATIONAL INSTRUMENTS

Constitution of the World Health Organization (WHO Constitution) (adopted 22 July 1946, entered into force 7 April 1948) 14 UNTS 185.

The World Congresses on Adult Guardianship Law 2010 and 2016, Yokohama Declaration (revised and amended) (16 September 2016).

UNGA, Convention Against Torture and Other Cruel, Inhuman or Degrading Treatment or Punishment (CAT) (adopted 10 December 1984, entered into force 26 June 1987) 1465 UNTS 85, art 1(1).

UNGA, Convention on the Elimination of All Forms of Discrimination against Women (CEDAW) (adopted 18 December 1979, entered into force 3 September 1981) 1249 UNTS 13.

UNGA, Convention on the Rights of Persons with Disabilities (adopted 13 December 2006, entered into force 3 May 2008) 2515 UNTS 3.

UNGA, Convention on the Rights of Persons with Disabilities (CRPD) (adopted 13 December 2006, entered into force 3 May 2008) 2515 UNTS 3.

UNGA, Convention on the Rights of the Child (CRC) (adopted 20 November 1989, entered into force 2 September 1990) 1577 UNTS 3.

UNGA, International Covenant on Civil and Political Rights (ICCPR) (adopted 16 December 1966, entered into force 23 March 1976) 999 UNTS 171.

UNGA, International Covenant on Economic, Social and Cultural Rights (ICESCR) (adopted 16 December 1966, entered into force 3 January 1976) 993 UNTS 3.

UNGA, Universal Declaration of Human Rights (UDHR) (10 December 1948) UNGA RES 217A (III).

UNGA, Vienna Declaration and Programme of Action (12 July 1993) UN Doc A/CONF.157/23.

World Medical Association, Declaration of Lisbon on the Rights of the Patient (revised) of 2005.

REGIONAL INSTRUMENTS

Africa

African Commission, 'Pretoria Declaration on Economic, Social and Cultural Rights in Africa' (2004).

African Union, Protocol to the African Charter on Human and Peoples' Rights on the Rights of Persons with Disabilities in Africa (adopted 29 January 2018).

Organization of African Unity, African Charter on Human and Peoples' Rights (Banjoul Charter) (adopted 27 June 1981, entered into force 21 October 1986) 1520 UNTS 271.

America

Organization of American States, Additional Protocol of the American Convention on Human Rights in the Area of Economic, Social and Cultural Rights (Protocol of San Salvador) (adopted 17 November 1988, entered into force 21 October 1986) 1520 UNTS 271.

Organization of American States, American Convention on Human Rights (adopted 22 November 1969, entered into force 18 July 1978) OAS Treaty Series No 36, 1144 UNTS 123.

Organization of American States, Inter-American Convention on the Elimination of All Forms of Discrimination Against Persons with Disabilities (adopted 7 June 1999, entered into force 4 September 2001) AG/RES. 1608 (XXIX-O/99).

Organization of American States, Inter-American Convention to Prevent and Punish Torture (9 December 1985) OAS Treaty Series, No 67.

Europe

CoE, Convention for the Protection of Human Rights and Dignity of the Human Being with regard to the Application of Biology and Medicine: Convention on Human Rights and Biomedicine (Oviedo Convention) (adopted 4 April 1997, entered into force 1 December 1999) ETS 164.

CoE, European Convention for the Protection of Human Rights and Fundamental Freedoms, as amended by Protocols Nos 11 and 14, 4 November 1950, ETS 5.

CoE, European Social Charter (revised) (adopted 3 May 1996, entered into force 1 July 1999) ETS 163.

EU, Charter of Fundamental Rights of the European Union (EUCFR).

NATIONAL INSTRUMENTS

Constitutions

Federal Republic of Germany, Grundgesetz (adopted 1949, amended 2020).
The Constitution of Kenya (adopted 2010).
The Constitution of Peru (adopted 1993, amended 2009).
The Constitution of the Republic of Ecuador (adopted 2008).
The Constitution of the Republic of Ghana (adopted 1992, amended 1996).
The Constitution of the Republic of Hungary (adopted 2011, amended 2013).
The Constitution of the Republic of Panama (adopted 1972, amended 2004).
The Constitution of the Republic of Serbia (adopted 2006).
The Constitution of the Republic of South Africa (adopted 1996).
The Constitution of the Republic of the Seychelles (adopted 1993, amended 2000).

Legislation

Argentina, Ministry of Health, Ley Nacional de Salud Mental. Ley N° 26.657 y su Decreto Reglamentario N° 603/13, 2 December 2010, sec 27.

Congress of Colombia, Law No 1996 of 2019, Por medio de la cual se establece el régimen para el ejercicio de la capacidad legal de las personas con discapacidad mayores de edad (adopted 2019).

Congress of the Philippines, Republic Act No 11036 (adopted 2017).

Federal Republic of Germany, Act on Proceedings in Family Matters and in Matters of Non-contentious Jurisdiction (adopted 2008, amended 2020).

Federal Republic of Germany, German Civil Code (adopted 1896, amended 2023).

Federal Republic of Germany, Sozialgesetzbuch (SGB IX) Neuntes Buch (adopted 2001, amended 2020).

Federal Republic of Germany, Strafgesetzbuch (adopted 1872, amended 2020).

India, Ministry of Law and Justice, Mental Healthcare Act, Law No 10 of 2017 (adopted 2017).

Italy, Basaglia Law, Law 180 of 1978, 13 May 1978.

Legislative Assembly of the Republic of Costa Rica, Law No 9379, Ley para la promoción de la autonomía personal de las personas con discapacidad (adopted 2016).

Ministry of Attorney General and Legislative Assembly of British Colombia, Representation Agreement Act [RSBC 1996] CHAPTER 405 (adopted in 1996).

Norway, Anti-Discrimination and Accessibility Act (No 42 of 2008).

Peru, Decreto Supremo que aprueba el Reglamento de la Ley N° 30947, Ley de Salud Mental, Decreto Supremo No 007–2020-SA, 5 March 2020, <https://busquedas.elperuano.pe/normaslegales/decreto-supremo-que-aprueba-el-reglamento-de-la-ley-n-30947-decreto-supremo-n-007–2020-sa-1861796–1/> accessed 14 November 2022.

Republic of Ghana, Mental Health Act (Act 846) of 2012.

The Republic of Ireland, Assisted Decision-Making (Capacity) Act 2015 (No 64 of 2015).

Tweede Kamer der Staten-Generaal, 32 399 Regels voor het kunnen verlenen van verplichte zorg aan een persoon met een psychische stoornis Wet verplichte geestelijke gezondheidszorg, Nr. 3, Memorie van Toelichting (2010), <https://zoek.officielebekendmakingen.nl/kst-32399–3.html> accessed 14 November 2022.

Uruguay, General Assembly, Salud Mental, Ley N° 19.529 (adopted 2017).

LIST OF CASES

INTERNATIONAL

A v New Zealand, Communication no 754/1997 (HRCtee, 3 August 1999).
Antonio Viana Acosta v Uruguay, Communication No 110/1981 (HRCtee, 29 March 1984).
CteeRPD, *HM v Sweden*, Communication No. 3/2011 (21 May 2012) UN Doc CRPD/C/7/D/3/2011.
CteeRPD, *Noble v Australia*, Communication No 7/2012 (10 October 2016) UN Doc CRPD/C/16/D/7/2012.
CteeRPD, *Mr X v Argentina*, Communication No 8/2012 (18 June 2014) UN Doc CRPD/C/11/D/8/2012.

REGIONAL

Africa

Purohit and Moore v The Gambia, Communication No. 241/2001, Sixteenth Activity report 2002–2003, Annex VII.

America

Luis Eduardo Guachalá Chimbó v Ecuador (Merits) IACHR Report No 111/18 (5 October 2018).
Rosario Congo v Ecuador, IACHR Report No 63/99 (13 April 1999).
Ximenes-Lopes v Brazil (Merits, Reparations, and Costs) IACtHR Series C no 149 (4 July 2006).

Europe

A v United Kingdom, App no 6840/74, 3 E.H.R.R. 131 (European Commission 1980).
Aggerholm v Denmark, App no 45439/18 (ECtHR, 15 September 2020).
AMV v Finland, App no 53251/13 (ECtHR, 23 March 2017).
AN v Lithuania, App no 17280/08 (ECtHR, 31 May 2016).
Arskaya v Ukraine, App no 45076/05 (ECtHR, 5 December 2013).
B v Romania, App no 1285/03 (ECtHR, 19 February 2013).
Bures v The Czech Republic, App no 37679/08 (ECtHR, 18 January 2013).
Çam v Turkey, App no 51500/08 (ECtHR, 23 February 2016).
DD v Lithuania, App no 13469/06 (ECtHR, 14 February 2012).
Fernandes de Oliveira v Portugal, App no 78103/14 (ECtHR, 31 January 2019).
Glass v the United Kingdom, App no 61827/00 (ECtHR, 9 March 2004).

Glor v Switzerland, App no 13444/04 (ECtHR, 30 April 2009).
Grare v France, App no 18835/91 (ECtHR, 2 December 1992).
Guberina v Croatia, App no 23682/13 (ECtHR, 22 March 2016).
Herczegfalvy v Austria, App no 10533/83 (ECtHR, 24 September 1992).
HL v The United Kingdom, App no 45508/99 (ECtHR, 5 October 2004).
Ireland v United Kingdom, App no 5310/71 (ECtHR, 18 January 1978).
Keenan v United Kingdom, App no 27229/95 (ECtHR, 3 April 2001).
Kiss v Hungary, App no 38832/06 (ECtHR, 20 May 2010).
Kudla v Poland, App no 30210/96 (ECtHR, 26 October 2000).
MS v Croatia (No 2), App no 75450/12 (ECtHR, 19 February 2015).
Murray v The Netherlands, App no 10511/10 (ECtHR, 26 April 2016).
PW v Austria, App no 10425/19 (ECtHR, 21 June 2022).
Rooman v Belgium, App no 18052/11 (ECtHR, 31 January 2019).
Shtukaturov v Russia, App no 44009/05 (ECtHR, 27 March 2008).
Stanev v Bulgaria, App no 36760/06 (ECtHR, 17 January 2012).
Storck v Germany, App no 61603/00 (ECtHR, 16 June 2005).
The Centre for Legal Resources On Behalf of Valentin Câmpeanu v Romania, App no 47848/08 (ECtHR, 17 July 2014).
Varbanov v Bulgaria, ECHR 2000-X 457.
Venken and Others v Belgium, App no 46130/14 (ECtHR, 6 April 2021).
Winterwerp v The Netherlands, App no 6301/73 (ECtHR, 24 October 1979).

NATIONAL

BayOlG NJW 1992, 2100.
Bundessozialgericht (2013): Order of 14 November 2013, B 9 SB 84/12 B. 113.
Bundesverfassungsgericht (1998): Order of 23 March1998, 2 Bvr 2270/96.
Bundesverfassungsgericht (2011): Order of 23 March 2011, 2 Bvr 882/09.
Bundesverfassungsgericht (2015): Order of 02 June 2015, 2 Bvr 2236/14.
Bundesverfassungsgericht (2016): Order of 26 July 2016, 1 BvL 8/15.
Bundesverfassungsgericht (2018): Order of 24 July 2018, 2 Bvr 309/15, Bvr 502/16.
Ghana Lotto Operators Association v National Lottery Authority [2007–2008] SCGLR 1089.

UNITED NATIONS DOCUMENTS

GENERAL COMMENTS

CAT, 'General comment No. 2, Implementation of article 2 by States parties' (General Comment 2) (24 January 2008) UN Doc CAT/C/GC/2.

CteeESCR, 'General Comment No. 14: The Right to the Highest Attainable Standard of Health (Art. 12)' (General Comment 14) (11 August 2000) UN Doc E/C.12/2000/4.

CteeESCR, 'General comment No. 21: The right of everyone to take part in cultural life (Art. 15, para 1(a))' (21 December 2009) Un Doc E/C.12/GC/21.

CteeESCR, 'General comment No. 22 on the right to sexual and reproductive health (Art. 12)' (2 May 2016) UN Doc E/C.12/GC/22.

CteeESCR, 'General Comment No. 3: The Nature of States Parties' Obligations (Art. 2, Para. 1, of the Covenant)' (14 December 1990) UN Doc E/1991/23.

CteeESCR, 'General Comment No. 5: Persons with Disabilities' (General Comment 5) (9 December 1994) UN Doc E/1995/22.

CteeRC, 'General comment No. 13: The right of the child to freedom from all forms of violence' (18 April 2011) UN Doc CRC/C/GC/13.

CteeRC, 'General Comment No. 15 (2013) on the right of the child to the enjoyment of the highest attainable standard of health (art. 24)' (17 April 2013) CRC/C/GC/15.

CteeRC, 'General Comment No. 4 (2003): Adolescent Health and Development in the Context of the Convention on the Rights of the Child' (1 July 2003) CRC/GC/2003/4.

CteeRC, 'General Comment No. 4: Adolescent Health and Development in the Context of the Convention on the Rights of the Child' (General Comment 4) (1 July 2003) UN Doc CRC/GC/2003/4.

CteeRC, 'General Comment No. 9 (2006): The rights of children with disabilities' (27 February 2007) UN Doc CRC/C/GC/9.

CteeRPD, 'General Comment No. 1 (2014) Article 12: Equal recognition before the law' (General Comment 1) (19 May 2014) UN Doc CRPD/C/GC/1.

CteeRPD, 'General comment No. 3 (2016) on women and girls with disabilities' (General Comment 3) (25 November 2016) UN Doc CRPD/C/GC/3.

CteeRPD, 'General comment No. 5 (2017) on living independently and being included in the community' (General Comment 5) (27 October 2017) UN Doc CRPD/C/GC/5.

CteeRPD, 'General Comment No. 6 (2018) on equality and non-discrimination' (General Comment 6) (26 April 2018) UN Doc CRPD/C/GC/6.

HRCtee, 'CCPR General Comment No. 18: Non-discrimination' (10 November 1989).

HRCtee, 'General comment No 20: Article 7 ((Prohibition of torture, or other cruel, inhuman or degrading treatment or punishment)' (27 May 2008), UN Doc HRI/GEN/1/Rev.9 (Vol. I).

HRCtee, 'General Comment No. 31, The nature of the general legal obligation imposed on States Parties to the Covenant' (26 May 2004) UN Doc CCPR/C/21/Rev.1/Add.13.

HRCtee, 'General Comment No. 35: Article 9 (Liberty and security of person)' (General Comment No. 35) (16 December 2014) UN Doc CCPR/C/GC/35.

REPORTS OF SPECIAL RAPPORTEURS

ECOSOC, 'Report of the Special Rapporteur on the right of everyone to the enjoyment of the highest attainable standard of physical and mental health, Paul Hunt' (11 February 2005) UN Doc E/CN.4/2005/51.

ECOSOC, 'The Concept and Practice of Affirmative Action, Final report submitted by Mr. Marc Bossuyt, Special Rapporteur, in accordance with Sub-Commission resolution 1998/5' (17 June 2002) UN Doc E/CN.4/Sub.2/2002/21.

OHCHR, 'Report of the Special Rapporteur on torture and other cruel, inhuman or degrading treatment or punishment' (5 March 2014) UN Doc A/HRC/25/60/Add.1.

OHCHR, 'Special Rapporteur on torture and other cruel, inhuman or degrading treatment or punishment, Statement by Mr. Juan E. Méndez' (4 March 2013), <www.madinamerica.com/wp-content/uploads/2013/03/torture.pdf > accessed 14 November 2022.

UNGA, 'Follow up report of the Special Rapporteur on torture and other cruel, inhuman or degrading treatment or punishment on his follow-up visit to the Republic of Ghana, Juan Méndez' (25 February 2015) UN Doc A/HRC/31/57/Add.2.

UNGA, 'Interim report of the Special Rapporteur on torture and other cruel, inhuman or degrading treatment or punishment, Manfred Nowak' (28 July 2008) UN Doc A/63/175.

UNGA, 'Report of the Special Rapporteur on the Right of Everyone to the Enjoyment of the Highest Attainable Standard of Physical and Mental Health, Paul Hunt' (31 January 2008) UN Doc A/HRC/7/11.

UNGA, 'Report of the Special Rapporteur on the right of everyone to the enjoyment of the highest attainable standard of physical and mental health, Dainius Pūras' (14 July 2017) UN Doc A/72/137.

UNGA, 'Report of the Special Rapporteur on the right of everyone to the enjoyment of the highest attainable standard of physical and mental health, Dainius Pūras' (15 April 2020) UN Doc A/HRC/44/48.

UNGA, 'Report of the Special Rapporteur on the right of everyone to the enjoyment of the highest attainable standard of physical and mental health, Dainius Pūras' (28 March 2017) UN Doc A/HRC/35/21.

UNGA, 'Report of the Special Rapporteur on the right of everyone to the enjoyment of the highest attainable standard of physical and mental health, Dainius Pūras' (12 April 2019) UN Doc A/HRC/41/34.

UNGA, 'Report of the Special Rapporteur on the right of everyone to the enjoyment of the highest attainable standard of physical and mental health, Dainius Pūras' (10 April 2018) UN Doc A/HRC/38/36.

UNGA, 'Report of the Special Rapporteur on the right of everyone to the enjoyment of the highest attainable standard of physical and mental health, Anand Grover' (10 August 2009) UN Doc A/64/272.

UNGA, 'Report of the Special Rapporteur on the right of everyone to the enjoyment of the highest attainable standard of physical and mental health, Dainius Pūras' (2 April 2015) UN Doc A/HRC/29/33.

UNGA, 'Report of the Special Rapporteur on the rights of persons with disabilities, Catalina Devandas-Aguilar, Rights of persons with disabilities' (16 July 2018) UN Doc A/73/161.
UNGA, 'Report of the Special Rapporteur on the rights of persons with disabilities, Catalina Devandas-Aguilar, Rights of persons with disabilities' (11 January 2019) UN Doc A/HRC/40/54.
UNGA, 'Report of the Special Rapporteur on torture and other cruel, inhuman or degrading treatment or punishment, Juan E. Méndez' (1 February 2013) UN Doc A/HRC/22/53.
UNGA, 'Report of the Special Rapporteur on torture and other cruel, inhuman or degrading treatment or punishment, Manfred Nowak' (5 February 2010) UN Doc A/HRC/13/39/Add.5.
UNGA, 'Report of the Special Rapporteur on torture and other cruel, inhuman or degrading treatment or punishment, Nils Melzer' (20 March 2020) UN Doc A/HRC/43/49.

CONCLUDING OBSERVATIONS

CAT, 'Concluding observations on the fourth periodic report of Azerbaijan' (27 January 2016) UN Doc CAT/C/AZE/CO/4.
CAT, 'Concluding observations on the seventh periodic report of Finland' (20 January 2017) UN Doc CAT/C/FIN/CO/7.
CAT, 'Concluding observations on the seventh periodic report of France' (10 June 2016) UN Doc CAT/C/FRA/CO/7.
Committee on the Elimination of Discrimination against Women, 'Concluding observations on the combined fourth and fifth periodic reports of India' (24 July 2014) UN Doc CEDAW/C/IND/CO/4–5.
CteeESCR, 'Concluding observations on sixth periodic report of Denmark' (12 November 2019) UN Doc E/C.12/DNK/CO/6.
CteeESCR, 'Concluding observations on the second periodic report of Lithuania' (24 June 2014) UN Doc E/C.12/LTU/CO/2.
CteeESCR, 'Concluding observations on the second periodic report of Kazakhstan' (29 March 2019) UN Doc E/C.12/KAZ/CO/2.
CteeRC, 'Concluding observations on the combined third to fifth periodic reports of Ghana' (13 July 2015) UN Doc CRC/C/GHA/CO/3–5.
CteeRPD, 'Concluding observations of the Committee on the Rights of Persons with Disabilities, India' (29 October 2019) UN Doc CRPD/C/IND/CO/1.
CteeRPD, 'Concluding observations of the Committee on the Rights of Persons with Disabilities, Tunisia' (13 May 2011) UN Doc CRPD/C/TUN/CO/1.
CteeRPD, 'Concluding observations of the Committee on the Rights of Persons with Disabilities, Greece' (29 October 2019) UN Doc CRPD/C/GRC/CO/1.
CteeRPD, 'Concluding Observations on the combined second and third periodic reports of Australia' (15 October 2019) UN Doc CRPD/C/AUS/CO/2–3.
CteeRPD, 'Concluding Observations on the combined second and third periodic reports of Spain' (13 May 2019) UN Doc CRPD/C/ESP/CO/2–3.
CteeRPD, 'Concluding Observations on the combined second and third periodic reports of Ecuador' (21 October 2019) UN Doc CRPD/C/ECU/CO/2–3.

CteeRPD, 'Concluding Observations on the initial Report of Albania' (14 October 2019) UN Doc CRPD/C/ALB/CO/1.

CteeRPD, 'Concluding Observations on the initial Report of Australia' (21 October 2013) UN Doc CRPD/C/AUS/CO/1.

CteeRPD, 'Concluding Observations on the initial Report of Austria' (30 September 2013) UN Doc CRPD/C/AUT/CO/1

CteeRPD, 'Concluding Observations on the initial Report of Bosnia and Herzegovina' (2 May 2017) UN Doc CRPD/C/BIH/CO/1.

CteeRPD, 'Concluding Observations on the initial Report of Chile' (13 April 2016) UN Doc CRPD/C/CHL/CO/1.

CteeRPD, 'Concluding Observations on the initial Report of Cuba' (10 May 2019) UN Doc CRPD/C/CUB/CO/1.

CteeRPD, 'Concluding Observations on the initial Report of Cyprus' (8 May 2017) UN Doc CRPD/C/CYP/CO/1.

CteeRPD, 'Concluding Observations on the initial Report of Denmark' (30 October 2014) UN Doc CRPD/C/DNK/CO/1.

CteeRPD, 'Concluding Observations on the initial Report of El Salvador' (1 October 2019) UN Doc CRPD/C/SLV/CO/2–3.

CteeRPD, 'Concluding Observations on the initial Report of Gabon' (2 October 2015) UN Doc CRPD/C/GAB/CO/1.

CteeRPD, 'Concluding observations on the initial report of Germany' (13 May 2015) UN Doc CRPD/C/DEU/CO/1.

CteeRPD, 'Concluding observations on the initial report of Greece' (29 October 2019) UN Doc CRPD/C/GRC/CO/1.

CteeRPD, 'Concluding Observations on the initial Report of Haiti' (13 April 2018) UN Doc CRPD/C/HTI/CO/1.

CteeRPD, 'Concluding Observations on the initial Report of Iraq' (23 October 2019) UN Doc CRPD/C/IRQ/CO/1.

CteeRPD, 'Concluding Observations on the Initial Report of Jordan' (15 May 2017) UN Doc CRPD/C/JOR/CO/1.

CteeRPD, 'Concluding Observations on the initial report of Kenya' (30 September 2015) UN Doc CRPD/C/KEN/ CO/1.

CteeRPD, 'Concluding observations on the initial report of Kuwait' (18 October 2019) UN Doc CRPD/C/KWT/CO/1.

CteeRPD, 'Concluding Observations on the initial Report of Malta' (17 October 2018) UN Doc CRPD/C/MLT/CO/1.

CteeRPD, 'Concluding Observations on the initial Report of Myanmar' (22 October 2019) UN Doc CRPD/C/MMR/CO/1.

CteeRPD, 'Concluding Observations on the initial Report of Nepal' (16 April 2018) UN Doc CRPD/C/NPL/CO/1.

CteeRPD, 'Concluding Observations on the initial Report of Norway (7 May 2019) UN Doc CRPD/C/NOR/CO/1.

CteeRPD, 'Concluding Observations on the initial Report of Poland' (29 October 2018), UN Doc CRPD/C/POL/CO/1.

CteeRPD, 'Concluding Observations on the initial Report of Rwanda' (3 May 2019) UN Doc CRPD/C/RWA/CO/1.

CteeRPD, 'Concluding Observations on the initial Report of Senegal' (13 May 2019) UN Doc CRPD/C/SEN/CO/1.

CteeRPD, 'Concluding Observations on the initial Report of Serbia' (23 May 2016) UN Doc CRPD/C/SRB/CO/1.

CteeRPD, 'Concluding Observations on the initial Report of Seychelles' (16 April 2018) UN Doc CRPD/C/SYC/CO/1.

CteeRPD, 'Concluding Observations on the initial Report of Slovakia' (17 May 2016) UN Doc CRPD/C/SVK/CO/1.

CteeRPD, 'Concluding Observations on the initial Report of South Africa' (23 October 2018) UN Doc CRPD/C/ZAF/CO/1.

CteeRPD, 'Concluding Observations on the initial Report of the Czech Republic' (15 May 2015) UN Doc CRPD/C/CZE/CO/1.

CteeRPD, 'Concluding observations on the initial report of the former Yugoslav Republic of Macedonia' (29 October 2018) UN Doc CRPD/C/MKD/CO/1.

CteeRPD, 'Concluding Observations on the initial Report of the Philippines' (16 October 2018) UN Doc CRPD/C/PHL/CO/1.

CteeRPD, 'Concluding Observations on the initial Report of Turkey' (1 October 2019) UN Doc CRPD/C/TUR/CO/1.

ECOSOC, 'Committee on Economic, Social and Cultural Rights Concluding observations on the fourth periodic report of the Republic of Korea' (19 October 2017) UN Doc E/C.12/KOR/CO/4.

ECOSOC, 'Committee on Economic, Social and Cultural Rights Concluding observations on the fourth periodic report of Argentina' (1 November 2018) UN Doc E/C.12/ARG/CO/4.

ECOSOC, 'Committee on Economic, Social and Cultural Rights Concluding observations on the fourth periodic report of Cameroon' (25 March 2019) UN Doc E/C.12/CMR/CO/4.

ECOSOC, 'Committee on Economic, Social and Cultural Rights Concluding observations on the second periodic report of Lithuania' (24 June 2014) UN Doc E/C.12/LTU/CO/2.

ECOSOC, 'Committee on Economic, Social and Cultural Rights Concluding observations on the fifth periodic report of Mauritius' (5 April 2019) UN Doc E/C.12/MUS/CO/5.

ECOSOC, 'Committee on Economic, Social and Cultural Rights Concluding observations on the second periodic report of Greece' (27 October 2015) UN Doc E/C.12/GRC/CO/2.

ECOSOC, 'Committee on Economic, Social and Cultural Rights Concluding observations on the initial report of Uganda' (8 July 2015) UN Doc E/C.12/UGA/CO/1.

ECOSOC, 'Committee on Economic, Social and Cultural Rights Concluding observations on the sixth periodic report of Bulgaria' (29 March 2019) UN Doc E/C.12/BGR/CO/6.

ECOSOC, 'Committee on Economic, Social and Cultural Rights Concluding observations on the initial report of Indonesia' (19 June 2014) UN Doc E/C.12/IDN/CO/1.

ECOSOC, 'Committee on Economic, Social and Cultural Rights Concluding observations on the sixth periodic report of the United Kingdom of Great Britain and Northern Ireland' (14 July 2016) UN Doc E/C.12/GBR/CO/6.

ECOSOC, 'Committee on Economic, Social and Cultural Rights Concluding observations on the second periodic report of Kazakhstan' (29 March 2019) UN Doc E/C.12/KAZ/CO/2.

ECOSOC, 'Committee on Economic, Social and Cultural Rights Concluding observations on the fifth periodic report of Australia' (11 July 2017) UN Doc E/C.12/AUS/CO/5.

ECOSOC, 'Committee on Economic, Social and Cultural Rights Concluding observations on the sixth periodic report of Poland' (26 October 2016) UN Doc E/C.12/POL/CO/6.

ECOSOC, 'Committee on Economic, Social and Cultural Rights Concluding observations on the sixth periodic report of Sweden' (14 July 2016) UN Doc E/C.12/SWE/CO/6.

ECOSOC, 'Committee on Economic, Social and Cultural Rights Concluding observations on sixth periodic report of Denmark' (12 November 2019) UN Doc E/C.12/DNK/CO/6.

ECOSOC, 'Committee on Economic, Social and Cultural Rights Concluding observations on the third periodic report of Slovakia' (14 November 2019) UN Doc E/C.12/SVK/CO/3.

ECOSOC, 'Committee on Economic, Social and Cultural Rights Concluding observations on the initial report of Cabo Verde' (27 November 2018) UN Doc E/C.12/CPV/CO/1.

HRCtee, 'Concluding observations on the initial reports of Ghana' (9 August 2016) UN Doc CCPR/C/GHA/CO/1.

GENERAL DOCUMENTS

Ad Hoc Committee, 7th Session, 'Draft Art 17 – Protecting the integrity of the person, International Disability Caucus' (19 January 2006), <www.un.org/esa/socdev/enable/rights/ahc7docs/ahc7idcchairamend1.doc> accessed 14 November 2022.

CteeRPD, 'General Comment on Equality and Non- discrimination (Article 5): First draft as at 31 August 2017' (31 August 2017), <www.ohchr.org/Documents/HRBodies/CRPD/GCArt5.docx> accessed 14 November 2022.

CteeRPD, 'Guidelines on article 14 of the Convention on the Rights of Persons with Disabilities, The right to liberty and security of persons with disabilities' (2014) UN Doc CRPD/C/12/2, Annex IV.

CteeRPD, 'Guidelines on deinstitutionalization, including in emergencies' (10 October 2022) UN Doc CRPD/C/5.

CteeRPD, 'Guidelines on treaty-specific document to be submitted by states parties under article 35, paragraph 1, of the Convention on the Rights of Persons with Disabilities' (18 November 2009) UN Doc CRPD/C/2/3.

OHCHR & CoE, 'The right of people with disabilities to live independently and be included in the community' (2012), <https://rm.coe.int/the-right-of-people-with-disabilities-to-live-independently-and-be-inc/16806da8a9> accessed 14 November 2022.

OHCHR Consultation Mental Health and Human Rights, HRC RES 43/13, 15 November 2021, speech of Michelle Bachelet, <https://conf.unog.ch/digitalrecordings/index.html?embed=-h&mrid=DE3A94BD-A240–450A-91DD-FC6323A179F1> accessed 14 November 2022.

OHCHR Consultation Mental Health and Human Rights, HRC RES 43/13, 15 November 2021, speech of Zsuzsanna Jakab, <https://conf.unog.ch/digitalrecordings/index.html?embed=-h&mrid=DE3A94BD-A240–450A-91DD-FC6323A179F1> accessed 14 November 2022.

OHCHR, 'Call for inputs: Draft guidance on Mental Health, Human Rights, and Legislation published jointly by WHO and OHCHR' (nd), <https://www.ohchr.org/en/calls-for-input/calls-input/draft-guidance-mental-health-human-rights-legislation-who-ohchr> accessed 14 November 2022.

OHCHR, 'Consultation on Human Rights and mental health: "Identifying strategies to promote human rights in mental health". Statement by UN High Commissioner of the United Nations for Human Rights Zeid Ra'ad Al Hussein' (14 May 2018), <https://www.ohchr.org/EN/NewsEvents/Pages/DisplayNews.aspx?NewsID=23080&LangID=E> accessed 14 November 2022.

OHCHR, 'Free, Prior and Informed Consent of Indigenous Peoples' (September 2013), <https://ohchr.org/Documents/Issues/ipeoples/freepriorandinformedconsent.pdf> accessed 14 November 2022.

OHCHR, 'Jurisprudence' (nd), <https://juris.ohchr.org/en/search/results?Bodies=9&sortOrder=Date> accessed 14 November 2022.

OHCHR, 'The Convention on the Rights of Persons with Disabilities, Training Guide, Professional Training Series No. 19' (2014), <https://www.ohchr.org/Documents/Publications/CRPD_TrainingGuide_PTS19_EN%20Accessible.pdf> accessed 14 November 2022.

SPT, 'Approach of the Subcommittee on Prevention of Torture and Other Cruel, Inhuman or Degrading Treatment or Punishment regarding the rights of persons institutionalized and treated medically without informed consent' (26 January 2016) UN Doc CAT/OP/27/2.

UN International Human Rights Instruments, 'Compilations of general comments and general recommendations adopted by Human Rights Treaty Bodies' (29 July 1994) UN Doc HRI/GEN/1/Rev.1, referring to General Comment 20.

UN Member States, 'Political Declaration of the High-level Meeting on Universal Health Coverage "Universal health coverage: moving together to build a healthier world"' (23 September 2019).

UN Sustainable Development Group, 'The Human Rights Based Approach to Development Cooperation Towards a Common Understanding Among UN Agencies' (2003), <https://unsdg.un.org/resources/human-rights-based-approach-development-cooperation-towards-common-understanding-among-un> accessed 14 November 2022.

UN, Ad Hoc Committee, Daily summary of discussion at the fifth session, Vol 6, No 5, the positions of Costa Rica, Trinidad and Tobago, the EU, Liechtenstein, and New Zealand (28 January 2005), <www.un.org/esa/socdev/enable/rights/ahc5sum31jan.htm> accessed 14 November 2022.

UNDP, 'Germany' (nd), <http://hdr.undp.org/en/countries/profiles/DEU> accessed 14 November 2022.

UNDP, *Human Development Report 2019, Beyond income, beyond averages, beyond today: Inequalities in human development in the 21st century* (UNDP 2019).

UNDP, *Human Development Report 2020. The next frontier: Human development and the Anthropocene* (UNDP 2020).

UNGA, 'Annual Report of the United Nations High Commissioner for Human Rights: Thematic Study on enhancing awareness and understanding of the Convention on the Rights of Persons with Disabilities' (26 January 2009) UN Doc A/HRC/10/48.

UNGA, 'Consideration of reports submitted by States parties under article 35 of the Convention, Initial reports of States parties, Germany' (7 May 2013) UN Doc CRPD/C/DEU/1.

UNGA, 'Declaration on the Rights of Disabled Persons' (9 December 1975) UN Doc A/RES/30/3447.

UNGA, 'Mental health and human rights, Report of the United Nations High Commissioner for Human Rights' (31 January 2017) UN Doc A/HRC/34/32.

UNGA, 'Report of the Ad Hoc Committee on a Comprehensive and Integral International Convention on the Protection and Promotion of the Rights and Dignity of Persons with Disabilities on its fifth session' (25 February 2005) UN Doc A/AC.265/2005/2.

UNGA, 'Report of the Ad Hoc Committee on a Comprehensive and Integral International Convention on the Protection and Promotion of the Rights and Dignity of Persons with Disabilities on its seventh session' (13 February 2006) UN Doc A/AC265/2006/2.

UNGA, 'Report of the Secretary-General, Progress of efforts to ensure the full recognition and enjoyment of the human rights of persons with disabilities' (24 July 2003) UN Doc A/58/181.
UNGA, 'Report of the United Nations High Commissioner for Human Rights, Mental health and human rights' (31 January 2017) UN Doc A/HRC/34/32.
UNGA, 'Report of the Working Group on Arbitrary Detention, United Nations Basic Principles and Guidelines on Remedies and Procedures on the Right of Anyone Deprived of Their Liberty to Bring Proceedings Before a Court' (6 July 2015) UN Doc A/HRC/30/37.
UNGA, 'Report of the Working Group on Arbitrary Detention' (19 July 2017) UN Doc A/HRC/36/37.
UNGA, 'Report of the Working Group to the Ad Hoc Committee on a Comprehensive and Integral International Convention on the Protection and Promotion of the Rights and Dignity of Persons with Disabilities' (27 January 2004) UN Doc A/AC265/2004/WG/1 Annex 1.
UNGA, 'Report of the Working Group to the Ad Hoc Committee' (27 January 2004) UN Doc A/AC.265/2004/WG/1, Annex I.
UNGA, 'Resolution adopted by the General Assembly on 25 September 2015, 70/1. Transforming our world: the 2030 Agenda for Sustainable Development' (21 October 2015) UN Doc A/RES/70/1.
UNGA, 'Resolution adopted by the Human Rights Council on 1 July 2016, 32/18. Mental health and human rights' (18 July 2016) UN Doc A/HRC/RES/32/18.
UNGA, 'Resolution adopted by the Human Rights Council on 19 June 2020, 43/13. Mental health and human rights' (1 July 2020) UN Doc A/HRC/RES/43/13.
UNGA, 'Resolution adopted by the Human Rights Council on 28 September 2017, 36/13. Mental health and human rights' (9 October 2017) UN Doc A/HRC/RES/36/13.
UNGA, 'Standard Rules on the Equalization of Opportunities for Persons with Disabilities' (20 December 1993) UN Doc A/RES/48/96, annex.
UNGA, 'The protection of persons with mental illness and the improvement of mental health care' (17 December 1991) UN Doc A/RES/46/119, annex.
UNGA, 'Thematic study on the right of persons with disabilities to live independently and be included in the community, Report of the Office of the United Nations High Commissioner for Human Rights' (12 December 2014) UN Doc A/HRC/28/37.
UNGA, Draft International Covenant on Human Rights: Report of the Third Committee (9 February 1957) UN Doc A/3525.
Working Group of the Ad hoc Committee on a Comprehensive and Integral International Convention on Protection and Promotion of the Rights and Dignity of Persons with Disabilities, Chair's Draft text (I-IV) Elements (December 2003), <https://www.un.org/esa/socdev/enable/rights/wgcontrib-chair1.htm> accessed 14 November 2022.
Working Group on Arbitrary Detention (WGAD), Opinion No. 8/2018 concerning Mr. N (Japan) (23 May 2018) UN Doc A/HRC/WGAD/2018/8.

DOCUMENTS OF OTHER BODIES

INTERNATIONAL

Human Rights Watch, 'Ghana should implement commitments on mental health issues' (2018), <https://www.hrw.org/news/2018/03/15/ghana-should-implement-commitments-mental-health-issues> accessed 14 November 2022.

Human Rights Watch, 'Like a death sentence: Abuses against persons with mental disabilities in Ghana' (2012) < https://www.hrw.org/report/2012/10/02/death-sentence/abuses-against-persons-mental-disabilities-ghana> accessed 14 November 2022.

Human Rights Watch, 'Living in Chains: Shackling of People with Psychosocial Disabilities Worldwide' (2020).

Human Rights Watch, 'Not everyone is celebrating on Independence Day in Ghana' (2019), <https://www.hrw.org/news/2019/03/13/not-everyone-celebrating-independence-day-ghana> accessed 14 November 2022

Human Rights Watch, 'World Report 2020, Events of 2019' (2020), <https://www.hrw.org/sites/default/files/world_report_download/hrw_world_report_2020_0.pdf> accessed 14 November 2022.

INTERIGHTS, 'The Centre for Legal Resources On Behalf of Valentin Câmpeanu v Romania' (nd), <www.interights.org/campeanu/index.html> accessed 14 November 2022.

Mental Disability Advocacy Center, 'Cage Beds and Coercion in Czech Psychiatric Institutions' (2014), <www.mdac.info/sites/mdac.info/files/cagebed_web_en_20140624_0.pdf> accessed 14 November 2022.

Mental Disability Advocacy Center, 'The Right to Legal Capacity in Kenya' (2014), <http://sro.sussex.ac.uk/id/eprint/48143/1/mdac_kenya_legal_capacity_2apr2014_0.pdf> accessed 14 November 2022.

QualityRights in Mental Health – Ghana Project (nd), <http://qualityrightsgh.com/> accessed 14 November 2022.

The World Bank, 'Countries and Economies' (nd), <https://data.worldbank.org/country> accessed 14 November 2022.

WHO 'Executive Board Resolution EB87.R24 (1991) Traditional medicine and modern health care', eighty-seventh session, 14–25 January 1991.

WHO and Commission on Social Determinants of Health, 'Closing the gap in a generation: Health equity through action on the social determinants of health' (2008), <https://www.who.int/social_determinants/final_report/csdh_finalreport_2008.pdf> accessed 14 November 2022.

WHO and the UN Children's Fund, 'A vision for primary health care in the 21st century' (2018), <https://www.who.int/docs/default-source/primary-health/vision.pdf> accessed 14 November 2022.

WHO Expert Committee on Mental Health & WHO, 'Expert Committee on Mental Health: report on the second session, Geneva, 11–16 September 1950' (1951) < https://apps.who.int/iris/handle/10665/37982> accessed 14 November 2022.

WHO, 'Comprehensive Mental Health Action Plan 2013–2030' (2021), <https://www.who.int/publications/i/item/9789240031029> accessed 14 November 2022.

WHO, 'Freedom from coercion, violence and abuse: WHO QualityRights core training: mental health and social services: course guide' (2019), <https://apps.who.int/iris/handle/10665/329582> accessed 14 November 2022.

WHO, 'Ghana, a very progressive mental health law' (2007), <https://www.who.int/mental_health/policy/country/GhanaCoutrySummary_Oct2007.pdf> accessed 14 November 2022.

WHO, 'Ghana' (nd), <https://www.who.int/mental_health/policy/country/ghana/en/> accessed 14 November 2022.

WHO, 'Global status report on violence and prevention' (2014), <https://www.who.int/violence_injury_prevention/violence/status_report/2014/en/> accessed 14 November 2022.

WHO, 'Guidance on community mental health services: Promoting person-centred and rights-based approaches' (2021), <https://www.who.int/publications/i/item/9789240025707> accessed 14 November 2022.

WHO, 'International Classification of Functioning, Disability and Health (ICIDH-2)' (2001), <https://www.who.int/standards/classifications/international-classification-of-functioning-disability-and-health> accessed 14 November 2022.

WHO, 'Legal capacity and the right to decide: WHO QualityRights core training: mental health and social services: course guide' (2019), < https://apps.who.int/iris/handle/10665/329539> accessed 14 November 2022.

WHO, 'Mental disorders' (8 June 2022), <https://www.who.int/news-room/fact-sheets/detail/mental-disorders> accessed 14 November 2022.

WHO, 'Mental Health Action Plan 2013–2020' (2013), <https://www.who.int/publications/i/item/9789241506021> accessed 14 November 2022, p 38.

WHO, 'Mental Health and COVID-19: Early evidence of the pandemic's impact: Scientific brief, 2 March 2022', <https://www.who.int/publications/i/item/WHO-2019-nCoV-Sci_Brief-Mental_health-2022.1> accessed 14 November 2022.

WHO, 'Mental Health Atlas 2017 Member State Profile; Germany' (2018), <https://www.who.int/publications/m/item/mental-health-atlas-2017-country-profile-germany> accessed 14 November 2022.

WHO, 'Mental Health Atlas 2020' (2021), <https://www.who.int/publications/i/item/9789240036703> accessed 14 November 2022.

WHO, 'Mental health care law: Ten basic principles' (1996), <https://www.who.int/gender-equity-rights/knowledge/mental-health-care-law/en/> accessed 14 November 2022.

WHO, 'Mental health, disability and human rights: WHO QualityRights core training – for all services and all people: course guide' (2019), <https://apps.who.int/iris/handle/10665/329546> accessed 14 November 2022.

WHO, 'Mental Health: A Call for Action by World Health Ministers, Ministerial Round Tables 2001, 54th World Health Assembly' (2001), <https://www.who.int/mental_health/advocacy/en/Call_for_Action_MoH_Intro.pdf> accessed 14 November 2022.

WHO, 'Mental health: strengthening our response' (17 June 2022), <https://www.who.int/news-room/fact-sheets/detail/mental-health-strengthening-our-response> accessed 14 November 2022.

WHO, 'Mental health: strengthening our response' (17 June 2022), <https://www.who.int/news-room/fact-sheets/detail/mental-health-strengthening-our-response> accessed 14 November 2022.

WHO, 'MiNDbank: More Inclusiveness Needed in Disability and Development; Country Resources: Germany' (nd), <www.mindbank.info/collection/country/germany> accessed 14 November 2022.

WHO, 'Strategies to end seclusion and restraint: WHO QualityRights Specialized training: course slides' (2019), <https://apps.who.int/iris/handle/10665/329747> accessed 14 November 2022.

WHO, 'Supported decision-making and advance planning: WHO QualityRights Specialized training: course guide' (2019), <https://apps.who.int/iris/handle/10665/329609> accessed 14 November 2022.

WHO, 'WHO QualityRights Tool Kit'(2012), <https://www.who.int/mental_health/publications/QualityRights_toolkit/en/> accessed 14 November 2022.

WHO, 'WHO QualityRights: Service standards and quality in mental health care' (nd), <https://www.who.int/mental_health/policy/quality_rights/infosheet_hrs_day.pdf> accessed 14 November 2022.

WHO, 'WHO traditional medicine strategy: 2014–2023' (2013), <https://www.who.int/medicines/publications/traditional/trm_strategy14_23/en/> accessed 14 November 2022.

WHO, 'WHO-AIMS Report on mental health system in Ghana' (2011).

WHO, 'World Mental Health Day on 10 October to highlight urgent need to increase investment in chronically underfunded sector' (5 October 2020), <https://www.who.int/news/item/05-10-2020-covid-19-disrupting-mental-health-services-in-most-countries-who-survey> accessed 5 July 2022.

WHO, *A Declaration of the Promotion of Patients' Rights in Europe* (WHO 1994).

WHO, Fact Sheet 'Mental disorders' (28 November 2019), <https://www.who.int/news-room/fact-sheets/detail/mental-disorders> accessed 14 November 2022.

WHO, *International Statistical Classification of Diseases and Related Health Problems, 10th Revision (ICD-10)-2015-WHO* (World Health Organization 2015).

WHO, OHCHR and other UN Agencies, Eliminating forced, coercive and otherwise involuntary sterilization: An interagency statement (WHO 2014).

WHO, *Organization of services for mental health: WHO mental health policy and service guidance package* (WHO 2003).

WHO, Seventy-fourth World Health Assembly, 'Resolution on strengthening WHO preparedness for and response to health emergencies' (31 May 2021), <https://apps.who.int/gb/ebwha/pdf_files/WHA74/A74_R7-en.pdf> accessed 14 November 2022.

World Network of Users and Survivors of Psychiatry, 'Position Paper on the Principles for the Protection of Persons with Mental Illness' (2001), <www.wnusp.net/index.php/position-paper-on-principles-for-the-protection-of-persons-with-mental-illness.html> accessed 14 November 2022.

REGIONAL

CoE Commissioner for Human Rights, 'Third party intervention, Application No. 47848/08 The Centre for Legal Resources on behalf of Valentin Câmpeanu v. Romania' (14 October 2011) CommDH(2011)37.

CoE Commissioner for Human Rights, *The right of people with disabilities to live independently and be included in the community* (Council of Europe Publishing 2012).

CoE, 'Committee of Ministers Recommendation No Rec(2004)10' (22 September 2004).

CoE, 'Explanatory Memorandum to Recommendation Rec (2004)10 of the committee of Minister to member states concerning the protection of human rights and dignity of persons with mental disorders' (22 September 2004) CM/Rec(2004)10.
CoE, 'Explanatory Report to the Protocol No. 12 to the Convention for the Protection of Human Rights and Fundamental Freedoms (ETS No 177)' (4 November 2000).
CoE, 'Report to the Bulgarian Government on the visit to Bulgaria carried out by the European Committee for the Prevention of Torture and Inhuman or Degrading Treatment or Punishment (CPT)' (10–21 August 2020) Doc CPT/Inf (2020).
CoE, 'Report to the Government of Ireland on the visit to Ireland carried out by the European Committee for the Prevention of Torture and Inhuman or Degrading Treatment or Punishment (CPT)' (23 September-4 October 2019) Doc CPT/Inf (2020).
CoE, 'Report to the Swedish Government on the visit to Sweden carried out by the European Committee for the Prevention of Torture and Inhuman or Degrading Treatment or Punishment (CPT),' (18–29 January 2021) Doc CPT/Inf (2021).
CoE, Committee of Ministers, 'Recommendation No R (99) 4 on principles concerning the legal protection of incapable adults' (23 February 1999), principle 25.
CoE, CPT, 'Involuntary placement in psychiatric establishments' (31 August 1998), <https://www.coe.int/en/web/cpt/psychiatry> accessed 14 November 2022.
CoE, CPT, 'The CPT standards' (8 March 2011) CPT/Inf/E (2002) 1 – Revised 2010.
CoE, Resolution ResAP(2005)1 on safeguarding adults and children with disabilities against abuse (2 February 2005).
Committee for the Prevention of Torture in Africa, 'Intersession Activity Report' (2016), <https://www.achpr.org/public/Document/file/English/59os_inter_session_report_comm_mute_eng.pdf> accessed 14 November 2022.
European Expert Group on the Transition from Institutional to Community-based Care, *Common European Guidelines on the Transition from Institutional to Community-based Care* (Brussels 2012).
European Joint Action on Mental Health and Well-being, 'Towards community-based and socially inclusive mental health care' (2017), <https://ec.europa.eu/health/sites/default/files/mental_health/docs/2017_towardsmhcare_en.pdf> accessed 14 November 2022.
European Union Agency for Fundamental Rights (FRA), *Involuntary placement and involuntary treatment of persons with mental health problems* (Publications Office of the European Union 2012).
European Union Agency for Fundamental Rights (FRA), *Legal capacity of persons with intellectual disabilities and persons with mental health problems* (FRA 2013).
Interreg North-West-Europe eMEN, 'Project Summary' (nd), <https://www.nweurope.eu/projects/project-search/e-mental-health-innovation-and-transnational-implementation-platform-north-west-europe-emen/> accessed 14 November 2022.
Mental Health Europe & Mental Health Initiative of the Open Society Foundations, 'Mapping Exclusion: Institutional and community-based services in the mental health field in Europe' (November 2012), <https://mhe-sme.org/wp-content/uploads/2017/11/mapping_exclusion_-_final_report_with_cover.pdf> accessed 14 November 2022.
Mental Health Europe & Tizard Centre at the University of Kent, 'Mapping and Understanding Exclusion: Institutional, coercive and community-based services and practices across Europe' (Mental Health Europe 2018), <https://mhe-sme.org/wp-content/uploads/2018/01/Mapping-and-Understanding-Exclusion-in-Europe.pdf> accessed 14 November 2022.

Mental Health Europe, 'Mapping and Understanding Exclusion: Institutional, coercive and community-based services and practices across Europe' (2017), <https://mhe-sme.org/wp-content/uploads/2018/01/Mapping-and-Understanding-Exclusion-in-Europe.pdf> accessed 14 November 2022.

Mental Health Europe, 'What we really need is support, not coercion' (10 December 2019), <https://www.mhe-sme.org/hrd19/> accessed 14 November 2022.

Organization of American States, *Principles and Best Practices on the Protection of Persons Deprived of Liberty in the Americas* (2008).

NATIONAL

Aktionsbündnis Seelische Gesundheit, 'EU project Interreg eMEN' (nd), <https://www.seelischegesundheit.net/themen/e-mental-health> accessed 14 November 2022.

American Psychiatric Association (APA), *Diagnostic and Statistical Manual of Mental Disorders, fifth edition* (APA Washington 2013).

Australian Human Rights Commission, 'Submission to the United Nations Committee on the Rights of Persons with Disabilities, Draft General Comment on Article 12 of the CRPD Committee' (28 February 2014), <https://humanrights.gov.au/our-work/legal/submissions-united-nations> accessed 14 November 2022.

Basic Needs 'Better Mental Health, Better Lives' (nd), <https://basicneedsghana.org/> accessed 14 November 2022.

Center for Human Rights and Humanitarian Law, *Torture in Healthcare Settings: Reflections on the Special Rapporteur on Torture's 2013 Thematic Report* (American University Washington College of Law 2014).

Centers for Disease Control and Prevention, 'CDC in Ghana' (nd), <https://www.cdc.gov/globalhealth/countries/ghana/pdf/Ghana_Factsheet.pdf> accessed 14 November 2022.

Deutsche Gesellschaft für Psychiatrie und Psychotherapie, Psychosomatik und Nervenheilkunde e. V. (DGPPN), 'DGPPN-Faktenblatt: Aktuelle Zahlen und Fakten der Psychiatrie und Psychotherapie' (2020), <https://www.dgppn.de/_Resources/Persistent/a2e357dac62be19b5050a1d89ffd8603cfdb8ef9/20201008_Factsheet.pdf> accessed 14 November 2022.

Deutscher Paritätischer Wohlfahrtsverband (Joint Welfare Association), *30 Jahre Mauerfall – Ein viergeteiltes Deutschland. Der Paritätische Armutsbericht 2019* (Der Paritätische Gesamtverband 2019).

Deutsches Institut für Menschenrechte, 'Entwicklung der Menschenrechtssituation in Deutschland Juli 2017-Juni 2018. Bericht an den Deutschen Bundestag gemäß §2 Absatz 5 DIMRG' (2018).

Federal Ministry of Justice and Consumer Protection, 'Referentenentwurf: Entwurf eines Gesetzes zur Reform des Vormundschafts- und Betreuungsrechts' (2020), <https://www.bmjv.de/SharedDocs/Gesetzgebungsverfahren/DE/Reform_Betreuungsrecht_Vormundschaft.html> accessed 14 November 2022.

Federal Ministry of Justice and Consumer Protection, *Qualität in der rechtlichen Betreuung. Abschlussbericht* (Bundesanzeiger Verlag 2018).

Federal Ministry of Justice and Consumer Protection, *Umsetzung des Erforderlichkeitsgrundsatzes in der betreuungsrechtlichen Praxis im Hinblick auf vorgelagerte „andere Hilfen"* (Bundesanzeiger Verlag 2018).

Federal Ministry of Labour and Social Affairs, 'Aktionswoche der Offensive Psychische Gesundheit' (nd), <https://inqa.de/DE/vernetzen/offensive-psychische-gesundheit/aktionswoche.html> accessed 14 November 2022.

Federal Office of Justice, 'Verfahren nach dem Betreuungsgesetz 1992 bis 2017' (nd), <https://www.bundesjustizamt.de/DE/Themen/Buergerdienste/Justizstatistik/Betreuung/Betreuung_node.html> accessed 14 November 2022.

Federal Republic of Germany, 'Depressive Erkrankungen: verhindern, früh erkennen, nachhaltig behandeln' (2006), <https://gesundheitsziele.de/cms/medium/261/Gesundheitsziele_Depression_BMG_01–03–06.pdf> accessed 14 November 2022.

Federal Republic of Germany, 'Nationaler Aktionsplan 2.0 der Bundesregierung zur UN-Behindertenrechtskonvention (UN-BRK)' (2016), <https://www.bmas.de/DE/Soziales/Teilhabe-und-Inklusion/Nationaler-Aktionsplan/nationaler-aktionsplan-2-0.html> accessed 14 November 2022.

Federal Republic of Germany, 'Strategie der Bundesregierung zur globalen Gesundheit' [Global Health Strategy] (2020), <https://www.bundesgesundheitsministerium.de/fileadmin/Dateien/5_Publikationen/Gesundheit/Broschueren/GlobaleGesundheitsstrategie_Web.pdf> accessed 14 November 2022.

German Alliance for Mental Health (nd), <https://www.seelischegesundheit.net/> accessed 14 November 2022; or Aktionsbündnis Seelische Gesundheit, 'Together for mental health against stigma' (nd), <https://www.seelischegesundheit.net/images/stories/buendnis/ABSG_FL_2017_en-web.pdf> accessed 14 November 2022.

Institut für transkulturelle Betreuung e.V., 'German Guardianship Law' (2010).

Republic of Ghana, Mental Health Authority, 'Annual Report, Mental Health Data' (2017).

Republic of Ghana, Mental Health Authority, 'Guidelines for Conducting Peer Reviews at Psychiatric Hospitals' (2018).

Republic of Ghana, Mental Health Authority, 'Guidelines for integrating mental health into general health care system including child and adolescent health care' (2018).

Republic of Ghana, Mental Health Authority, 'Guidelines for Traditional and Faith-based Healers in Mental Health' (2018).

Republic of Ghana, Mental Health Authority, 'Psychiatrists in Ghana as at 2nd December, 2019' (2019), <https://mhaghana.com/publications/> accessed 14 November 2022.

Republic of Ghana, Ministry of Health, 'Code of Ethics and Standards of Practice for Alternative Medicine Practitioners in Ghana' (2006).

Republic of Ghana, Ministry of Health, 'Ten Year Mental Health Policy 2018–2027: Ensuring a mentally healthy population' (2018).

Republic of Ghana, Ministry of Health, 'The mental health system in Ghana' (2013).

Republic of Ghana, Ministry of Health, Mental Health Regulation (L.I. 2385) of 2019.

Staatliche Koordinierungsstelle, 'Das deutsche Betreuungsrecht im Lichte der UN-Behindertenrechtskonvention: Positionspapier der Staatlichen Koordinierungsstelle nach Art. 33 UN-BRK (Fachausschuss Freiheits- und Schutzrechte)' (2017).

US Department of Health and Human Services, *Mental Health: Culture, Race, and Ethnicity – A Supplement to Mental Health: A Report of the Surgeon General* (US Public Health Services 2001).

We Shall Overcome, 'Forced psychiatric interventions as disability-based discrimination. Parallel Report to the 5th Periodic Report of Norway to the UN Committee on Economic, Social and Cultural Rights for the 51 session (4 – 29 November 2013)' (September 2013).

LIST OF TABLES

Table 2.1: Overview of the various terms and their definitions as adopted in this book 24
Table 3.1: Major international human rights treaties recognising mental health as human right 46
Table 3.2: Human rights to ensure the protection and promotion of mental health .. 55
Table 4.1: The right to the highest standard of health interpreted as including... 63
Table 4.2: Core obligations under the right to health 68
Table 5.1: Overview of sections and respective CRPD Articles 86
Table 5.2: Summary of the scope of, and obligations arising from, Article 5 CRPD 100
Table 5.3: Summary of the scope of, and obligations arising from, Article 12 CRPD 119
Table 5.4: Summary of the scope of, and obligations arising from, Articles 17, 15 and 16 CRPD 158
Table 5.5: Mapping of the right to access mental healthcare obligations derived from the CRPD 189
Table 6.1: Overview of interviewees (case study on Ghana) 200
Table 7.1: The right to mental health in detail 273

SAMENVATTING (DUTCH SUMMARY)

De COVID-19 pandemie, gevolgd door de oorlog in Oekraïne, heeft van geestelijke gezondheid een wereldwijde prioriteit gemaakt. De boodschap is duidelijk: er is geen gezondheid zonder geestelijke gezondheid. Ondanks de groeiende erkenning van het belang van geestelijke gezondheid, blijft het onduidelijk hoe mensenrechten kunnen worden gebruikt en begrepen om geestelijke gezondheid te bevorderen en te beschermen.

Dit onderzoek is erop gericht bij te dragen aan de ontwikkeling van "het recht op geestelijke gezondheid". Daarbij behandelt dit boek zowel (1) de geestelijke gezondheidscomponenten van het recht op de hoogst haalbare standaard van gezondheid, als (2) andere onderling afhankelijke mensenrechten afgeleid uit het Verdrag inzake de rechten van personen met een handicap (VN-verdrag Handicap) die gekoppeld kunnen worden aan geestelijke gezondheid, en die kunnen worden geïntegreerd in een juridisch kader over het "recht op geestelijke gezondheid". De centrale onderzoeksvragen van deze studie zijn: *Welke rechten en plichten bestaan er in het kader van de bescherming van geestelijke gezondheid op grond van internationale mensenrechten? Hoe moet de toegang tot geestelijke gezondheidszorg worden geregeld, bezien vanuit mensenrechtenperspectief?* Als onderdeel van de analyse worden juridische uitdagingen besproken en wordt de invloed van tradities in de context van geestelijke gezondheidszorg belicht. Naast het identificeren van de inconsistenties tussen internationale mensenrechtennormen en nationale wetgeving, verkennen de landenstudies van Ghana en Duitsland hoe nationale normen en praktijken mogelijk (praktische) oplossingen kunnen bieden voor de juridische uitdagingen. Deze landen zijn ten eerste gekozen omdat beide landen zogenaamde *best practice* landen zijn op het gebied van wetgeving inzake geestelijke gezondheid. Ten tweede waren in beide landen geschikte lokale onderzoeksmogelijkheden. Ten slotte vertegenwoordigen de landen lage-, midden- en hoge-inkomenslanden. Daarmee zijn alle inkomensniveaus van de wereld gedekt. Dit onderzoek heeft tot doel een uitputtend en constructief mensenrechtenkader op te stellen om wetgevers en beleidsmakers op internationaal, regionaal en nationaal niveau te helpen bij het waarborgen van het recht op geestelijke gezondheid in overeenstemming met mensenrechten.

Deel 1 legt de basis voor het onderzoek. **Hoofdstuk 2** zet de achtergrond en inhoud van geestelijke gezondheid, geestelijke beperking en geestelijke gezondheidszorg uiteen en verschaft conceptuele duidelijkheid. Dit hoofdstuk legt uit waarom en hoe verschillende terminologieën worden gebruikt in dit onderzoek en gaat dieper in op de verhouding tussen cultuur en geestelijke gezondheid. Verder identificeert dit hoofdstuk aanhoudende mensenrechtenproblemen waarmee personen met psychische stoornissen

Samenvatting (Dutch Summary)

in de context van de geestelijke gezondheidszorg worden geconfronteerd, waarbij onderscheid wordt gemaakt tussen "belemmeringen voor de toegang tot geestelijke gezondheidszorg" en "specifieke mensenrechtenschendingen in instellingen voor geestelijke gezondheidszorg". De geïdentificeerde vormen de basis van de rest van het onderzoek en de normatieve analyse.

Deel 2 omvat de belangrijkste normatieve analyse van dit onderzoek. Het brengt belangrijke mensenrechtennormen en de daaruit afgeleide verplichtingen van staten om uitvoering te geven aan het recht op geestelijke gezondheid in kaart. **Hoofdstuk 3** analyseert het evoluerende kader van geestelijke gezondheid als mensenrecht en beschrijft wat het recht op geestelijke gezondheid inhoudt. Het toont aan hoe het Internationaal Verdrag inzake economische, sociale en culturele rechten (IVESCR) een juridisch bindend recht op een zo goed mogelijke lichamelijke en geestelijke gezondheid kent dat wordt aangevuld met normen uit het recht op gezondheid, zoals neergelegd in het VN-Verdrag Handicap en het VN-Kinderrechtenverdrag. Uit deze internationale mensenrechtenverdragen vloeit de verplichting van de staten voort om de geestelijke gezondheid als mensenrecht te eerbiedigen, beschermen en verwezenlijken. Op basis van de in hoofdstuk 2 beschreven uitdagingen in het kader van mensenrechten, stelt dit onderzoek dat andere relevante mensenrechtennormen noodzakelijk zijn om het recht op geestelijke gezondheid te bevorderen en volledig te beschermen. In dat verband wordt een kader voor het recht op geestelijke gezondheid vastgesteld dat bestaat uit het recht om vrij te zijn van discriminatie; het recht op gelijke erkenning voor de wet; het recht op respect voor iemands lichamelijke en geestelijke integriteit; het recht om vrij te zijn van foltering of wrede, onmenselijke of onterende behandeling of bestraffing; het recht om vrij te zijn van uitbuiting, geweld en misbruik; het recht op vrijheid en veiligheid van de persoon; en het recht om onafhankelijk te leven en in de maatschappij te worden opgenomen; naast het recht op de hoogst haalbare gezondheidsstandaard.

Hoofdstuk 4 onderzoekt op systematische wijze het recht op de hoogst haalbare standaard van gezondheid als essentieel onderdeel van het bredere recht op geestelijke gezondheid. Het hoofdstuk analyseert in hoeverre met name het recht op een zo goed mogelijke lichamelijke en geestelijke gezondheid, zoals neergelegd in artikel 12 van het IVESCR, de geestelijke gezondheid als zelfstandige norm respecteert, beschermt en vervult. Volgens dit onderzoek omvat het recht op de hoogst haalbare gezondheidsstandaard het recht op onderliggende determinanten van geestelijke gezondheid en het recht op (tijdige) toegang tot passende faciliteiten, goederen en diensten voor de bevordering van geestelijke gezondheid. Naast determinanten die betrekking hebben op de fysieke omgeving (drinkwater, voedsel, huisvesting, sanitaire voorzieningen, et cetera) blijken de onderliggende determinanten van de geestelijke gezondheid ook psychosociale, structurele en politieke determinanten te omvatten. Hoewel het recht op de hoogst bereikbare gezondheidsstandaard geleidelijk mag worden gerealiseerd, waarbij rekening wordt gehouden met de beschikbare middelen, hebben staten kernverplichtingen om aan minimumnormen te voldoen. De kernverplichtingen die voortvloeien uit het recht op de hoogst bereikbare gezondheidsstandaard omvatten (i) toegang tot essentiële gezondheidsdiensten, (ii) het waarborgen van de vrijheid van medische behandeling en experimenten zonder toestemming, (iii) de onmiddellijke uitbreiding van rechtmatige en niet-dwingende behandelingsalternatieven, (iv) toegang tot maatschappelijke geestelijke gezondheidszorg, (v) toepassing van strategieën met stappenplannen om van dwangbehandeling over te gaan op passende, aanvaardbare en rechtmatige geestelijke gezondheidszorg en rechtmatige geestelijke ondersteuning vi) het verlenen van diensten ter bevordering van de geestelijke gezondheid, vii) het bevorderen van anti-stigmacampagnes, en viii) het opnemen van de erkenning, de zorg en de behandeling van geestelijke gezondheidsaandoeningen in het opleidingscurriculum van alle gezondheidswerkers. Hoofdstuk 4 bestaat verder uit een beschrijving van internationale en regionale jurisprudentie die verschillende manieren toont waarop geestelijke gezondheid kan worden geïnterpreteerd als een justitiabel element van het recht op gezondheid. De analyse in hoofdstuk 4 laat ten slotte zien dat er meer aandacht moet worden besteed aan andere mensenrechtennormen, met name om de toegang tot geestelijke gezondheidszorg te waarborgen.

Hoofdstuk 5 analyseert de aanvullende mensenrechten (zoals uiteengezet in hoofdstuk 3 in het kader van het recht op geestelijke gezondheid) en de daaruit voortvloeiende verplichtingen uit het VN-Verdrag Handicap, voor zover deze relevant zijn voor het garanderen van een humane en waardige geestelijke gezondheidszorg. Dit wordt gedaan vanuit een mensenrechtenbenadering met een focus op handicaps. Het VN-Verdrag Handicap introduceert een paradigmaverschuiving in de geestelijke gezondheidszorg, waarbij zorggebruikers niet langer erkend worden als louter ontvangers van zorg, maar als rechthebbenden. Uit de analyse van artikel 5 van het VN-Verdrag Handicap blijkt dat het verdrag transformatieve gelijkheid bevordert. Om gelijkheid te bevorderen en de nadelen die personen met een geestelijke handicap ondervinden te verhelpen, verplicht de gelijkheids- en non-discriminatienorm uit het VN-Verdrag Handicap haar lidstaten tot individuele en structurele aanpassingen. Hierbij introduceert hoofdstuk 5 de leerstukken van de redelijke aanpassingen [measures of reasonable accommodation] en specifieke maatregelen [specific measures]. De bedoeling van artikel 12 VN-Verdrag Handicap is om van een tijdperk van plaatsvervanging en paternalistische voogdijregimes over te gaan naar een tijdperk van ondersteuning. In plaats van een persoon met een geestelijke handicap onbekwaam te verklaren en een vervangende beslisser aan te wijzen die namens de persoon beslissingen neemt in het belang van de persoon, dringt Artikel 12 VN-Verdrag Handicap aan op invoering van een ondersteunde beslissingsregeling waarbij personen die niet over de mentale capaciteit beschikken om zelf beslissingen te nemen, worden ondersteund om hun wensen en voorkeuren met betrekking tot geestelijke gezondheidszorg interventies kenbaar te maken. Hoewel het een zeer omstreden artikel is, wordt het beëindigen van vervangende besluitvorming beschouwd als een centraal element voor de vermindering van het risico op een breder scala aan mensenrechtenschendingen. Het onderdeel "vrij zijn van niet-consensuele inmenging" wordt beheerst door artikelen 17, 15 en 16 van het VN-Verdrag Handicap. Deze artikelen bieden een recht om niet willekeurig te worden blootgesteld aan niet-consensuele inmenging, om een klacht in te dienen wanneer dit recht wordt geschonden, en om verhaal en herstel te zoeken. Hun aspirationele karakter

Samenvatting (Dutch Summary)

onderstreept de bestaande complexiteit en laat onopgeloste spanningen bestaan, vooral wat betreft niet-consensuele behandeling in noodsituaties. Wanneer de redenen voor de interventie echter worden losgekoppeld van de geestelijke handicap en er geen alternatieven voorhanden zijn, mogen er volgens dit onderzoek zo min mogelijk beperkende maatregelen worden toegepast. Het laatste deel van hoofdstuk 5 analyseert de bescherming tegen onvrijwillige plaatsing in een instelling en behandelt de kwesties van onvrijwillige opname, alsmede deïnstitutionalisering en regelingen voor zelfstandig wonen. Het hoofdstuk illustreert ten eerste hoe het recht op vrijheid en veiligheid (artikel 14 van het VN-Verdrag Handicap) sterkere waarborgen biedt ten aanzien van personen met een geestelijke handicap. Ten tweede laat het zien hoe het recht om onafhankelijk te leven en deel uit te maken van de maatschappij (artikel 19) een wettelijke codificatie biedt voor maatschappelijke geestelijke gezondheidsdiensten om zelfstandig te wonen te ondersteunen met als doel het uitbannen van institutionalisering in de context van de geestelijke gezondheidszorg.. Hoofdstuk 5 maakt duidelijk dat het VN-Verdrag Handicap bestaande juridische kaders op verschillende manieren uitdaagt. Dit geeft aanleiding tot verscheidene controversiële debatten. Enkele van deze debatten worden in hoofdstuk 5 beschreven, waaronder die over "nadelen van universele handelingsbekwaamheid", "rechtvaardiging voor restrictieve interventies" en "suïcidepreventie versus het recht op vrijheid". Er wordt een weg vooruit aangeboden die wellicht niet geheel in overeenstemming is met het ethos van het VN-Verdrag Handicap zoals omarmd door het Comité voor de rechten van mensen met een handicap. In deze discussies en in andere delen van het hoofdstuk komt het afwegen van verschillende mensenrechten aan de orde. De benadering van het VN-Verdrag Handicap brengt uitdagingen met zich mee, vooral wat betreft het omgaan met crisis- of noodsituaties. In dergelijke situaties zijn regionale mensenrechtenhoven en internationale mensenrechtenorganen het niet altijd eens met de door het VN-Verdrag Handicap ingevoerde normen. De moeilijkheid zit in het vinden van oplossingen die in overeenstemming zijn met de mensenrechten van de betrokkenen. Een aantal oplossingen worden in hoofdstuk 5 voorgesteld en andere worden in detail behandeld in de landenstudies in hoofdstuk 6.

Met de landenstudies in **deel 3** stapt dit onderzoek af van een klassiek-juridische benadering ter evaluatie van de nakoming van de verplichting van Ghana en Duitsland om het recht op geestelijke gezondheid te realiseren en de praktische uitvoering. In **hoofdstuk 6** wordt onderzocht in hoeverre geestelijke gezondheid als mensenrecht in Ghana en Duitsland gestalte heeft gekregen door wetgevende of beleidsmaatregelen. Na een beoordeling van de geestelijke gezondheidszorg in de landen op basis van de AAAQ-norm, vindt een analyse van hun wetgevend kader inzake geestelijke gezondheid plaats. In beide landenanalyses focust dit onderzoek op aanhoudende belangrijke uitdagingen binnen de nationale context. Dit legt de normen van het VN-Verdrag Handicap en hun tekortkomingen bloot. Er wordt tevens gezocht naar praktische, op mensenrechten gebaseerde oplossingen die zijn ontleend aan nationale wetgeving en goede ervaringen uit andere landen. Dit resulteert in een beschrijving van hoe de gekozen casestudies als voorbeeld kunnen dienen om het begrip van het recht op geestelijke gezondheid in het algemeen, en een mensenrechtenbenadering van de toegang tot geestelijke gezondheidszorg in het bijzonder, verder te bevorderen. Met betrekking tot Ghana analyseert dit onderzoek de juridische context van gezondheidsinterventies die neerkomen op mishandeling en geeft zij richtlijnen voor het reguleren van afzondering en dwangmaatregelen op een manier die in overeenstemming is met mensenrechten. Aangezien informele geestelijke gezondheidszorg een prominente rol speelt in de dienstverlening, bevordert de analyse van Ghana het recht op geestelijke gezondheid door richtlijnen voor te stellen voor de informele geestelijke gezondheidszorg. Informele geestelijke gezondheidszorg, ook buiten Ghana, staat in de schijnwerpers vanwege verschillende mensenrechtenschendingen die op dit gebied plaatsvonden. Hoofdstuk 6 doet voorstellen om humane en waardige zorg in de informele geestelijke gezondheidszorg te garanderen door samenwerking tussen formele en informele aanbieders van geestelijke gezondheidszorg. De landenstudie naar Duitsland richt zich op de voogdijregeling en bestudeert de juridische context van beschikkingsonbevoegdheid en ondersteunde besluitvorming, met inbegrip van waarborgen voor wettelijke vertegenwoordiging. Daarnaast vestigt de landenstudie naar Duitsland de aandacht op formele en informele ondersteunende maatschappelijke diensten als wenselijke alternatieven voor wettelijke vertegenwoordiging.

In **deel 4** en **hoofdstuk 7** van de studie worden de belangrijkste bevindingen gepresenteerd en wordt een reeks aanbevelingen gedaan over hoe een mensenrechtenbenadering van geestelijke gezondheid kan bijdragen tot de verwezenlijking van het recht op geestelijke gezondheid in de praktijk. De eerste en belangrijkste aanbeveling is dat staten en overheidsactoren het recht op geestelijke gezondheid uitdrukkelijk erkennen in hun nationale wetgeving en ervoor zorgen dat de houders van rechtennaar de rechter kunnen stappen in geval van een schending. Ten tweede moeten staten en overheidsactoren binnenlandse beleidsrichtlijnen instellen en uitvoeren met precieze instructies voor de tenuitvoerlegging van het recht op geestelijke gezondheid, met inbegrip van actieplannen en de verantwoordelijkheden van de verschillende actoren. Ten slotte moeten de staten hun rapportageverplichtingen ten aanzien van de VN-verdragsorganen serieus nemen. De tweede reeks aanbevelingen is gericht aan het Comité voor de rechten van personen met een handicap en houdt in dat deze praktische oplossingen voor kwesties die tot controversiële debatten hebben geleid, beter moet uitleggen. Het Comité zou staten precies moeten informeren hoe zij kunnen omgaan met situaties waarin rechten tegen elkaar moeten worden afgewogen, en zou dergelijke oplossingen moeten behandelen in slotopmerkingen of een Algemene Aanbeveling over het recht op gezondheid. De laatste aanbevelingen houden in dat niet-gouvernementele organisaties (NGO's) zich bewust moeten zijn van de technische en inhoudelijke implicaties van het recht op geestelijke gezondheid, en het recht op geestelijke gezondheid in hun activiteiten moeten betrekken. NGO's moeten verder informatie delen over het recht op geestelijke gezondheid en het publiek er meer bewust van maken.

Om de centrale onderzoeksvragen te beantwoorden, stelt dit onderzoek een kader op voor het recht op geestelijke gezondheid dat alle relevante mensenrechtennormen

Samenvatting (Dutch Summary)

omvat, met inbegrip van hun specifieke onderdelen en waarborgen. Het kader behandelt de bestaande mensenrechtenproblemen in de context van de geestelijke gezondheid in het algemeen, en de problemen in de geestelijke gezondheidszorg in het bijzonder. De verschillende mensenrechtendimensies die in deze studie worden besproken, kunnen de geestelijke gezondheid bevorderen en beschermen. Door het recht op geestelijke gezondheid te implementeren in het nationale rechtssysteem, kunnen de mensenrechtennormen de verwezenlijking van het recht op geestelijke gezondheid voor iedereen in de samenleving bevorderen.

SELECTED BIBLIOGRAPHY

Abbo C, 'Profiles and outcome of traditional healing practices for severe mental illnesses in two districts of Eastern Uganda' (2011) 4 Global Health Action.

Ahonen M, 'Ancient philosophers on mental illness' (2019) 30(1) History of Psychiatry 3.

Aichele V & Degener T, 'Frei und gleich im rechtlichen Handeln – Eine völkerrechtliche Einführung zu Artikel 12 UN-BRK' in Valentin Aichele (ed), *Das Menschenrecht auf gleiche Anerkennung vor dem Recht: Artikel 12 der UN-Behindertenrechtskonvention* (Nomos 2013) 49.

Aichele V, 'Germany' in Lisa Waddington & Anna Lawson (eds), *The UN Convention on the Rights of Persons with Disabilities in Practice: A Comparative Analysis of the Role of Courts* (Oxford University Press 2018).

Alexandrov NV & Schuck N, 'Coercive interventions under the new Dutch mental health law: Towards a CRPD-compliant law?' (2021) 76(59) International Journal of Law and Psychiatry.

Allen J and others, 'Social determinants of mental health' (2014) 26(4) International Review of Psychiatry 392.

Andión Ibañez X & Dekanosidze T, 'The State's obligation to regulate and monitor private health care facilities: the Alyne da Silva Pimentel and the Dzebniauri cases' (2017) 38(17) Public Health Reviews 1.

Angermeyera MC and others, 'Changes in the perception of mental illness stigma in Germany over the last two decades' (2014) 29(6) European Psychiatry 390.

Anokye R and others, 'Knowledge of mental health legislation in Ghana: a case of the use of certificate of urgency in mental health care' (2018) 12(37) International Journal of Mental Health Systems.

Arambulo K, Strengthening the Supervision of the International Covenant on Economic, Social and Cultural Rights. Theoretical and Procedural Aspects (Intersentia 1999).

Arnardóttir OM, 'The rights of persons with disabilities in the context of healthcare' in Brigit Toebes, Mette Hartlev, Aart Hendriks & Janne Rothmar Herrmann (eds), Health and Human Rights in Europe (Intersentia 2012).

Arstein-Kerslake A & Flynn E, 'The General Comment on Article 12 of the Convention on the Rights of Persons with Disabilities: A Roadmap for Equality Before the Law' (2016) 20(4) The International Journal of Human Rights 471.

Arstein-Kerslake A, Restoring voice to people with cognitive disabilities: realizing the right to equal recognition before the law (Cambridge University Press 2017).

Audet CM and others 'Mixed methods inquiry into traditional healers' treatment of mental, neurological and substance abuse disorders in rural South Africa' (2017) 12(12) PLoS ONE.

Awenva DA and others, 'From Mental Health Policy Development in Ghana to Implementation: What are the Barriers?' (2010) 13(3) African Journal of Psychiatry 184.

Babalola E and others, 'The biopsychosocial approach and global mental health: Synergies and opportunities' (2017) 33(29) Indian Journal of Social Psychiatry 291.

Selected Bibliography

Barlett P and others, 'Urgently awaiting implementation: The right to be free from exploitation, violence and abuse in Article 16 of the Convention on the Rights of Persons with Disabilities (CRPD)' 53 (2017) The International Journal of Law and Psychiatry 2.

Barlett P, 'The Right to Life and the Scope of Control: Fernandes de Oliveira v Portugal' (18 March 2019), <https://strasbourgobservers.com/2019/03/18/the-right-to-life-and-the-scope-of-control-fernandes-de-oliveira-v-portugal/> accessed 14 November 2022.

Barlow DH & Durand VM, Abnormal Psychology: An Integrative Approach, eighth edition (Cengage Learning 2017).

Bartlett P & Schulze M, 'Urgently awaiting implementation: The right to be free from exploitation, violence and abuse in Article 16 of the Convention on the Rights of Persons with Disabilities (CRPD)' (2017) 53 International Journal of Law and Psychiatry 2.

Bartlett P and others, Mental Disability and the European Convention on Human Rights (International Studies in Human Rights Volume 90) (Martinus Nijhoff Publishers 2007).

Bartlett P, 'Implementing a Paradigm Shift: Implementing the Convention on the Rights of Persons with Disabilities in the Context of Mental Disability Law' in Torture in Healthcare Settings: Reflections on the Special Rapporteur on Torture's 2013 Thematic Report (Centre for Human Rights and Humanitarian Law, American University Washington College of Law 2014).

Bartlett P, 'The United Nations Convention on the Rights of Persons with Disabilities and Mental Health Law' (2012) 75(5) Modern Law Review 752.

Bertolote J & Sartorius N, 'WHO initiative of support to people disabled by mental illness: Some issues and concepts related to rehabilitation' (1996) 11(2) European Psychiatry 56.

Bertolote J, 'The roots of the concept of mental health' (2008) 7(2) World Psychiatry 113.

Bhugra D and others (eds), 'The right to mental health and parity' 57(2) (2015) Indian Journal of Psychiatry 117.

Boye M, 'Inside Accra Psychiatric Hospital: The good, the bad, the ugly!' (7 September 2017), GhanaWeb, <https://www.ghanaweb.com/GhanaHomePage/health/Inside-Accra-Psychiatric-Hospital-The-good-the-bad-the-ugly-578188> accessed 14 November 2022.

Bramesfeld A and others, 'Managing Mental Health Service Provision in the Decentralized, Multi-layered Health and Social Care System of Germany' (2004) 7(1) The Journal of Mental Health Policy and Economics 3.

Bratan T and others, 'Implementation of the UN Convention on the Rights of Persons with Disabilities: A Comparison of Four European Countries with Regards to Assistive Technologies' (2020) 10(74) Societies.

Brosey D, 'Supported Decision-making and the German Law of Betreuung. A legal perspective on supported and substitute decision-making regarding Art. 12 CRPD', in Dagmar Coester-Waltjen, Volker Lipp & Donovan WM Waters (eds), Liber Amicorum Makoto Arai (Nomos 2015).

Brus M, 'Soft Law in Public International Law: A Pragmatic or a Principled Choice? Comparing the Sustainable Development Goals and the Paris Agreement' in Pauline Westerman, Jaap Hage, Stephan Kirste & Anne Ruth Mackor (eds), *Legal Validity and Soft Law* (Springer 2018).

Bühring P, 'Psychotherpaeutische Versorgung: Die Frage der Gerechigkeit' (2021) 2 Deutsches Ärzteblatt 55.

Byrne M and others, 'A new tool to assess compliance of mental health laws with the convention on the rights of persons with disabilities' (2018) 58 International Journal of Law and Psychiatry 122.

Selected Bibliography

Caivano N, 'Conceptualizing Capacity: Interpreting Canada's Qualified Ratification of Article 12 of the UN Disability Rights Convention' (2014) 4(1) Western Journal of Legal Studies.

Cera R, 'Article 5 [Equality and Non-Discrimination]' in Della Fina, Rachele Cera & Giuseppe Palmisano (eds), *The United Nations Convention on the Rights of Persons with Disabilities* (Springer International Publishing 2017).

Chapman A and others, 'Reimagining the Mental Health Paradigm for Our Collective Well-Being' (2020) 22(1) Health and Human Rights Journal 1.

Chapman A, 'Conceptualizing the Right to Health: A Violations Approach' (1998) 65 Tennessee Law Review 389.

Chisholm B, 'Outline for a study group on World Health and the survival of the human race: material drawn from articles and speeches' (1951), <https://apps.who.int/iris/handle/10665/330666> accessed 14 November 2022.

Cohen J & Ezer T, 'Human rights in patient care: A theoretical and practical framework' (2013) 15(2) Health and Human Rights Journal 7.

Coomans F & van Hoof F (eds), *The right to complain about economic, social and cultural rights: proceedings of the expert meeting on the adoption of an optional protocol to the International covenant on economic, social and cultural rights held from 25–28 January 1995 in Utrecht* (SIM 1995).

Corsi JL, 'Article 5: Equality and Non-Discrimination' in Ilias Bantekas, Michael Ashley Stein & Dimitris Anastasiou (eds), *The UN Convention on the Rights of Persons with Disabilities: A Commentary* (Oxford University Press 2018) 142.

Craven MCR, *The International Covenant on Economic, Social and Cultural Rights: A Perspective on its Development* (Clarendon Press 1998).

Dawson J, 'A realistic approach to assessing mental health laws' compliance with the UN-CRPD' (2015) 40 International Journal of Law and Psychiatry 70; and George Szmukler, '"Capacity", "best interests", "will and preferences" and the UN Convention on the Rights of Persons with Disabilities' (2019) 18(1) World Psychiatry 34.

Dhanda A, 'Legal Capacity in the Disability Rights Convention: Stranglehold of the Past or Lodestar for the Future' (2007) 34(2) Syracuse Journal of International Law & Commerce.

Dinerstein R, 'Emerging international trends for practices in guardianship laws for people with disabilities' (2016) 22 ILSA Journal of International and Comparative Law 435.

Doku V and others, 'Implementing the Mental Health Act in Ghana: Any Challenges Ahead?' (2012) 46(4) Ghana Medical Journal 241.

Donnelly J, 'The Relative Universality of Human Rights' (2007) 29(2) Human Rights Quarterly 281.

Dove N, 'A Return to traditional healthcare practices; A Ghanaian study' (2010) 40(5) Journal of Black Studies 823.

Drew N and others 'Human rights violations of people with mental and psychosocial disabilities: an unresolved global crisis' (2011) 378(9803) The Lancet 1664.

Eaton J & Ohene S, 'Providing Sustainable Mental Health Care in Ghana: A Demonstration Project' in Sheena Posey Norris, Erin Hammers Forstag & Bruce M Altevogt (eds), *Providing Sustainable Mental and Neurological Health Care in Ghana and Kenya* (National Academies Press 2016)

Egan S, 'The doctrinal approach in international human rights law scholarship' in Lee McConnell and Rhona Smith (eds), *Research Methods in Human Rights* (Routledge 2018).

Intersentia 311

Selected Bibliography

Elgeti H, 'Sozialpsychiatrische Dienste in Deutschland: Ein großes Versprechen' (2019) 43(2) Soziale Psychatrie 16.

Engman T and others, 'A New Profession is Born – Personligt ombud, PO' (2008), <https://www.personligtombud.se/publikationer/pdf/A%20New%20Proffession%20is%20Born.pdf> accessed 14 November 2022.

Enoch J and others, 'Human Rights in the Fourth Decade of the HIV/AIDS Response' 19(2) (2017) Health and Human Rights Journal 177.

Fallon-Kund M and others, 'Balancing autonomy and protection: A qualitative analysis of court hearings dealing with protective measures' (2017) 53 International Journal of Law and Psychiatry 69.

Fennell P, 'Article 15: Protection against Torture and Cruel or Inhuman or Degrading Treatment or Punishment' in Ilias Bantekas, Michael Ashley Stein & Dimitris Anastasiou (eds), *The UN Convention on the Rights of Persons with Disabilities: A Commentary* (Oxford University Press 2018).

Fernando S, *Mental health worldwide: Culture, globalization and development* (Palgrave Macmillan 2014).

Ferri D, 'Reasonable accommodation as a gateway to the equal enjoyment of human rights: from New York to Strasbourg' (2018) 6(1) Social Inclusion.

Fiala-Butora J and others, 'Article 19: Living Independently and Being Included in the Community' in Ilias Bantekas, Michael Ashley Stein and Dimitris Anastasiou (eds), *The UN Convention on the Rights of Persons with Disabilities: A Commentary* (Oxford University Press 2018).

Flynn E and others (eds), *Global perspectives on legal capacity reform: our voices, our stories* (Routledge 2018)

Flynn E and others, 'Report on disability-specific forms of deprivation of liberty' (2019), <https://www.nuigalway.ie/media/centrefordisabilitylawandpolicy/files/DoL-Report-Final.pdf> accessed 14 November 2022.

Flynn E, From Rhetoric to Action: Implementing the UN Convention on the Rights of Persons with Disabilities (CUP 2011).

Forman L and others, 'What could a strengthened right to health bring to the post-2015 health development agenda?: interrogating the role of the minimum core concept in advancing essential global health needs' (2016) 13 BMC International Health and Human Rights 1.

Fredman S, Discrimination Law, second edition (Oxford University Press 2011).

Freeman M and others, 'Reversing hard won victories in the name of human rights: a critique of the General Comment on Article 12 of the UN Convention on the Rights of Persons with Disabilities' (2015) 2 Lancet Psychiatry 844.

Gaebel W and others, 'Psychisch Kranke: Stigma erschwert Behandlung und Integration' (2004) 48 Deutsches Ärzteblatt 553.

Gaebel W, 'Pro und Kontra: Machen Antistigmakampagnen Sinn? [For and Against: Do Anti-Stigma Campaigns Make Sense?]' (2005) 32(5) Psychiatrische Praxis 218.

Gispen ME, Human Rights and Drug Control: Access to Controlled Essential Medicines in Resource-constrained Countries (Intersentia 2017).

Goffman E & Helmreich WB, 'On the Characteristics of Total Institutions' in Erving Goffman (ed), Asylum (Anchor Books 1961).

Gopalkrishnan N, 'Cultural Diversity and Mental Health: Considerations for Policy and Practice' (2018) 6(179) Frontiers in Public Health 179.

Gostin L, Global Health Law (Harvard University Press 2014).

Greer S, The Margin of Appreciation: Interpretation and Discretion under the European Convention on Human Rights (Council of Europe 2000).

Guarnizo-Peralta D, 'Disability rights in the Inter-American System of Human Rights: An expansive and evolving protection' (2018) 36(1) Netherlands Quarterly of Human Rights.

Gureje O and others, 'The role of global traditional and complementary systems of medicine in treating mental health problems' (2015) 2(2) Lancet Psychiatry 168.

Hendriks A, 'UN Convention on the Rights of Persons with Disabilities' (2007) 14(3) European Journal of Health Law 273.

Hernandez M and others, 'Cultural Competence: a literature review and conceptual model for mental health services' (2009) 60(8) Psychiatric Services 1046.

Herring J, Vulnerable Adults and the Law (Oxford University Press 2016).

Hesselman M and others (eds), Socio-Economic Human Rights for Essential Public Services Provision (Routledge 2017).

Heymann J and others, 'Constitutional rights to health, public health and medical care: the status of health protections in 191 countries' (2013) 8(6) Global Public Health 639.

Howard E, 'Indirect Discrimination, Reasonable Accommodation and Religion' in Daniël Cuypers & Jogchum Vrielink (eds), Equal is not Enough (Cambridge University Press 2018).

Hunt P & Mesquita J, 'Mental Disabilities and the Human Right to the Highest Attainable Standard of Health' (2006) 28(2) Human Rights Quarterly 332.

Hunt P and others, 'Implementation of Economic, Social and Cultural Rights' in Schott Sheeran and Nigel Rodley (eds), Routledge Handbook of International Human Rights Law (Routledge 2013).

Incayawar M, 'Efficacy of Quichua healers as psychiatric diagnosticians' (2008) 192(5) British Journal of Psychiatry 390.

Kallert T and others, 'Coerced hospital admission and symptom change – a prospective observational multi-centre study' (2011) 6(11) PLOS One 1

Kaspers J, 'Germany's mental health system in a nutshell. Shedding light on the confusing German therapy system' (2016), <www.jan-kaspers.de/articles/download/german_mental_health_nutshell.pdf> accessed 14 November 2022.

Kayess R & French P, 'Out of darkness into light? Introducing the Convention on the rights of persons with disabilities' (2008) 8(1) Human Rights Law Review 1.

Kazou K, 'Analysing the Definition of Disability in the UN Convention on the Rights of Persons with Disabilities: is it really based on a 'Social Model' approach?' (2017) 23 International Journal of Mental Health and Capacity Law 25.

Keeling A, 'Article 16: Freedom from Exploitation, Violence, and Abuse' in Ilias Bantekas, Michael Ashley Stein & Dimitris Anastasiou (eds), The UN Convention on the Rights of Persons with Disabilities: A Commentary (Oxford University Press 2018).

Kelly BD, 'The Assisted Decision-Making (Capacity) Act 2015: what it is and why it matters' (2017) 186(2) Irish Journal of Medical Science 351.

Kelly BD, Dignity, Mental Health and Human Rights (Ashgate 2015).

Keys M, 'Article 17 [Protecting the Integrity of the Person]' in Valentina Della Fina, Rachele Cera & Giuseppe Palmisano (eds), The United Nations Convention on the Rights of Persons with Disabilities (Springer International Publishing 2017).

Knapp M and others, 'Economic barriers to better mental health practice and policy' (2006) 21(3) Health Policy and Planning 157.

Knibbe M and others 'Bianca in the neighborhood: moving beyond the 'reach paradigm' in public mental health' (2016) 26(4) Critical Public Health Journal 434.

Kovess-Masfety V and others, 'Evolution of Our Understanding of Positive Mental Health' in Helen Herrman, Shekhar Saxena & Rob Moodie (eds), Promoting Mental Health: concepts, emerging evidence, practice (World Health Organization 2005).

Kpobi LNA and others, 'Traditional herbalists' methods of treating mental disorders in Ghana' (2019) 56(1) Transcultural Psychiatry 250.

Kraepelin E, 'Comparative psychiatry' (reprinted; originally published in 1904) in Roland Littlewood & Simon Dien (eds), Cultural psychiatry and medical anthropology: In introduction and reader (The Athlone Press 2000).

Lachwitz K, 'Funktion und Anwendungsbereich der"Unterstützung"("support") bei der Ausübung der Rechts- und Handlungsfähigkeit gemäß Artikel 12 UN-BRK – Anforderungen aus der Perspektive von Menschen mit geistiger Behinderung', in Valentin Aichele (ed), Das Menschenrecht auf gleiche Anerkennung vor dem Recht: Artikel 12 der UN-Behindertenrechtskonvention (Nomos 2013)

Laing J, 'Preventing violence, exploitation and abuse of persons with mental disabilities: Exploring the monitoring implications of Article 16 of the United Nations Convention on the Rights of Persons with Disabilities' (2017) 53 International Journal of Law and Psychiatry 27.

Lawson A and Waddington L (eds), Domestic Interpretation of the UN Convention on the Rights of Persons with Disabilities: A Comparative Analysis (Oxford University Press 2017).

Leary VA, 'Justiciability and Beyond: Complaint Procedures and the Right to Health' (1995) 55 International Commission of Jurists Review.

Leenen HJJ and others, Handboek gezondheidsrecht (Boom Uitgevers Den Haag 2020).

Lees S & Leicht-Miranda M, 'Legal Opinion on Article 12 of the CRPD' (2008), <https://disability-studies.leeds.ac.uk/library/author/legalopiniononarticleofthecrpd/> accessed 14 November 2022.

Lewis O & Campbell A, 'Violence and abuse against people with disabilities: A comparison of the approaches of the European Court of Human Rights and the United Nations Committee on the Rights of Persons with Disabilities' (2017) 53 International Journal of Law and Psychiatry 45.

Lewis O, 'Stanev v. Bulgaria: On the Pathway to Freedom' (2012) 19(2) Human Rights Brief.

Lipp V, 'Erwachsenenschutz, gesetzliche Vertretung und Artikel 12 UN-BRK', in: Valentin Aichele (ed), Das Menschenrecht auf gleiche Anerkennung vor dem Recht: Artikel 12 der UN-Behindertenrechtskonvention (Nomos 2013).

Lipp V, 'Kritik und Reform des Betreuungsrechts' (2017), <https://docplayer.org/124708824-Kritik-und-reform-des-betreuungsrechts.html accessed 12 April 2021> accessed 14 November 2022.

Lipp V, 'Legal Protection of Adults in Germany – An Overview' (2016), <https://www.bgt-ev.de/fileadmin/Mediendatenbank/Themen/Einzelbeitraege/Lipp/Lipp_Legal_Protection_Adults.pdf> accessed 14 November 2022.

Litins'ka Y, Assessing capacity to decide on medical treatment: On human rights and the use of medical knowledge in the laws of England, Russia and Sweden (Uppsala University 2018).

Lord JE, 'Shared Understanding or Consensus – Masked Disagreement? The Anti-Torture Framework in the Convention on the Rights of Persons with Disabilities' (2010) 33 Loyala of Los Angeles International and Comparative Law Review.

Mammeri-Latzel M, 'Overview of German Adult Guardianship Law from the Perspective of a German Judge (1st instance)' in Makoto Arai, Ulrich Becker, Volker Lipp (eds), Adult Guardianship Law for the 21st Century (Nomos 2013).

Marchesi A, 'Article 15 [Freedom from Torture or Cruel, Inhuman or Degrading Treatment or Punishment]' in Valentina Della Fina, Rachele Cera & Giuseppe Palmisano (eds), The United Nations Convention on the Rights of Persons with Disabilities (Springer International Publishing 2017).

Marks S, 'The Emergence and Scope of the Human Right to Health' in José Zuniga, Stephen Marks and Lawrence Gostin (eds), Advancing the Human Right to Health (Oxford University Press 2013).

Marschner R, 'Menschen in Krisen: Unterbringung und Zwangsbehandlung in der Psychiatrie', in Valentin Aichele (ed), Das Menschenrecht auf gleiche Anerkennung vor dem Recht: Artikel 12 der UN-Behindertenrechtskonvention (Nomos 2013).

Marsella AJ & Yamada AM, 'Culture and mental health: An introduction and overview of foundations, concepts and issues' in Israel Cuéllar & Freddy Paniagua (eds), Handbook of multicultural mental health (Academic Press 2000).

Martin W and others, 'The Essex Autonomy Project Three Jurisdictions Report: Towards Compliance with CRPD Art. 12 in Capacity/Incapacity Legislation across the UK' (2016), <https://autonomy.essex.ac.uk/resources/eap-three-jurisdictions-report/> accessed 14 November 2022, p 58.

Matta V and others, Qualität in der rechtlichen Betreuung (Bundesanzeiger Verlag 2018).

McInerney S, 'Introducing the biopsychosocial model for good medicine and good doctors' (2002) 324(1533) BMJ.

McSherry B, 'Protecting the Integrity of the Person: Developing Limitations on Involuntary Treatment' (2008) 26(2) Law in Context: Socio-Legal Journal 111.

McSherry B, 'Regulating seclusion and restraint in health care settings: The promise of the Convention on the Rights of Persons with Disabilities' (2017) 53 International Journal of Law and Psychiatry 39.

Mégret F, 'The Disabilities Convention: Human Rights of Persons with Disabilities or Disability Rights?' (2008) 30(2) Human Rights Quarterly 494.

Meier B, 'Making Health a Human Right: The World Health Organisation and the United Nations Programme on Human Rights and Scientific and Technological Developments' (2012) 13 Journal of the Historical Society 195.

Memon A and others, 'Perceived barriers to accessing mental health services among black and minority ethnic (BME) communities: a qualitative study in Southeast England' (2016) 6(11) BMJ Open.

Merry SE, 'Changing rights, changing culture' in Jane Cowan, Marie-Bénédicte Dembour and Richard Wilson (eds), Culture and Rights: Anthropological Perspectives (Cambridge University Press 2012).

Mfoafo-M'Carthy M & Grishow JD, 'Mental illness, stigma and disability rights in Ghana' (2017) 5 African Disability Rights Yearbook 84.

Minkovitz T, 'Prohibition of Compulsory Mental Health Treatment and Detention Under the CRPD' (2011) SSRN Electronic Journal.

Selected Bibliography

Minkowitz T, 'A Response to the Report by Juan E. Méndez, Special Rapporteur on Torture, Dealing with Torture in the Context of Health Care, as it Pertains to Nonconsensual Psychiatric Interventions' in Center for Human Rights and Humanitarian Law, Torture in Healthcare Settings: Reflections on the Special Rapporteur on Torture's 2013 Thematic Report (American University Washington College of Law 2014).

Minkowitz T, 'The United Nations Convention on the Rights of Persons with Disabilities and the Right to Be Free from Nonconsensual Psychiatric Interventions' (2007) 34(2) Syracuse Journal of International Law and Commerce.

Moeckli D, 'Equality and Non-Discrimination' in Daniel Moeckli, Sangeeta Shah, and Sandesh Sivakumaran (eds), International Human Rights Law, second edition (Oxford University Press 2013).

Moitra M and others, 'The global gap in treatment coverage for major depressive disorder in 84 countries from 2000–2019: a systematic review and Bayesian meta-regression analysis' (2022) 19(2) PLoS Med.

Moleón Ruiz A & Fuertes Rocañín JC, 'Psychiatrists' opinion about involuntary outpatient treatment' (2020) 20(1) Revista Española de Sanidad Penitenciaria 39.

Molodynski A and others, 'Coercion in mental healthcare: time for a change in direction' (2016) 13(1) BJPsych International 1.

Murphy R and others, 'Service Users' Experiences of Involuntary Hospital Admission Under the Mental Health Act 2001 in the Republic of Ireland' (2017) 68(11) Psychiatric Services 1127.

Nortje G and others, 'Effectiveness of traditional healers in treating mental disorders: a systematic review' (2016) 3(2) Lancet Psychiatry 154.

Nys H and others, 'Patient Capacity in Mental Health Care: Legal Overview' (2005) 12(4) Health Care Analysis 329.

Offergeld J, Unterstützung der Selbstbestimmung oder fremdbestimmende Stellvertretung? Rechtliche Betreuung aus der Perspektive von Menschen mit Lernschwierigkeiten (Beltz Juventa 2021).

Okeke CN, 'The use of international law in the domestic courts of Ghana and Nigeria' (2015) 32 Arizona Journal of International and Comparative Law 372.

Okyerefo MPK, 'The gospel of public image in Ghana' in H Englund (ed), Christianity and Public Culture in Africa (Ohio University Press 2011).

Osei A and others, 'The new Ghana mental health bill' (2011) 8(1) Psychiatry International 8.

Palmisano G, 'Article 19 [Living Independently and Being Included in the Community]' in Valentina Della Fina, Rachele Cera & Giuseppe Palmisano (eds), The United Nations Convention on the Rights of Persons with Disabilities (Springer International Publishing 2017).

Patel V & Prince M, 'Global Mental Health' (2010) 303(19) The Journal of the American Medical Association 1976

Patel V, 'Rethinking mental health care. Bridging the credibility gap' (2014) 12 Intervention Journal 15.

Pauwelyn J and others, Informal International Lawmaking (Oxford University Press 2012).

Pavone IR, 'Article 25 [Health]' in Valentina Della Fina, Rachele Cera & Giuseppe Palmisano (eds), The United Nations Convention on the Rights of Persons with Disabilities (Springer International Publishing 2017).

Peltzer K and others, 'HIV/AIDS/STI/TB knowledge, beliefs and practices of traditional healers in KwaZulu-Natal, South Africa' (2006) 18(6) AIDS Care 608.

Selected Bibliography

Perehudoff K, Health, Essential Medicines, Human Rights & National Constitutions (WHO 2008).

Perlin M & Szeli E, 'Article 14: Liberty and Security of the Person' in Ilias Bantekas, Michael Ashley Stein & Dimitris Anastasiou (eds), The UN Convention on the Rights of Persons with Disabilities: A Commentary (Oxford University Press 2018).

Potts H, 'Accountability and the Right to the Highest Attainable Standard of Health' (2008), <http://repository.essex.ac.uk/9717/1/accountability-right-highest-attainable-standard-health.pdf> accessed 14 November 2022.

Quinn G & Degener T, 'Human rights and disability: the current use and future potential of United Nations human rights instruments in the context of disability' (2002), <https://www.ohchr.org/Documents/Publications/HRDisabilityen.pdf> accessed 14 November 2022.

Ramos Pozón S, 'The convention on the rights of persons with disabilities and mental health law: A critical review' (2016) 10 ALTER, European Journal of Disability Research 301.

Raustiala K & Victor DG, 'The Regime Complex for Plant Genetic Resources' (2004) 58 (2) International Organization 277.

Read U, 'Rights as Relationships: Collaborating with Faith Healers in Community Mental Health in Ghana' (2019) 43 Culture, Medicine and Psychiatry 613.

Read UM and others, 'Local suffering and the global discourse of mental health and human rights: An ethnographic study of responses to mental illness in rural Ghana' (2009) 5 Globalization and Health.

Retief M & Letšosa R, 'Models of disability: A brief overview' (2018) 74(1) HTS Teologiese Studies/ Theological Studies.

Rosenthal E & Rubenstein LS, 'International human rights advocacy under the "Principles for the Protection of Persons with Mental Illness.' (1993) 16(3–4) International Journal of Law and Psychiatry 257.

Salize HJ and others, 'Mental health care in Germany' (2007) 257 European Archives of Psychiatry and Clinical Neuroscience 92.

Sam DL & Moreira V, 'Revisiting the Mutual Embeddedness of Culture and Mental Illness' (2012) 10(2) Online Readings in Psychology and Culture.

Sambrook Smith M and others, 'Barriers to accessing mental health services for women with perinatal mental illness: systematic review and meta-synthesis of qualitative studies in the UK' (2019) 9(1) BMJ Open.

San Giorgi M, The Human Right to Equal Access to Health Care (Intersentia 2012).

Saul B and others, The International Covenant on Economic, Social and Cultural Rights. Commentary, Cases, and Materials (Oxford University Press 2014).

Saxena S & Hanna F, 'Dignity- a fundamental principle of mental health care' (2015) 142(4) Indian Journal of Medical Research 355.

Schabas W, The Universal Declaration of Human Rights: The Travaux Préparatoires (Cambridge University Press 2013).

Scholten M & Gather J, 'Adverse consequences of article 12 of the UN Convention on the Rights of Persons with Disabilities for persons with mental disabilities and an alternative way forward' (2017) 4 Journal of Medical Ethics.

Scholten M and others, 'Equality in the informed consent process: competence to consent, substitute decision-making, and discrimination of persons with mental disorders' (2021) 46(1) Journal of Medicine and Philosophy 108.

Selected Bibliography

Schuck N, 'Mental health and exploitation, violence and abuse: the domestication of articles 5 and 16 of the African Charter on Human and Peoples' Rights in Ghana and its implication for conventional and traditional mental healthcare' (2019) 3 African Human Rights Yearbook 179.

Schulze M, Freedom from exploitation, violence and abuse of persons with disabilities (Council of Europe 2017).

Schulze M, Understanding the UN Convention On The Rights Of Persons With Disabilities (Handicap International 2010).

Seatzu F, 'Article 17: Protecting the Integrity of the Person' in Ilias Bantekas, Michael Ashley Stein & Dimitris Anastasiou (eds), The UN Convention on the Rights of Persons with Disabilities: A Commentary (Oxford University Press 2018).

Series L & Nilsson A, 'Article 12 CRPD: Equal Recognition before the Law' in Ilias Bantekas, Michael Ashley Stein & Dimitris Anastasiou D (eds), The UN Convention on the Rights of Persons with Disabilities: A Commentary (Oxford University Press 2018).

Shorter E, A History of Psychiatry: From the Era of the Asylum to the Age of Prozac (John Wiley & Sons, Inc. 1997).

Sinding Aasen H and Hartlev M, 'Human Rights Principles and Patient Rights' in Brigit Toebes, Mette Hartlev, Aart Hendriks, Katharina O Cathaoir, Janne Rothmar Herrmann & Henriette Sinding Aasen (eds), Health and Human Rights. Global and European Perspectives, second edition (Intersentia 2022).

Slide M, 'The contribution of mental health services to recovery' (2009) 18(5) Journal of Mental Health 367.

Smith R & McConnell L, 'Introduction to human rights research methods' in Lee McConnell and Rhona Smith (eds), Research Methods in Human Rights (Routledge 2018).

Smith R, 'Human rights based approaches to research' in Lee McConnell and Rhona Smith (eds), Research Methods in Human Rights (Routledge 2018).

Smith RC and others, 'An evidence-based Patient centered method makes the biopsychosocial model scientific' (2013) 91(3) Patient Education and Counseling 185.

Solomon A, 'Depression, Too, is a Thing with Feathers' (2008) 44(4) Contemporary Psychoanalysis 509.

Ssenyonjo M, 'The influence of the International Covenant on Economic, Social and Cultural Rights in Africa' (2017) 64 Netherlands International Law Review 259.

Stavert J & McGregor R, 'Domestic legislation and international human rights standards: the case of mental health and incapacity' (2018) 22(1) The International Journal of Human Rights 70.

Sulaberidze L and others, 'Barriers to delivering mental health services in Georgia with an economic and financial focus: informing policy and acting on evidence' (2018) 18(1) BMC Health Services Research 108.

Szmukler G and others, 'Mental health law and the UN Convention on the rights of persons with disabilities' (2014) 37(3) International Journal of Law and Psychiatry 245.

Szmukler G, 'Coercion in Psychiatric Treatment and Its Justification' in D Moseley & G Gala (eds), Philosophy and Psychiatry (Routledge 2016).

Szwed M, 'The notion of 'a person of unsound mind' under Article 5 §1(e) of the European Convention on Human Rights' (2020) 38(4) Netherlands Quarterly of Human Rights 283.

Thakker J & Ward T, 'Culture and classification: The cross-cultural application of the DSM-IV' (1998) 18(5) Clinical Psychology Review 501.

Thornicroft G and others, 'Capacity Building in Global Mental Health Research' (2012) 20(1) Harvard Review of Psychiatry 13.
Tobin J, The right to health in international law (Oxford University Press 2012).
Toebes B and others (eds), The Right to Health: a Multi-Country Study of Law, Policy and Practice (Springer 2014).
Toebes B, 'Introduction: Health and Human Rights in Europa' in Brigit Toebes, Mette Hartlev, Aart Hendriks & Janne Rothmar Herrmann (eds), Health and Human Rights in Europe (Intersentia 2012).
Toebes B, 'The right to health and other health-related rights' in Brigit Toebes, Mette Hartlev, Aart Hendriks & Janne Rothmar Herrmann (eds), Health and Human Rights in Europe (Intersentia 2012).
Toebes B, The Right to Health as a Human Right in International Law (Intersentia/Hart 1999).
Trilsch M, Die Justiziabilität wirtschaftlicher, sozialer und kultureller Rechte im innerstaatlichen Recht (Springer 2012).
Venkatapuram S, Health Justice: An Argument from the Capabilities Approach (Polity Press 2011).
Vogt I, 'Gesundheitsberufe und stigmatisierende Tendenzen gegenüber psychisch Kranken: Ein systematischer Überblick' (2018) as part of the dgvt congress presentations on Stigmatisierung von Menschen mit psychiatrischen Diagnosen: Beständigkeit und Wandel, <https://www.dgvt-kongress.de/rueckblick/programm/programmuebersicht-2018/samstag-03-maerz-2018/stigmatisierung-von-menschen-mit-psychiatrischen-diagnosen-bestaendigkeit-und-wandel/> accessed 14 November 2022.
Waddington L & Broderick A, Promoting equality and non-discrimination for persons with disability, Contribution to the Council of Europe Strategy on the Rights of Persons with Disabilities (Council of Europe 2017).
Walker G, 'Ghana Mental Health Act 846 2012: a qualitative study of the challenges and priorities for implementation' (2015) 49(4) Ghana Medical Journal.
Walker GH & Osei A, 'Mental health law in Ghana' (2017) 14(2) British Journal of Psychiatry International 38.
Wallsten T and others, 'Short-term outcome of inpatient psychiatric care – impact of coercion and treatment characteristics' (2006) 41(12) Social Psychiatry and Psychiatric Epidemiology 975.
Weller P, 'Article 25: Health' in Ilias Bantekas, Michael Ashley Stein & Dimitris Anastasiou (eds), The UN Convention on the Rights of Persons with Disabilities: A Commentary (Oxford University Press 2018).
White R & Sashidharan SP, 'Towards a more nuanced global mental health' (2014) 204(6) British Journal of Psychiatry 415.
Wildeman S, 'Protecting Rights and Building Capacities: Challenges to Global Mental Health Policy in Light of the Convention on the Rights of Persons with Disabilities' (2013) 41(1) Journal of Law, Medicine & Ethics.
Wolfrum R and others, 'The reception of international law in the German legal order: An introduction' in Erika de Wet, Holger Hestermeyer & Rüdiger Wolfrum (eds), The implementation of international law in Germany and South Africa (Pretoria University Law Press 2015).
Yamin A, 'Beyond Compassion: The Central Role of Accountability in Applying a Human Rights Framework to Health' (2008) 10(2) Health and Human Rights 1.

Yazdi-Feyzabadi V and others, 'The World Health Organization's Definition of Health: A Short Review of Critiques and Necessity of A Shifting Paradigm' (2018) 13(5) Iranian Journal of Epidemiology 155.

Zabow T, 'Traditional healers and mental health in South Africa' (2007) 4(4) International Psychiatry 81.

Zhang MWB & Ho RCM, 'Specific Mental Health Disorders: Child and Adolescent Mental Disorders' in Stella R Quah (ed), International Encyclopedia of Public Health, second edition (Elsevier 2017).

Zhang Y, Advancing the Right to Health Care in China towards Accountability (Intersentia 2019).

Zielasek J & Gaebel W, 'Mental health law in Germany' (2015) 12(1) British Journal of Psychiatry International 14.

Zinkler M, 'Germany without Coercive Treatment in Psychiatry – A 15 Month Real World Experience' (2016) 5(1) Laws, 15.

CURRICULUM VITAE

Natalie Abrokwa carried out her PhD research on human rights and mental health at the Department of Transboundary Legal Studies at the University of Groningen, the Netherlands. She currently works at the Groningen Centre for Health Law at the University of Groningen, where she regularly teaches in various LLM and minor programmes, and she works with the Policy, Law and Human Rights Unit (PLR) of the Department of Mental Health and Substance Use of the World Health Organization. She is also a member of the Netherlands Network for Human Rights Research. Alongside her PhD research, Natalie has lectured in summer schools across Europe and presented her research at various international conferences. Previously, Natalie worked as legal consultant and researcher at the Human Rights Advocacy Centre, a renowned human rights organisation in Accra, Ghana. She obtained her Master's degree (LL.M.) in international human rights and humanitarian law from the European University Viadrina Frankfurt (Oder), Germany in 2017.

HUMAN RIGHTS RESEARCH SERIES

The Human Rights Research Series' central research theme is the nature and meaning of international standards in the field of human rights, their application and promotion in the national legal order, their interplay with national standards, and the international supervision of such application. Anyone directly involved in the definition, study, implementation, monitoring, or enforcement of human rights will find this series an indispensable reference tool.

The Series is published together with the world famous Netherlands Network for Human Rights Research (formerly School of Human Rights Research), a joint effort by human rights researchers in the Netherlands.

Editorial Board: Prof. dr. Antoine Buyse (Utrecht University), Prof. dr. Fons Coomans (Maastricht University), Prof. dr. Yvonne Donders (Chair – University of Amsterdam), Dr. Antenor Hallo de Wolf (University of Groningen), Prof. dr. Kristin Henrard (Erasmus University Rotterdam), Prof. dr. Nicola Jägers (Tilburg University), Prof. Titia Loenen (Leiden University) Prof. dr. Janne Nijman (T.M.C. Asser Instituut) and Prof. dr. Brigit Toebes (University of Groningen). For previous volumes in the series, please visit http://shr.intersentia.com.

Published titles within the Series:

91. Getahun A. Mosissa, *A Re-examination of Economic, Social and Cultural Rights in a Political Society in the Light of the Principle of Human Dignity*
    ISBN 978-1-78068-987-6
92. Veronika Flegar, *The Transformative Potential of a Vulnerability Focus in Basic Assistance Policies*
    ISBN 978-1-83970-039-2
93. Marieke J. Hopman, *Looking at Law through Children's Eyes*
    ISBN 978-1-83970-101-6
94. Daniela Heerdt, *Blurred Lines of Responsibility and Accountability. Human Rights Abuses at Mega-Sporting Events*
    ISBN 978-1-83970-117-7
95. Annick Pijnenburg, *At the Frontiers of State Responsibility. Socio-economic Rights and Cooperation on Migration*
    ISBN 978-1-83970-148-1
96. Amy Weatherburn, *Labour Exploitation in Human Trafficking Law*
    ISBN 978-1-83970-154-2
97. Caia Vlieks, *Nationality and Statelessness in Europe. European Law on Preventing and Solving Statelessness*
    ISBN 978-1-83970-261-7
98. Claire Loven, *Fundamental Rights Violations by Private Actors and the Procedure before the European Court of Human Rights. A Study of Verticalised Cases*
    ISBN 978-1-83970-283-9
99. Mary Jessie Dickson, *Leaving, Entering, and Remaining: Seeking Asylum in an Extraterritorial World*
    ISBN 978-1-83970-353-9